PSYCHOLOGY OF COUNSELING

PSYCHOLOGY RESEARCH PROGRESS

Additional books in this series can be found on Nova's website
under the Series tab.

Additional e-books in this series can be found on Nova's website
under the e-book tab.

PSYCHOLOGY OF EMOTIONS, MOTIVATIONS AND ACTION

Additional books in this series can be found on Nova's website
under the Series tab.

Additional e-books in this series can be found on Nova's website
under the e-book tab.

PSYCHOLOGY RESEARCH PROGRESS

PSYCHOLOGY OF COUNSELING

ANNAMARIA DI FABIO
EDITOR

New York

NOTICE TO THE READER

The Publisher has taken reasonable care in the preparation of this book, but makes no expressed or implied warranty of any kind and assumes no responsibility for any errors or omissions. No liability is assumed for incidental or consequential damages in connection with or arising out of information contained in this book. The Publisher shall not be liable for any special, consequential, or exemplary damages resulting, in whole or in part, from the readers' use of, or reliance upon, this material. Any parts of this book based on government reports are so indicated and copyright is claimed for those parts to the extent applicable to compilations of such works.

Independent verification should be sought for any data, advice or recommendations contained in this book. In addition, no responsibility is assumed by the publisher for any injury and/or damage to persons or property arising from any methods, products, instructions, ideas or otherwise contained in this publication.

This publication is designed to provide accurate and authoritative information with regard to the subject matter covered herein. It is sold with the clear understanding that the Publisher is not engaged in rendering legal or any other professional services. If legal or any other expert assistance is required, the services of a competent person should be sought. FROM A DECLARATION OF PARTICIPANTS JOINTLY ADOPTED BY A COMMITTEE OF THE AMERICAN BAR ASSOCIATION AND A COMMITTEE OF PUBLISHERS.

Additional color graphics may be available in the e-book version of this book.

Library of Congress Cataloging-in-Publication Data

Psychology of counseling / editor, Annamaria Di Fabio (Department of Psychology, University of Florence, Italy).
    pages cm
 Includes index.
 ISBN 978-1-62618-388-9 (hardcover)
 1. Counseling psychology. I. Di Fabio, Annamaria.
 BF636.6.P82 2013
 158.3--dc23
                          2013008993

Published by Nova Science Publishers, Inc. † New York

"This book has been independently peer reviewed by national and international academics who are experts in the field. The reviews included all contributions that appear in the published book and peer reviews were exceptionally positive."

Contents

Preface

The book presents a review of current research perspectives and intervention in the field of psychology of counseling. The aim is to stimulate virtuous circularity between scientifically based methodological frameworks, perspectives of interventions and innovation both on theoretical and applicative levels.

In order to respond to this challenge, from the point of view of its structure the volume is divided into two parts. The first part presents some theoretical perspectives to enrich the level of reflections and stimuli, the second part presents research and interventions with a view to trace new horizons of the discipline and to expand these horizons to fertilize the discipline and open new opportunities for intervention.

In this perspective, the first chapter by Annamaria Di Fabio recovers the roots of psychology of counseling to highlight relevant aspects of the present and to make a contribution in building the future. Ample space is given to the issues of internationalization and the quantitative and qualitative approaches from research to intervention. The chapter configures the psychology of counseling as a creative discipline in constant evolution, capable of progressively intercepting new needs and able to reach contributions of innovative intervention in relation to social, economic and cultural changes, responding through useful interventions to the challenges of contemporary society.

The second chapter by Maureen E. Kenny and Mary Beth Medvide points out very clearly the imperative of prevention and the great contribution which in this direction is required to offer to psychology of counseling. The necessity is underlined for counselors to more fully prepare for and engage in prevention relying on the importance of the efficacy and cost-effectiveness of prevention. Primary prevention provides a strategy for realizing social justice reinforcing strengths across individual, family, school, community and societal risks and consequently promoting psychological and physical well-being. For this reason counselors should develop varied skills, as multicultural competence, knowledge of unique ethical challenge, and skills in diagnosis and intervention in complex systems. This chapter shows the rationale for increased engagement in prevention, presenting an overview of relevant issues related to prevention, and identifying the types of skills needed for competence in prevention.

The third chapter by Jasmine M. Terwilliger, Nicholas Bach, Carli G. Bryan and Monnica T. Williams deals with the issue of multicultural approach or colorblind with respect to different cultural groups. This chapter presents a comprehensive review of the literature indicating that multiculturalism, embracing different cultural groups, is psychologically healthier than colorblindness correlated with a worst mental health. Counselors are encouraged therefore to use a multicultural approach in various environments as organizations, workplace, and schools to facilitate relationships and enrich outcomes.

The fourth chapter by Bar-On introduces one of the most innovative theoretical construct in the last years, emotional intelligence, on the one hand exploring in detail and on the other hand with a broad vision, its application in counseling within the perspective of counseling and clinical psychology. This chapter aims at discussing the possible application of emotional intelligence (EI) in clinical psychology but also in psychiatry, social work and counseling. In the first part there is a description on traditional focus of clinical psychology and EI. The subsequent part considering the key findings related to the impact of emotional intelligence on psychological health and well-being, justifies the application of EI in clinical psychology and shows the ways in which it can be used in assessment, intervention and controlling therapeutic progress. Then the chapter examines the needed empirically support and strengthen the use of EI in clinical work.

The fifth chapter by Terri Duck, Jay Middleton, Deborah Simpson, Jennifer Thibodeaux, Janelle McDaniel and Walter Buboltz enriches the volume with an appeal to the importance of exploring deeply the interconnections between family of origin and career development in terms of research and intervention. This chapter examines the literature in relation to important family of origin variables such as parental education, parental career choice and satisfaction, socioeconomic status of family, family dynamics, culture of origin and parenting styles and their impact on career development outcomes such as vocational identity, career self-efficacy, career exploration and career aspirations. As the aforementioned family of origin variables may have a long-lasting impact on an individual's approach to own career and potentially own lifespan satisfaction with career, the authors remind the importance to support individuals in achieving a satisfying career and life.

The sixth chapter by Jean-Luc Bernaud introduces an innovative theory, the adaptive counseling theory (ACT) as a new perspective for career counseling. The ACT provides frameworks for caring different aspects but also for taking into account the evolution of clients during counseling sessions.

This chapter presents the theoretical foundations in three steps: 1) the different approach of clients to understand the career issues, 2) the characteristic-treatment interaction model shown by recent research, 3) the adaptive counseling model illustrated in terms of interventions.

The second part of the volume is aimed at exploring the new boundaries of the discipline and new possible interventions.

The seventh chapter by Janet Usinger presents a longitudinal study to understand deeply how adolescents give meaning to the role that education plays in their own personal development, in relation to the funded project State Gaining Early Awareness and Readiness for Undergraduate Programs (GEAR UP). From the qualitative interview, using an interview approach, that followed a cohort of 60 students from seventh grade to twelfth grade, who lived in economically disadvantaged urban and rural communities, five main themes emerge (a) determination to succeed; (b) things happen magically; (c) school is a place of happiness; (d) I can show my pride; and (e) learning is secondary to more important things. In the study the needs associate with self-determination theory are explored, namely autonomy, competence, and relatedness, showing the implication for practice.

The eighth by Renée A. Middleton, Bengü Ergüner-Tekinalp, Elena A. Petrova, Natalie F. Williams and Thomandra Sam increases the understanding of the racial identity issue of mental health practitioners and its bearing on the therapeutic dyad. Using a mixed-method approach, researchers have identified racial patterns analyzing the implications for the research and the future practice.

The ninth chapter by Jacobus G. Maree and Esta Hansen through a case study, underlines the usefulness of a life design approach in helping counselors identify and deal with the adaptability needs of a pregnant teenager. The intervention aimed to enhance the participant's involvement in her life design process and to facilitate co-constructive conversation, gathering quantitative data gathering using the *Myers-Briggs Type Inventory* and the *Career Adapt-Abilities Scale* and qualitative data using *Career Interest Profile*. Findings show the effectiveness of using a qualitative life design counseling within the career counseling process in enhancing the ability to design own life. This approach enables counselor and clients to develop awareness of clients' Self and uncover their major life themes and subthemes.

The tenth chapter by Nancy Slater explores deeply the role of process of art-making as the change agent for psychological and emotional healing across clinical populations. Through clinical practitioner observations of a client's therapeutic art-making and the client's responses to the process of art-making, understanding increases about client behavior, mental functioning and influences of stressful life experiences. Taking into account the process of art-making as an integral part of using art in treatment can enhance counseling practice and suggests the analysis of treatment outcomes.

The eleventh chapter by Annamaria Di Fabio and Letizia Palazzeschi explores some possibilities of emotional intelligence in mediation reflecting on new perspectives for psychological counseling intervention in this context. The literature relative to relationships between emotions and mediation is analyzed in particular underlining the role of emotional intelligence in mediation. After tracing the evolution of emotional intelligence construct presenting the most significant and relevant theoretical model and tools for measuring, the interest in the promotion of emotional intelligence is clarified as a variable that can be increased trough specific training. The importance of emotional intelligence in mediation and the possible implications for training of mediators and psychological counseling intervention in mediation is highlighted.

The twelfth chapter by Jessica M. Choplin, Debra Pogrund Stark and Joseph A. Mikels describes the cognitive steps that consumers need to go trough to make wise conventional and unconventional decisions in mortgage counseling. The aim is to facilitate clients develop adaptive coping strategies to help them actually through greater awareness about the steps involved in the decision. These steps include: 1) learning about and understanding how mortgage operates; 2) estimating future income and the ongoing expenses of home ownership, insurance, real estate taxes and repairs; 3) evaluating known attributes of the mortgage such as the interest rate and monthly payment for fixed-rate mortgages; 4) identifying how important those attributes are; 5) judging the likelihood of events such as the likelihood of unemployment in the case of younger consumers; 6) integrating all of that information to make a decision. The authors describe cognitive and social psychological barriers that impede consumers' abilities to enact each step, making it difficult for consumers to integrate and evaluate all of the information needed to make wise decisions. Recognition and awareness of these cognitive steps and the barriers consumers face in taking these steps will help counselors dealing effectively with clients' needs.

The hope is that this book can really help to enhance in the 21st century the great possibilities that the discipline of counseling has always demonstrated as a valuable aid to protection and valorisation of individual resources to the advantage not only of the individual belonging realities but of the whole society.

Annamaria Di Fabio

Theoretical Perspectives

In: Psychology of Counseling
Editor: Annamaria Di Fabio

ISBN: 978-1-62618-388-9
© 2013 Nova Science Publishers, Inc.

Chapter 1

Counseling: From the Past through the Present towards the Future

Annamaria Di Fabio[*]
Department of Psychology, University of Florence, Italy

ABSTRACT

The present chapter aims to offer some reflections in relation to the actual and future perspectives in the field of psychology of counseling. It starts with a review of the literature from past to present to build the future. Then it deals with the issues of internationalization of psychology of counseling and subsequently with quantitative and qualitative approaches in the psychology of counseling from research to intervention. Furthermore it describes promising research and intervention areas in the psychology of counseling: narrative career counseling, counseling at school, counseling for work and relationships, counseling for health and wellbeing, online counseling and new technologies. It also deals with the theme of the effectiveness of counseling interventions and finally with the issue of training of professionals in the psychology of counseling. The present chapter shows how the psychology of counseling is configured as a discipline that progressively intercepts new needs or adaptively restructures the intervention in relation to social, economic and cultural changes, expressing fully the nature of magmatic and creative discipline in relation to many challenges that contemporary society proposes.

1. THE PSYCHOLOGY OF COUNSELING: A GLANCE AT THE EVOLUTION

The Society for Counseling Psychology Division 17 of American Psychological Association defines psychology of counseling as "a psychological specialty facilitates personal and interpersonal functioning across the life span with a focus on emotional, social,

---

[*] Corresponding author: E-mail address: adifabio@psico.unifi.it.

vocational, educational, health-related, developmental, and organizational concerns". Through the integration of theory, research and practice, and with a sensitivity to multicultural issues, this discipline involves a wide range of interventions to promote individual well-being, alleviate suffering, and overcome the critical moments. The psychology of counseling focuses on both the normal developmental issues and the disorders associated with physical, emotional and mental problems. The Society for Counseling Psychology emphasizes that counseling psychologists carry out their activities in different fields including teaching, research, psychotherapy and counseling, career development, evaluation, supervision, and consulting. Counseling psychologists use a variety of methods closely tied to theory and research to help individuals, groups and organizations to function at their best, and to intervene on the dysfunctional aspects (Society for Counseling Psychology Division 17, 2012).

For tracing the historical evolution that over the years regarded the psychology of counseling there are different perspectives. Whiteley (1984) traditionally refers to five phases: 1) the work of Frank Parsons (1909) and the development of vocational guidance; 2) the movement for mental health that has been proposed to promote mental health and prevent mental illness through the application of psychiatry and psychology; 3) the study of psychometrics and individual differences; 4) the emergence of counseling and psychotherapy, according to a non-medical and non-psychoanalytic perspective, in particular the classic work of Carl Rogers, *Counseling and Psychotherapy* (1942); 5) socio-economic developments in the United States, during and after the Second World War, when it emerges the need for adequate services for veterans.

Another perspective is that of Heppner, Casas, Carter, and Stone (2000) who point out that the history of the psychology of counseling concerns essentially the history of Division 17 of APA, which was born in 1943 initially as Division of Personnel and Guidance, whose primary interests addressed guidance, training and selection in schools, colleges and guidance agencies. Since 1946 the 17th Division was renamed Division of Counseling and Guidance. Heppener et al. (2000) proposed an evolution of psychology of counseling in three time periods through which the thematic of diversity issues in Division 17 is declined. The first time period "Pre 1980: Early Beginnings" focuses on the elderly and people with disabilities, tackles the problem of racial/ethnic minority and gender differences. The second time period "1980-1991: Growing Awareness and Developments" next to an ever greater attention to the issues addressed in the previous period, emphasizes the importance of including lesbian, gay, and bisexual issues in research and training programs and opens in a particular manner to multicultural issues. The third time period "1992-1999: Increased Awareness and Stronger Commitments" is characterized by an increasing emphasis on multicultural issues and in particular for multicultural training, attention also underlined by the election in 1997 of Rosie Bingham, the first black president of Division 17.

The historical evolution of the psychology of counseling has been drawn recently by Munley, Duncan, McDonnell, and Sauer (2004) who identified eight periods from the thirties of last century until the beginning of this century. The first period is characterized essentially by the birth of the major American associations in the field of psychology and the psychology of counseling. After the establishment of the American Psychological Association (APA) in 1892, centered on basic research and the Association of Counseling Psychologist (ACP) in 1931, in 1937 the American Association of Applied Psychology (AAAP), which focused on applied research, was formed. However, the lack of a unifying organization for Psychologists led in 1945 to bring together AAAP in APA in order "to advance psychology as a science, as a profession, and as a means of promoting human welfare" (Wolfe, 1946, p. 3), thus at the same time focusing on research and intervention. The following the Division 17 centered on personnel psychology and guidance was born. The second period "Clinical psychology" is placed in the Forties of the last century and it is particularly related to advances in training for clinical psychologists (Shakow, 1942) that prepared the development of psychology of counseling in the Fifties. Following the Second World War, institutional standards have indeed been developed for the training of professional psychologists, the accreditation of doctoral training programs (Baker & Benjamin, 2000) until arriving at the Boulder Conference (APA, 1949), which recommended an equal emphasis on research and practice. The third period "Veterans Administration (VA) influence" played an important role in the development of clinical psychology and counseling in the United States, trying to create new positions for psychologists outside the traditional medical setting. Yet since 1946, the VA had in fact initiated a comprehensive national training and employment program for clinical psychologists (Miller, 1946), which provided four-year paid traineeships in hospitals of the VA for students working on their Doctor of Philosophy (PhD) degrees in clinical psychology.

The fourth period, during the 1950s, is characterized by the appearance of the terms "counseling psychology" and "counseling psychologist" proposed during the Northwestern Conference on the Training of Counseling Psychologists in 1951. In 1952, the VA announced a new training program for counseling psychologists and required the APA to provide a list of universities qualified to conduct doctoral training in counseling psychology. Furthermore in 1954, the Journal of Counseling Psychology (JCP), which has become one of the leading journals of empirical research in the United States for the psychology of counseling was published for the first time (Wrenn, 1966). In 1955 the name of the APA Division 17, until that moment Division of Counseling and Guidance, was changed to Counseling Psychology (APA, 1956). The fifth period corresponds to the Sixties of last century and has seen a life-threatening identity crisis of psychology of counseling because in 1959 the Education and Training Board of APA decided to eliminate the psychology of counseling as recognized and approved specialty and therefore requested a special report on the status of such discipline. The report on the status of psychology of counseling was extremely critical and had as its main focus an unfavorable comparison with clinical psychology. Such report resulted in the need to outline the status and identity of psychology of counseling, and this led to the second National Conference on Psychology of Counseling in the United States, the Greyston Conference of 1964. The final conference report included specific recommendations for counselors and psychologists, Division 17, APA and universities, practicum and internship agencies, employers, training and supporting agencies. These recommendations concerned the steps to improve the quality of professional training of counseling psychologists and the affirmation of psychology of counseling as a profession. Furthermore in 1969, John Whiteley founded the journal, The Counseling Psychologist (TCP), with the support of Division 17 of APA. In the sixth period, between the Seventies and Eighties of last century, the development of professional identity of the psychology of counseling was stressed (Fretz & Simon, 1992; Kagan et al., 1988; Sprinthall, 1990; Tyler, 1992; Watkins, 1983; Whiteley & Fretz, 1980) in response to social, cultural and professional changes in the United States. During the Eighties many academic courses on psychology of counseling were developed and accredited. Furthermore, since mental health care becomes an important part of the activities of the health system and legislation ensured the right to psychologists to provide health services reimbursable independently, increasingly more psychologists became self-employed (Watkins, Lopez, Campbell, & Himmel, 1986). During this period, the third national conference of psychology of counseling was held in 1987 in Atlanta, which proposed the following topics: public image, professional practice in various settings, training and accreditation, research, and organizational and political issues in psychology of counseling (Weissberg et al., 1988). Important issues have covered the value of scientist-practitioner/scientist-professional model, prevention, development of life-long learning, building skills, attention to culture, ethnicity, gender and diversity (Kagan et al., 1988). In the Eighties and Nineties, multiculturalism also emerges as a significant aspect of psychology of counseling in the United States, guidelines were outlined and then operationalized (Arredondo et al., 1996) and specific skills were included in training programs (Heppner, et al. 2000; Sue et al., 1982) that held less and less within the biomedical paradigm and increasingly included qualitative research methodology in psychology of counseling (Hill & Gronsky, 1984; Hoshmand, 1989; Howard, 1984; Polkinghorne, 1984), reflecting a growing pluralism in theory and intervention (Morrow & Smith, 2000). In the seventh period, during the 1990s, the psychology of counseling continued to be influenced by economic and social forces and events. The counseling psychologists were increasingly working in health and private sectors. The conference took place in Atlanta in 1987 after which there was a reorganization of the APA Division 17 between 1992 and 1996 (Carter & Davis, 2001) with the nomination of four vice-presidents for the following areas: diversity and public interest area; education and training area; intervention area; science area. The Commission for the Recognition of Specialties and Proficiencies in Professional Psychology (CRSPPP) was established in 1995 to undertake a formal process through which the APA could recognize the distinctive features and skills in the profession of psychology (Nelson, 1999) and psychology of counseling (APA, 1999).

In the eighth and final period corresponding to the first decade of this century, the APA Division 17 changed its name to The Society of Counseling Psychology to affirm a greater organizational autonomy and professional identity (APA Division 17, 2000). The Fourth National Counseling Psychology Conference was held in Houston in 2001 and its theme was Counseling Psychologists: Making a Difference with the following objectives: a) to hold a conference open to everyone; b) establish relations with the APA; c) develop closer links with organizations of psychology of counseling; d) establish a better match between training and practice; e) focus on social advocacy through the Social Action groups (SAGs; they are groups that meet for seven days and center on specific areas for social action for example multiculturalism; Fouad et al., 2004) for the promotion of social justice and the ethical principles of practice of psychology of counseling. Thus, at the beginning of twenty-first century the psychology of counseling appeared as a complex, continuous change and proactive discipline to respond timely and effectively to changes in postmodern society (Munley et al., 2004).

Furthermore, it is possible to delineate the historical evolution of the psychology of counseling, using both content analysis of the principal journals in the filed of psychology of counseling (Scheel et al., 2011) which allow us to trace the change of the research themes in such field and the surveys addressed to counseling psychologists (Watkins, 2008) which allow us to highlight the point of view of professionals.

Regarding the content analysis of the principal scientific journal in the field of psychology of counseling, the analysis of the first 19 volumes of The Journal of Counseling

Psychology (JCP), carried out by Munley (1974), highlighted that the main categories of published research can be brought back first to a counseling process and outcome, and secondly to vocational behavior, and test development and evaluation.

Twenty-five years later, Buboltz, Miller, and Williams (1999) replicated the study of Munley in 1974 re-doing a content analysis of the JCP, using the volumes from 1973 to 1998. Again, process and outcome research emerge as the two main content areas of the publications of the journal during the investigated period of 26 years, with vocational behavior research and tests and measures as the third and fourth main area. In fact, during this period, the 44% of research published in the JCP was categorized as outcome, process, and process outcome research. Thus, from the birth of the journal until the end of the Nineties the most prolific research categories in JCP was counseling process and outcome research. This maintenance over time of the research focus in counseling on outcomes and processes had important benefits for the advancement of knowledge in the psychology of counseling.

Furthermore, it is possible to highlighted that in the field of psychology of counseling there was a progressive differentiation both in the research field and in the professional activities. Hill, Nutt, and Jackson (1994) compared the research on the counseling processes published in JCP and in the Journal of Consulting and Clinical Psychology (JCCP), analyzing the research published in both journals between 1978 and 1992. Research on counseling processes are prevalent in the JCP: 42% of the articles on this topic compared to 19% of the articles of JCCP. Furthermore, Hill et al. (1994) noted a decreasing trend over time in the publications on the JCP: research on processes representing 55% of the articles were published within the first five years, 37% of articles were published over the next five years and 32% of articles were published in last five years, whereas publications related to research on processes in the JCCP remained stable at around 19% in the analyzed period of fifteen years. Scheel et al. (2011) underlined that these results highlighted a greater fluidity in the identity of psychology of counseling with respect to clinical psychology and showed a shift in emphasis in recent years by process and outcome research into new research topics in the field of psychology of counseling.

Recently Scheel et al. (2011) effected a research coauthored by Society of Counseling Psychology Section for the Promotion of Psychotherapy Science (SPPS) with the aim of investigating, through a content analysis, a perceived decreasing trend in the amount of research related to counseling in the fundamental journals for psychology of counseling, the Counseling Psychologist (TCP) (the official journal of the Society for Counseling Psychology) and the Journal of Counseling Psychology (JCP) (the Journal of Psychology of Counseling published by the American Psychological Association).

Scheel et al. (2011) hypothesized that the current research in the field of psychology of counseling is changing its themes of study, dealing with a lesser extent to the traditional aspects linked to the study outcomes and processes in counseling in favor of issues like social justice and cultural competence in counseling.

The results of content analysis of the article in TCP and in JCP, which covers a period of 30 years from 1979 to 2008 (excluded the issue 4 of 1987 and the issue 2 of 2005 that was completely dedicated to statistics) carried out by Scheel et al. (2011), underline that such decline hypothesized by authors in the number of articles relative to outcomes and processes of counseling in JCP and in TCP, the most prestigious journals in psychology of counseling in the United States, in favor of articles linked to the issues of social justice and cultural competence in counseling. Overall, the publications in the two journals indicated a decrease of attention on the issues of outcomes and processes in counseling. In the period between 1979 and 1983, 152 studies were related to the category analogue studies involving research on attitudes, expectations and preferences of clients who had no real experience with counseling intervention. In the subsequent period of five years (1984-1988), the number of analogue studies was practically halved ($n = 72$). The decline was not arrested during the 30-year period examined, until reaching 18 studies between 2004 and 2008. According to Scheel et al. (2011), a possible explanation for this decline is the shift in psychology of counseling from the dominance of counseling outcome and process research to issues such as those of social justice and cultural competence in counseling that characterizes current research in the psychology of counseling.

With regard to surveys addressed to counseling psychologists, Watkins (2008) compared the survey data collected in the 1985 survey of Watkins, Lopez, Campbell, and Himmel (1986), in the 2000 survey of Goodyear et al. (2008) and in the 2000/2003 survey of Munley, Pate, and Duncan (2008), emphasizing that these data showed both continuity and change, highlighting aspects of the rich heritage of psychology of counseling on one hand, on the other hand the present opportunities for growth and future prospects. Watkins (2008) identified the following main aspects in common between the data of the three surveys: 1) The majority of counseling psychologists have a PhD, are licensed as psychologists, provide individual therapy, and are to a certain extent satisfied with their graduate training, internship training, and with having chosen psychology of counseling as their profession. 2) Counseling psychologists, SCP members or not, provide a wide range of therapy activities (including marital, family, and group), employment activities (including education and educational services, management/administration, and to some extent research), and work in various employment settings (including private practices, universities and colleges, human services, hospitals, and clinics). 3) A large part of counseling psychologists is identified primarily with the role of clinical practitioner, choosing the eclecticism, the cognitivism, and the psychodynamic as main theoretical approaches. The principal differences between the data of the three surveys are instead the following (Watkins, 2008): 1) The representation of women within the SCP increased significantly since 1985 and also the number of psychologists who identify their major area of intervention as psychology of counseling increased significantly within the APA in general. 2) The representation of ethnic minorities increased in the SCP since 1985 and also the number of ethnic minorities that identify their major area of intervention as the psychology of counseling increased within the APA in general. 3) Although there are similarities between SPC members and nonmembers, there are differences in relation to the fact that SPC members belong more to college and university settings whereas nonmembers come mainly from private practice settings. Watkins (2008) therefore highlights the aspects of continuity in counseling over the years but also the changes that occurred, noting in particular a greater presence of women and ethnic minorities among the counseling psychologists and an increase of professionals working in private practice settings than in the past.

Currently the guidelines of the American Psychological Association (Hage et al., 2007) emphasize the importance of issues related to prevention and social justice in the field of psychology of counseling. Prevention, recognized as a means to prevent the development of psychological problems and reduce suffering (Kenny, 2009), can produce significant and lasting changes, increasing the resources of individuals and reducing social inequities (Kenny, 2011). Paying attention to the historical development of the discipline, prevention was recognized as one of the main features of the identity of counseling (Gelso & Fretz, 2001). The current focus to evidence-based practice can identify and promote specific prevention activities, especially in light of the recent interest in prevention research, training and counseling intervention (Albee, 2000; Romano & Hage, 2000; Vera, 2000). Specifically, the members of the Prevention Section of the Society of Counseling Psychology (SCP, Division 17 of American Psychological Association) outlined fifteen international guidelines on the prevention, aimed at giving greater emphasis on prevention in the field of counseling (Hage et al., 2007), organized in four sections: interventions in the field of prevention; research and evaluation on prevention; education and training in prevention; political and social responsibility for prevention. They constitute a framework for stimulating professionals to actions that favor the wellbeing of individuals and communities, also through increasing of one's own knowledge, abilities and experiences in the field of prevention (Hage et al., 2007). The guidelines of the American Psychological Association (Hage el al., 2007) constitute therefore a stimuli for a greater application of research and practice by counseling psychologists, for offering an adequate and prompt answer to the different needs of postmodern society. It is possible to identify strategies which can be included in prevention activities with the aim of promoting social justice (Kenny, 2011). There is in fact a high probability that many of the people with a greater need for psychological intervention for mental health problems cannot access services or not seek psychological intervention, since they do not have the resources to identify such services (for example in the United States, people of color, immigrants, and people belonging to lower socio-economic classes; Weisfeld & Perlman, 2005). It is thus crucial to develop prevention strategies to reduce the occurrence of mental health problems, instead of treatments which can only act on the problems already acclaimed (Albee, 2000). Preventive interventions should be addressed to improve the socio-economic conditions at the base of many physical and mental health problems to empower individuals and communities themselves (Kenny & Hage, 2009). On the base of incidence formula (ratio of organic factors, stress, environmental factors that increase the disadvantages conditions, the strengths and resources of the individuals or groups that resist the negative effects of disadvantage; Albee & Ryan-Finn, 1993), that shows the link between social conditions, distress and various types of discomfort, it is possible to design preventive interventions. They can act on elements of social context (social support, nutrition, water, housing conditions) that support healthy lifestyles, rather than physical aspects. Prevention interventions can also promote protective factors (development of personal resources, coping strategies, self-esteem) that can reinforce the resilience against social stress and enable individuals to identify and achieve personal goals, once social barriers are reduced. Career development interventions that help people to improve their ability in identifying and reaching satisfying professional goals, constitute an important strategy in prevention of social injustice (Kenny & Di Fabio, 2009). Therefore prevention can represent an instrument for the realization of social justice, eliminating factors of oppression through a system change and supporting the development of strengths and resources of individuals and community that facilitate self-determination (Kenny & Romano, 2009). It is important that counseling psychologists know the mechanisms through with social injustice, power and cultural factors can cause distress (Crethar, Rivera, & Nash, 2008): since social injustice can contribute to feelings of powerlessness, interventions should focus on increasing self-esteem and feelings of self-efficacy (Goodman et al., 2004) so that strategies can be developed to address the various complex situations of their lives in an adaptive way also without the help of a professional. Furthermore, the importance of multidisciplinary collaboration between different professionals (physicians, lawyers, psychologists, economists) and with key figures in the territory to effectively solve complex social problems as they emerge (Hage et al., 2007). It is important to consider that, to be an expert psychologist, is necessary to regard psychological and political elements related to wellbeing and social justice (Prilleltensky & Fox, 2008). For this reason it is important that counseling psychologists integrate traditional centered-on-person approaches with interventions focusing on systemic changes, at a level of community, institutions, and society (Constantine, Hage, Kindaichi, & Bryant, 2007). Such integrated interventions can be realized thanks to abilities such as outreach, advocacy, social justice education, social actions, and media advocacy (Cohen, Chavez, & Chehimi, 2007) that should be developed through specific training. Therefore prevention and social justice represent future research and intervention perspectives of great relevance in the field of psychology of counseling. As stressed by Brown and Lent (2000) in the third edition of the Handbook of Counseling Psychology, important current research areas in the psychology of counseling concern qualitative research methods, preventive interventions with school-age youth, promotion of school-to-work transitions that accompany in-depth studies about cultural issues, career and educational topics, implications of gender, race, ethnicity, sexual orientation, social class, and culture in counseling.

2. MOVING TOWARDS AN INTERNATIONALIZATION OF PSYCHOLOGY OF COUNSELING

The internationalization of psychology of counseling represents a current challenge particularly relevant for researchers and professionals (Leong & Savickas, 2007). Savickas (2007a) in his contribution to the special issue on International Perspectives on Counseling Psychology of "Applied Psychology: An International Review" identified four fundamental objectives for counseling at the world level: 1) define the psychology of counseling according to an international perspective; 2) crystalize a cross-national professional identity; 3) encourage the construction of indigenous models, methods and materials, and 4) promote international collaboration.

Concerning the first objective, Savickas (2007a) calls for the construction of a shared definition psychology of counseling, which is transversal across the different countries and significant for the international community. In this regard he suggests the formation of a task force within the Counseling Psychology Division 16 in the International Association of Applied Psychology in order to define the psychology of counseling according to an international perspective, developing a cross-national concept of the discipline that is consensual and convergent. In relation to the second objective, Savickas (2007a) underlines the difficult in crystalizing a professional cross-nation identity since counseling psychologists have a diffused identity as they are engaged in a wide variety of activities with different groups of clients in different life situations and in different types of settings using a wide range of theories and techniques. Also in this case, the author advocates the formation of a task force of Division 16 with the task of examining, in the different parts of the world, who the counseling psychologists are and how they differ from other professionals that are clearly defined as social workers and clinical psychologists. Regarding the third objective, Savickas

(2007a), while emphasizing the need for a shared definition of psychology of counseling and for a coherent professional identity, highlights that the psychology of counseling cannot assume the same form in all countries. In regard to promoting the progress of psychology of counseling at a world level, the author suggests formulating and implementing strategies which facilitate the development of indigenous psychological theory and research which are based on specific cultural context where they were applied. In this regard, Maree and Molepo (2007) underline the importance of modifying the approaches to counseling in disadvantaged contexts, such as the South African context where, highlighting for example, operating a postmodern career construction approach in counseling can lead to more satisfying results with respect to traditional approaches. Taking up the fourth goal, Savickas (2007a) underlines as "indigenous development does not mean isolation" (p. 186) and highlights as the globalization of the economy and the progressive internationalization of psychology of counseling allow the promotion of contacts and exchanges between counseling psychologists of different parts of the world. Therefore, the importance of promoting the interaction between counseling psychologists of different countries is stressed (Savickas, 2007a).

Leung and Tsoi-Hoshmand (2007) underline that the objectives proposed by Savickas (2007a) could be used as a general guide also for internationalization of counseling psychology journals, favoring the development of different international counseling scholarships. According to the authors, such internationalization can be promoted through various modalities: the counseling journals should: give impulse to deal with central issues for the development of psychology of counseling at a world level; favor submissions of contributions on thematic topics of common interest for counseling psychologists in different parts of the world; consider different formats for the theme-based discussion (for example, case studies and the use of online formats for discussion and documentation) which accompany conventional ways to bring conceptual and empirical works. Furthermore, Leung and Tsoi-Hishmand (2007) highlighted the significant role that the Asian Journal of Counseling continues to have in the development of an indigenous and international scholarship in counseling in Asia and other parts of the world.

The internationalization can not ignore the indigenization which assumes a particular relevance in the field of psychology of counseling (Savickas, 2007a). Indigenous psychology develops at the beginning of the Eighties in Asia among Filipino psychologists, under the leadership of Virgilio Enriquez (Pe-Pua & Protacio-Marcelino, 2000) and grew up over the past two decades, up to permeate Western psychology (Ho, Peng, Lai, & Chan, 2001) in research and practice.

Ho (1998) defines indigenous psychology as the study of human behavior and mental processes within a cultural context that is based on values, conceptions, belief systems, methodologies, and other internal resources to specific analyzed cultural groups. Indigenous psychology aims to understand the functions of people in their context, including knowledge, skills and belief that individuals have in relation to themselves (Ho, 1998; Kim, Yang, & Hwang, 2006; Sinha, 1997), using a bottom-up model-building paradigm (Kim, 2000).

Concerning the ecologic and contextual base of behavior, which pays attention to indigenous psychology, a coincidence emerges with the developmental–contextual perspective of counseling psychology) (Walsh, Galassi, Murphy, & Park-Taylor, 2002): the development is seen as a process which is grounded in the family, neighborhood, community, school, and society, which cannot be considered isolated from that context (Walsh et al.,

2002). In addition, individuals and their contexts are considered active and dynamic agents of change, able to mutually influence development outcomes (Lerner, 2002).

Further deepening, the term indigenization refers to the process of use of the developments made elsewhere (as in U.S. psychology) and of introduction of changes to make it suitable to the new culture (Adair, 1992). Indigenization regards the significant analysis of theories, concepts and measures of a culture for adapting them to another culture (Stead, 2004). In other terms indigenization is presented as a necessary step for achieving a synthesis between unity and diversity (Ho et al., 2001).

Enriquez (1993) suggests that two ways for indigenization in psychology in local context exist, that is indigenous from without and indigenous from within. The indigenous from without model includes a process in which the existing psychological theories, concepts and methods are modified for adapting to local cultural context. This perspective could discover universal psychological aspects in social cultural and ecologic contexts (Draguns, 2003; Kim & Berry, 1993; Kim et al., 2006). A process for examining the existing psychological theories has the following objectives: a) adapt and develop such theories and concepts on the base of the knowledge of local researchers and professionals; b) analyze the adapted counseling psychological theories and concepts using local samples and multiple research methods (qualitative and quantitative traditions and mixed-method research methods (Ægisdóttir, Gerstein, & Cinarbas, 2008); c) generate alternative models and frameworks of the psychology of counseling in which indigenous aspects and universal aspects are integrated. Regarding the possibility that research produces significant results and is relevant at a social level, Stead (2004) suggests the use of participatory action research, which is collaborative and try to give more power to those that are oppressed.

In the indigenous model from within, researchers develop theories, concepts and methods, included those relative to psychology of counseling, specific for a cultural context, using indigenous information. Referring to the conceptualization of Blowers (1996), firstly, the first level of indigenous model from within is local and aims at the clarification of processes that form the normal and abnormal personality, emotions and behavior as defined by the culture of belonging, useful for the development of relevant theories and application methods. The second level of indigenous from within model is national: it refers to the understanding and development of psychology as a institutionalized discipline "influenced and structured by the history and politics of a nation" (Blowers, 1996, p. 2). It is necessary to reflect on the cultural appropriateness of professional and ethical guidelines and principles to guide professional practice (Mok, 2003). Counseling psychologists should be open to as many cultural perspectives as possible (Gergen, 2001). For example, the recognized role of the self-determination principle: in reality a client, in making a decision related to their career must examine not only their own needs and desires but also those parts of which feel responsible, like his/her parents and society (Mok, 2003). Social constructionism can be a useful perspective for facing the need to understand the cultural meanings that people have when they interact in the workplace (Stead, 2004). The third level of indigenous model from within regards the application of psychological method to the study of culture-specific practices, which reflect beliefs, values and preferences, grounded in a specific culture (Blowers, 1996).

In an increasingly globalized world, scholars in the field of psychology of counseling should collaborate more and more in research to examine the convergence and divergence of their communities (Leung & Chen, 2009). At a professional level, it is important that counseling psychologists focus on the importance of indigenous practices which are used through the years in a specific community for maintaining their physical and psychological health and wellbeing (Leung & Chen, 2009).

Concerning the developmental modalities of psychology of counseling, in national and international contexts among the individuated as central aspects just emerge the following: culture, indigenization, globalization, conceptual frameworks, transfer of knowledge and emerging definitions in psychology of counseling (Young, 2010; Young & Lalande, 2011; Young & Valach, 2009). For promoting the process of psychology of counseling in specific communities, specific actions for training, research and practice that should be conceived at the same time international and indigenous perspectives are necessary (Ho et al., 2001; Hwang, 2009).

In her address, Forrest (2010), as past president of the Society of Counseling Psychology, underlines in particular the importance of linking internationalization of psychology of counseling to professional competence. Whether or not, the internationalization and the competence of professionals will be integrated properly, the U. S. psychology will run the risk of remaining increasingly isolated from the psychology of other countries and shared international themes will be not individuated (Forrest, 2010). The author underlines in many cases the psychology leaders of different parts of the world refer to the American Psychological Association for the guidelines relative to different fields, such as for example, ethics, accreditation, and model licensing law, among others. In this regard Forrest (2010) shows the risk of possible unintentional damage both for professionals and for clients, in the case in which standards of U.S. psychology are exported without an accurate revision and attention to the influence of the national culture in which they could be applied. The long term consequences of such actions could contribute in continuing and increasing criticism against U.S. hegemony in psychology. The author also highlights the increasing globalization can create the need to have at least some common standards between different countries to facilitate the mobility of counseling psychologists and ensure provision of quality services for clients in different parts of the world. A lack of shared standards reduces the possibility of mobility for counseling psychologists and reduces their freedom to be able to work and live in different countries (Forrest, 2010). A further effort at an international level, according to Forrest (2010), is that of working together to identify universal ethical principles according to the Universal Declaration of Ethical Principles for Psychologists, a document developed and adopted by the International Union of Psychological Sciences (2008), by IAAP and International Association for Cross-Cultural Psychology. The aim of the document is to "provide a moral framework and generic set of ethical principles for psychology organizations worldwide" (p. 1). It underlines the importance of global thinking to ethical shared principles in counseling on the one side, on the other side encouraging ethical actions which are sensitive and answer the need of local communities (Forrest, 2010). Another aspect of attention in relation to the internationalization highlighted by the author concerns the complex attempt promoted by the Taskforce on APA's Role in International Quality Assurance of establishing common international professional standards. The author underlines the importance of continuing to promote in the next years the internationalization of psychology of counseling as a fundamental mission for researchers and professionals in such field. In particular the invitation that Forrest (2010) addresses to counseling psychologists is "to become partners/learning leaders who will bring together efforts to internationalize psychology with efforts to codify the competencies of professional practice in ways that are respectful of the many cultures and countries of the world" (p. 97).

The current president of the Society of Counseling Psychology Y. Barry Chung (2012), in his presidential welcome, underlined the fundamental objectives of the Association: 1) guide the training of specialists in the psychology of counseling; 2) encourage and disseminate research in the field of psychology of counseling; 3) support ethical and competent counseling interventions in various application contexts; 4) promote diversity within the Association and the application of the psychology of counseling for the public interest; 5) support the effective communication among counseling psychologists and between the Association and other organizations. Chang (2012) also argues that the Association emphasizes developmental, strength-based, multicultural, and social justice principles and the principles of positive psychology, continuing to promote international perspectives in the psychology of counseling.

3. QUANTITATIVE AND QUALITATIVE APPROACHES IN PSYCHOLOGY OF COUNSELING: FROM RESEARCH TO INTERVENTION

An analysis of the literature relative to psychology of counseling reveals that it is possible to underline how such discipline is characterized by the presence of two approaches: quantitative approaches and qualitative approaches (Maree & Pietersen, 2007a; Ponterotto, 2005). Quantitative approaches focus on quantification of observed data and on control of empirical variables (Kerlinger, 1986; Maree & Pietersen, 2007a; Mouton & Marais, 1990; Nieuwenhuis, 2007; Ponterotto, 2005; Valle, King, & Halling, 1989). Therefore quantitative research uses a wide number of participants and applies statistical procedures which examine mean and variance of groups (Gravetter & Forzano, 2003; Maree & Pietersen, 2007a, 2007b; Mouton, 2001; Ponterotto & Grieger, 1999).

Quantitative study deals with correlation and causal links between variables (Tabachnick & Fidell, 2007) from the one side, from the other side it refers to a wide range of empirical procedures which aim to describe and interpret the experiences of research participants in a context-specific setting (Denzin & Lincoln, 2000; Merriam, 2009; Parker, 1994; Smith, 2008). Results of qualitative studies are in general presented using verbal extracts which often correspond to the words that participants use for describing an event, an experience or a psychological phenomenon (Taylor & Bogdan, 1998). Both qualitative approaches and qualitative approaches are characterized by collection, analysis and interpretation of the observed data (Nieuwenhuis, 2010; Ponterotto, 2005).

In the review by Neville, Carter, Spengler, and Hoffman (2006), which emerged in the last two decades, many articles about methodological progresses in the field of psychology of counseling both in relation to quantitative methods and in relation to qualitative methods were published. The development of increasingly sophisticated research methods allowed researchers to analyze more in-depth complexities of relationships between variables in the field of psychology of counseling (Neville et al., 2006). In 2006 The Counseling Psychologist published a Special Issue about quantitative approaches which focused in particular on the empirical method in psychology of counseling and aimed to underline use, progress, and best practice of specific methods and research designs. The five articles that composed the Special Issue of 2006 regarded relevant issues relative to research design and methodology as good practices for analyzing, interpreting, and using reliability data (Helms, Henze, Sass, & Mifsud, 2006), discriminant analysis (Sherry, 2006), factor analysis (Kahn, 2006), structural equation models (Weston & Gore, 2006), and effect size (Henson, 2006).

Helms et al. (2006) individuated seven categories relative to good practices for analyzing, interpreting, and using reliability data essential to guarantee the reliability of measures in quantitative research in psychology of counseling: 1) calculate and reported reliability coefficients for each tool used; 2) determine whether conceptual and structural properties of the scale support the use of Cronbach's alpha; 3) when the researcher chooses to eliminate some items of a scale, provide the numbers of items of the short version and of the original version of the scale and insert the indices of sample variability and the sub-scale inter-correlation; 4) describe participants characteristics; 5) interpret the data reliability, sharing the analytical process in details; 6) analyze the data reliability, calculating and reporting confidence intervals for all coefficients of reliability; 7) use the Cronbach's Alpha coefficient, specifying the use of a priori of reliability coefficients.

Along with established modalities of analysis in the field of psychology of counseling, as Cronbach's alpha for reliability, further modalities show significant possibilities of intervention in such fields have emerged (Neville et al., 2006): discriminant analysis, Exploratory Factor Analysis (EFA), Confirmatory Factor Analysis (AFC), and Structural Equation Models (SEM).

Discriminant analysis is presented by Sherry (2006) as one of the alternative approach to more traditional ANOVA or Student t test for comparison between two or more groups. Discriminant analysis is composed of two approaches for analyzing differences among groups: Predictive Discriminant Analysis (PDA) and Descriptive Discriminant Analysis (DDA). PDA uses continuous or interval response variables for predicting group membership. DDA instead uses group membership for predicting or describing scores on continuous variables. DDA reduces the probability of committing a Type I error because it can indicate where the groups differ on some variables with a statistical procedure. Furthermore DDA preserves the complexity of interrelated research variables since it considers these variables simultaneously in the analysis.

Kahn (2006) describes the possible applications of Exploratory Factor Analysis (EFA) and of Confirmatory Factor Analysis (CFA) in psychology of counseling. A common objective of two types of analysis is constituted of the reduction of several variables into a smaller number of groups or categories. Factor analysis, both exploratory and confirmatory, aim therefore to describe, as a limited number of latent constructs are able to explain, covariation among numerous variables. Reduced data in groups or categories can solve many problems facing counseling psychologists, which can be relative to clients (for example, reducing a complex set of presented problems in themes), to students in a training program (for example, reducing a long list of targets in nucleus), to participants in a research (for example to find the factors common to the various items of a new instrument). Furthermore, factor analysis has a long tradition in the classical theory of measurement (Nunnally & Bernstein, 1994) and its use has spread for research on the development of scales and for assessing the validity of psychological instruments. The factorial analysis can also be used to create factor scores as a means to reduce data (Tinsely & Tinsley, 1987) and to develop and evaluate theories (Russell, 2002; Thompson, 2004). Thus factor analysis has the potential to advance the work of counseling psychologists in many areas, especially by helping to simplify the data.

Weston and Gore (2006) underline the importance of using Structural Equation Models (SEM) in research in the field of psychology of counseling. Authors highlight that as the introduction of SEM allowed counseling psychologists to respond to complex and multidimensional issues that until a few decades ago could not be addressed because we did not have adequate methods for analyzing multivariate models. According to Weston and Gore (2006) to prevent incorrect use of SEM, researchers must carefully choose the number of participants, with large samples needed to specify complex models; they must report the indices of fit, standardized parameter estimates with the significance; they must include a covariance matrix or correlations with mean and standard deviation to allow others to replicate the results and test the health of the model in an independent manner.

Another important aspect in quantitative research in the field of psychology of counseling is the importance of the effect size for the interpretation of results and synthesis through empirical studies (Henson, 2006): the evaluation of statistical significance has historically dominated the determination of the importance of the findings by psychologists and the importance of effect size and confidence intervals continues to be crucial in quantitative research in the field of psychology of counseling.

An analysis of the literature shows, however, that the field of psychology in general and the psychology of counseling in particular, is witnessing a gradual shift from the main significance of quantitative methods to qualitative methods and to a perspective which integrates such quantitative methods and qualitative methods (Ivankova, Creswell, & Clark, 2010; Morgan & Sklar, 2012; Ponterotto, 2005). The interest in qualitative methods in the field of psychology of counseling is testified by the recent publications on this subject such as the 2005 Special Issue "Knowledge in Context: Qualitative Methods in Counseling Psychology Research" of Journal of Counseling Psychology and by the works that call for the use of mixed method approaches in the psychology of counseling (Hanson, Creswell, Plano Clark, Petska, & Creswell, 2005; Haverkamp, Morrow, & Ponterotto, 2005; Haverkamp & Young, 2007; Suzuki, Ahluwalia, Mattis, & Quizon, 2005).

The purpose of qualitative research is to understand and describe the processes and meanings that people attribute to their behavior and that of others (Patton, 1984). In qualitative research, knowledge is not passively observed, but actively constructed by participants (Heppner, Kivlighan, & Wampold, 1999). According to Yeh and Inman (2007), the multiple possibilities of qualitative research have not been fully realized in the psychology of counseling. The authors report the data by Ponterotto (2005) who points out that only 10% of counseling psychology programs offer a qualitative research course for doctoral students, a median percent of approximately 10% of the doctoral dissertation in counseling psychology are qualitative. Ponterotto (2005) also points out that although in the field of psychology of counseling, numerous articles have been published on various aspects of qualitative research (Gomez et al., 2001; Ladany, Hill, Corbett, & Nutt, 1996; Timlin-Scalera, Ponterotto, Blumberg, & Jackson, 2003; Yeh, Inman, Kim, & Okubo, 2006; Yeh, Ma, et al., 2005), quantitative studies are still particularly represented.

Yeh and Inman (2007) outline nine principal qualitative approaches that can be applied in the field of psychology of counseling. 1) *Case study*, focuses on a detailed and thorough analysis of a single case or multiple cases over time through the use of multiple sources such as interviews, observations, audio-visual materials (Creswell, 2002; Merriam, 1988; Stake

1995). 2) *Consensual qualitative research*, is a constructivist approach (which is created between the researcher and research participants) with post-positivist elements (quasi-statistical or numerical classification of results). This approach has, as a key aspect, the consensus among more researchers and the use of external auditors to carry out a data collection as objective as possible (Hill et al., 2005; Hill, Thompson, & Williams, 1997). 3) *Discovery oriented*, is an exploratory method which employs the in depth and naive study of a phenomenon to obtain information in relation to a new situation, which is not yet known. The main aspect of this method is the emphasis on the consistency between the cases and the use of consensus among multiple judges (Mahrer, 1988; Mahrer & Boulet, 1999).

4) *Grounded theory*, an approach in which researchers do not test hypotheses but rather they construct a theory from raw data or extend an existing theory. In this approach, ideas and themes emerge from the data and are therefore more connected with reality (Fassinger, 2005; Strauss & Corbin, 1998). 5) *Ethnography*, this is an approach where the researcher is involved in long-term observation and immersion in the daily lives of a group. In this approach, behaviors, customs, values and interactions of the group are explored and described (Bernard, 2002; Creswell, 1998; Suzuki, et al., 2005). 6) *Long interview*, is a constructivist approach which regards the cultural contexts and shared meanings rather than individual affective states. It uses a highly focused interview that allows researchers to obtain detailed information, without a repeated and prolonged involvement in the lives of participants (McCracken, 1988). 7) *Narrative approach*, which includes the "linguistic and structural characteristics of narrated text" and more recently the "meanings and relationships found in narratives as well as the social, historical, and cultural contexts of narratives" (Hoshmand, 2005, p. 179). 8) *Phenomenological approach*, focuses on describing the central conscious meaning or on the essence of the lived experience of the phenomenon under study. In this approach the meaning of the phenomenon is conceptualized within the consciousness of the individual (Creswell, 1998, 2002; Moustakas, 1994; Polkinghorne, 1989). 9) *Participatory action research*, as for other constructivist research action methods the meaning is co-constructed between researchers and participants in participatory action research (PAR). In this approach participants in the study represent collaborators in the research (Fine et al., 2003; Kidd & Kral, 2005). At the end of their contribution Yeh and Inman (2007) emphasize the importance of conducting qualitative research in the field of psychology of counseling and of increasing in professionals the self-awareness and self-exploration of self-locations in the qualitative analysis as an important aspect of skills of a multicultural counselor.

In the field of qualitative approaches, in the psychology of counseling, this assumes a particular relevance regarding the question of data analysis in qualitative research and in particular the validity of the research (Di Fabio & Maree, 2012a). In qualitative research, the validity is conceived as trustworthiness with reference to the mode in which data are collected, selected and classified, especially if they are verbal and textual data (Perakyla, 1993). Trustworthiness is conceived in terms of credibility, transferability, dependability and confirmability (Di Fabio & Maree, 2012a; Maree & Van der Westhuizen, 2009). Credibility corresponds to internal validity, the transferability to external validity, the dependability to reliability, and the trustworthiness to objectivity (Maree & Van der Westhuizen, 2009). Credibility of the data refers to factors such as the significance of the results and their truthfulness for participants (Miles & Huberman, 1994). External verification (audit) of the results by researchers who have not participated in the research allows evaluation of the credibility of the findings (Lincoln & Guba, 1985). Transferability refers to the degree in which the results can be generalized to other contexts (Lincoln & Guba, 1985; Maree & Van der Westhuizen, 2009). The characteristics of research, from the theoretical model underlying the method of collecting and analyzing data, must be described to allow researchers to assess whether the qualitative results are transferable to other contexts. Only then can one express an informed opinion, taking into account the specific conditions under which the results have been achieved (Maree & Van der Westhuizen, 2009). Dependability regards stability and consistency of process and methods of research during time and influences the degree of control in one study (Goetz & LeCompte, 1984; Maree & Van der Westhuizen, 2009). For increasing the validity of the procedure, the researcher should monitor the quality of the recording and the transcription of data, documentation and methods of observation and interviews (Hoepfl, 1997). Confirmability refers to the objectivity of the data and the absence of errors in the research. The results can be considered to be confirmed when they are derived from participants and conditions of research, rather than by the (subjective) opinion of the researcher (Lincoln & Guba, 1985; Maree & Van der Westhuizen, 2009). For checking the confirmability of data, an external researcher who was not involved in the study should assess whether the methods and procedures of the study are described sufficiently clearly and in sufficient detail to allow verification of the data (audit) (Schwandt & Halpern, 1988). The validity of qualitative research can be improved by increasing the number of sources of validation (Maree & Van der Westhuizen, 2009).

This process defined triangulation (Denzin, 1978; Denzin & Lincoln, 2003) is essential to ensure the validity of the interpretation of the data (Terre Blanche & Durrheim, 2004) and to establish their reliability (McMillan & Schumacher, 2001). The triangulation includes the use of different information sources (for example, people, times and settings), methods (for example, observations, interviews and documents), research, theories and data types (for example, tests and recordings) (Maree & Van der Westhuizen, 2009). Crystallization is another way to achieve quality assurance in qualitative data (Maree & Van der Westhuizen, 2009) and to validate the results using different methods for collecting and analyzing data. The implication is that researchers should consider different perspectives to ensure quality assurance in the research. Triangulation and crystallization can be used individually or jointly in research on counseling based on individual choice of the researcher (Di Fabio & Maree, 2012a).

If in the past, quantitative and qualitative approaches had to be separated in research in the field of psychology of counseling (Tashakkori & Teddlie, 2003; Teddlie & Tashakkori, 2003), currently they are attempts of integration (Castro, Kellison, Boyd, & Kopak, 2010; Hanson et al., 2005). Combined research methods are established (Creswell, 2002, 2003; Greene, Caracelli, & Graham, 1989; Tashakkori & Teddlie, 1998, 2003). These methods include the collection, analysis and integration of quantitative and qualitative data in a single or multiphase study (Hanson et al., 2005). The use of both types of data allows researchers to obtain a more thorough understanding of the phenomenon of interest (Hanson et al., 2005). Mertens (2003) and Punch (1998) suggested that investigations with mixed methods can be used for a) better understanding of a research problem by converging numeric trends from quantitative data and specific details from qualitative data; b) identify variables/constructs that can be measured through the use of existing tools or developing new ones; c) obtain quantitative statistical data and results from a sample of the population and use them to identify individuals who can explore these results through qualitative data; d) reflect the needs of individuals or marginalized or underrepresented groups.

In the field of intervention in an attempt to integrate qualitative and quantitative approaches, the stimuli that come from the specific field of career counseling are of particular interest. In this filed, to understand in depth the challenge posed by the use of research approaches and innovative and effective intervention, consideration should be given the distinction made by Savickas (2010b) between vocational guidance and career counseling. The first belongs to a more traditional and slightly obsolete formulation since it constitutes an assessment made on the person by the operator: its focus is on content (for example which occupation is expected to carry the person), its main function is to administer the tests and their interpretation to do the profiling that is for obtaining the person's profile in terms of skills, interests and characteristics. Career counseling is instead an interaction aimed at the client's problem appraisal: its focus is on process, that is how the client chooses an occupation, is responsible to identify the difficulties in choosing a career, modalities to facilitate the process and helps clients to make their choice, increasing in them an interest in the world of work and the theme of career; adaptive forms of management of one's own careers; curiosity about the various opportunities and options and the confidence in self for career choice.

In postmodern society, psychologists and counselors are called upon to design and implement complex differentiated and integrated services to respond to what could be described emblematically the transition from scores to stories (McMahon, 2010; McMahon & Patton, 2002). This is connected with a change in the practice of career counseling through the influence of constructivism and postmodern philosophies, passing from a perspective previously inspired to the metaphor of tests and tell, to a perspective inspired to the narrative metaphor, based on a postmodern approach to counseling. In this perspective, life-story counseling is proposed as one of the identities of career counseling, considered a multi-storied approach (Maree, 2007). In this regard Savickas et al. (2009) highlighted the value of combining qualitative and quantitative approaches in career counseling, emphasizing the value of the qualitative assessment in addition to quantitative measures. Also Diemer and Gore (2009) emphasized the benefits to be gained in career counseling using simultaneously the ideographic approaches centered on the individual and on one's own specific characteristics and the nomothetic approaches which instead emphasize the possibility of making inferences based on groups of individuals for which the career development constructs are defined a priori and considered as relatively stable in the different cultural groups.

The Life Design paradigm (Savickas et al., 2009) provides a framework for appropriate identity interventions which promote the intention and action through storytelling. The primary objective is to find a way to equip clients and counselors by eliciting and designing life stories of clients during career counseling. Qualitative instruments can thus provide a structure for career counselors through which clients can tell their stories and in so doing, allow career counselors to listen, elaborate and clarify the stories of clients. In other words, processes of co-construction between clients and career counselors are promoted (Rehfuss, 2009).

Narrative perspective thus provides the stimulus for the development of instruments of qualitative assessment but also quantitative and not traditional, which will become increasingly innovative in order to facilitate the identification of the guide theme, facilitate the reconstruction of the story in proactive terms and thus help the person to deal with transitions that will meet throughout the course of life in a changing environment (Maree,

2007; Di Fabio, 2009; Di Fabio & Maree, 2012b). It is important to develop quantitative tools with a new mode of administration and restitution anchored to what Lemoine already in 2007 defined as the perspective of focused self-determination facilitated by a third party (story inspires action, story is reconstructed with psychological facilitation. Therefore, in view of the counselor as a "change agent", less and less a diagnostic modality and increasingly a reflective modality through the use of tools, that is not likely to inhibit the search for meaning of the person nor to function as a response or a self-determining prophecy (Di Fabio, 1998, 2002, 2009; Lemoine, 2007). Thus the new and innovative application modality of testing, the facilitated narrative reconstruction, within career counseling intervention, is the methodological mainstay capable of responding to the complexity involved in globalization and in new realities in the labor market prevailing on the international scenario and is configured as an attractive intervention modality which could be extended with the necessary adaptations to other areas of the psychology of counseling. As Savickas (2004) recalls the future is "to enable rather then just fit".

4. PROMISING RESEARCH AND INTERVENTION AREAS IN PSYCHOLOGY OF COUNSELING

4.1. Narrative Career Counseling

At the beginning of the Twenty-first century a new social work as a result of market globalization and the rapid development of information technology emerged. Work prospects are not definitive and predictable and, in contrast, are characterized by frequent changes. Savickas (2007b) points out that currently individuals can expect to work in at least ten different organizations in the course of their existence. Workers are encouraged to develop knowledge and skills continuously, using increasingly sophisticated technologies, to accept flexibility, to be open to change and create their own opportunities. These new concepts of a working life designate a type of career related more to the person and than to the organization (Duarte, 2004). In this new work environment, career counseling and career counseling psychology have become increasingly contextualized in line with the different theories and methods of intervention (Metz & Guichard, 2009). In the world of work characterized by instability and unpredictability, therefore the importance of the new paradigm Life Designing for the 21st century emerges (Savickas et al., 2009). The theoretical framework for interventions of Designing Life is well summarized by Guichard (2010) and includes as two fundamental pillars the career construction model developed by Savickas (2001, 2005) and the Self-construction model proposed by Guichard (2004, 2005, 2008).

Referring to these two models, the career construction model (Savickas, 1998, 2005, 2007a, 2011) and the self-construction models (Guichard, 2004, 2005, 2008, 2010), and to their complementarily and specificity it is important to underline the following aspects. Both models refer to the epistemology of social constructionism by arguing that knowledge and identity of an individual are the product of social and cognitive processes that take place in the context of interactions between individuals and groups and negotiating with each other, and that the meaning which an individual gives to reality is constructed in a social and cultural history using dialogue through which relationships are formed (Guichard, 2010). The main difference between the two models is that the Self-construction model does not specifically focus on constructing career but its goal is more general, in terms of constructing the individual's life in its different domains, whereas the career construction model by Savickas (2005) gives instead more emphasis to the means by which the individual constructs one's own career path.

The career construction model (Savickas, 2005) describes a career path according to a dynamic perspective which is based on personal meanings and past memories, present experiences and future aspirations that come together in a theme of life in progressive evolution. This self-construction model gives greater emphasis to the role of individual identity which is seen as multiple and is described as a system of subjective identity forms (SFIS) in evolution (Guichard, 2010).

The two models can therefore differentiate in these terms: the career construction model describes a person more unified, who is part of a certain continuity, while the Self-construction model presents a plural person characterized by different present experiences in the different life domains, looking for future perspectives that can unify one's life.

Whether the principal question on which Savickas' (2005) model is based is the following: "What is the meaning of my career in my life?"; the fundamental question regarding Guichard's (2010) model is instead: "What in my life (could) give it a meaning for me?". According to Guichard (2010), it is possible to hypothesize that in North America and in Europe the first question can be more adequate for adult clients and that the second question can be more adequate for adolescents and emerging adults. In light of the new paradigm Life Designing (Savickas et al., 2009) the role of career counseling consists in helping clients to elaborate one's own identity with one's own words, played roles, and to outline one's own underlying skills through comparative and probabilistic reflections. This is a non linear process but it is addressing the exploration of the self, of the environment and of the relationships between self and environment (Guichard, 2004, 2005; Guichard & Dumora, 2008).

The new paradigm Life Designing for career construction in the 21st century (Savickas et al., 2009) furthermore introduces in its definition a perspective life-long, holistic, contextual and preventive. In this perspective the counselor should favor the rooting of relative planning for the client. Vocational guidance is seen therefore as a "discipline of change" and counselors as "agents of change" rather than as specialists able to formulate a more or less predictive diagnosis (Savickas et al., 2009).

According to a constructionist perspective, career implies putting themselves in a non-static condition which leads to reinterpret the past memories, present experiences and future aspirations. The story of their life connects the individual with their constellations of complexity, offering a "biographic" bridge for constructing, reconstructing, and containing self, especially in a context of increasingly work transitions (Savickas et al., 2009). Narratability constitutes therefore an indispensable construct for Life Designing interventions: for helping clients revitalize their story, revisiting them with a greater sense of coherence, continuity and complexity; it is necessary for counselors to have narrative skills (Savickas et al., 2009).

The Life Designing paradigm in the 21st century (Savickas et al. 2009) is an identity intervention which promotes the intention and action through story telling. The process of narrating and reflecting on their stories helps individuals to integrate their personal story to construct their life themes and come to the cohesion of their lives, providing a direction to continue to live (Rehfuss 2009). The focus of the narrative is to understand and strengthen the power of the individual story.

This process moves from a positivist tradition based on objective observations to a tradition which regards the individual subjective qualitative commitment (Sarbin 1986; White & Epston 1990). Scholars argue that the narrative approach have developed theories and interventions that use storytelling as a main element in the conceptualization of career paths. The narrative should be built in career counseling to promote the success of individuals in the 21st century (Reid 2005). The purpose of the whole narrative theory and related interventions is to change the story of the individual as to change one's own life or one's own identity can change one's own story (Maree 2007; Rehfuss 2009).

Since narratives are qualitative in nature, it is important to have in career counseling also qualitative narrative tools used to measure changes in individuals' career narratives in relation to the actions carried out (Rehfuss, 2009). In this regard, Rehfuss (2009) pioneered and developed the Future Career Autobiography (FCA), an instrument able to detect changes in the professional career stories as a result of interventions from the perspective of the new paradigm for the 21st century (Savickas et al., 2009). The FCA allows detection of personal and professional motives, value and direction of individuals in narrative form. The FCA is constituted by a sheet of paper entitled "Future Career Autobiography" which contains specific instructions. If, for example, it refers to an intervention aimed at a college student the instructions are as follows: "Please use this page to write a brief paragraph about where you hope to be in life and what you hope to be doing occupationally five years after graduating from college". These instructions are intended to facilitate the development of narratives of the participants leading them to reflect on current and future goals of life, personal and professional. The FCA is administered at the beginning and at a Life Designing intervention to see if there have been changes in personal and professional stories of individuals, who are given ten minutes to write the autobiography. The FCA indeed provides for a limited space of time in the belief that it is just a short, focused and concise story forming the desired outcome for the evaluations.

A brief narrative allows more easily identified current personal and professional goals and can facilitate subsequent comparisons between the before and after individual narratives and the changes or lack of changes in the descriptions of identity of individuals (Rehfuss, 2009). FCA is configured as a first and useful new tool for evaluating the effectiveness of the intervention from the perspective of the new paradigm Life Designing for the 21st century.

On this same line of personalized intervention, since the life stories are central in the Designing Life Counseling (Savickas et al., 2009), Savickas prepared since 1989, and then progressively refined by subsequent developments, a trace interview which has now reached its complete form in its version Career Construction Interview (2010a), allows professionals to work on the construction of identity with their clients, facilitating people to give meaning to their personal and professional life. Following the indications of the author, in the commentary he provided on the use of the Career Construction Interview (Savickas, 2008), the following considerations emerged as key points of the conceptual framework of reference.

Knowing one's own story helps client achieve a clear and stable self-image. The process of self-construction is realized by the construction of the self as story, in that the self constitutes an internal compass to cross transitions. In this sense, the story is the fundamental meaning that is given in recording the personal experience and in pursuing the goal. In this context there is the value of narratability (Savickas, 2005; Savickas et al., 2009): it serves to place the issue in the larger scheme of meaning experienced in constructing the narrative of life patterns and constellations of choices, using the narrative to reduce confusion and resolve the doubt and to clarify the choices to increase the ability to decide. Indecision about career must be cleared; it is often the hesitation that comes before the transformation, because the process can result in a potential loss of position and indecision can be a response to an oscillating search for meaning, rather than a stalemate. Then, it is essential to build an ensemble which gives clarity to the parties: the stories can be the means to resolve the indecision, they take on special significance through the explanation of a deviation, or a difference, and can account for the change from beginning to end. The stories inspire action: when they tell their story, clients are building a possible future. They, in fact, tell counselors the stories that they themselves want to hear because of all the possible stories they tell the goals to current aims and inspire action; rather than remember, people reconstruct the past so that events support the today's choices and prepare the ground for future steps (Savickas, 2008).

4.2. Counseling at School

American School Counseling Association (2004) points out how the school counseling psychologists propose to help students tackle their academic, personal/social, career, and developmental needs (2004). Interventions include individual and group counseling, career counseling and guidance, classroom guidance, consultation with teachers and parents, intervention, crisis prevention and response, developing teacher workshops, working with community programs, developing transition plans and post-secondary options (American School Counseling Association, 2004).

Professionals should help students gain cohesive educational and occupational goals, helping them understand how their educational experiences can prepare them to be competitive in the labor market and achieve their goals (Gore & Metz, 2008). In the present historical period where higher levels of academic performance are pre-requisites to enter and advance in meaningful work, the relationship with the career development of academic commitment as well as with psychological well-being is particularly relevant (American College Health Association, 2004; Fouad et al., 2006; Multon, Heppner, Gysbers, Zook, & Ellis-Kalton, 2001). In view of the positive youth development (Catalano, Berglund, Ryan, Lonczak, & Hawkins, 2004; Pittman, Irby, Tolamn, Yohalem, & Ferber, 2001) is recognized in accordance with the objectives of primary prevention, that the personal skills needed as protective factors in reducing the likelihood of developing psychological dysfunction (Kenny & Hage, 2009; Kenny et al., 2009). School counselors thus have a unique role in promoting the success and wellbeing of students and facilitate their development (Metz, 2009).

In particular with regard to the transition from school to university, studies focus on the examination of resilience factors that promote adaptive transitions (Kenny & Bledsoe, 2005; Kenny, Blustein, Chaves, Grossman, & Gallagher, 2003; Kenny, Blustein, Haase, Jackson, & Perry, 2006; Kenny et al., 2007), highlighting the role of engagement, motivation, education and social support as resources to overcome the barriers perceived by young people in education and training (Kenny et al., 2006; Kozan, Di Fabio, Blustein, & Kenny, in press). It also stresses the importance of promoting career decision-making satisfaction, career planning, and teacher support as related to school engagement (Kozan et al., in press).

A further area of in-depth study for school counselors in promoting transition from school to university regards the use of non-cognitive factors, such as attitudes, behaviors, other psychosocial components that affect performance and motivation of students to encourage academic success and college readiness (Metz, Hu, & Mitton, 2011). College readiness, which can be defined as the degree to which an individual is prepared to enroll and follow successful university-level courses, is a construct that provides opportunity for intervention for counseling psychologists in schools (Conley, 2007; Metz et al., 2011). The school counselors can promote aspects of college readiness which join with knowledge of specific content and relevant key strategies, context knowledge, and academic behaviors (Metz et al., 2011).

In the field of scholastic counseling a growing interest is emerging for issues in multicultural counseling both in terms of research and intervention. In the United States, where multicultural counseling has been particularly developed, students within the education system are increasingly differentiated from the ethnic point of view, while the school counseling psychologists continue to be a homogenous group consisting predominantly of Caucasians (Loe & Miranda, 2005). It is underlined therefore that to provide effective services, it is necessary that the school counseling psychologists develop multicultural skills (Oakland, 2005; Ridley & Kleiner, 2003; Sue, Arredondo, & McDavis, 1992). It is necessary that the school counseling psychologists have the skills necessary to work with people of different ethnic groups in individual and group counseling (Ridley & Kleiner, 2003; Sue, et al., 1992). These skills are particularly related to personal beliefs and attitudes, knowledge of other cultural perspectives and practices and the ability to apply culturally sensitive interventions (Holcomb-McCoy, 1999; Sue et al., 1992).

Although much progress is being made in the field of school psychology, many aspects of the research and intervention require further study. Between 1990-1999, only 10.6% of articles (Miranda & Gutter, 2002) in the four major school psychology journals had multicultural content. More recently, Brown, Shriberg, and Wang (2007) show that between 2000 and 2003, 16.9% of the articles published were about multicultural content, underlining an increase in articles devoted to this type of content.

School counseling psychologists are a culturally homogenous group in which only 5.5% are people of color (Curtis, Hunley, Walker, & Baker, 1999). In this regard, Loe and Miranda (2005) point out that while the students come from a wide variety of groups and ethnic minorities, the school counseling psychologists are still largely homogenous from an ethnic point of view.

An analysis of the literature shows the importance of having adequate knowledge of different cultures to create appropriate counseling interventions (Brown et al., 2007; Loe & Miranda, 2005, Miranda & Gutter, 2002). The most important thing to learn for school counseling psychologist is awareness. It is through awareness that school counseling psychologists can reflect on the possible bias due to ethnic differences. With a solid understanding of their identity, the school counselor psychologists are also better able to understand the client's identity and world view that the client owns. So the school counseling psychologists are called to deepen their level of multicultural bias, since only in this way will they be able to understand the cultural identity of clients and provide appropriate interventions. In summary the need to develop multicultural competence of school counseling psychologists emerge (Brown et al., 2007; Loe & Miranda, 2005, Miranda & Gutter, 2002). If the school counseling psychologists have more multicultural skills, they are better able to provide services for students belonging to different ethnic groups. Further research on multicultural content is necessary to provide adequate services to students in the current multicultural setting.

Another area that in recent years is strongly characterized in a particularly relevant manner is research on school counseling that regards the specific aspects of intervention outcomes. This is probably due to the fact that especially in the United States it is increasingly required for school counseling psychologists not only to provide a range of services but also to evaluate the developed programs to improve the academic and professional success of students (Gore, 2008). The constraints imposed by local and national government policies have led to a particular zeal for the "responsibility" of professionals and consequently to verify the effectiveness of interventions in schools (Gore, 2008).

Baskin et al. (2010) investigated the effectiveness of 132 counseling interventions for students considering 107 studies. Recent literature in fact highlighted the need for a more active role of school counseling psychologists, indicating empirically the most effective interventions in schools (Gysbers, 2004; Romano & Kachgal, 2004; Sabella, 2004, Whiston, 2004) and increasing resources for multicultural interventions (Coleman, 2004) aimed particularly at young people from ethnic minorities (Yeh, 2004). It should also take into consideration the factors that act as moderators on the effectiveness of interventions in schools. Aspects concerning participants include: age, gender, ethnicity (Casey & Berman, 1985; Stice, Shaw, Bohon, Marti, & Rohde, 2009; Weisz, Weiss, Alicke, & Klot, 1987; Weisz, Weiss, Han, Granger, & Morton, 1995). Aspects of intervention include: training of professionals (Stice et al., 2009; Weisz et al., 1995), the mode of intervention (Prout & De Martino, 1986; Prout & Prout, 1998), the number of participants in the intervention. The meta-analysis conducted by Baskin et al. (2010) shows the effectiveness of counseling interventions implemented in schools, encouraging the work of school counseling psychologists in this area, supported by empirical research. However, it is necessary to consider factors that can affect the intervention outcomes: age (counseling is more effective with adolescents than in children), readiness for psychological interventions, cognitive and emotional abilities, similar groups (greater depth and openness to others of the same gender in group interventions), training of professionals who develop more knowledge and skills. Therefore school counseling psychologists are encouraged to design, implement, and do research on effective interventions in schools, modeling them on the needs and characteristics of specific targets, promoting a network of partnerships to implement actions that are responsive to the well-being needs of young people, especially in disadvantaged conditions or otherwise reduce access to services (Baskin et al., 2010).

In this regard, Bryan, Moore-Thomas, Day-Vines and Holcomb-McCoy (2011) examined data from the Educational Longitudinal Study of 2002 (Ingles, Pratt, Rogers, Siegel, & Stutts, 2004), showed that the contact of school students with high school counselor psychologists in relation to information about the university, has an influence on the college application rates in line with previous studies (Cabrera & La Nasa, 2000, 2001; McDonough, 2005a, 2005b; Pema, 2000; Pema et al., 2008; Pema & Titus, 2005). Bryan et al. (2011) refers to the concept of social capital in terms of resources related to the relations (Coleman, 1998): they can be considered a micro-personal level (relations with family members, teachers and counselors) or a macro level in terms of social networks or institutions (churches, schools, local organizations). The sources of social capital for students are: family, especially for education (Hetherington, 1998), school, as the main institution that involves social relationships outside the family or social network helpful for improving individual success (Lin, 2001). The role of school counseling psychologists is particularly important for low-income families less able to provide care and stimulation of technical, psychological, cognitive and informative types (Stanton-Salazar & Dornbusch, 1995). Academic support, good guidance about school programs and support by school counseling psychologists, can offer a social network that can surmount the limitations of families with limited resources. Counseling services in high school, however, appear to differ according to different ethnic groups of students: people of color, and Latin Americans can benefit from interventions by sometimes less trained counselors who do not give much emphasis to preparation for college (Corwin, Venegas, Oliverez, & Colyar, 2004; McDonough, 2005b; Plank & Jordan, 2001), realized by many activities designed for White people (Powell, 1996). The results of the study by Bryan et al. (2011) have implications for counselors, school administrators and politicians who have the responsibility to design and implement strategic counseling interventions that can improve school and academic achievement (Brown & Trusty, 2005).

4.3. Counseling for Work and Relationships

Work represent a very important component of the individual's life with which psychology of counseling deals together with other aspects of relationships, family, personal growth, and wellbeing (Hesketh, 2000).

As Hesketh stated (2000), the importance of work for the wellbeing of individuals was traditionally demonstrated both theoretically and empirically through studies that emphasize the role of work-related factors in life satisfaction in general (Near, Rice, & Hunt, 1978). Currently, two perspectives can be identified in counseling for work that recall the importance of relationships and of individual multiple roles: counseling according to the new inclusive psychology for working by Blustein (2006) and counseling for work and relationships (Richardson, 2009). According to Blustein (2006, 2011) work is central to understanding human behavior and context that contains life experience. The work has the following three basic functions: 1) work as a tool for survival and power, 2) work as an instrument for social relationship, 3) work as a means of self-determination (Blustein, 2006; Blustein, McWhirter, & Perry, 2005). In the field of counseling, Blustein (2006, 2011) highlights that it is necessary a cross a multi-dimensional inclusiveness which helps all people of every social class, race and gender to find meaning and satisfaction in their working lives, whether as workers or potential workers (Blustein, 2006). Also with regard to the relationship between caregiving and work, the inclusive perspective by Blustein (2006) proposes to give dignity to the caregiving considering a real form of work.

Blustein (2006) underlines that there are overlaps between the two processes of professional counseling and personal counseling (Heppner & Heppner, 2003; Swanson, 1995). The meta-perspective that Blustein and Spengler (1995) detected in this regard, called the domain-sensitive approach, refers to a way of intervening on clients that involves the whole range of human experiences. From the perspective of counseling intervention, the new perspective of inclusive psychology for working emphasizes the importance of helping clients improve their support structure, revitalizing the relational and community aspects of based-on-work transitions and helping clients resolve difficult relationship issues, and also of providing supportive working alliances, using the secure base of counseling for easy browsing and finding solutions when necessary (Blustein, 2006). One of the main themes of inclusive psychology for working is that changes in the social and political world as a whole are needed, in order to reduce those inequalities that still exist in education, training and work (Blustein, 2006; Blustein et al., 2005). In this perspective, another goal would be to stimulate the critical consciousness of clients (Blustein, 2006; Blustein et al., 2005). The new inclusive psychology for working shows the constellations of complexity that characterizes our age and provides an opportunity to contribute and to advance the implementation of measures that would facilitate a better quality of life for clients, encouraging growth of the community, and recognizing the inclusive dimensions of the working individual (Blustein & Di Fabio, 2009).

Another current proposal is counseling for work and relationship by Richardson (2012), which is based on the perspective of social constructionism, along with the values of feminism and social justice, in response to changes of life in contemporary society that led to a shift in vocational psychology from helping people develop their careers to build their lives through work and relationships.

The main proposal of this perspective (Richardson, 2012) is a new way to describe the construction of social life through four main contexts: market work, personal care work, personal relationships, and market work relationships. In this proposal, the traditional focus on work and career in vocational psychology is included in a more holistic concept that includes different relational aspects of personal and professional life. Market work is "the work that people do for pay in public spheres of life as well as the work that they do in educational institutions to prepare for market work" (Richardson, 2012, p. 191). Personal care work regards "work that is done to care for the self, for dependents, for relationships, and for communities in personal lives. This includes, for example, parenting, caring for older relatives, caring for one's own personal needs, and volunteering in community organizations". Personal relationships are referred to "the ongoing relationships with friends, spouses or partners, parents, children, and siblings" (Richardson, 2012, p. 191). Market work relationships regard "relationships with others such as mentors, bosses and supervisors, colleagues, teachers, and students" (Richardson, 2012, p. 191). In addition, each of the four major life contexts can include many work and relationships contexts.

The perspective by Richardson (2012) is part of social constructionism, which refers to the ways in which personal experience and human development are co-constructed by the actions of individuals and the social reality in which people are involved (Gergen, 1991, 1999, 2009; Gergen & Davis, 1995). Richardson (2012) also refers to the values of feminism and social justice that are becoming increasingly important in the psychology of counseling and vocational psychology (Blustein et al., 2005; Goodman et al., 2004; Vera & Speight, 2003). Richardson (2012) states that counseling for work and relationship perspectives are consistent with the feminist standpoint theorists (Haraway, 1997; Harding, 1991) who oppose the existence of a single objective point of view on reality and argue that the perceived reality depends on the perspective from which one observes. According to feminist theorists knowledge based on the perspective and experience of women is very different from that of men. Richardson (2012) shares this aspect and emphasizes the female experience, which requires greater attention to care work traditionally done by women to a greater extent (Haraway, 1997; Harding, 1991). In this perspective, it is also necessary to recognize the importance of care work as real work and give it dignity as proposed by the inclusive psychology for working by Blustein (2006). Counseling for work and relationships is therefore a holistic perspective that does not focus only on work in the traditional sense but includes care work, attributing importance not only to professional but also personal relations.

A further proposal of the work and counseling relationship (Richardson, 2012), which is based on career construction by Savickas (2005), is represented by the centrality of the narrative theory to understand how life is built by individual and how agentic and intentional action represents a critical process in the construction of existence. The relevance of narrative theory in vocational psychology can be strengthened in two ways: by underlining that narrative theory is fundamental to understanding how life and professional paths are constructed; arguing that the narrative theory is able to highlight how culture influences the construction of individuals' lives.

According to Richardson (2012), counseling for work and relationship shows implications for research, intervention and training. The field of research opens interesting perspectives for further work in relation to personal care, agentic action, life transitions and turning points, using narrative inquiry research, and research on critical consciousness. In the field of intervention, counseling for work and relationship shows implications for different types of intervention, both for career counseling in a specific manner and for counseling and psychotherapy in general. The most significant implication for career counseling is that counseling for work and relationship perspective expands the holistic aspect in the professional area since such perspective aims to help people in building their lives and not just their career. In the wider context of counseling and psychotherapy, it is necessary to consider all the issues that clients face in the major social contexts of their lives including the market work. A second implication for intervention, for both career counseling and for counseling and psychotherapy in general, is the centrality of the narrative theory to understand how people construct their lives.

In the field of training, counseling for work and relationship perspective has several implications. First, this perspective introduces a change in the objectives of vocational courses taught as part of most master's and doctoral-level counseling and counseling psychology programs since helping people build their lives involves training students to help people considering the various aspects of life and not only issues related to work addressed in traditional curricula. A second implication concerns the need for counselor psychologists who have expertise both within the context of career counseling and counseling in general. A further implication is that narrative theory should be regarded as a core theory in vocational course curricula with the aim to teach students how to encourage clients in the examination of their internal world, and strengthen clients' agentic action for the construction of their lives through work and relationships.

4.4. Counseling for Health and Wellbeing

According to the Ottawa Charter for Health Promotion (WHO, 1986), health is achieved when individuals develop and employ the best resources, both personal (physical and psychological) and external (social and material). According to the bio-psycho-social (Engel, 1977) conditions of health and illness resulting from the interaction between biological, psychological and social factors, it is necessary to keep in mind that they are always interconnected, even in design and implementation of intervention to favor health and wellbeing. With the adoption of the resolution The Counseling Profession as Advocates for

Optimum Health and Wellness (1989), the practice of counseling has increasingly focused on prevention (Derzon, 2006), development (American School Counselor Association [ASCA], 2003) and wellbeing (Myers & Sweeney, 2005a), implementing interventions based on rigorous research methodologies (American Counseling Association, 2005). There are two models of wellbeing as the framework of interventions to promote wellbeing. The first Wheel of Wellness model (Hettler, 1984) focused exclusively on physical health. Subsequent developments (Sweeney & Witmer, 1991; Witmer & Sweeney, 1992) in an ecological perspective, led to a second model of wellbeing based on counseling IS-Wel (Myers, Sweeney, & Witmer, 2000), meaning wellbeing as an optimal state of health that everyone is able to reach in which body, mind and spirit are integrated by the individual to live a fuller life in the community. The philosophy of wellbeing, holistic and positive, offers a new way of looking at disease according to a developmental, strength-based perspective (Gerstein, 2006; Ivey, Ivey, Myers, & Sweeney, 2005) which can promote growth and human development. It configures the need to empirically validate these current theoretical approaches for offering to counseling psychologists a framework in which to place interventions for promoting individuals' wellbeing.

In the field of counseling for wellbeing, current perspectives emerge such as that of Prilleltensky, Dokecki, Frieden, and Wang (2007) who propose a perspective in counseling, which underlines the connection between wellbeing and justice, highlighting that wellbeing is a positive condition which can be obtained through the simultaneous satisfaction of needs at the individual, relational, and collective level (Prilleltensky, Nelson, & Peirson, 2001a, 2001b; Schneider Jamner & Stokols, 2000), which cannot be separated from justice and, conversely, justice is meaningless without wellbeing.

In this perspective, the counselling should be addressed simultaneously to both wellbeing and promotion of justice. Recently, a growing number of researchers and practitioners stressed the importance of developing a value-based approach to counseling (Prilleltensky et al., 2001a, 2001b; Schneider et al., 2000). Counselors are carriers of a set of values which cannot be ignored and are faced with ethical issues: if they don't challenge the status quo of society remaining passive, they are likely to support it tacitly, to privilege intrapsychic dynamics, and to deny the origins of social suffering and distress (Dokecki, 1996). Additional issues include: the conduct more "right" to be held with the clients about social issues; which responsibilities counselors have as professionals for addressing these social issues although using training mainly aimed at helping individuals; which are the limits of their expertise when trying to work simultaneously at an individual, relational and collective level.

The important aspects for the individual wellbeing are hope, optimism (Seligman, 2002), intellectual stimulation, cognitive growth (Shonkhoff & Phillips, 2000), control (Marmot, 1999; Rutter, 1987), physical health (Smedley & Syme, 2000), psychological wellbeing (Nelson, Lord, & Ochocka, 2001; Nelson & Prilleltensky, 2005), meaning and spirituality (Kloos & Moore, 2000; Powell, Shahabi, & Thoresen, 2003), alongside supportive social relationships.

The relational wellbeing is characterized by affection, care, ties, support (Cohen, Underwood, & Gottlieb, 2000; Gottman & DeClaire, 2001; Ornish, 1997; Rhoades & Eisenberg, 2002; Stansfeld, 1999); respect for diversity (Dudgeon , Garvey, & Pickett, 2000; Goodman, 2001; Trickett, Watts, & Birman, 1994), meaning of participation in family, work and civic life (Klein, Ralls, Smith-Major, & Douglas, 2000; Nelson et al., 2001; Putnam, 2000, 2001).

It is also necessary to have satisfaction of social needs and political rights, free from economic exploitation and abuse of human rights to achieve quality of life (Felice, 2003; George, 2002; Korten, 1995, 1999; Sen, 1999a, b). Health, safety, self-determination and opportunities for growth are useful to health, access to water, non-criminal environment, fair distribution of resources and economic prosperity (Carr & Sloan, 2003; Frey & Stutzer, 2002; Keating & Hertzman, 1999; Kim, Millen, Irwin, & Gersham, 2000; Marmot & Wilkinson, 1999; Wilkinson, 1996). For facilitating empowerment of disadvantaged people, we should be aware of the differences in power between different groups based on socioeconomic class, race, gender, skills, psycho-physical privilege (Smedley & Syme, 2000; Stokols, 2000, 2003).

Four new practices of counseling (Prilleltensky et al., 2007) should be contextualized within the framework of the relationship between wellbeing and justice, since the counseling goes towards more proactive, holistic and consciousness at political level approaches. 1) Counseling psychologists have to pay equal attention to personal, relational, and collective well-being areas, without favoring one over another until the specific context of a client or a group has been explored in depth. It is essential that clients be informed about the values and processes that will face the justice-based counseling. 2) Counseling psychologists provide an opportunity for themselves and clients to engage in groups and/or in causes that promote social justice. The counselor has to pay equal attention to the reactive and proactive practices. It is necessary to keep in mind the preferences of clients, because the groups can be contraindicated for some; it is important to make selection procedures for entering groups in locations that ensure clients the opportunity to participate in social justice groups. 3) Counseling psychologists offer experiences that promote the protection, action-based research, prevention, community wellbeing and social justice. 4) Counseling psychologists have to pay equal attention to intra-psychic forces, injustice and power dynamics that can potentially oppress clients inside and outside. The internalized oppression is often a manifestation of external oppression and cannot be eradicated without considering the second.

Another area of particular interest, in the field of psychology for health and wellbeing, is counseling for lesbian, gay and bisexual (LGB) clients, particularly people of color, emphasizing the need to broaden qualitative and quantitative studies in psychological literature (Moradi, DeBlaere, & Huang, 2010). The LGB people of color are characterized by the integration of different identities (ethnic and sexual minorities) and often feel hetero-sexist stigma in communities of color (Moradi et al., 2010). The issues relating to LGB people of color have not been adequately addressed in the literature and there is a relative lack of appropriate and effective interventions (Stoltenberg et al., 2000). In addition there are two perspectives that deserve further study (Moradi et al., 2010; Parks, 2005; Phillips, 2005): the greater risk perspective suggests that people of color can experience more hetero-sexist stigma and its deleterious consequences than LGB white people; the resilience perspective that indicates how LGB people of color can be more resilient in dealing with this stigma.

A content analysis of non-empirical and empirical literature of the last ten years on LGB people of color (Singh & Shelton, 2011) allowed the identification of methodological limitations (related to recruitment, sample sizes, and inadequate training of counselors) (Mays, Cochran, & Zamudio, 2004; Morrow, 2003; Worthington & Navarro, 2003; Zea, Reisen, & Diaz, 2003) and areas of methodological innovation needed for research, which can support the activities of the counseling psychologists toward this target. Furthermore, since people rely heavily on LGB services for mental health (Bieschke, McClanahan, Tozer, Grzegorek, & Park, 2007), it is important to expand research in psychology of counseling primarily using a qualitative methodology supported by trustworthiness and credibility (Yeh & Inman, 2007), to explore the everyday experiences and understanding that participants have of a certain phenomenon and to avoid misunderstandings by policy makers (Hunt et al., 2006). Singh and Shelton (2011) provide recommendations for future research on the LGB population: explore the experiences of LGB people of color; use meaningful standards for the studies; identify and discuss the influence of subjective factors related to research on the outcomes of the studies; increase attention to research on transgender and bisexuality; provide more opportunities for training on qualitative research; using the range of qualitative methods as a function of the specific target of the study (LGB person); examine how interventions aimed at LGB people have evolved over time.

4.5. Online Counseling and New Technologies

At the beginning of the XXI century there is the birth of a new social work asset, as a result of the globalization of markets and the exorbitant development of information technology (Di Fabio, 2009; Guichard, 2009; Savickas, 2000, 2005). In this new scenario, the Internet is a tool that has a fundamental position and can influence or even revolutionize counseling and the psychology of counseling (Bernaud & Di Fabio, 2011).

Recently, much attention was paid to the use of online counseling. Gore and Leuwerke (2000) among others (see Herr, 1996; Lent, 1996; Watts, 1996), push counselors to the new and modern services that take advantage of innovations in computer technology and communications, since many applications of technology, although interesting, have not yet achieved widespread application or attention in psychological literature.

There are different methods for distance counseling: telephone, email, chat (written), videoconferencing, or chat and audiochat. These modes provide a wide range of responses that meet the needs of an audience at a distance. It is necessary to note that these emerging practices are yet to be formalized in reference to the principles of quality of service (Barak & Bloch, 2006; Mallen & Vogel, 2005).

As pointed out by Gore and Leuwerke (2009), in reviews by Barak and Bloch (2006) and Mallen and Vogel (2005), it became evident that counseling via e-mail allows both client and counselor to interact and respond according to their own time, asynchronously, and allows time for elaboration and reflection. The synchronous chat is when both participants are at the computer at the same time and communicate via instant messaging or web chat systems, which allows a more immediate interaction between client and counselor. Blogs can send information according to various formats, stories, images, videos, comments and documents that can be viewed by other people. Finally, the video conference is very close to the face-to-face counseling, but can take place remotely using a webcam and a computer.

Providing a counseling service through internet offers many advantages: functional techniques, economic costs, accessibility of the service (McCrickard & Butler, 2005). Online counseling can reach a greater number of potential clients by offering potentialities not provided by traditional interventions (McCrickard & Butler, 2005). The Internet eliminates the problem of distance as an impediment to the counseling service. Clients can work with professionals from another country (Maples & Han, 2008), from rural areas or places where there is a limited number of counselors. This aspect could be very important for those who are forced to stay indoors because of psychological problems, such as agoraphobia or mental disabilities (Barnett & Scheetz, 2003). The counseling at distance could help to increase access for groups that are traditionally under-represented and not served (Leong, 1993).

It is important to stress that at present many challenges are configured for online counseling (Gore & Leuwerke, 2009). Research has not yet clearly established the effectiveness of online counseling with respect to face-to-face counseling (Gore & Leuwerke, 2009; Manhal-Baugus, 2001; Recupero & Rainey, 2005) considering also that online counseling can preclude to counselors in part the access to non-verbal information. In fact communication via text does not convey emotions, tone of voice or body movements that often provide crucial information. Another limitation is relative to the training of counselors, because many programs do not provide specific training exercises or supervised experience in client service through the Internet (Berger, 2004; Bobek et al., 2005).

Some consensus seems to emerge among professional organizations and experts regarding the acceptability of offering online services, provided that the professionals follow the standards of professional ethics, such as the Code of Ethics of the American Association of Psychologists (APA, 2003), the Code of Ethics of the National Career Development Association (NCDA, 2007), which argues that counselors who offer their services via Internet should ensure that client needs are met. In this regard, some recommendations that Gore and Leuwerke (2009) propose are the following: online counselors should be vigilant about the potential lack of communication during their service, which could lead to errors in counseling intervention. It is possible that some aspects of online communication can, on one hand, encourage the use of a very emotional language and, on the other hand, inhibit the mechanisms that, when interacting face-to-face, regulate the emotional content of communication. As Bernaud and Di Fabio (2011) remember, while they are online, some people reveal something about themselves or express themselves more frequently or intensely than they would in person (Suler, 2004). Another issue for counselors regards online security and the processing of information transmitted via computer: e-mail between a client and the counselor can be transmitted via Internet through a network system which is not secure (Barnett & Scheetz, 2003; Kanz, 2001) and they could be seen by others.

The review by Sampson (2002) on issues related to quality and ethical use of internet-based resources also emphasizes the lack of professional online counseling for individuals with low readiness that can require specific interventions. Counselors who venture into online counseling have to be particularly careful to make sure it continues to work properly with this new medium (Fisher & Fried, 2003). They have to take additional training, which includes helping clients to overcome any frustrations experienced at the beginning of online counseling service (Glueckauf, Pickett, Ketterson, Loomis, & Rozensky, 2002), as for example technical difficulties, communication delays when writing and the feeling of lack of contact with the counselor (Haberstroh et al., 2007). Counselors, when working online, must also know that they must clearly identify themselves, so that clients can make an informed choice when engaging in a counseling service and make sure clients are old enough to take advantage of counseling (Fisher & Fried, 2003; Shaw & Shaw, 2006).

In the filed of career guidance and counseling, Sampson (2009) states that a central objective in public policy is to ensure that effective services are truly accessible to people who need them in different moments of their lives. In reference to this matter, the task of professionals is to provide effective career interventions that are truly accessible to promote social justice. Given the limited availability of funds and the growing demand for career guidance, public policy should focus on providing career guidance interventions that people need.

Sampson (2009) emphasizes the need to increase the cost/effectiveness of vocational guidance intervention through the use of ICT. This has led to some innovations, as for example: the provision of resources for career self-help websites (Sampson, 2008); the use of assessment based on Internet (Barak, 2006; Fassinger, 2005); the provision of services that combine face-to-face interventions and Internet-based interventions, including social networks (Barnes, 2008). A relevant issue concerns the importance of using differentiated vocational guidance and career counseling interventions to help individuals in choosing the career services that best meet their needs at a specific moment (Sampson, 2008). Probably individuals who have higher levels of readiness for career choice can be better able to benefit from career guidance interventions with limited assistance, while individuals who show lower levels of readiness cannot be ready to receive interventions without the assistance of a professional (Sampson, 2008). Only limited evidence of the effectiveness of the use of self-help computer-based career interventions have emerged (Miller & Brown, 2005). In Sampson's (2008) perspective, the limited effectiveness of these interventions seems to be due to individuals who have a low to moderate readiness. But it is important to ask whether this is really true because there is not enough available research on this issue (Bernaud & Di Fabio, 2011). In any case, when professionals provide the client with assistance, they greatly increase the effectiveness of the intervention (Miller & Brown, 2005; Whiston, 2003; Whiston, Sexton, & Lasoff, 1998).

Bernaud and Di Fabio (2011) suggest caution and stress the need to continue to increase knowledge through empirical research. Authors report, for example, a need for further in-depth studies on Suler's (2004) hypothesis, which refers to the idea of disinhibition in the use of the network. According to Suler (2004) criteria for the facilitation of disinhibition are: anonymity, invisibility, asynchronicity of the exchange, the magic of technology use, attractive character of the exchange, perception of fairness in the exchange. Moreover, Bernaud (as cited in Di Fabio, 2010a) emphasizes the possibility of a paradoxical implication for those who use Internet. If in online counseling, clients are characterized from the ease in the use of interventions (implication) on the one hand, on the other hand from the ease of leaving them without explanation, sometimes without giving signals before (disimplication), this phenomenon would seem to configure in terms of a consumer attitude on Internet.

In conclusion it is possible to state that the new and promising use of Internet in counseling shows the following development areas: developing research in particular on effectiveness of interventions, developing new models of online counseling, promotion of quality standards, training of e-counselors (Bernaud & Di Fabio, 2011).

5. Effectiveness of Counseling Interventions

The evaluation of counseling interventions represents an area of traditional research in counseling and psychotherapy (Oliver & Spokane, 1988; Truax & Carkhuff, 2008; Whiston et al., 1998). Current studies on the effectiveness of counseling interventions can be particularly found in relation to school counseling intervention and to career counseling intervention.

In relation to school counseling interventions, Whiston, Lee Tai, Rahardja, and Eder (2011) recently conducted two meta-analyses with the aim of reducing the gap in research on counseling, examining studies on school counseling interventions with a quantitative approach. The first meta-analysis, using the traditional approach, which is to compare the experimental group and the control group based on standardized mean difference procedures (Chambers, 2004), producing an effective size as an indicator of the effectiveness of intervention obtained from the experimental group compared to that of the control group. The second meta-analysis has instead used standardized gain scores obtained from pre-post test comparisons. Furthermore, authors investigated the influence of moderator variables on effect size, such as quality of research methods, characteristics of sample, and type of intervention (Lipsey, 2003). Whiston (2002) highlighted the importance of doing research, so far limited, to analyze the effects of counseling interventions at a school level as empirical support for economic investment by politicians, school administrators, and families. The need for a programmatic approach to school counseling emerges instead of the simple activation of services, to respond more effectively and timely to the needs of students (Gysbers & Henderson, 1988, 1994, 2000, 2006; Gysbers & Moore, 1974, 1981). The activities that according to Whiston et al. (2011) should be included in school curricula are: guidance curriculum (which favors guidance and prevention), individual planning (individual meetings client-counselor for academic and professional planning), responsive services (individual or group work, peer counseling or mentoring to support students at risk of dropping out), and system support (management, maintenance, reinforcement of school counseling programs). The results of the meta-analysis by Whiston et al. (2011) indicate positive effects of counseling interventions in schools, including an increased ability toward problem-solving skills, school attendance, social skills, and reduced behavior problems of students. The need also emerges to conduct further research on the effectiveness of counseling in schools, in particular, to understand what interventions are most effective with which clients (considering different backgrounds), and under what circumstances for fostering personal, social, academic development and school success.

The study on the intervention effectiveness is currently an important area also in the field of career counseling (Brown et al., 2003; Heppner & Heppner, 2003; Oliver & Spokane, 1988; Whiston, Brecheisen, & Stephens, 2003; Whiston et al., 1998). Research on the effects of career counseling interventions remain limited, especially compared to research on the effectiveness of psychotherapy, which has a long tradition of research (Barkham, 2003). Career counseling is a different intervention with respect to psychotherapy, but has some common features with it. The primary focus of career counseling are career or work-related issues but the process takes place within a relational context in which career issues presented by the client will inevitably overlap with personal issues (Richardson, in press; Whiston & Oliver, 2005). To ensure the effectiveness of intervention, the career counselor has to possess interpersonal skills along with specific technical skills for career counseling.

Moreover, Heppner (2005) underlines that, although there are numerous studies on the effectiveness of guidance in general, much less is known about career counseling in particular and research in career counseling processes is very limited. The author argues that research in this area is lacking for several reasons: in particular a priori belief that career counseling is very effective; the idea that career counseling does not refer to specific processes; the slow contribution that research on processes provides to base knowledge. It configures the importance of examining the processes during counseling in relation to the characteristics of professionals, micro-techniques and effectiveness of the intervention (Heppner, Multon, Gysbers, Ellis , & Zook, 1998; Multon, Ellis-Kalton, Heppner, & Gysbers, 2003). The study by Heppner et al. (1998) focused on the impact of career counselor self-efficacy on career counseling, stressing that most general characteristics of the career counselor, for example, the level of experience, showed fewer relationships with the career counseling process and results, while more specific characteristics, for example, the level of self-efficacy, cultural competence, or style of solving problems, seem to be promising factors for further research on career counseling. Subsequent research conducted by Multon et al. (2003) on counselor self-disclosure showed that the total number of self-disclosures correlate negatively with the working alliance measured at the end of the interviews, stressing that counselor self-disclosures are perceived by the client as a restraint to the relationship.

In general, the meta-analysis related to research on the effectiveness of career counseling showed a positive impact, although the effect size varied in different studies. A classical meta-analysis carried out by Oliver and Spokane (1988), for example, showed an overall average effect size of .82, while a more recent meta-analysis conducted by Brown and Ryan Krane (2000) showed a modest average effect size of only .34. A subsequent meta-analysis carried out by Whiston et al. (1998) still showed a small average effect size of .30, although individual career counseling produced a more robust .75. Whiston et al. (2003) underlined that career interventions were often studied as an overall category that includes workshops, computer applications, classes, and self-administered workbooks and inventories and not only individual counseling, suggesting that the observed variation in effect observed in meta-analyses could be explained by the range of included intervention modalities. A number of studies showed greater effects for individual career counseling with respect to interventions without the presence of a counselor (Whiston, 2002; Whiston et al., 2003), suggesting the importance of relationship in counseling. In light of these different results, Heppner (2005) suggests the importance of conducting further research to fully understand how specific aspects of career counseling are related to different outcomes. Whiston and Oliver (2005) argue furthermore that it is important not only to know that the career counseling is effective, but knowing what processes contribute to this effect.

Regarding the process, research examined the role of relationship between career counselor and client during the intervention, as well as other technical components of career counseling. Research documented the importance of relationships with the client in counseling (Heppner & Hendricks, 1995; Kirschner, Hoffman, & Hill, 1994), although the relevance for the outcome of career counseling was less evident (Heppner et al, 1998; Whiston & Oliver, 2005). Regarding other dimensions of career counseling, Anderson and Niles (2000) showed that clients valued emotional support, as well as self-exploration and ability to obtain information on career paths. Healy (2001) similarly reported that in career counseling clients attributed value to the relational support, such as being listened to and clarification of feelings, but also to individualized test interpretations and feedback and acquisition of useful information. Brown and Ryan Krane (2000) found that in addition to providing support, the use of workbooks and written exercises, world of work information, and counselor modeling were important to help clients make a decision about their career path. These components of counseling were not, however, assessed in relation to different outcomes of counseling.

In relation to outcomes, client satisfaction was frequently considered as an index of intervention effectiveness (Brown & Brooks, 1990; Crites, 1981; Mau & Fernandes, 2001).

Despite the limitations of self-report as an outcome assessment, Zysberg (2010) argues that client satisfaction remains an important indicator, since counseling is usually undertaken in response to a request of a client and a client can decide not to participate or continue if dissatisfied. Zysberg (2010) also underlines that the perceived relationship with the career counselor has an important role in client satisfaction, supporting the value of the relational skills of the counselor.

Maguire (2004) challenged researchers to provide more robust evidence of different outcomes of career counseling for both the individual client and for society in a broader perspective. Wider outcomes for society, such as organizational and economic benefits emerge over time, while the individual benefits in terms of attitudinal, motivational, and learning changes of client are more immediate (Maguire, 2004). Regarding the expected results for career counseling, Savickas (2002) argues that in addition to customer satisfaction, change or development of the client should also be considered. Ryan (1999) identified growth in career maturity, congruence, and vocational identity of the client as a key outcome for career counseling, while Kidd, Jackson, and Hirsch (2003) identify, through interviews with adult workers, a set of motivational and learning outcomes, including self-awareness or self-insight, and awareness of opportunities, transition skills, and a sense of future direction, as relevant outcomes for career counseling interventions.

Another modality traditionally taken into account in the French-speaking countries to detect career counseling outcomes refers to the vocational and professional development model developed by Pelletier, Noiseux, and Bujold (1974). This model identifies four fundamental career counseling outcomes for individuals: knowledge of self and knowledge of school and career pathways; the mastery of skills for seeking and obtaining work and school entry, and the presence of motivational dispositions to advance in school and at work. These outcomes reflect the importance of motivational and learning dimensions, similar to those identified by Kidd et al., 2003. In line with this method of defining career counseling outcomes, a study conducted with university students in France (Bernaud, Di Fabio, & Saint-Denis, 2010) showed how both client satisfaction and perceived effects of career counseling, according to the model by Pelletier et al. (1974), were explained by both technical skills of the career counselor, which included academic guidance, the quality of information and materials provided, use of testing, relational skills of career counseling, including self-disclosure, openness, and the use of non-directive and non evaluative counseling. In following a study among Italian high school students and university students (Di Fabio, Bernaud, & Palazzeschi, 2008), client satisfaction was best explained by perceived relational behaviors of the career counselor, while perceived effects of career counseling defined according to the model by Pelletier et al. (1974) are better explained by perceived technical behaviors of the career counselor. These results were confirmed by a subsequent study (Di Fabio, Bernaud, & Kenny, in press) conducted with Italian university students, highlighting the importance of both relational and technical competencies of career counseling for both client satisfaction and perceived effects of career counseling across multiple dimensions.

Currently in the theoretical framework of Life Designing paradigm for the 21st century (Savickas et al., 2009), it is important to use qualitative assessment and intervention in a perspective that emphasizes the transition from scores to stories (McMahon & Patton, 2002). The Life Designing paradigm in the 21st century (Savickas et al., 2009) is a framework for identity interventions that promote intention and action through storytelling. Current narrative career interventions and instruments try to help both client and counselor to work with life stories: these qualitative interventions and instruments provide a structure that enable clients to narrate their stories and also offer career counselors more opportunities to listen, clarify or change the co-constructed with client story (Rehfuss, 2009).

It is therefore configured in the research the necessity to verify the effectiveness of career counseling interventions and qualitative instruments (Di Fabio, 2012). In that regard the validity of Future Career Autobiography, as an assessment instrument for measuring change in personal and occupational life narratives resulting from typical career interventions, was verified (FCA, Rehfuss, 2009). The study by Rehfuss and Di Fabio (in press) carried out on Italian female entrepreneurs with a control group, showed a significant change from general to more specific life and occupational themes after Life Designing career counseling intervention in the experimental group while the control group did not reveal any changes. Moreover, the number of words used in the FCA increased after the intervention in the experimental group revealed expanded narrative expression.

The effectiveness of some modalities of qualitative intervention according to the Life Designing paradigm perspective (Savickas et al., 2009) was verified through the FCA (Rehfuss, 2009). In some studies (Di Fabio & Maree, in press, 2012b), the effectiveness of such modalities of qualitative intervention has been verified through quantitative tools since traditionally effective career counseling interventions are those which diminish the career decision-making difficulties and enhance the career decision-making self-efficacy of clients (Whiston, 2008).

The effectiveness of the Construction Career Interview (CCI, Savickas, 2010a) was verified in Italian university students with the use of control group (Di Fabio, in press a). The results of the study (Di Fabio, in press a) showed: an increase in the number of words produced in the FCA after the intervention in the experimental group, and an increase of change themes relative to personal and occupational areas in the experimental group. These results emphasize the effectiveness of the Construction Career Interview.

Similar results were obtained in relation to the Career Construction Genogram (Di Fabio, 2010b), whose effectiveness was demonstrated with Italian female entrepreneurs also in this case using an experimental design with control group (Di Fabio, in press b). The results of the study (Di Fabio, in press b) showed: an increase in the number of words produced in FCA after the intervention in the experimental group, and an increase of change themes relative to personal and occupational areas in the experimental group.

The effectiveness of the Career Interest Profile (CIP, Maree, 2010), a qualitative instrument for deepening professional interests, was also verified (Di Fabio & Maree, submitted). The effectiveness of the CIP was verified through a quali-quantitative approach in Italian university students with the use of control group (Di Fabio & Maree, submitted). From a qualitative point of view the results showed: an increase in the number of words produced in the FCA after the intervention in the experimental group; an increase in change themes relative to personal and occupational areas in the experimental group (Di Fabio & Maree, submitted). From a quantitative point of view, the intervention with the CIP led to a decrease in career decision-making difficulties measured through the Career Decision-Making Difficulties Questionnaire (CDDQ, Gati, Krausz, & Osipow, 1996) and an increase in career decision-making self-efficacy measured by the Career decision self-efficacy Scale - Short Form (SF-CDSES, Betz & Taylor, 2000), tools traditionally used to verify the effectiveness of interventions (Whiston, 2008; Di Fabio & Maree, 2012b).

Another study (Di Fabio & Maree, 2012) verified the effectiveness of a Group-based Life Designing Counseling in Italian female entrepreneurs with a control group using a quantitative approach. The results showed that the Group-based Life Designing Counseling intervention was effective, producing a decrease in the career decision-making difficulties (Gati et al., 1996) and an increase in the career decision-making self-efficacy (Di Fabio & Maree, 2012).

The presented studies showed that the analyzed interventions (The Career Construction Interview, the Construction Career Genogram, the Career Interest Profile, the Group-based Life Designing Counseling) were effective for the development of self-awareness through a process of continuous construction and reconstruction with the use of narrative in a storied approach (Maree 2007; Savickas 1989, 2005, 2010a).

Another area of current research in the field of counseling is relative to the aspect of motivation of the client to counseling intervention within the self-determination theory (Deci & Ryan, 1985) theoretical framework. Ryan, Lynch, Vansteenkiste, and Deci (2010) extensively covered the issue of motivation of clients in counseling and psychotherapy, using the self-determination theory. Some clients are resistant to change (Engle & Arkowitz, 2006; Greenberg, 2004; MacKinnon, Michaels, & Buckley, 2006) for several reasons: sending or pressure from others, seeking approval, lack of interest. Therefore it is important to work toward increasing motivation of the client, as positive and lasting results occur when clients are actively and personally involved in change (Overholser, 2005; Ryan & Deci, 2008). The empirical evidence showed that the motivation of client was predictive of intervention effectiveness (Ryan et al., 2010). Therefore the motivation of client to counseling intervention should be considered a component of the process rather than separate, and motivational strategies should be integrated into practice through non-specific factors (Ryan et al., 2010). Lynch, Vansteenkiste, Deci, and Ryan (2011), again in the self-determination theory framework, make a distinction between intrinsic and extrinsic motivation (from external regulation to full volition). So if the motivation of the client to counseling is integrated (autonomous) it is more likely that client will continue the path and receive greater benefits regardless of time spent in the intervention, compared to the client whose level of motivation (in purely quantitative terms) can be equally high, but at a qualitative level is externally regulated (controlled). This is because the changes of clients who are more motivated on their own are more likely to be self-selected, deep, consistent with their values, maintained over time and generalized to various spheres of their lives.

With regard to the multicultural counseling perspective, it is important to consider the motivation to the intervention of clients with backgrounds different from that of the counselor, which can affect the relationship between client and counselor and the counseling process itself. For this reason, the respect of clients and their autonomy is important (Kim, 2011). Counseling psychologists may address ethical issues related to supporting the autonomy of clients and the implications for multicultural counseling: it is important to respect the different backgrounds, perspectives, value systems and beliefs of others (Leong & Lee, 2006; Lynch, 2002; Pedersen, 1991; Sue et al., 1992).

In conclusion, the motivation of the client to counseling intervention as the construction of autonomy becomes a positive outcome with universal value with respect to individuation and independent culturally dependent processes, regardless of the approach used, as an indicator of higher individual functioning. This is especially true in times of multicultural applications in counseling (Ryan et al., 2010).

6. TRAINING OF PROFESSIONALS IN PSYCHOLOGY OF COUNSELING

For analyzing the issue of training of professionals in psychology of counseling, we refer to a current study conducted by Pieterse, Evans, Risner-Butner, Collins, and Mason (2009). The authors conducted a content analysis of 54 multicultural and diversity-related course syllabi from programs of counseling and counseling psychology accredited by the American Psychological Association and by the Accreditation of Counseling and Related Programs.

The results show that most of the course emphasizes the importance of multicultural skills, highlighting social justice as one of the main contents. In the past three decades, in the field of counseling psychology, an increasing emphasis is recognized on racial and cultural variables in research, training and intervention. The claim that multicultural work required a distinct set of skills was introduced in 1982 by Sue et al. and revised in 1992 by Sue et al. The multicultural competencies are highlighted by the attitudes and beliefs, knowledge, attitudes and skills in three areas (Arredondo et al., 1996; APA, 2003): Awareness of the counselor about values and personal biases, understanding the perspective of the "culturally different" and development of strategies and intervention techniques. Pedersen (1991) believes that multiculturalism is "a wide range of multiple groups without grading, comparing, or ranking them as better or worse than one another and without denying the very distinct and complementary or even contradictory perspectives that each group brings with it" (p. 4). According to Abreu, Chung and Atkinson (2000) representation more widespread in multicultural counseling includes knowledge, awareness and ability to work in societies characterized by multiple raids, ethnic groups and cultures (Arredondo et al., 1996). The focus of social justice is to respond to inequalities in the system that lead to marginalization of various groups of people (Vera & Speight, 2003), racism, oppression, sexism and classism (Smith, Baluch, Bernabei, Robohm, & Sheehy, 2003). Goodman et al. (2004) conceptualized the role of social justice as "the scholarship and professional action designed to change societal values, structures, policies, and practices, such that disadvantaged or marginalized groups gain increased access to these tools of self determination" (p. 795). While multiculturalism focuses on the diversity (age, race, gender, language, country of origin, religion, sexual orientation, socioeconomic status) in a perspective of inclusion and acceptance, social justice focuses more on oppression and marginalization in context of diversity at a society level (Vera & Speight, 2003). The accreditation standards promoted by the Council on the Accreditation of Counseling and Related Programs (CACREP, 2001) emphasized that training for multicultural counseling should include courses related to: social justice, conflict resolution, cultural awareness, nature of biases, prejudices, processes of intentional or unintentional oppression and discrimination, other culturally oriented behaviors which can be negative for growth of the person, multicultural counseling theories, identity development and multicultural skills. Many scholars emphasized the need to introduce multiculturalism, considering three main areas of knowledge, awareness and development of specific skills, in training programs for counseling (Collins & Pieterse, 2007; D'Andrea & Daniels, 1991; Reynolds, 1995); however, these aspects are often treated through single courses (Abreu et al., 2000; Ponterotto, 1997). Some of the challenges of multicultural training include broad definitions of ethnographic and cultural variables, as well as wide differences in the degree to which the contextual variables of people are emphasized (Ancis &

Rasheed, 2005). There is not a training more effective than another, and this shows a lack of consensus in defining terms and a framework, a lack which hinders efforts to achieve effective training for multicultural counseling (Ancis & Rasheed, 2005). Fouad (2006) identified some critical elements such as the need for an explicit commitment to the institutional and program level, an active recruitment and retention of diverse faculty, an examination of course content for a culture-centered emphasis. A resistance from the students of counseling emerged to study in-depth issues relative to multicultural counseling (Carter, 2001; Helms et al., 2003). There are also several approaches, including training for self-awareness, skill development, and multicultural experiences of cultural "immersion" (Kim & Lyons, 2005).

Recently, social justice is increasingly recognized as a critical aspect of the training programs for counseling psychologists (Constantine et al., 2007; Goodman et al., 2004; Kiselica & Robinson, 2001; Talleyrand, Chung, & Bemak, 2006) so that the American Counseling Association accepted the new division of Counselors for Social Justice (Lewis, Arnold, House, & Toporek, 2002). The counselor, in fact, has a role in the process of social change, particularly in teaching strategies for social change (Pieterse et al., 2008). Key issues in the training occurred in peace education, political ideology, freedom of conscience, social activism, economic systems of oppression, poverty, principles of democracy, transformative learning, full and fair participation of all groups to society, mental health interventions focused on prevention (Bell, 1997; Fox & Prilleltensky, 1997; Friere, 1970; Lalas, 2007; Vera & Speight, 2007). Thus the central aspects of a training program regards individual diversity, multiculturalism and social justice to respond effectively and timely to the multiple needs of a postmodern society (Pieterse et al., 2008).

Also Collins and Arthur (2007), focusing on a Canadian counselor, demonstrated that they are increasingly working with different targets that require the development of new approaches, particularly taking the cultural aspects into account. A key question is how to develop attitudes, knowledge and skills for effective practice based on skills and ethical conduct. By a large point of view, all interactions are multicultural (Pedersen, 1991). The populations in the postmodern society are becoming increasingly multicultural and the definition of culture (and the population-specific approach) now includes many factors such as age, gender, sexual orientation, ability, religion, socioeconomic status and social class (Arredondo & Perez, 2006; Arthur & Collins, 2005; Mollen, Ridley, & Hill, 2003). Each counselor brings one's own cultural identity that influences how they interact with clients (Ho, 1995; James, 1996). According to the model by Collins and Arthur (2007) there are three main areas, each characterized by specific core competencies. Each of them can be implemented through specific strategies.

1) Cultural Awareness-Self: Active awareness of personal assumptions, values, and biases: the counselor is the starting point for the development of multicultural competence (American Psychological Association [APA], 2002b; Arredondo et al., 1996; Sue et al., 1992), that is, by changing the definition of culture it is possible to deepen self-knowledge. The five core competencies are the following. 1. Demonstrate awareness of your own cultural identities. 2. Demonstrate awareness of differences between your own cultural identities and those of individuals from other dominant or non-dominant groups. 3. Demonstrate awareness of the impact of culture on the theory and practice of counseling/psychology. 4. Demonstrate

awareness of the personal and professional impact of the discrepancy between dominant and non-dominant cultural groups in North America. 5. Demonstrate awareness of your level of multicultural competence.

2) Cultural Awareness-Other: Understanding the worldview of the client: it is important to know the point of view of the client. The three core competencies are as follows. 1. Demonstrate awareness of the cultural identities of your clients. 2. Demonstrate awareness of the relationship of personal culture to health and well-being. 3. Demonstrate awareness of the socio-political influences that impinge on the lives of non-dominant populations.

3) Culturally Sensitive Working Alliance: the meeting point between the awareness of one's own culture and that of the client is the development of a working alliance that has three components: a) a relationship of trust and respect; b) agreement on the objectives, c) agreement on tasks (Collins & Arthur, 2005a, 2006a). Three core competencies should be developed by the counselor. 1. Establish trusting and respectful relationships with clients that take into account cultural identities. 2. Collaborate with clients to establish counseling goals that are responsive to salient dimensions of cultural identity. 3. Collaborate with clients to establish client and counselor tasks that are responsive to salient dimensions of cultural identity.

It should be noted that cultural competence does not refer to mere possession of knowledge, information about the culture and behavioral skills that can or cannot disrupt the psychologist from a personal point of view. It is rather to internalize this knowledge so deeply, that it becomes a part of person and not something added to the behavioral repertoire (Fowers & Davidov, 2006). Moreover to effectively translate the skills acquired in practice and ethical standards requires judgment (ability to assess when to apply particular knowledge or skill, for example, with such clients, in what circumstances, such as focusing on particular aspects) and diligence (self-reflection and attention to both the level of multicultural competence of an individual and to apply the appropriate level of intercultural competence in all areas of intervention; Collins & Arthur, 2005b). Counselors are therefore required to contribute to the wellbeing of all members of society including the non-dominant populations that often have reduced access to services and have fewer resources. Also it is necessary to develop research about multicultural competence of counselors to validate the traditional framework (Atkinson & Israel, 2003; D'Andrea, Daniels, & Noonan, 2003; Reynolds & Pope, 2003), about barriers and development facilitators, about application in intervention and about the maintenance of multicultural competence and training (Parham & Whitten, 2003). Counselor psychologists as practitioners with multicultural skills could be able to stimulate a change in the broader social, economic and political system, to influence client distress and emotional and psychological well-being (Collins & Arthur, 2007). In recent years the need has emerged for multiculturally competent career counseling (Fouad, 1993, 1995; Fouad & Arbona, 1994; Metz, Fouad, & Ihle-Helledy, 2009; Spokane, Fouad, & Swanson, 2003; Vespia, Fitzpatrick, Fouad, Kantamneni, & Chen, 2010). In the field of vocational psychology, a growing recognition of need has emerged for context-sensitive career counseling that recognizes the role of the cultural contexts of one's own career in clients behavior (Blustein, 2001; Chung, 2003; Cook, Heppner, & O'Brien, 2002; Fouad, 2001; Fouad et al., 2008; Fouad & Walker, 2005; Kantamneni & Fouad, 2011; Whiston, 2003). Within a perspective that sees career counseling as a context sensitive, it is necessary to pay attention not only to the cultural contexts of clients but also to the cultural contexts of counselors, stressing the importance for career counselors to consider metacognitive processes for addressing counselor-related cultural factors (Byars-Winston & Fouad, 2006). Even Richardson (2012), in her counseling for work and relationship perspectives, supports the importance of training career counselors to consider the various aspects of their clients' lives and not only work-related problems.

The guidelines for prevention of the American Psychological Association (Hage et al., 2007) point out further aspects of the training of professionals. In particular, the twelfth guideline identifies the following significant aspects for the formation of counseling psychologists for prevention (Conyne, 1994, 1997, 2004; Durlak, 2003; Romano & Hage, 2000): understand the difference between a prevention perspective and a restorative view; develop and conduct educational programs; evaluate community needs and establish programs to meet them; implement systemic interventions; take an ecological approach, working with multidisciplinary teams; develop marketing actions, pay attention to positive psychology and that of positive youth development; strengthen individuals and their communities; assess the implications of local and national policies and political influences. In this regard Conyne, Newmeyer, Kenny, Romano, & Matthews (2008) identify three key teaching strategies in prevention: 1) establish specific courses or sequence of courses in prevention programs offered by the home or departments; 2) insert the concepts of prevention within existing courses of the program or department, 3) develop support area possibilities in prevention integrating courses in other disciplines.

Within the inclusive psychology for working perspective by Blustein (2006, 2011) and their domain-sensitive approach perspective (Blustein & Spengler, 1995) appears essential for training the career counselor to acquire competences to help clients improve their support structure, revitalizing relational and community aspects and providing a secure base in counseling to facilitate exploration and individuate possible solutions (Blustein, 2006). Career counselors should be able to increase the choice for clients who believe they have no chance because of their socio-economic disadvantage conditions promoting social justice (Blustein, 2006). Blustein (2006) also stresses the importance for career counselors to acquire abilities to promote social and political changes to reduce inequalities in the field of education, training and work.

A further aspect relative to training of professionals in psychology of counseling is the evaluation of training interventions. Ridley and Mollen (2010) evaluated the status of training programs for counselors, trying to understand if they can achieve the set objectives, that is to bring benefits to clients and not be detrimental to them (the first principle of the Ethical Principles of Psychologists and the Code of Conduct; American Psychological Association, 2002a). In particular authors focus on the limited purpose of micro-skills training (Ridley, Kelly, & Mollen, 2011), and propose a multilevel model for the development of counseling skills (Ridley, Mollen, & Kelly, 2011a) and discuss the implications (Ridley, Mollen, & Kelly, 2011b). The psychology of counseling is facing important issues as the adequacy of training especially for young people who are being trained as counselors (Bein et al., 2000; Binder, 2004; Boswell & Castonguay, 2007). According to the authors this is a problem that goes beyond the individual, the members of the faculty and the training programs. Moreover, the relational skills of the counselor, developed with formal training, are comparable to those developed through informal courses (O'Donovan, Bain, & Dyck, 2005); styles of response of advanced students are similar to those of novices (Tracey, Hays, Malone, & Herman, 1988);

postdoctoral students show greater flexibility, immediacy of response styles to clients, greater ability to establish objectives for intervention, agreement on tasks and understanding of the intervention, assessment and evaluation, but that does not support greater effectiveness of the intervention conduit (Tracey et al., 1988). And yet the relationship between experience and expertise is not significant (Goodyear, 1997; Lichtenberg, 1997), for example, as regards the ability to build a bond with the client, there are no differences between the advanced and beginning students (Mallinckrodt & Nelson, 1991). It is necessary develop valid methods for assessing complex skills of the counselor in training as well as those for microskills (Baker & Daniels, 1989).

Advanced students do not seem to be able to promote positive outcomes of the interventions compared to beginners (Strupp & Hadley, 1979). The experience does not warrant the respect of ethical standards by the counselor, interconnected with the skills of multicultural counseling (Goh, 2005; Jennings, Sovereign, Bottorff, Mussell, & Vye, 2005). It is especially important to consider how counselors resolve the problems (expertise) than what they do (skills). How is it referred to cognitive and affective approaches to the intervention of counselors, including how to conceptualize the case, determining the approach with clients, developing and supporting the motivation over time (Goodyear, 1997).

In conclusion, it can proceed with the research to foster the development of the profession of counseling psychology, critically evaluating the methods used so far in practice and encouraging new models for training (Ridley & Mollen, 2010).

Norcross, Evans and Ellis (2010) collected information on the rates of acceptance of applications, standards for admission, financial assistance, student characteristics, and theoretical research on the outcome of selection on the American Psychological Association-accredited counseling programs. The practice-oriented programs have more applicants accepted (29%) compared to research-based programs (17%).

Average Graduate Record Examination Scores (594 quantitative, 552 verbal) and average grade point averages (3.57) are consistent and similar across programs. About 70% of students are women, 29% belong to ethnic and racial minorities, 8% are international students. 89% of students have an internship as part of the five-year programs.

In the past two decades research showed significant differences among the programs accredited by the APA along the continuum of research-practice (Cherry, Messenger, & Jacoby, 2000; Gaddy, Charlot-Swilley, Nelson, & Reich, 1995; Mayne, Norcross, & Sayette, 1994; Norcross, Castle, Sayette, & Mayne, 2004).

The research-oriented programs accept fewer applications, higher scores on the Graduate Record Examination (GRE), longer training and get more funding. The practice-oriented programs accept about 29% of the applications, admit 8-9 students per year and offer full financial support to 30% of students (Stoltenberg et al., 2000).

These programs are linked to universities. Models of counseling psychology training are rooted in institutional contexts that influence them for a good part (Stoltenberg et al., 2000). About 95% of programs are research-oriented at university as opposed to 75% of those equal-emphasis and 33% of those practice-oriented. In conclusion, echoing the words of Stoltenberg et al. (2000): "The history of counseling psychology has been one of examining and reexamining the utility of integrating science and practice" (p. 622).

CONCLUSION

The present chapter aimed to offer the reader a theoretical framework with ideas for reflection in relation to the actual perspective in the field of psychology of counseling as a stimulus that opens to the richness of contributions that we will deal with in the next chapters of this volume. Since review of the literature, it has emerged that psychology of counseling seems a variegated, dynamic and flexible framework in response to multiple and different requests of current postmodern scenarios.

In response to an increasingly globalized and multicultural society and to an increasingly changing labor market which encourages people to deal with an increasing number of transitions (Guichard, 2009; Savickas et al., 2009), psychology of counseling opens in new issues and research related to that discipline moves from traditional themes relative to processes and outcomes of counseling intervention to challenges of internationalization (Leong & Savickas, 2007; Savickas, 2007a) and indigenization (Leung & Chen, 2009; Ho et al., 2001; Pée-Pua & Protacio-Maecelino, 2000), multiculturalism (American School Counseling Association, 2004; Oakland, 2005; Ridley & Kleiner, 2003; Fouad, 1993, 1995; Fouad & Arbona, 1994; Metz et al., 2009), prevention (Kenny & Hage, 2009; Kenny et al., 2009), social justice (Kenny, 2011; Kenny & Hage, 2008; Weisfeld & Perlman, 2005), and online counseling (Gore & Leuwerke, 2009; Herr, 1996; Lent, 1996; Watts, 1996).

In fact, the psychology of counseling encompasses different needs, the necessity to have a framework increasingly internationalized that is cross-national, consensual, convergent and shares definitions, theoretical and intervention aspects (Leong & Savickas, 2007; Savickas, 2007) on one hand, on the other hand the need to implement strategies that facilitate the development of indigenous theory and research based on the specific cultural context in which they are applied (Leung & Chen, 2009; Pée-Pua & Protacio-Maecelino, 2000; Savickas, 2007a). As Savickas (2007) underlines, indigenization doesn't mean isolation and the auspice is to promote a real international collaboration.

Faced with an always more multiethnic society, the questions about multicultural counseling arise primarily in the school (American School Counseling Association, 2004), as well as in particular fields, for example, the promotion of health and wellbeing of lesbian, gay and bisexual people where there emerges an always increasing necessity to amply research both qualitative and quantitative studies (Moradi et al., 2010; Singh & Shelton, 2011).

In relation to social justice (Kenny, 2011; Kenny & Hage, 2008) the importance is emphasized for counseling psychologists to address, in particular, those that have more difficulties in access psychological services, underlying the role of prevention to foster the development of protective factors which can strengthen the resilience against social stress in order to empower the individuals and the community (Kenny & Hage, 2008). Also the theories on wellbeing unite with justice issues (Prilleltnsky et al., 2001a, 2001b), pointing out that wellbeing can be achieved through the simultaneous satisfaction of needs at individual, relational and collective levels.

Current society is characterized by new technologies that open interesting perspectives for online counseling (Gore & Leuwerke, 2009; Herr, 1996; Lent, 1996; Watts, 1996), allowing counselors to provide effective action that is accessible to a major number of people in order to promote social justice (Sampson, 2009).

In the actual work context, life is ever-changing and workers are stimulated to continuously develop knowledge and skills, to always use more sophisticated technologies, to accept flexibility, to be available to change and to create alone one's own opportunity (Guichard, 2009; Savickas et al., 2009). The career counselor becomes the Life Designing counselor (Savickas et al., 2009) where the narrative takes the form of a fundamental construct capable of allowing the clients to revitalize their stories, revisiting them with a greater sense of coherence, continuity and complexity.

It is also understandable that in this changed scenario of the labor market, theories that support the importance of counseling for work and relations as inclusive work psychology by Blustein (2006), which supports the importance of changes in the social and political world to reduce existing inequalities and where the principal goal of the counselor must be to stimulate the critical conscience of the clients to assume importance. To this perspective, the counseling for work and relationship by Richardson (2012) is added, which supports that the central purpose of vocational psychology is to help people to develop their career path and to build their lives through work and their relationships in several fields.

Referring to the theoretical perspectives delineated in the present chapter, there are configured ideas of reflection in relation to the training of professionals in psychology of counseling. In relation to the aspects of indigenization and internationalization, research and practice should be designed in a perspective both indigenous and international to promote the psychology of counseling in specific communities (Ho et al., 2001; Hwang, 2009). To counseling psychologists, it is asked to focus on the indigenous practice utilized in a specific community to promote health and wellbeing (Leung & Chen, 2009) from one side, and from the other side to share skills, ethic principles, and professional standards built on an international level (Forrest, 2010).

It is also underlined that the counseling psychologists always assume major importance and have multicultural skills to work with people from different ethnic groups (Collins & Arthur, 2007; Ridley & Kleiner, 2003). As Collins and Arthur (2007) show, it is essential that counseling psychologists have cultural self-awareness, show awareness of their cultural identity, awareness of the impact of the culture in theory and in practice of psychology of counseling, awareness of the personal and professional impact of the discrepancy between dominant and non-dominant cultural groups, and awareness of one's own level of multicultural competence.

It is also essential that counseling psychologists know the mechanisms through which social injustice helps to create feelings of powerlessness and implement interventions focused on self-esteem and consequently on self-efficacy to enable clients to deal in an adaptive way with the complex and varied problems of their life without having to apply to the support of the professional (Goodman et al., 2004). For promoting social justice and consequently, wellbeing and empowerment of disadvantaged people, counseling psychologists are required to simultaneously consider individual psychological aspects and political aspects, integrating traditional approaches centered on the person with interventions focused on systemic change at the community, institutions, and society level (Constantine et al., 2007).

Moreover, there are interesting perspectives in relation to online counseling, but this means for professionals, as suggested by Sampson (2002), the need to apply additional training that allows counseling psychologists to continue to work properly with this new medium.

Faced with this variety of perspectives and ways of intervention, it is important to emphasize the need for counseling psychologists to master research methods both quantitative and qualitative for analyzing psychological phenomena in a qualitative and quantitative dual perspective that can quantify the observed data and to apply statistical procedures to examine the correlational and causal links between variables (Neville et al., 2006) on one hand, and on the other hand to describe and interpret the experiences of the participants in a content-specific setting (Denzin & Licoln, 2000). In this framework, the field of Life Designing Counseling (Savickas et al., 2009) requires career counseling psychologists to master narrative tools and interventions. Career counseling, according to a psychological perspective of Life Designing intervention, is an identity intervention that promotes the intent and action through story telling (Savickas et al., 2009) and the career counselor is seen as an agent of change.

Furthermore, the evaluation of the effectiveness of intervention assumes more and more relevance first in the scholastic field (Whiston et al., 2011) but also in the field of career counseling. Within the new approach of Life Designing (Savickas et al., 2009), which marks the passage from scores to stories (McMahon & Patton, 2002) is configured the need to verify the effectiveness of qualitative career counseling interventions and instruments through a qualitative-quantitative approach. This accounts for an accredited evaluation of intervention, in quantitative terms, relative to the reduction of the perception of career decision-making difficulties of the client and increased career decision-making self-efficacy perceived by the client on the one hand (Whiston, 2008), and on the other hand for changes in the clients' life stories (Di Fabio, 2012, in press a, in press b; Di Fabio & Maree, 2012b; Rehfuss & Di Fabio, in press).

As outlined in this chapter it is understandable how the psychology of counseling is configured as a discipline that progressively intercepts new needs and adaptively restructures the intervention in relation to social, economic and cultural changes, expressing fully the nature of magmatic and creative discipline relating to the many challenges that contemporary society proposes.

REFERENCES

Abreu, J. M., Chung, R. H. G. & Atkinson, D. R. (2000). Multicultural counseling training: Past, present and future directions. *The Counseling Psychologist*, *28*, 64-656.

Adair, J. G. (1992). Empirical studies of indigenisation and development of the discipline in developing countries. In S. Iwawaki, Y. Kashima, & K. Leung (Eds.). *Innovations in cross-cultural psychology* (pp. 62-74). Amsterdam: Swets & Zeitlinge.

Ægisdóttir, S., Gerstein, L. H. & Cinarbas, D. C. (2008). Methodological issues in cross-cultural counseling research: Equivalence, bias, and translations. *The Counseling Psychologist*, *36*, 188-219.

Albee, G. W. & Ryan-Finn, K. D. (1993). An overview of primary prevention. *Journal of Counseling and Development*, *72*, 115-123.

Albee, G. W. (2000). The future of primary prevention. *Journal of Primary Prevention*, *21*, 7-9.

American College Health Association (2004). *Healthy campus 2010*. Retrieved from http://www.acha.org/info_resources/hc2010.cfm.

American Psychological Association (1999). Archival description of counseling psychology. *The Counseling Psychologist, 27,* 589-592.

American Psychological Association (2002a). Ethical principles of psychologists and code of conduct. *American Psychologist, 57,* 1060-1073.

American Psychological Association (2003). *Ethical principles of psychologists and code of conduct.* Washington, D.C.: Author.

American Psychological Association Division 17 (2000). Division of counseling psychology: Minutes of the incoming executive board meeting, August 21, 1999. *The Counseling Psychologist, 28,* 579-583.

American Psychological Association, Committee on Training in Clinical Psychology (1949). Doctoral training in programs in clinical psychology: 1949. *American Psychologist, 4,* 331-341.

American Psychological Association, Division of Counseling and Guidance, Committee on Counselor Training (1952a). Recommended standards for training counseling psychologists at the doctoral level. *American Psychologist, 7,* 175-181.

American Psychological Association, Division of Counseling and Guidance, Committee on Counselor Training (1952b). The practicum training of counseling psychologists. *American Psychologist, 7,* 182-188.

American Psychological Association, Division of Counseling And Guidance, Committee on Definition (1956). Counseling Psychology as a specialty. *American Psychologist, 11,* 282-285,

American Psychological Association. (2002b). *Guidelines on multicultural education, training, research, practice, and organizational change for psychologists.* Retrieved from http://www.apa.org/pi/ multicultural guidelines.pdf.

American School Counseling Association (2004). *The role of the professional school counselor.* Retrieved from www.schoolcounselor.orglcontent.asp?pl=325&sl=133& contentid=133.

American School Counselor Association (2003). *The ASCA National Model: A framework for school counseling programs.* Alexandria, VA: Author.

Ancis, J. R. & Rasheed, S. A. (2005). Multicultural counseling training approaches: Implications for pedagogy. In C. Z. Enns & A. L. Sinacore (Eds.), *Teaching and social justice: Integrating multicultural and feminist theories in the classroom* (pp. 85-97). Washington, DC: American Psychological Association.

Anderson, W. P. Jr. & Niles, S. G. (2000). Important events in career counseling: Client and counselor descriptions. *The Career Development Quarterly, 48,* 251-263.

Arredondo, P. & Perez, P. (2006). Historical perspectives on the multicultural guidelines and contemporary applications. *Professional Psychology: Research and Practice, 37*(1), 1-5.

Arredondo, P., Toporek, R., Brown, S. P., Jones, J., Locke, D. C., Sanchez, J. & Stadler, H. (1996). Operationalization of the multicultural counseling competencies. *Journal of Multicultural Counseling and Development, 24,* 42-78.

Arthur, N. & Collins, S. (2005). Introduction to culture-infused counselling. In N. Arthur & S. Collins (Eds.), *Culture-infused counselling: Celebrating the Canadian mosaic* (pp. 3-40). Calgary, AB: Counselling Concepts.

Atkinson, D. R. & Israel, T. (2003). The future of multicultural counselling competence. In D. B. Pope-Davis, H. L. K. Coleman, W. M. Liu, & R. L. Toporek (Eds.), *Handbook of multicultural competencies in counseling and psychology* (pp. 591-606). Thousand Oaks, CA: Sage.

Baker, D. B. & Benjamin, L. T. Jr. (2000). The affirmation of the scientist-practitioner: A look back at Boulder. *American Psychologist, 55,* 241-247.

Baker, S. B. & Daniels, T. G. (1989). Integrating research on the microcounseling program: A meta-analysis. *Journal of Counseling Psychology, 36,* 213-222.

Barak, A. & Bloch, N. (2006). Factors related to perceived helpfulness in supporting highly distressed individuals through an online support chat. *CyberPsychology and Behavior, 9,* 60-68.

Barak, A. (2006). Internet career assessment. In J. Greenhaus & G. Callanan (Eds.), *Encyclopedia of career development* (pp. 404-405). Thousand Oaks, CA: SAGE.

Barkham, M. (2003). Quantitative research on psychotherapeutic interventions: Methods and findings across four research generations. In R. Woolfe, W. Dryden, & S. Strawbridge (Eds.), *Handbook of counseling psychology* (pp. 25-73). London: Sage.

Barnes, A. (2008). *Workforce development and the use of ICT in delivering career guidance in the UK: ICT2 Skills for E-Guidance Practitioners Project.* Retrieved from http://www.crac.org.uk/crac_new/pdfs/ICTSkills2_Report.pdf

Barnett, J. E. & Scheetz, K. (2003). Technological advances and telehealth: Ethics, law, and the practice of psychotherapy. *Psychotherapy: Theory, Research, Practice, Training, 40,* 86-93.

Baskin, T. W., Slaten, C. D., Crosby, N. R., Pufahl, T., Schneller, C. L. & Ladell, M. (2010). Efficacy of counseling and psychotherapy in schools: A meta-analytic review of treatment outcome studies. *The Counseling Psychologist, 38*(7) 878-903.

Bein, E., Anderson, T. & Strupp, H. H., Henry, W. P., Schact, T. E., Binder, J. L., ... Butler, S. F. (2000). The effects of training in time-limited dynamic psychotherapy: Changes in therapeutic outcome. *Psychotherapy Research, 10,* 119-132.

Bell, L. (1997). Theoretical foundations for social justice education. In M. Adams, L. Bell, & P. Griffin (Eds.), *Teaching for diversity and social justice* (pp. 3-16). New York: Routledge.

Berger, T. (2004). Computer-based technological applications in psychotherapy training. *Journal of Clinical Psychology, 60,* 301-315.

Bernard, H. R. (2002). *Research methods in anthropology: Qualitative and quantitative approaches* (3rd ed.). Walnut Creek, CA: Alta Mira.

Bernaud, J. L., Di Fabio, A. & Saint-Denis, C. (2010). Effets subjectifs du conseil en orientation et satisfaction des usagers: Une analyse des processus et des determinants [Subjective effects of career counseling and client satisfaction: An analysis of the process and determinants]. *Revue Canadienne de Counseling, 44*(3), 307-325.

Bernaud, J.-L. & Di Fabio, A. (2011). New technology and career development in vocational guidance and career counseling: What is the challenge? *Risorsa Uomo. Rivista di Psicologia del Lavoro e dell'Organizzazione, 16,* 151-162.

Betz, N. E. & Taylor, K. M. (2000). *Manual for the Career Decision Making Self-Efficacy Scale (CDMSES) and CDMSES – Short Form.* Unpublished manuscript, Ohio State University, Columbus, OH.

Bieschke, K. J., Parrish, P. L. & Blasko, K. A. (2007). Review of empirical research focused on the experience of lesbian, gay, and bisexual clients in counseling and psychotherapy. In K. J. Bieschke, R. M. Perez, & K. A. DeBord (Eds.), *Handbook of counseling and psychotherapy with lesbian, gay, bisexual, and transgender clients* (2nd ed., pp. 293-315). Washington, DC: American Psychological Association.

Binder, J. L. (2004). *Key competencies in brief dynamic psychotherapy: Clinical practice beyond the manual.* New York, NY: Guilford.

Blowers, G. H. (1996). The prospect for a Chinese psychology. In M. H. Bond (Ed.), *Handbook of Chinese psychology* (pp. 1-14). Oxford, UK: Oxford University Press.

Blustein, D. (2001). Extending the reach of vocational psychology. Toward an inclusive and integrative psychology of working. *Journal of Vocational Behavior, 59*, 171-182.

Blustein, D. L. & Di Fabio, A. (2009). The new inclusive perspective of working psychology: Its significance in the Italian context. *Risorsa Uomo. Rivista di Psicologia del Lavoro e dell'Organizzazione, 15*, 231-240.

Blustein, D. L. & Spengler, P. M. (1995). Personal adjustment: Career counseling and psychotherapy. In W. B. Walsh & S. H. Osipow (Eds.), *Handbook of vocational psychology* (2nd ed., pp. 217–259). Mahwah, NJ: Erlbaum.

Blustein, D. L. (2006). *The psychology of working: A new perspective for career development, counseling, and public policy.* Mahwah, NJ: Erlbaum.

Blustein, D. L. (2011). A relational theory of working. *Journal of Vocational Behavior, 79*, 1-17.

Blustein, D. L., McWhirter, E. H. & Perry, J. (2005). An emancipatory communitarian approach to vocational development theory, research, and practice. *The Counseling Psychologist, 33*, 141-179.

Bobek, B. L., Robbins, S. B., Gore, P. A., Jr., Harris-Bowlsbey, J., Lapan, R., Dahir, C. & Jepsen, D. (2005). Training counselors to more effectively use computer-assisted career guidance systems: A model curriculum. *The Career Development Quarterly, 53*, 363-371.

Boswell, J. F. & Castonguay, L. G. (2007). Guest editors' introduction. *Psychotherapy: Theory, Research, Practice, and Training, 44*, 363.

Brown, D. & Brooks, L. (1990). *Career choice and development.* San Francisco, CA: Jossey-Bass.

Brown, D. & Trusty, J. (2005). School counselors, comprehensive school counseling programs, and academic achievement: Are school counselors promising more than they can deliver? *Professional School Counseling, 9*, 1-8.

Brown, S. D. & Lent, R.W. (Eds.) (2000). *Handbook of counseling psychology* (3rd ed.). New York: Wiley.

Brown, S. D. & Ryan Krane, N. E. (2000). Four (or five) sessions and a cloud of dust: Old assumptions and new observations about career counseling. In S. D. Brown, R. W. Lent (Eds.), *Handbook of counseling psychology* (3rd ed., pp. 740-766). New York: Wiley.

Brown, S. D., Ryan Krane, N. E., Brecheisen, J., Castelino, P., Budisin, I., Miller, M. & Edens, L. (2003). Critical ingredients of career choice interventions: More analyses and new hypotheses. *Journal of Vocational Behavior, 62*(3), 411-428.

Brown, S. L., Shriberg, D. & Wang, A. (2007). Diversity research literature on the rise? A review of school psychology journals from 2000 to 2003. *Psychology in the Schools, 44*(6), 639-650.

Bryan, J., Moore-Thomas, C., Day-Vines, N. L. & Holcomb-McCoy, C. (2011). School counselors as social capital: The effects of high school college counseling on college application rates. *Journal of Counseling & Development, 89*, 190-199.

Bubolz, W. C., Miller, M. & Williams, D. J. (1999). Content analysis of research in the Journal of Counseling Psychology (1973-1998). *Journal of Counseling Psychology, 46*, 496-503.

Byars-Winston, A. & Fouad, N.A. (2006). Metacognitions and multicultural competence: Expanding the culturally appropriate career counseling model. *The Career Development Quarterly*, 54, 187-201.

Cabrera, A. F, & La Nasa, S. M. (2001). On the path to college: Three critical tasks facing America's disadvantaged. *Research in Higher Education, 42*, 119-150.

Cabrera, A. F, & La Nasa, S. M. (Eds.). (2000). *Understanding the college choice of disadvantaged students: New directions for institutional research (No. 107)*. San Francisco, CA: Jossey-Bass.

Carr, S. & Sloan, T. (Eds.). *Poverty and psychology: Emergent critical practice*. Boston, MA: Kluwer/Plenum.

Carter, J. A. & Davis, K. L. (2001). Revitalizing the Division: The reorganization of Division 17. *The Counseling Psychologist, 29*, 882-906.

Carter, R. T. (2001). Back to the future in cultural competence training. *The Counseling Psychologist, 29*, 787-789.

Casey, R. J. & Berman, J. S. (1985). The outcome of psychotherapy with children. *Psychological Bulletin, 98*, 388-400.

Castro, F. G., Kellison, J. G., Boyd, S. J. & Kopak, A. (2010). A methodology for conducting integrative mixed methods research and data analyses. *Journal of Mixed Methods Research, 4*, 342-360.

Catalano, R. F., Berglund, M. L., Ryan, J. A. M., Lonczak, H. S. & Hawkins, J. D. (2004). Positive youth development in the United States: Research findings on evaluations of positive youth development programs. *Annals of the American Academy of Political and Social Science Special Issue: Positive Development: Realizing the Potential of Youth, 591*, 98-124.

Chambers, E. A. (2004). An introduction to meta-analysis with articles from *The Journal of Educational Research* (1992-2002). *The Journal of Educational Research, 98*, 35-44.

Cherry, D. K., Messenger, L. C. & Jacoby, A. M. (2000). An examination of training model outcomes in clinical psychology programs. *Professional Psychology: Research and Practice, 31*, 562-568.

Chung, Y. B. (2003). Career counseling with lesbian, gay, bisexual, and transgendered persons: The next decade. *The Career Development Quarterly, 52*, 78-86.

Chung, Y. B. (2012). *Presidential welcome*. Retrieved from http://www.div 17.org/about_president.html.

Cohen, L., Chávez, V. & Chehimi, S. (Eds.) (2007). *Prevention is primary: Strategies for community well-being*. San Francisco, CA: Jossey Bass.

Cohen, S., Underwood, L. G. & Gottlieb, B. H. (Eds.). (2000). *Social support measurement and intervention: A guide for social and health scientists*. Oxford: Oxford University Press.

Coleman, H. L. K. (2004). Toward a well-utilized partnership. *The Counseling Psychologist, 32*, 216-224.

Coleman, J. S. (1988). Social capital in the creation of human capital. *American Journal of Sociology, 94*, 95-120.

Collins, N. M. & Pieterse, A. L. (2007). Critical incident analysis based learning: An approach to training for active racial and cultural awareness. *Journal of Counseling and Development, 85*, 14-23.

Collins, S. & Arthur, N. (2005a). Enhancing the therapeutic alliance in culture-infused counselling. In N. Arthur & S. Collins (Eds.), *Culture-infused counselling: Celebrating the Canadian mosaic* (pp. 103-149). Calgary, AB: Counselling Concepts.

Collins, S. & Arthur, N. (2005b). Multicultural counselling competencies: A framework for professional development. In N. Arthur & S. Collins (Eds.), *Culture-infused counselling: Celebrating the Canadian mosaic* (pp. 41-102). Calgary, AB: Counselling Concepts.

Collins, S. & Arthur, N. (2007). A framework for enhancing multicultural counselling competence. *Canadian Journal of Counselling, 47*(1), 31-49.

Conley, D. (2007). *Toward a comprehensive conception of college readiness.* Eugene, OR: Educational Policy Improvement Center.

Constantine, M. G., Hage, S. M., Kindaichi, M. M. & Bryant, R. M. (2007). Social justice and multicultural issues: Implications for the practice and training of counselors and counseling psychologists. *Journal of Counseling and Development, 85*, 24-29.

Conyne, R. K. (1994). Preventive counseling. *Counseling and Development, 27*, 1-10.

Conyne, R. K. (1997). Educating students in preventive counseling. *Counselor Education and Supervision, 36*, 259-269.

Conyne, R. K. (2004). *Preventive counseling: Helping people to become empowered in systems and settings.* New York: Brunner-Routledge.

Conyne, R. K., Newmeyer, M. D., Kenny, M. E., Romano, J. L. & Matthews, C. R. (2008). Two key strategies for teaching prevention: Specialized course and infusion. *Journal of Primary Prevention, 29*, 375-401.

Cook, E., Heppner, M. & O'Brien, K. (2002). Career development of women of color and White women: Assumptions, conceptualization, and interventions from an ecological perspective. *The Career Development Quarterly, 50*, 291-305.

Corwin, Z. B., Venegas, K. M., Oliverez, R. M. & Colyar, J. E. (2004). School counsel: How appropriate guidance affects educational equity. *Urban Education, 39*, 442-457.

Council for Accreditation of Counseling and Related Educational Programs. (2001). *CACREP accreditation manual: 2001 standards.* Alexandria, VA: Author.

Creswell, J. (1998). *Qualitative inquiry and research design: Choosing among five traditions.* Thousand Oaks, CA: Sage.

Creswell, J. (2002). *Research design: Qualitative, quantitative, and mixed methods approaches.* Thousand Oaks, CA: Sage.

Creswell, J. W. (2003). *Research design: Quantitative, qualitative, and mixed methods approaches* (2nd ed.). Thousand Oaks, CA: Sage.

Crethar, H. C., Rivera E. T. & Nash, S. (2008). In search of common threads: Linking multicultural, feminist, and social justice counseling paradigms. *Journal of Counseling and Development, 86*, 269-278.

Crites, J. O. (1981). *Career counseling.* New York: McGraw Hill.

Curtis, M. J., Hunley, S. A., Walker, K. J. & Baker, A. C. (1999). Demographic characteristics and professional practices in school psychology. *School Psychology Review, 28*, 104-116.

D'Andrea, J., Daniels, J. & Noonan, M. J. (2003). New developments in the assessment of multicultural competencies. In D. B. Pope-Davis, H. L. K. Coleman, W. M. Liu, & R. L. Toporek (Eds.), *Handbook of multicultural competencies in counseling and psychology* (pp. 154-167). Thousand Oaks, CA: Sage.

D'Andrea, M. D. & Daniels, J. (1991). Exploring the different levels of multicultural training in counselor education. *Journal of Counseling and Development, 70,* 78-85.

Deci, E. L. & Ryan, R. M. (1985). *Intrinsic motivation and self-determination in human behavior.* New York: Plenum.

Denzin, N. K. & Lincoln, Y. S. (2000). Introduction: The discipline and practice of qualitative research. In N. K. Denzin & Y. S. Lincoln (Eds.), *Handbook of qualitative research* (2nd ed., pp. 1-28). Thousand Oaks, CA: Sage.

Denzin, N. K. & Lincoln, Y. S. (2003). Introduction: The discipline and practice of qualitative research. In N. K. Denzin & Y. S. Lincoln (Eds.), *Strategies of qualitative inquiry* (2nd ed., pp. 1-45). Thousand Oaks, CA: Sage.

Denzin, N. K. (1978). *The research act: A theoretical introduction to sociological methods.* New York: McGraw-Hill.

Derzon, J. (2006). How effective are school-based violence prevention programs in preventing and reducing violence and other antisocial behaviors? A meta-analysis. In S. R. Jimerson & M. J. Furlong (Eds.), *Handbook of school violence and school safety: From research to practice* (pp. 429-442). Mahwah, NJ: Lawrence Earlbaum.

Di Fabio, A. & Maree, J. G. (2012a). Ensuring quality in scholarly writing. In J. G. Maree (Ed.), *Complete your thesis or dissertation successfully: Practical guidelines* (pp. 137-145). Cape Town: Juta.

Di Fabio, A. & Maree, J. G. (2012b). Group-based Life Design Counseling in an Italian context. *Journal of Vocational Behavior, 80,* 100-107.

Di Fabio, A. & Maree, J. G. (submitted). Effectiveness of the Career Interest Profile (CIP). *Journal of Employment Counseling.*

Di Fabio, A. (1998). *Psicologia dell'orientamento. Problemi, metodi e strumenti* [*Vocational guidance. Problems, methods, instruments*]. Firenze: Giunti.

Di Fabio, A. (2002). *Bilancio di competenze e orientamento formativo. Il contributo psicologico* [*Competence assessment and formative guidance. The psychological contribution*]. ITER Organizzazioni Speciali, Firenze: Giunti.

Di Fabio, A. (2009). *Manuale di psicologia dell'orientamento e career counseling nel XXI secolo* [*Handbook of vocational psychology and career counseling in the XXI century*]. Firenze: Giunti O.S.

Di Fabio, A. (2010a, June). *ICT in vocational guidance and career counseling: Which challenge?* Paper presented at IAEVG-NCDA-SVP International Symposium "Bridging International Perspectives of Career Development" (Techniques and Technologies for Career development), San Francisco, California.

Di Fabio, A. (2010b). Life designing in 21st Century: Using a New, Strengthened Career Genogram. *Journal of Psychology in Africa, 20*(3), 381-384.

Di Fabio, A. (2012, July). *Narratability and career construction: Empirical evidence of intervention effectiveness.* State-of-the-Science Address Invitation Lecture in the field of *Psychology of Counseling* presented at International Congress of Psychology (ICP) 2012, Cape Town, South Africa.

Di Fabio, A. (in press a). The effectiveness of the Career Story Interview from the perspective of Life Designing. *South African Journal of Psychology.*

Di Fabio, A. (in press b). Evaluation of the effectiveness of the New Career Construction Genogram. *Cypriot Journal of Educational Sciences.*

Di Fabio, A., Bernaud, J. -L. & Kenny, M. E. (in press). Perceived career counselor relational and technical behaviors and outcomes among Italian university students. *Journal of Career Assessment.*

Di Fabio, A., Bernaud, J.-L. & Palazzeschi, L. (2008). Efficacia percepita dell'intervento di career counseling in studenti italiani [Perceived efficacy of the career counseling intervention in Italian students]. *Counseling. Giornale Italiano di Ricerca e Applicazioni, 1*, 315-326.

Diemer, M. A. & Gore, P. A. Jr. (2009). Culture and assessment: Nomothetic and idiographic considerations. *The Career Development Quarterly, 57*, 342-347.

Dokecki, P. (1996). *The tragi-comic professional: Basic considerations for ethical reflective generative practice.* Pittsburgh, PA: Duquesne University Press.

Draguns, J. G. (2003). Universal and cultural aspects of counseling and psychotherapy. In J. G. Ponterotto, J. M. Casas, L. A. Suzuki, & C. M. Alexander (Eds.), *Handbook of multicultural counseling* (pp. 93-122). Thousand Oaks, CA: Sage.

Duarte, M. E. (2004). O individuo e a organização: Perspectivas de desenvolvimento [The individual and the organization: Perspectives of development]. *Psychologica, (extra-série)*, 549-557.

Dudgeon, P., Garvey, D. & Pickett, H. (Eds.). (2000). *Working with Indigenous Australians: A handbook for psychologists.* Perth, Western Australia: Gunada Press.

Durlak, J. (2003). Effective prevention and health promotion programming. In T. P. Gullotta & M. Bloom (Eds.), *Encyclopedia of primary prevention and health promotion* (pp. 61-69). New York: Kluwer.

Engel, G. L. (1977). The need for a new medical model: A challenge for biomedicine. *Science, 196*, 701-708.

Engle, D. E. & Arkowitz, H. (2006). *Ambivalence in psychotherapy: Facilitating readiness to change.* New York: Guilford.

Enriquez, V. G. (1993). Developing a Filipino psychology. In U. Kim & J. W. Berry (Eds.), *Indigenous psychologies: Research and experience in cultural context* (pp. 152-169). Newbury Park, CA: Sage.

Fassinger, R. E. (2005). Paradigms, praxis, problems, and promise: Grounded theory in counseling psychology research. *Journal of Counseling Psychology, 52*, 156-166.

Felice, W. (2003). *The global new deal: Economic and social human rights in world politics.* New York, NY: Rowman and Littlefield.

Fine, M., Torre, M. E. & Boudin, K., Bowen, I., Clark, J., Hylton, D., Upuegui, D. (2003). Participatory action research: From within and beyond prison bars. In P. M. Camic, J. E. Rhodes, & L. Yardley (Eds.), *Qualitative research in psychology: Expanding perspectives in methodology and design* (pp. 173-198). Washington, DC: American Psychological Association.

Fisher, C. B. & Fried, A. L. (2003). Internet-mediated psychological services and the American Psychological Association Ethics Code. *Psychotherapy: Theory, Research, Practice, Training, 40*, 103-111.

Forrest, L. (2010). Linking international psychology, professional competence, and leadership: Counseling psychologists as learning partners. *The Counseling Psychologist*, *38*, 96-120.

Fouad, N. A. & Arbona, C. (1994). Careers in a cultural context. *The Career Development Quarterly*, *43*, 96-104.

Fouad, N. A. & Walker, C. M. (2005). Understanding cultural influences in career choices: Differential item analysis of the Strong Interest Inventory. *Journal of Vocational Behavior*, *66*, 104-123.

Fouad, N. A. (1993). Cross-cultural vocational assessment. *The Career Development Quarterly*, *42*, 4-13.

Fouad, N. A. (1995). Career linking: An intervention to promote math and science career awareness. *Journal of Counseling and Development*, *73*, 527-534.

Fouad, N. A. (2001). The future of vocational psychology: Aiming high. *Journal of Vocational Behavior*, *59*, 183-191.

Fouad, N. A. (2006). Multicultural guidelines: Implementation in an urban counseling psychology program. *Professional Psychology: Research and Practice*, *37*, 6-13.

Fouad, N. A., Guillen, A., Harris-Hodge, E., Henry, C., Novakovic, A., Terry, S., Kantamneni, N. (2006). Need, awareness, and use of career services for college students. *Journal of Career Assessment*, *14*, 407-420.

Fouad, N. A., Kantamneni, N., Smothers, M., K., Chen, Y. L., Fitzpatrick, M. E., Guillen, A. & Terry, S. (2008). Asian American Career Development: A qualitative analysis. *Journal of Vocational Behavior*, *72*, 43-59.

Fouad, N. A., Mcpherson, R. H., Gerstein, L., Blustein, D. L., Ellman, N., Helledy, K. I. & Metz, A. J. (2004). Houston, 2001: Context and legacy. *The Counseling Psychologist*, *32*, 15-77.

Fowers, B. J. & Davidov, B. J. (2006). The virtue of multiculturalism: Personal transformation, character, and openness to the other. *American Psychologist*, *61*(6), 581-594.

Fox, D. & Prilleltensky, I. (1997). *Critical psychology: An introduction*. Thousand Oaks, CA: Sage.

Fretz, B. R. & Simon, N. P. (1992). Professional issues in counseling psychology: Continuity, change, and challenge. In S. D. Brown & Robert W. Lent (Eds.), *Handbook of counseling psychology* (2nd ed., pp. 3-36). New York: John Wiley.

Frey, B. & Stutzer, A. (2002). *Happiness and economics: How the economy and institutions affect human well-being*. Princeton, NJ: Princeton University Press.

Friere, P. (1970). *Pedagogy of the oppressed*. New York: Continuum International.

Gaddy, C. D., Charlot-Swilley, D., Nelson, P. D. & Reich, J. N. (1995). Selected outcomes of accredited programs. *Professional Psychology: Research and Practice*, *26*, 507-513.

Gati, I., Krausz, M. & Osipow, S. H. (1996). A taxonomy of difficulties in career decision making. *Journal of Counseling Psychology*, *43*(4), 510-526.

Gelso, C. & Fretz, B. (2001). *Counseling psychology* (2nd ed.). Tokyo: Harcourt College.

George, R. E. (2002). *Socioeconomic democracy: An advanced socioeconomic system*. London: Praeger.

Gergen, K. J. & Davis, K. E. (1985). *The social construction of the person*. New York, NY: Springer-Verlag.

Gergen, K. J. (1991). *The saturated self: Dilemmas of identity in contemporary life*. New York, NY: Basic Books.

Gergen, K. J. (1999). *An invitation to social construction*. London, UK: Sage.

Gergen, K. J. (2001). *Social construction in context*. London: Sage.

Gergen, K. J. (2009). *Relational being: Beyond self and community*. New York, NY: Oxford University Press.

Gerstein, L. H. (2006). Counseling psychology's commitment to strengths: Rhetoric or reality? *Journal of Counseling Psychology, 34*, 276-292.

Glueckauf, R. L., Pickett, T. C., Ketterson, T. U., Loomis, J. S. & Rozensky, R. H. (2002). Preparation for the delivery of telehealth services: A self-study framework for expansion of practice. *Professional Psychology: Research and Practice, 34*, 159-163.

Goetz, J. P. & LeCompte, M. D. (1984). *Ethnography and qualitative design in educational research*. New York: Academic Press.

Goh, M. (2005). Cultural competence and master therapists: An inextricable relationship. *Journal of Mental Health Counseling, 27*, 71-81.

Gomez, M. J., Fassinger, R. E., Prosser, J., Cooke, K., Meija, B. & Luna, J. (2001). Voces abriendo caminos [Voices foraging paths]: A qualitative study of the career development of notable Latinas. *Journal of Counseling Psychology, 48*, 286-300.

Goodman, D. (2001). *Promoting diversity and social justice*. London: Sage.

Goodman, L., Liang, B., Helms, J., Latta, R., Sparks, E. & Weintraub, S. R. (2004). Training counseling psychologists as social justice agents: Feminist and multicultural principles in action. *The Counseling Psychologist, 32*, 793-836.

Goodyear, R. K. (1997). Psychological expertise and the role of individual differences: An exploration of issues. *Educational Psychology Review, 9*, 251-265.

Goodyear, R. K., Murdock, N., Lichtenberg, J. W., McPherson, R., Koetting, K. & Petren, S. (2008). Stability and change in counseling psychologists' identities, roles, functions, and career satisfaction across fifteen years. *The Counseling Psychologist, 36*, 220-249.

Gore, P. A. Jr. & Leuwerke, W. C. (2000). Information technology for career assessment on the Internet. *Journal of Career Assessment, 8*, 3-20.

Gore, P. A. Jr. & Leuwerke, W. C. (2009). Il career counseling nell'era informatica [career counseling in the information era]. *Career counseling e bilancio di competenze. Prospettive internazionali [Career counseling and competences assessment: International perspectives]* (pp. 50-68). Firenze: Giunti O.S. Organizzazioni.

Gore, P. A. Jr. & Metz, A. J. (2008). Advising for career and life planning. In V. N. Gordon, W. R. Habley, & T. J. Grites (Eds.), *Academic advising: A comprehensive handbook* (2nd ed., pp. 103-117). San Francisco, CA, US: Jossey-Bass; US.

Gore, P. A., Jr. (2008). Counseling e successo accademico (Post-secondary student success). *Counseling: Giornale Italiano di Ricerca e Applicazioni, 1*, 119-137.

Gottman, J. & DeClaire, J. (2001). *The relationship cure*. New York: Crown.

Gravetter, F. J. & Forzano, L. B. (2003). *Research methods for the behavioral sciences*. Belmont, CA: Wadsworth/Thomson.

Greenberg, R. P. (2004). Essential ingredients for successful psychotherapy: Effects of common actors. In M. J. Dewan, B. N. Steenbarger, & R. P. Greenberg (Eds.), *The art and science of brief psychotherapies* (pp. 231-242). Washington, DC: APPI.

Greene, J. C. & Caracelli, V. J. (Eds.). (1997). *Advances in mixed-method evaluation: The challenges and benefits of integrating diverse paradigms.* (New Directions for Evaluation, No. 74). San Francisco: Jossey-Bass.

Guichard, J. (2004). Se faire soi. *L'Orientation Scolaire et Professionnelle, 33,* 499-534.

Guichard, J. (2005). Life-long self-construction. *International Journal for Educational and Vocational Guidance, 5,* 111-124.

Guichard, J. (2008). Proposition d'un schéma d'entretien constructiviste de conseil en orientation pour des adolescents ou de jeunes adultes. *L'Orientation Scolaire et Professionnelle, 37,* 413-440.

Guichard, J. (2009). Problematiche e sfide dell'orientamento nelle società industriali globalizzate all'inizio del XXI secolo [Issues and challenges of guidance in industrial globalized societies at the beginning of XXI century]. In A. Di Fabio (Ed.), *Career counseling e bilancio di competenze. Prospettive internazionali [Career counseling and competence assessment: International perspectives].* Firenze: Giunti O.S. Organizzazioni Speciali.

Guichard, J. (2010, March). *Les théories de la construction des parcours professionnels et de la construction de soi: Deux approches de la construction de la vie individuelle [Theories of career construction and Self construction : Two approaches to the construction of individual life].* Paper presented at International INETOP Congress, Paris, France.

Guichard, J. E. & Dumora, B. (2008). A constructivist approach to ethically-grounded vocational development interventions for young people. In J. Athansou & R. Van Esbroeck (Eds.), *International Handbook of Career Guidance.* Dordrecht: Springer Science.

Gysbers, N. C, & Henderson, P. (1988). *Developing and managing your school guidance program.* Alexandria, VA; American Counseling and Development Association.

Gysbers, N. C, & Henderson, P. (1994). *Developing and managing your school guidance program* (2nd ed.). Alexandria, VA; American Counseling Association.

Gysbers, N. C, & Henderson, P. (2000). *Developing and managing your school guidance program* (3rd ed.). Alexandria, VA; American Counseling Association.

Gysbers, N. C, & Henderson, P. (2006). *Developing and managing your school guidance program* (4th ed.). Alexandria, VA; American Counseling Association.

Gysbers, N. C, & Moore, E. J. (1974). *Career guidance, counseling, and placement: Elements of an illustrative guide.* Columbia: Career Guidance, Counseling Project, University of Missouri-Columbia.

Gysbers, N. C, & Moore, E. J. (1981). *Improving guidance programs.* Englewood Cliffs, NJ; Prentice Hall.

Gysbers, N. C. (2004). Counseling psychology and school counseling partnership: Overlooked? Under-utilized? But needed! *The Counseling Psychologist, 32,* 245-252.

Haberstroh, S., Duffey, T., Evans, M., Gee, R. & Trepal, H. (2007). The experience of online counseling. *Journal of Mental Health Counseling, 29,* 269-282.

Hage, S. M., Romano, J. L., Conyne, R. K., Kenny, M., Matthews, C., Schwartz, J. P. & Waldo, M. (2007). Best practice guidelines on prevention practice, research, training, and social advocacy for psychologists. *The Counseling Psychologist, 35,* 493-566.

Hanson, W. E., Creswell, J. W., Plano Clark, V. L., Petska, K. S. & Creswell, J. D. (2005). *Mixed methods research designs in counseling psychology.* Retrieved from http:// digitalcommons.unl.edu/psychfacpub/373.

Haraway, D. J. (1997). Situated knowledge: The science question in feminism and the privilege of partial perspective. *Feminist Studies, 14*, 575-599.

Harding, S. (1991). *Whose science, whose knowledge?* Milton Keynes, UK: Open University Press.

Haverkamp, B. E., Morrow, S. L. & Ponterotto, J. G. (2005). A time and place for qualitative and mixed methods in counseling research. *Journal of Counseling Psychology, 52*, 123-125.

Healy, C. C. (2001). A follow-up of adult career counseling clients of a university extension center. *The Career Development Quarterly, 49*, 363-373.

Helms, J. E., Henze, K. T., Sass, T. L. & Mifsud, V. A. (2006). Treating Cronbach's alpha reliability coefficients as data in counseling research. *The Counseling Psychologist, 34*, 630-660.

Helms, J. E., Shakes Malone, L. T., Kevin, H., Satiani, A., Perry, J. & Warren, A. (2003). First annual diversity challenge: "How to survive teaching courses on race and culture." *Journal of Multicultural Counseling & Development, 31*, 3-11.

Henson, R. K. (2006). Effect-size measures and meta-analytic thinking in counseling psychology research. *The Counseling Psychologist, 34*, 601-629.

Heppner, M. J. & Hendricks, F. (1995). A process and outcome study examining career indecision and indecisiveness. *Journal of Counseling & Development, 73*, 426-437.

Heppner, M. J. & Heppner, P. P. (2003). Identifying process variables in career counseling: A research agenda. *Journal of Vocational Behavior, 62*, 429-452.

Heppner, M. J. (2005). *I fattori che caratterizzano un processo di career counseling efficace [The factors that characterize a process of effective career counseling].* Paper presented at VII National Congress *Choice guidance: research, training, applications,* Padova, Italy.

Heppner, M. J., Multon, K. D. & Gysbers, N. C. (2001, August). Informing career counseling training through programmatic empirical research. In K. M. O'Brien & M. Heppner (Co-Chairs), *Career counseling training: Empirical models, social justice settings, diverse populations.* Symposium presented at the annual meeting of the American Psychological Association, San Francisco.

Heppner, M. J., Multon, K. D., Gysbers, N. C., Ellis, C. A. & Zook, C. E. (1998). The relationship of trainee self-efficacy to the process and outcome of career counseling. *Journal of Counseling Psychology, 45*, 393-402.

Heppner, P. P., Casas, J. M., Carter, J. & Stone, G. L. (2000). The maturation of counseling psychology: Multifaceted perspectives, 1978-1998. In S. D. Brown & R. W. Lent (Eds.), *Handbook of counseling psychology* (3rd ed., pp. 3-49). New York: John Wiley & Sons.

Heppner, P. P., Kivlighan, D. M., Jr. & Wampold, B. E. (1999). *Research design in counseling* (2nd ed.). Belmont, CA: Wadsworth.

Herr, E. L. (1996). Perspectives on ecological context, social policy, and career guidance. *The Career Development Quarterly, 45*, 5-19.

Hesketh, B. (2000). Prevention and development in the workplace. In S. D. Brown & R. W. Lent (Eds.), *Handbook of counseling psychology* (3rd ed., pp. 471-498). New York: John Wiley.

Hetherington, M. J. (1998). The political relevance of trust. *American Political Science Review, 92*, 791-808.

Hettler, W. (1984). Wellness: Encouraging a lifetime pursuit of excellence. *Health Values: Achieving High Level Wellness, 8*, 13-17.

Hill, C. E. & Gronsky, B. R. (1984). Research: Why and how? In J. M. Whiteley, N. Kagan, L. W. Harmon, B. R. Fretz, & F. Tanney (Eds.), *The coming decade in counseling psychology* (pp. 149-159). Schenectady, NY: Character Research.

Hill, C. E., Knox, S., Thompson, B. J., Williams, E. N., Hess, S. A. & Ladany, N. (2005). Consensual qualitative research: An update. *Journal of Counseling Psychology, 52*, 196-205.

Hill, C. E., Nutt, E. A. & Jackson, S. (1994). Trends in psychotherapy process research: Samples, measures, and classic publications. *Journal of Counseling Psychology, 41*, 364-377.

Hill, C. E., Thompson, B. J. & Williams, E. N. (1997). A guide for conducting consensual qualitative research. *The Counseling Psychologist, 25*, 517-572.

Ho, D. Y. F. (1995). Internalized culture, culturocentrism, and transference. *Counseling Psychologist, 23*(1), 4-24.

Ho, D. Y. F. (1998). Indigenous psychologies: Asian perspectives. *Journal of Cross-Cultural Psychology, 29*, 88-103.

Ho, D. Y. F., Peng, S., Lai, A. C. & Chan, S. (2001). Indigenization and beyond: Methodological relationalism in the study of personality across cultural traditions. *Journal of Personality, 69*(6), 926-953.

Hoepfl, M. C. (1997). Choosing qualitative research: A primer for technology education researchers. *Journal of Technology Education, 9*(1), 47-63.

Holcomb-McCoy, C. (1999). Multicultural competence and counselor training: A national survey. *Journal of Counseling and Development, 77*(3), 294-306.

Hoshmand, L. T. (1989). Alternate research paradigms: A review and teaching proposal. *The Counseling Psychologist, 17*, 3-79.

Hoshmand, L. T. (2005). Narratology, cultural psychology, and counseling research. *Journal of Counseling Psychology, 52*, 178-186.

Howard, G. S. (1984). A modest proposal for a revision of strategies for counseling research. *Journal of Counseling Psychology, 31*, 430-431.

Hunt, B., Matthews, C, Milsom, A. & Lammel, J. A. (2006). Lesbians with physical disabilities: A qualitative study of their experiences with counseling. *Journal of Counseling & Development, 84*, 163-173.

Hwang, K. K. (2009). The development of indigenous counseling in contemporary Confucian communities. *The Counseling Psychologist, 37*, 930-943.

Ingels, S. J., Pratt, D. J., Rogers, J. E., Siegel, P. H. & Stutts, E. S. (2004). *Education Longitudinal Study of 2002: Base year data file user's manual (NCES 2004-405)*. Washington, DC: Department of Education, National Center for Education Statistics.

International Union of Psychological Science (2008). *Universal declaration of ethical principles for psychologists*. Retrieved from http://www.am.org/iupsys/resources/ethics/index.html.

Ivankova, N. V., Creswell, J. W. & Clark, V. L. P. (2010). Foundations and approaches to mixed methods research. In K. Maree (Ed.), *First steps in research* (pp. 256-280). Pretoria, South Africa: Van Schaik.

Ivey, A. E., Ivey, M. B., Myers, J. E., & Sweeney, T. J. (2005). *Developmental counseling and therapy: Promoting wellness over the lifespan.* NY: Houghton-Mifflin/Lahaska.

James, C. E. (1996). Race, culture and identity. In C. E. James (Ed.), *Perspectives on racism and the human services sector: A case for change* (pp. 5-35). Toronto, ON: University of Toronto Press.

Jennings, L., Sovereign, A., Bottorff, N., Mussell, M. P. & Vye, C. (2005). Nine ethical values of master therapists. *Journal of Mental Health Counseling, 27,* 32-47.

Kagan, N., Armsworth, M. W. & Altmaier, E. M., Dowd, E. T., Hansen, J. C., Mills, D. H., … Vasquez, M. J. T. (1988). Professional practice of counseling psychology in various settings. *The Counseling Psychologist, 16,* 347-365.

Kahn, J. H. (2006). Factor analysis in counseling psychology research, training, and practice: Principles, advances, and applications. *The Counseling Psychologist, 34,* 684-718.

Kantamneni, N. & Fouad, N. (2011). Structure of vocational interests for diverse groups on the 2005 strong interest inventory. *Journal of Vocational Behavior, 78,* 193-201.

Kanz, J. E. (2001). Clinical-supervision.com: Issues in the provision of online supervision. *Professional Psychology: Research and Practice, 32,* 415-420.

Keating, D. P. & Hertzman, C. (Eds.). (1999). *Developmental health and the wealth of nations: Social, biological, and educational dynamics.* New York: The Guilford Press.

Kenny, M. & Di Fabio, A. (2009). Prevention and career development. *Risorsa Uomo. Rivista di Psicologia del Lavoro e dell'Organizzazione, 15,* 361-374.

Kenny, M. E. & Bledsoe, M. (2005). Contributions of the relational context to career adaptability among urban adolescents. *Journal of Vocational Behavior, 66*(2), 257-272.

Kenny, M. E. & Hage, S. M. (2009). The next frontier: Prevention as an instrument of social justice. *The Journal of Primary Prevention, 30,* 1-10.

Kenny, M. E. & Romano, J. (2009). Promoting positive development and social justice through prevention: A legacy for the future. In M. E. Kenny, A. M. Horne, P. Orpinas, & L. E. Reese (Eds.), *Realizing social justice: The challenge of preventive interventions* (pp. 17-35). Washington, DC: American Psychological Association.

Kenny, M. E. (2009). Verso l'avanzamento della prevenzione nel Counseling. *Counseling: Giornale Italiano di Ricerca e Applicazioni, 2,* 127-137.

Kenny, M. E. (2011). Prevention approaches for advancing social justice. *Counseling: Giornale Italiano di Ricerca e Applicazioni, 4,* 7-12.

Kenny, M. E., Blustein, D. L., Chaves, A., Grossman, J. & Gallagher, L. (2003). The role of perceived barriers and relational support in educational and vocational lives of urban high school students. *Journal of Counseling Psychology, 50,* 142-155.

Kenny, M. E., Blustein, D. L., Haase, R. F., Jackson, J. & Perry, J. C. (2006). Setting the stage: Career development and the student engagement process. *Journal of Counseling Psychology, 53*(2), 272-279.

Kenny, M. E., Gualdron, L., Scanlon, D., Sparks, E., Blustein, D. & Jernigan, M. (2007). Urban adolescents' construction of supports and barriers to their educational and career attainment. *Journal of Counseling Psychology, 54,* 336-343.

Kenny, M. E., Horne, A. M., Orpinas, P. & Reese, L. E. (2009). Social justice and the challenge of preventive interventions: An introduction. In M. E. Kenny, A. M. Horne, P. Orpinas, & L. E. Reese (Eds.), *Realizing social justice: The challenge of preventive interventions* (pp. 3-14). Washington, DC: American Psychological Association.

Kerlinger, F. N. (1986). *Foundations of behavioral research* (3rd ed.). Fort Worth, TX: Holt, Rinehart, and Winston.

Kidd, J. M., Jackson, C. & Hirsh, W. (2003). The outcomes of effective career discussions at work. *Journal of Vocational Behavior, 62*, 119-133.

Kidd, S. A. & Kral, M. J. (2005). Practicing participatory action research. *Journal of Counseling Psychology, 52*, 187-195.

Kim, B. S. K. & Lyons, H. Z. (2005). Experiential activities and multicultural counseling competence training. *Journal of Counseling & Development, 81*, 400-408.

Kim, B. S. K. (2011). Client motivation and multicultural counseling. *The Counseling Psychologist, 39*, 267-275.

Kim, J. K., Millen, J. V., Irwin, A. & Gersham, J. (Eds.). (2000). *Dying for growth: Global inequality and the health of the poor.* Monroe, ME: Common Courage Press.

Kim, U. & Berry, J. W. (1993). *Indigenous psychologies: Research and experience in cultural context.* Newbury Park, CA: Sage.

Kim, U. (2000). Indigenous, cultural, and cross-cultural psychology: A theoretical, conceptual, and epistemological analysis. *Asian Journal of Social Psychology, 3*, 265-287.

Kim, U., Yang, K. S. & Hwang, K. K. (2006). *Indigenous and cultural psychology.* New York: Springer.

Kirschner, T., Hoffman, M. A. & Hill, C. E. (1994). Case study of the process and outcome of career counseling. *Journal of Counseling Psychology, 41*, 216-226.

Kiselica, M. S. & Robinson, M. (2001). Bringing advocacy counseling to life: The history, issues, and human dramas of social justice work in counseling. *Journal of Counseling & Development, 79*, 387-397.

Klein, K., Ralls, R. S., Smith Major, V. & Douglas, C. (2000). Power and participation in the workplace: Implications for empowerment theory, research, and practice. In J. Rappaport & E. Scidman (Eds.), *Handbook of community psychology* (pp. 273-295). New York: Klewer Academic/Plenum.

Kloos, B. & Moore, T. (Eds.). (2001). Spirituality, religion, and community psychology II: Resources, pathways and perspectives [Special issue]. *Journal of Community Psychology, 29*(5), 487-613.

Korten, D. (1995). *When corporations rule the world. San Francisco:* Berrett-Koehler/ Kumarian Press.

Korten, D. (1999). *The post corporate world.* San Francisco: Berrett-Koehler/Kumarian Press.

Kozan, S., Di Fabio, A., Blustein, D. L. & Kenny, M. E. (in press). The role of social support and work-related factors on the school engagement of Italian high school students. *Journal of Career Assessment.*

Ladany, N., Hill, C. E., Corbett, M. M. & Nutt, E. A. (1996). Nature, extent, and importance of what psychotherapy trainees do not disclose to their supervisors. *Journal of Counseling Psychology, 43*, 10-24.

Lalas, J. (2007). Teaching social justice in multicultural urban schools: Conceptualization and classroom implication. *Multicultural Education, 14*, 17-21.

Lemoine, C. (2007). Organizzare l'auto-attenzione durante i test e i questionari [Organising self-attention during tests and questionnaires]. *Risorsa Uomo, 13*, 443-454.

Lent, R. W. (1996). Career counseling, science, and policy: Revitalizing our paradigms and roles. *The Career Development Quarterly, 45*, 58-64.

Leong, F. T. L. & Lee, S. H. (2006). A cultural accommodation model for cross-cultural psychotherapy: Illustrated with the case of Asian Americans. *Psychotherapy: Theory, Research, Practice, Training, 43*, 410-423.

Leong, F. T. L. & Savickas, M. L (2007). Introduction to the Special Issue on international perspectives on counseling Psychology. *Applied Psychology, 56*(1), 1-6.

Leong, F. T. L. (1993). The career counseling process with racial/ethnic minorities. The case of Asian Americans. *The Career Development Quarterly, 42*, 26-40.

Lerner, R. M. (2002). *Concepts and theories of human development* (3rd ed.). Mahwah, NJ: Lawrence Erlbaum.

Leung, S. A. & Chen, P. H. (2009). Counseling psychology in Chinese communities in Asia: Indigenous, multicultural, and cross-cultural considerations. *The Counseling Psychologist, 37*, 944-966.

Leung, S. A. & Tsoi-Hoshmand, L. (2007). Internationalization and international publishing: Broadening the impact of scholarly work in counseling. *The Hong Kong Professional Counselling Association, 14*, 141-154.

Lewis, J., Arnold, M. S., House, R. & Toporek, R.L. (2002). *ACA advocacy competencies.* Alexandria, VA: American Counseling Association, Advocacy Task Force. Retrieved from http://www.counseling.org/Content/NavigationMenu/RESOURCES/ADVOCACY COMPETENCIES/advocacy_competencies1.pdf.

Lichtenberg, J. W. (1997). Expertise in counseling psychology: A concept in search of support. *Educational Psychology Review, 9*, 221-238.

Lin, N. (2001). *Social capital: A theory of social structure and action.* New York, NY: Cambridge University Press.

Lincoln, Y. S. & Guba, E. G. (1985). *Naturalistic inquiry.* Beverly Hills, CA: Sage.

Lipsey, M. W. (2003). Those confounded moderators in meta-analysis: Good, bad, and ugly. *Annals of the American Academy of Political and Social Science, 587*, 69-81.

Loe, S. A. & Miranda, A.H. (2005). An examination of ethnic incongruence in school based psychological services and diversity-training experiences among school psychologists. *Psychology in the Schools, 42*(4), 419-432.

Lynch, M. F. (2002). The dilemma of international counselor education: Attending to cultural and professional fits and misfits. *International Journal for the Advancement of Counseling, 24*, 89-100.

Lynch, M. F., Vansteenkiste, M., Deci, E. L. & Ryan, R. M. (2011). Autonomy as process and outcome: Revisiting cultural and practical issues in motivation for counseling. *The Counseling Psychologist, 39*(2), 286-302.

MacKinnon, R. A., Michaels, R. & Buckley, P. J. (2006). *The psychiatric interview in clinical practice.* Washington, DC: American Psychiatric Publishing.

Maguire, M. (2004). Measuring the outcomes of career guidance. *International Journal for Educational and Vocational Guidance, 4*, 179-192.

Mahrer, A. R. & Boulet, D. B. (1999). How to do discovery-oriented psychotherapy research. *Journal of Clinical Psychology, 55*, 1481-1493.

Mahrer, A. R. (1988). Discovery-oriented psychotherapy research: Rational, aims, and methods. *American Psychologist, 43*, 694-702.

Mallen, M. J. & Vogel, D. L. (2005). Online counseling: A need for discovery. *Counseling Psychologist, 33*, 910-921.

Mallinckrodt, B. & Nelson, M. L. (1991). Counselor training level and the formation of the psychotherapeutic working alliance. *Journal of Counseling Psychology, 38*, 133-138.

Manhal-Baugus, M. (2001). E-therapy: Practical, ethical, and legal issues. *CyberPsychology and Behavior, 4*, 551-563.

Maples, M. F. & Han, S. (2008). Cybercounseling in the United States and South Korea: Implication for counseling college students of the millennial generation and the networked generation. *Journal of Counseling and Development, 86*, 1778-183.

Maree, J. & Pietersen, J. (2007a). The quantitative research process. In K. Maree (Ed.), *First steps in research* (pp. 144-153). Pretoria, South Africa: Van Schaik.

Maree, J. & Pietersen, J. (2007b). Sampling. In K. Maree (Ed.), *First steps in research* (pp. 171-181). Pretoria, South Africa: Van Schaik.

Maree, J. & van der Westhuizen (2009). *Head start in designing research proposals in the social science*. Cape Town, South Africa: Juta and Company.

Maree, J. G. & Molepo, J. M. (2007). Changing the approach to career counseling in disadvantaged context: A case study. *Australian Journal of Career Development, 16*(3), 62-70.

Maree, J. G. (2010). *The Career Interest Profile* (3rd ed.). Randburg: Jopie van Rooyen & Partners.

Maree, K. (Ed.). (2007). *Shaping the story: A guide to facilitating narrative career counseling*. Pretoria: Van Schaik Publishers.

Marmot, M. & Wilkinson, R. (Eds.). (1999). *Social determinants of health*. New York: Oxford University Press.

Marmot, M. (1999). Introduction. In M. Marmot & R. Wilkinson (Eds.), *Social determinants of health* (pp. 1-16). New York: Oxford University Press.

Mau, W. C. & Fernandes, A. (2001). Characteristics and satisfaction of students who use career counseling services. *Journal of College Students Development, 42*(6), 581-588.

Mayne, T. J., Norcross, J. C. & Sayette, M. A. (1994). Admission requirements, acceptance rates, and financial assistance in clinical psychology programs: Diversity across the practice-research continuum. *American Psychologist, 49*, 605-611.

Mays, V. M., Cochran, S. D. & Zamudio, A. Z. (2004). HIV prevention research: Are we meeting the needs of African American men who have sex with men? *Journal of Black Psychology, 30*, 78-105.

McCracken, G. (1988). *The long interview: Quantitative research methods* (Vol. 13). New Delhi, India: Sage.

McCrickard, M. P. & Butler, L. T. (2005). Cybercounseling: A new modality for counselor training and practice. *International Journal for the Advancement of Counselling, 27*, 101-110.

McDonough, P M. (2005b). Counseling matters: Knowledge, assistance, and organizational commitment in college preparation. In W. G. Tiemey, Z. B. Corwin, & J. E. Colyar (Eds.), *Preparing for college: Nine elements of effective outreach* (pp. 69-87). Albany: State University of New York Press.

McDonough, P. M. (2005a). *Counseling and college counseling in America's high schools*. Alexandria, VA: NACAC. Retrieved from http://www.nacacnet.org/Publications Resources/Research/Documents/WhitePaper_ McDonough.pdf.

McMahon, M. & Patton, W. (2002). Using qualitative assessment in career counseling. *International Journal for Educational and Vocational Guidance, 2*, 51-66.

McMahon, M. (2010). Career counseling and story telling: Constructing a 21st narrative for practice. In H. Ohlsson & H. Borg (Ed.), *Career development* (pp. 1-23). New York, United States: Nova Science.

McMillan, J. H. & Schumacher, S. (2001). *Research in education: A conceptual introduction.* New York: Longman.

Merriam, S. B. (1988). *Case study research in education: A qualitative approach.* San Francisco: Jossey-Bass.

Merriam, S. B. (2009). *Qualitative research: A guide to design and implementation.* San Francisco: John Wiley and Sons.

Mertens, D. M. (2003). Mixed methods and the politics of human research: The transformative-emancipatory perspective. In A. Tashakkori & C. Teddlie (Eds.), *Handbook of mixed methods in social and behavioral research* (pp. 135-164). Thousand Oaks, CA: Sage.

Metz, A. J. & Guichard, J. (2009). Vocational psychology and new challenge. *The Career Development Quarterly, 57*, 310-318.

Metz, A. J. (2009). The role and function of professional school counselors in the United States. *Counseling. Giornale Italiano di Ricerca e Applicazioni, 3*, 279-294.

Metz, A. J., Hu, Q. & Mitton, S. (2011). Using non-cognitive factors to promote academic success and college readiness. *Counseling: Giornale Italiano di Ricerca e Applicazioni, 4*, 241-255.

Metz, A.J., Fouad, N. A., Ihle-Helledy, K. (2009). Career aspirations and expectations of college students. Demographic and labor market influences. *Journal of Career Assessment, 17*(2), 155-171.

Miles, M. B. & Huberman, A. M. (1994). *Qualitative data analysis: A sourcebook of new methods* (2nd ed.). London, UK: Sage.

Miller, J. G. (1946). Clinical psychology in the Veterans Administration. *American Psychologist, 1*, 181-189.

Miller, M. J. & Brown, S. D. (2005). Counseling for career choice: Implications for improving interventions and for working with diverse populations. In S. D. Brown & R. W. Lent (Eds.), *Career development and counseling: Putting theory and research to work* (pp. 441-465). New York: Wiley & Sons.

Miranda, A. H. & Gutter, P. B. (2002). Diversity research literature in school psychology: 1990-1999. *Psychology in the Schools, 39*(5), 597-604.

Mok, D. S. (2003). Multiple/dual relationship in counseling: Implications for Asian context. *Asian Journal of Counseling, 10*, 95-125.

Mollen, D., Ridley, C. R. & Hill, C. L. (2003). Models of multicultural counseling competence. In D. B. Pope-Davis, H. L. K. Coleman, W. M. Liu, & R. L. Toporek (Eds.), *Handbook of multicultural competencies in counseling and psychology* (pp. 21-37). Thousand Oaks, CA: Sage.

Moradi, B., DeBlaere, C. & Huang, Y. P. (2010). Centralizing the experiences of LGB people of color in counseling psychology. *The Counseling Psychologist, 38*, 322-330.

Morgan, B. & Sklar, R. (2012). Sampling and research paradigm. In J. G. Maree (Ed.), *Complete your thesis or dissertation successfully: Practical guidelines* (pp. 69-80). Cape Town: Juta.

Morrow, S. L. & Smith, M. L. (2000). Qualitative research for counseling psychology. In S. D. Brown & R.W. Lent (Eds.), Handbook of counseling psychology (3rd ed., pp. 199–230). New York: John Wiley.

Morrow, S. L. (2003). Can the master's tools ever dismantle the master's house? Answering silences with alternative paradigms and methods. *The Counseling Psychologist, 31*, 70-77.

Moustakas, C. E. (1994). *Phenomenological research methods.* Thousand Oaks, CA: Sage.

Mouton, J. & Marais, H.C. (1990). *Basic concepts in the methodology of the social sciences* (Revised ed.). Pretoria, South Africa: Human Sciences Research Council.

Mouton, J. (2001). *How to succeed in your Master's and Doctoral Studies, A South African Guide and Resource Book.* Pretoria: Van Schaik Publishers.

Multon, K. D., Ellis-Kalton, C. A., Heppner, M. J. & Gysbers, N. C. (2003). The relationship between counselor verbal response modes and the working alliance in career counseling. *The Career Development Quarterly, 51*, 259-273.

Multon, K. D., Heppner, M. J., Gysbers, N. C., Zook, C. & Ellis-Kalton, C. A. (2001). Client psychological distress: An important factor in career counseling. *The Career Development Quarterly, 49*, 324-335.

Munley, P. H. (1974). A content analysis of the Journal of Counseling Psychology. *Journal of Counseling Psychology, 21*(4), 305-310.

Munley, P. H., Duncan, L. E., McDonnell, K. A. & Sauer, E. M. (2004). Counseling psychology in the United States of America. *Counselling Psychology Quarterly, 17*(3), 247-271.

Munley, P. H., Pate, W. E., II, & Duncan, L. E. (2008). Demographic, educational, employment and professional characteristics of counseling psychologists. *The Counseling Psychologist, 36*, 250-280.

Myers, J. E., Sweeney, T. J. & Witmer, J. M. (2000). The Wheel of Wellness counseling for wellness: A holistic model for treatment planning. *Journal of Counseling & Development, 78*, 251-266.

Myers, J. E., & Sweeney, T. J. (2005a). *Counseling for wellness: Theory, research, and practice.* Alexandria, VA: American Counseling Association.

National Career Development Association (1997). *NCDA guidelines for the use of the Internet for provision of career information and planning services.* Columbus, OH: Author.

Near, J. P., Rice, R. W. & Hunt, R. G. (1978). Work and extra-work correlates of life and job satisfaction. *Academy of Management Journal, 21*, 248-264.

Nelson, G. & Prilleltensky, I. (Eds.) (2005). *Community psychology: In pursuit of liberation and well-being.* New York, NY: Palgrave MacMillan.

Nelson, G. Lord, J. & Ochocka, J. (2001). *Shifting the paradigm in community mental health: Towards empowerment and community.* Toronto: University of Toronto Press.

Nelson, P. D. (1999). *The historical roots of CRSPPP and its mission to recognize specialties and proficiencies in professional psychology.* Retrieved from http://www.apa.org/crsppp/history.html.

Neville, H. A., Carter, R. T., Spengler, P. M. & Hoffman, M. A. (2006). Quantitative research designs and counseling psychology: Historical development, current application, and best practices. *The Counseling Psychologist, 34*, 597-600.

Nieuwenhuis, J. (2007). Introducing qualitative research. In K. Maree (Ed.), *First steps in research* (pp. 46-68). Pretoria, South Africa: Van Schaik.

Nieuwenhuis, J. (2010). *Qualitative research designs and data gathering techniques*. In K. Maree (Ed.), *First steps in research* (pp. 70-92). Pretoria, South Africa: Van Schaik.

Norcross, J. C., Castle, P. H., Sayette, M. A. & Mayne, T. J. (2004). The PsyD: Heterogeneity in practitioner training. *Professional Psychology: Research and Practice, 35*, 412-419.

Norcross, J. C., Evans, K. L. & Ellis, J. L. (2010). The Model Does Matter II: Admissions and training in APA - accredited counseling psychology programs. *The Counseling Psychologist, 38*, 257-268.

Nunnally, J. C. & Bernstein, I. H. (1994). *Psychometric theory* (3rd ed.). New York: McGraw-Hill.

O'Donovan, A., Bain, J. D. & Dyck, M. J. (2005). Does clinical psychology education enhance the clinical competence of practitioners? *Professional Psychology: Research and Practice, 36*, 104-111.

Oakland, T. (2005). Commentary # 1: What is multicultural school psychology? In Frisby, C. L. & Reynolds, C. R. (Eds.), *Comprehensive handbook of multicultural school psychology* (pp. 3-13). Hoboken, NJ: John Wiley & Sons Inc.

Oliver, L. W. & Spokane, A. R. (1988). Career intervention outcome: What contributes to client gain? *Journal of Counseling Psychology, 35*, 447-462.

Ornish, D. (1997). *Love and survival: The scientific basis for the healing power of intimacy*. New York, NY: Harper and Collins.

Overholser, J. C. (2005). Contemporary psychotherapy: Promoting personal responsibility for therapeutic change. *Journal of Contemporary Psychotherapy, 35, 369-376*

Parham, T. A. & Whitten, L. (2003). Teaching multicultural competencies in continuing education for psychologists. In D. B. Pope-Davis, H. L. K. Coleman, W. M. Liu, & R. Torporek (Eds.), *Handbook of multicultural competencies in counseling and psychology* (pp. 562-574). Thousand Oaks, CA: Sage.

Parker, I. (1994). Discourse Analysis. In Bannister, P., Burman, E., Parker, I., Taylor, M. & Tindall, C. (Eds.), *Qualitative methods in psychology: A research guide*. USA: Open University Press.

Parks, C. W. (2005). Black men who have sex with men. In J. L. Chin (Ed.), *The psychology of prejudice and discrimination: Bias based on gender and sexual orientation* (Vol. *3*, pp. 227-248). Westport, CT: Praeger/ Greenwood.

Parsons, F. (1909). *Choosing a vocation*. Boston, MA: Houghton Mifflin.

Patton, M. Q. (1984). *Qualitative evaluation methods*. Beverly Hills: SAGE.

Pelletier, D., Noiseux, G. & Bujold, C. (1974). *Développment personnel et croissance personnelle* [*Personal development and personal growth*]. Montréal: McGraw-Hill.

Pema, L. W. & Titus, M. A. (2005). The relationship between parental involvement as social capital and college enrollment: An examination of racial/ethnic group differences. *Journal of Higher Education, 76*, 485-518.

Pema, L. W. (2000). Differences in the decision to attend college among African Americans, Hispanics, and Whites. *Journal of Higher Education, 71*, 117-141.

Pema, L. W., Rowan-Kenyon, H., Thomas, S. L., Bell, A., Anderson, R. & Li, C. (2008). The role of college counseling in shaping college opportunity: Variations across high schools. *Review of Higher Education, 31*, 131-160.

Pe-Pua, R. & Protacio-Marcelino, E. (2000). Sikolohiyang Pilipino (Filipino psychology): A legacy of Virgilio G. Enriquez. *Asian Journal of Social Psychology, 3,* 49-71.

Peräkylä, A. (1993). Reliability and validity in research based on tapes and transcripts. In D. Silverman (Ed.), *Qualitative research. Theory, method and practice* (pp. 201-220). London, UK: Sage.

Phillips, L. (2005). Deconstructing "down low" discourse: The politics of sexuality, gender, race, AIDS, and anxiety. *Journal of African American Studies, 9,* 3-15.

Pieterse, A. L., Evans, S. A., Risner-Butner, A., Collins, N. M. & Mason, L. B. (2009). Multicultural competence and social justice training in counseling psychology and counselor education: A review and analysis of a sample of multicultural course syllabi. *The Counseling Psychologist, 37,* 93-115.

Pittman, K. J., Irby, M., Tolamn, J., Yohalem, N. & Ferber, T. (2001). *Preventing problems, promoting development, encouraging engagement: Competing priorities or inseparable goals.* Retrieved from http://forumforyouthinvestment.org/preventproblems.pdf.

Plank, S. B. & Jordan, W. J. (2001). Effects of information, guidance, and actions on post-secondary destinations: A study of talent loss. *American Educational Research Journal, 38,* 947-979.

Polkinghorne, D. E. (1984). Further extensions of methodological diversity for counseling psychology. *Journal of Counseling Psychology, 31,* 416-429.

Polkinghorne, D. E. (1989). Phenomenological research methods. In R. S. Balle & S. Halling (Eds.), *Existential–phenomenological perspectives in psychology: Exploring the breadth of human experience* (pp. 41-60). New York: Plenum Press.

Ponterotto, J. G. & Grieger, I. (1999). Merging qualitative and quantitative perspectives in a research identity. In M. Kopala & L. A. Suzuki (Eds.), *Using qualitative methods in psychology* (pp. 49-62). Thousand Oaks, CA: Sage.

Ponterotto, J. G. (1997). Multicultural training: A competency model and national survey. In D. B. Pope-Davis & H. L. K. Coleman (Eds.), *Multicultural counseling competencies: Assessment, education, training, and supervision* (pp. 111-130). Thousand Oaks, CA: Sage.

Ponterotto, J. G. (2005). Qualitative research in counseling psychology: A primer on research and paradigms and philosophy of science. *Journal of Counseling Psychology, 52,* 126-136.

Powell, A. G. (1996). *Lessons from privilege: The American prep school tradition.* Cambridge, MA: Harvard University Press.

Powell, L., Shahabi, L. & Thoresen, C. (2003). Religion and spirituality: Linkages to physical health. *American Psychologist, 58,* 36-52.

Prilleltensky, I. & Fox, D. R. (2007). Psychopolitical literacy for wellness and justice, *Journal of Community Psychology, 35,* 793-805.

Prilleltensky, I. Nelson, G. & Peirson, L. (Eds.). (2001a). *Promoting family wellness and preventing child maltreatment: Fundamentals for thinking and action.* Toronto: University of Toronto Press.

Prilleltensky, I., Dokecki, P., Frieden, G., Wang, V. O. (2007). Counseling for wellness and justice: Foundations and ethical dilemmas. In E. Aldarondo (Ed.), *Practical ethics for psychologists: A positive approach* (pp. 19-42). Mahwah, NJ: Lawrence Erlbaum.

Prilleltensky, I., Nelson, G. & Peirson, L. (2001b). The role of power and control in children's lives: An ecological analysis of pathways towards wellness, resilience, and problems. *Journal of Community and Applied Social Psychology, 11*, 143-158.

Prout, H. T. & DeMartino, R. A. (1986). A meta-analysis of school-based studies of psychotherapy. *Journal of School Psychology, 24*, 285-292.

Prout, S. M. & Prout, H. T. (1998). A meta-analysis of school-based studies of counseling and psychotherapy: An update. *Journal of School Psychology, 36*, 121-136.

Punch, K. F. (1998). *Introduction to social research: Quantitative and qualitative approaches*. Thousand Oaks, CA: Sage.

Putnam, R. (2000). *Bowling alone: The collapse and revival of American community*. New York, NY: Simon & Schuster.

Putnam, R. (2001). Social capital: Measurement and consequences. *Isuma: Canadian Journal of Policy Research, 2*, 41-51.

Recupero, P. R. & Rainey, S. E. (2005). Informed consent to e-therapy. *American Journal of Psychotherapy, 59*, 319-331.

Rehfuss, M. & Di Fabio, A. (in press). Validating the Future Career Autobiography as a measure of narrative change. *Journal of Career Assessment*.

Rehfuss, M. C. (2009). The Future Career Autobiography: A narrative measure of career intervention effectiveness. *The Career Development Quarterly, 58*(1), 82-90.

Reid, H. L. (2005). Narrative and career guidance: Beyond small talk and towards useful dialogue for the 21st century. *International Journal for Educational and Vocational Guidance, 5*, 125-136.

Reynolds, A. L. & Pope, R. L. (2003). Multicultural competence in counseling centers. In D. B. Pope-Davis, H. L. K. Coleman, W. M. Liu, & R. L. Toporek (Eds.), *Handbook of multicultural competencies in counseling and psychology* (pp. 365–382). Thousand Oaks, CA: Sage.

Reynolds, A. L. (1995). Challenges and strategies for teaching multicultural counseling courses. In J. G. Ponterotto, J. M. Casas, L. A. Suzuki, & C. M. Alexander (Eds.), *Handbook of multicultural counseling* (pp. 312-330). Thousand Oaks, CA: Sage.

Rhoades, L. & Eisenberg, R. (2002). Perceived organizational support: A review of the literature. *Journal of Applied Psychology, 87*, 698-714.

Richardson, M. S. (2009). Another way to think about the work we do: Counselling for work and relationship. *International Journal for Educational and Vocational Guidance, 9*, 75-84.

Richardson, M. S. (2012). Counseling for work and relationship. *The Counseling Psychologist, 40*(2), 190-242.

Richardson, M. S. (in press). Counseling for work and relationship. *The Counseling Psychologist*.

Ridley, C. R, & Kleiner, A. J. (2003). Multicultural counseling competence. In B. Pope-Davis, H. L. Coleman, W. Ming Liu, & R L. Toporek, (Eds.), *Handbook of multicultural competencies in counseling and psychology* (pp. 3-20). Thousand Oaks, CA: Sage Publications.

Ridley, C. R, & Mollen, D. (2010). Training in counseling psychology: An introduction to the major contribution. *The Counseling Psychologist, 39*(6), 793-799.

Ridley, C. R., Kelly, S. & Mollen, D. (2011). Microskills training: Evolution, reexamination, and call for reform. *The Counseling Psychologist, 39*, 800-824.

Ridley, C. R., Mollen, D. & Kelly, S. (2011a). Beyond microskills: Toward a model of counseling competence. *The Counseling Psychologist, 39*(6), 825-864.

Ridley, C. R., Mollen, D. & Kelly, S. (2011b). Counseling competence: Implications and applications of a model. *The Counseling Psychologist, 39*(6), 865-886.

Rogers, C. R. (1942). *Counseling and psychotherapy*. Boston, MA: Houghton Mifflin.

Romano, J. L. & Hage, S. M. (2000). Prevention and counseling psychology: Revitalizing commitments for the 21st century. *The Counseling Psychologist, 28*, 733-763.

Romano, J. L. & Kachgal, M. M. (2004). Counseling psychology and school counseling: An underutilized partnership. *The Counseling Psychologist, 32*, 184-215.

Russell, D. W. (2002). In search of underlying dimensions: The use (and abuse) of factor analysis in personality and social psychology bulletin. *Personality and Social Psychology Bulletin, 28*, 1629-1646.

Rutter, M. (1987). Psychosocial resilience and protective mechanisms. *American Journal of Orthopsychiatry, 57*, 316-331.

Ryan, N. E. (1999). *Career counseling and career choice goal attainment: A meta-analytically derived model for career counseling practice* (Unpublished doctoral dissertation). Loyola University, Chicago.

Ryan, R. M. & Deci, E. L. (2008). A self-determination approach to psychotherapy: The motivational basis for effective change. *Canadian Psychology, 49*, 186-193.

Ryan, R. M., Lynch, M. F., Vansteenkiste, M. & Deci, E. L. (2010). Motivation and autonomy in counseling, psychotherapy, and behavior change: A look at theory and practice. *The Counseling Psychologist, 39*(2), 193-260.

Sabella, R. A. (2004). A reaction to counseling psychology and school counseling: An underutilized partnership. *The Counseling Psychologist, 32*, 263-269.

Sampson, J. P. (2002). Quality and ethics in internet-based guidance. *International Journal for Educational and Vocational Guidance, 2*, 157-171.

Sampson, J. P. (2008). *Designing and implementing career programs: A handbook for effective practice*. Broken Arrow, OK: National Career Development Association.

Sampson, J. P. (2009, June). *Translating career theory to practice: The risk of unintentional social justice*. Paper presented at International Association of Educational and Vocational Guidance conference, Jyvaskyla, Finland.

Sarbin, T. R. (1986). The narrative as a root metaphor for psychology. In T. R. Sarbin (Ed.), *Narrative psychology: The storied nature of human conduct*. New York: Praeger.

Savickas, M. L. (2008, May). Career as story. Lecture at 10th International Congress *Choice guidance: research, training, applications*, 15-17 may, Florence, Italy.

Savickas, M. L. (1989). Career-style assessment and counseling. In T. Sweeney (Ed.), *Adlerian counseling: A practical approach for a new decade* (3rd ed.). Muncie, IN: Accelerated Development Press.

Savickas, M. L. (1998). Career style assessment and counseling. In T. J. Sweeney (Ed.), *Adlerian counseling: A practitioner's approach* (4th ed., pp. 329-359). Philadelphia, PA: Accelerated Development.

Savickas, M. L. (2004). Vocational psychology. In C. Spielberger (Ed.), *Encyclopedia of Applied Psychology* (pp. 655-667). Amsterdam, Netherlands: Elsevier.

Savickas, M. L. (2000). Renovating the psychology of careers for the twenty-first century. In A. Collin, & R. A. Young (Eds.), *The future of career* (pp. 53–68). New York: Cambridge University Press.

Savickas, M. L. (2001). Toward a comprehensive theory of career development: Dispositions, concerns, and narratives. In F. T. L. Leong & A. Barak (Eds.), *Contemporary models in vocational psychology: A volume in honor of Samuel H. Osipow* (pp. 295-320). Mahwah, NJ: Lawrence Erlbaum.

Savickas, M. L. (2002). Quality outcomes for career development: Practice perspective. In L. Bezanson & E. O'Reilly (Eds.), *Making Waves: Connecting Career Development with Public Policy* (Vol. 2, pp. 18-20). Ottawa: Canadian Career Development Foundation.

Savickas, M. L. (2005). The theory and practice of career construction. In S. D. Brown & R. W. Lent (Eds.), *Career development and counseling: Putting theory and research to work* (pp. 42-70). Hoboken, NJ: Wiley.

Savickas, M. L. (2007a). Internationalisation of counseling psychology: Constructing cross-national consensus and collaboration. *Applied Psychology: An International Review, 56*(1), 182-188.

Savickas, M. L. (2007b). Prologue Reshaping the story of career counseling. In K. Maree (Ed.), *Shaping the story. A guide to facilitating narrative counselling* (pp. 1-3). Pretoria, South Africa: Van Schaik.

Savickas, M. L. (2010a). *Life Designing: Framework and introduction.* Paper presented at the 27th International Congress of Applied Psychology, Melbourne, Australia.

Savickas, M. L. (2010b). Vocational counseling. In I. B. Weiner & W. E. Craighead (Eds.), *Corsini's encyclopedia of psychology* (4th ed., pp. 1841-1844). Hoboken, NJ: John Wiley & Sons.

Savickas, M. L. (2011). *Career counseling.* Washington: American Psychological Association.

Savickas, M. L., Nota, L. & Rossier, L., Dauwalder, J. P., Duarte, M. E., Guichard, J.,...van Vianen, A. E. M. (2009). Life designing: A paradigm for career construction in the 21th century. *Journal of Vocational Behavior, 75*, 239-250.

Scheel, M. J.,Berman, M., Friedlander, M. L., Conoley, C. W., Duan, C. & Whiston, S C. (2011). Whatever happened to counseling in counseling psychology? *The Counseling Psychologist, 39*(5), 673-692.

Schneider Jamner, M. & Stokols, D. (Eds.). (2000). *Promoting human wellness.* Berkeley, CA: University of California Press.

Schwandt, T. A. & Halpern, E. S. (1988). *Linking Auditing and metaevaluation: Enhancing quality in applied research.* Thousand Oaks, CA: Sage.

Seligman, M. E. (2002). *Authentic happiness.* New York, NY: Free Press.

Sen, A. (1999a). *Beyond the crisis: Development strategies in Asia.* Singapore: Institute of Southeast Asian Studies.

Sen, A. (1999b). *Development as freedom.* New York, NY: Anchor Books.

Shakow, D. (1942). The training of the clinical psychologist. *Journal of Consulting Psychology, 6*, 277-288.

Shaw, H. E. & Shaw, S. F. (2006). Critical ethical issues in online counseling: Assessing current practices with an ethical intent checklist. *Journal of Counseling and Development, 84*, 41-53.

Sherry, A. (2006). Discriminant analysis in counseling psychology research. *The Counseling Psychologist, 34*, 661-683.

Shonkhoff, J. & Phillips, D. (Eds.). (2000). *From neurons to neighbourhoods: The science of early childhood development.* Washington, DC: National Academy Press.

Singh, A. A. & Shelton, K. (2011). A content analysis of LGBTQ qualitative research in counseling: A ten-year review. *Journal of Counseling & Development, 89*, 217-226.

Sinha, D. (1997). Indigenous psychology. In J. W. Berry, Y. H., Poortinga, & J. Pandey (Eds.). *Handbook of cross-cultural psychology* (Vol. 1, pp. 129-170). Boston: Allyn & Bacon.

Smedley, B. D. & Syme, S. L. (Eds.). (2000). *Promoting health: Intervention strategies from social and behavioral research.* Washington, DC: National Academy Press.

Smith, L. T. (2008). On tricky ground: Researching the native in the age of uncertainty. In N. K. Denzin & Y. S. Lincoln (Eds.), *The landscape of qualitative research,* (3rd ed., pp. 113-143). Thousand Oaks, CA: Sage.

Smith, L., Baluch, S., Bernabei, S., Robohm, J. & Sheehy, J. (2003). Applying a social justice framework to college counseling centers. *Journal of College Counseling, 6*, 3-13.

Society for Counseling Psychology Division 17 (2012). *About counseling psychologists.* Retrieved from http://www.div17.org/students_defining. html

Spokane, A. R., Fouad, N. A. & Swanson, J. L. (2003). Culture-centered career intervention. *Journal of Vocational Behavior, 62*, 453-458.

Sprinthall, N. A. (1990). Counseling psychology from Greyston to Atlanta: On the road to Armageddon? *The Counseling Psychologist, 18*, 455-463.

Stake, R. E. (1995). *The art of case study research.* Thousand Oaks, CA: Sage.

Stansfeld, S. (1999). Social support and social cohesion. In M. Marmot & R. Wilkinson (Eds.), *Social determinants of health* (pp. 155-178). New York: Oxford University Press.

Stanton-Salazar, R. D. & Dombusch, S. M. (1995). Social capital and the reproduction of inequality: Information networks among Mexican origin high school students. *Sociology of Education, 68*, 116-135.

Stead, G. B. (2004). Culture and career psychology: A social constructionist perspective. *Journal of Vocational Behavior, 64(3)*, 389-406.

Stice, E., Shaw, H., Bohon, C., Marti, C. N. & Rohde, P. (2009). A meta-analytic review of depression prevention programs for children and adolescents: Factors that predict magnitude of intervention effects. *Journal of Consulting and Clinical Psychology, 77*, 486-503.

Stokols, D. (2000). The social ecological paradigm of wellness promotion. In M. S. Jamner & D. Stokols, (Eds.), *Promoting human wellness* (pp. 21-37). Los Angeles, CA: University of California Press.

Stokols, D. (2003). The ecology of human strengths. In L. Aspinwall & U. Staudinger (Eds.), *A psychology of human strengths: Fundamental questions and future directions for a positive psychology* (pp. 331-343). Washington, DC: American Psychological Association.

Stoltenberg, C. D., Pace, T. M., Kashubeck-West, S., Biever, J. L., Patterson, T. & Welch, I. D. (2000). Training models in counseling psychology: Scientist-practitioner versus practitioner-scholar. *The Counseling Psychologist, 28*, 622-640.

Strauss, A. & Corbin, J. (1990). *Basics of qualitative research: Grounded theory procedures and techniques.* Newbury Park, CA: Sage.

Strupp, H. H. & Hadley, S. W. (1979). Specific versus nonspecific factors in psychotherapy. *Archives of General Psychiatry, 36*, 1125-1136.

Sue, D. W., Bernier, J. E., Durran, A., Feinberg, L., Pedersen, P., Smith, E. J. & Vasquez-Nuttall, E. (1982). Position paper: Cross-cultural counseling competencies. *The Counseling Psychologist*, *10*, 45-52.

Sue, D., Arredondo, P. & McDavis, J. (1992). Multicultural counseling competencies and standards: A call to the profession. *Journal of Counseling and Development*, *70*, 477-486.

Suler, J. (2004). The online disinhibition effect. *Cyberpsychology & Behavior*, *7*(3), 321-326.

Suzuki, L. A., Ahluwalia, M. K., Mattis, J. S. & Quizon, C. A. (2005). Ethnography in counseling psychology research: Possibilities for application. *Journal of Counseling Psychology*, *52*(2), 206-214.

Swanson, J. (1995). The process and outcome of career counseling. In W. B. Walsh & S. H. Osipow (Eds.), *Handbook of vocational psychology: Theory practice and research* (2nd ed., pp. 217-260). Mahwah, NJ: Lawrence Erlbaum.

Sweeney, T. J. & Witmer, J. M. (1991). Beyond social interest: Striving toward optimum health and wellness. *Individual Psychology*, *47*, 527-540.

Tabachnick, G. G. & Fidell, L. S. (2007). *Experimental Designs Using ANOVA*. Belmont, CA: Duxbury.

Talleyrand, R. M., Chung, R. C. & Bemak. F. (2006). Incorporating social justice in counselor training programs: A case study example. In R. L. Toperk., L. H. Gerstein., N. A. Fouad., G. Roysircar, & T. Israel (Eds.), *Handbook of social justice in counseling psychology* (pp. 44-58). Thousand Oaks, CA: Sage.

Tashakkori, A. & Teddlie, C. (1998). *Mixed methodology: Combining qualitative and quantitative approaches*. Thousand Oaks, CA: Sage.

Tashakkori, A. & Teddlie, C. (Eds.) (2003). *Handbook of mixed methods in social and behavioral research*. Thousand Oaks, CA: Sage.

Taylor, S. J. & Bogdan, R. (1998). *Introduction to qualitative research methods: A guidebook and resource* (3rd ed.). New York: Wiley.

Teddlie, C. & Tashakkori, A. (2003). Major issues and controversies in the use of mixed methods in the social and behavioral sciences. In A. Tashakkori & C. Teddlie (Eds.), *Handbook of mixed methods in social & behavioral research* (pp. 3-50). Thousand Oaks, CA: Sage.

Terre Blanche, M. S. & Durrheim, K. (2004). *Research in practice: Applied methods for the social sciences*. Cape Town, South Africa: University of Cape Town.

Thompson, B. (2004). *Exploratory and confirmatory factor analysis: Understanding concepts and applications*. Washington, DC: American Psychological Association.

Timlin-Scalera, R. M., Ponterotto, J. G., Blumberg, F. C. & Jackson, M. A. (2003). A grounded theory study of help-seeking behaviors among White male high school students. *Journal of Counseling Psychology*, *50*, 339-350.

Tinsley, H. E. A. & Tinsley, D. J. (1987). Uses of factor analysis in counseling psychology research. *Journal of Counseling Psychology*, *34*, 414-424.

Tracey, T. J., Hays, K. A., Malone, J. & Herman, B. (1988). Changes in counselor response as a function of experience. *Journal of Counseling Psychology*, *35*, 119-126.

Trickett, E. J., Watts, R. J. & Birman, D. (Eds.). (1994). *Human diversity: Perspectives on people in context*. San Francisco: Jossey-Bass.

Truax, C. B. & Carkhuff, R. (2008). *Toward effective counseling and psychotherapy: Training and practice*. Chicago IL: Aldine.

Tyler, L. (1992). Counseling psychology—Why? *Professional Psychology: Research and Practice, 3*, 342-344.

Valle, R., King, M. & Halling, S. (1989). An introduction to existential-phenomenological thought in psychology. In R. Valle & S. Halling (Eds.), *Existential-phenomenological perspective in psychology* (pp. 3-16). New York: Plenum Press.

Vera, E. M. & Speight, S. L. (2003). Multicultural competence, social justice, and counseling psychology: Expanding our roles. *The Counseling Psychologist, 31*, 253-272.

Vera, E. M. & Speight, S. L. (2007). Advocacy, outreach, and prevention: Integrating social action roles in professional training. In E. Aldarondo (Ed.), *Advancing social justice through clinical practice* (pp. 373-390). Mahwah, NJ: Lawrence Erlbaum.

Vera, E. M. (2000). A recommitment to prevention work in counseling psychology. *The Counseling Psychologist, 28*, 829-837.

Vespia, K. M., Fitzpatrick, M. E., Fouad, N. A., Kantamneni, N. & Chen, Y. L. (2010). Multicultural career counseling: a national survey of competencies and practices. *The Career Development Quarterly, 59*(1), 54-71.

Walsh, M. E., Galassi, J. P., Murphy, J. A. & Park-Taylor, J. (2002). A conceptual frame work for counseling psychologists in schools. *The Counseling Psychologist, 30*(5), 682-704.

Watkins, C. E. Jr. (2008). A counseling psychology for the New Millennium. *The Counseling Psychologist, 36*, 290-293.

Watkins, C. E. Jr., Lopez, F. G., Campbell, V. L. & Himmell, C. D. (1986). Contemporary counseling psychology: Results of a national survey. *Journal of Counseling Psychology, 33*, 301-309.

Watkins, C. E., Jr. (1983). Counseling psychology versus clinical psychology: Further explorations on a theme or once more around the ''Identity'' Maypole with gusto. *The Counseling Psychologist, 11*, 76-92.

Watts, A. G. (2005). Career guidance policy: An international review. *The Career Development Quarterly, 54*, 66-77.

Watts, A.G. (1996). Careers guidance and public policy. In A.G. Watts, B. Law, J. Killeen, J. M. Kidd, & R. Hawthorn (Eds.), *Rethinking careers education and guidance: Theory, policy and practice* (pp. 380-391). London: Routledge.

Weisfeld, A. & Perlman, R. L. (2005). Disparities and discrimination in health care: An introduction. *Perspectives in Biology and Medicine, 48*, S1-S9.

Weissberg, M., Rude, S. S. & Gazda, G. M., Bozarth, J. D., Mcdougal, K. S., Slavit, M. R., … Walsh, D. J. (1988). An overview of the third national conference for counseling psychology: Planning the future. *The Counseling Psychologist, 16*, 325-331.

Weisz, J. R., Weiss, B., Alicke, M. D. & Klotz, M. L. (1987). Effectiveness of psychotherapy with children and adolescents: A meta-analysis for clinicians. *Journal of Consulting and Clinical Psychology, 55*, 542-549.

Weisz, J. R., Weiss, B., Han, S. S., Granger, D. A. & Morton, T. (1995). Effects of psychotherapy with children and adolescents revisited: A meta-analysis of treatment outcome studies. *Psychological Bulletin, 117*, 450-468.

Weston, R. & Gore, P. A. Jr. (2006). A brief guide to structural equation modeling. *The counseling Psychologist, 34*, 719-751.

Whiston, S. C, Brecheisen, B. K. & Stephens, J. (2003). Does treatment modality affect career counseling effectiveness? *Journal of Vocational Behavior, 62*, 390-410.

Whiston, S. C. & Oliver, L.W. (2005). Career counseling process and outcome. In W. B. Walsh & M. L. Savickas (Eds.), *Handbook of vocational psychology: Theory, research, and practice* (3rd ed., pp. 155-194). Mahwah, NJ: Lawrence Erlbaum.

Whiston, S. C. (2002). Response to the past, present, and future of school counseling: Raising some issues. *Professional School Counseling, 5,* 148-155.

Whiston, S. C. (2003). Career counseling: 90-years-old yet still healthy and vital. *The Career Development Quarterly, 52,* 35-42.

Whiston, S. C. (2004). Counseling psychology and school counseling: Can a stronger partnership be forged? *The Counseling Psychologist, 32,* 270-277.

Whiston, S. C. (2008). *Principles and applications of assessment in counseling* (3rd ed.). Belmont, CA: Brooks/Cole.

Whiston, S. C., Lee Tai, W., Rahardja, D. &Eder, K. (2011). School counseling outcome: A meta-analytic examination of interventions. *Journal of Counseling & Development, 89,* 37-55.

Whiston, S. C., Sexton, T. L. & Larsoff, D. L. (1998). Career intervention outcome: A replication and extension. *Journal of Counseling Psychology, 45,* 150-165.

White, M. & Epston, D. (1990). *Narrative means to therapeutic ends.* New York: Norton.

Whiteley, J. N. & Fretz, B. R. (1980). *The present and future of counseling psychology.* Monterey, CA: Brooks/Cole.

Whiteley, J. N. (1984). *Counseling psychology: A historical perspective.* New York: Character Research Press.

Wilkinson, R. G. (1996). *Unhealthy societies: The afflictions of inequality.* London: Routledge.

Witmer, J. M., & Sweeney, T. J. (1992). A holistic model for wellness and prevention over the life span. *Journal of Counseling & Development, 71,* 140-148.

Wolfe, D. (1946). The reorganized American Psychological Association. *American Psychologist, 1,* 3-6.

World Health Organization (1986, November). *The Ottawa Charter for Health Promotion.* First International Conference on Health Promotion, Ottawa, Canada.

Worthington, R. L. & Navarro, R. L. (2003). Pathways to the future: Analyzing the contents of a content analysis. *The Counseling Psychologist, 31,* 85-92.

Wrenn, C. G. (1966). Birth and early childhood of a journal. *Journal of Counseling Psychology, 13,* 485-488.

Yeh, C. J. & Inman, A. G. (2007). Qualitative data analysis and interpretation in counseling psychology: Strategies for best practices. *The Counseling Psychologist, 35,* 369-403.

Yeh, C. J. (2004). Multicultural and contextual research and practice in school counseling. *The Counseling Psychologist, 32,* 278-285.

Yeh, C. J., Inman, A., Kim, A. B. & Okubo, Y. (2006). Asian American families' collectivistic coping strategies in response to 9/11. *Cultural Diversity and Ethnic Minority Psychology, 12,* 134-148.

Yeh, C. J., Ma, P. W., Madan, A., Hunter, C. D., Jung, S., Kim, A., et al. (2005). The cultural negotiations of Korean immigrant youth. *Journal of Counseling and Development, 83,* 172-181.

Young, R. A. & Lalande, V. (2011). Canadian counselling psychology: From defining moments to ways forward. *Canadian Psychology/Psychologie canadienne, 52*(4), 248-255.

Young, R. A. & Valach, L. (2009). Evaluating the processes and outcomes of vocational counselling: An action theory perspective. *Orientation Scolaire et Professionnelle, 38*(3), 281-306.

Young, R. A. (2010, July). *Counselling Psychology: The ways forward*. Paper presented at 27th International Congress of Applied Psychology 2010 (ICAP 2010), 11-16 July, Melbourne, Australia.

Zea, M. C., Reisen, C. A. & Díaz, R. M. (2003). Methodological issues in research on sexual behavior with Latino gay and bisexual men. *American Journal of Community Psychology, 31*, 281-291.

Zysberg, L. (2010). Factors associated with satisfaction in career counseling. *International Journal of Psychology and Counseling, 2*(5), 80-84.

In: Psychology of Counseling
Editor: Annamaria Di Fabio

ISBN: 978-1-62618-388-9
© 2013 Nova Science Publishers, Inc.

Chapter 2

The Prevention Imperative and the Work of the Counselor

Maureen E. Kenny * *and Mary Beth Medvide*
Boston College, Chestnut Hill, MA, US

ABSTRACT

With evidence mounting as to the efficacy and cost-effectiveness of prevention and the ethical and social justice mandates for preferring prevention to remediating problems after they have developed, counselors need to more fully prepare for and engage in prevention. Primary prevention, by stopping problems before they occur, prevents human suffering and offers a strategy for eliminating existing disparities in levels of psychological and physical well-being by social class and race. Prevention programs that strive to realize these lofty goals need to simultaneously reduce individual, family, school, community and societal risks and to reinforce and build strengths across all of these areas.

Drawing from the developmental contextual framework (Lerner, 1986), it is evident that psychological and physical wellness are multi-determined and that efforts to address one set of factors without addressing others, will lead to temporary and ineffective effects. Recent prevention efforts focused on reducing levels of obesity and major depression illustrate the array of factors that should be considered in prevention program design.

The counselor who seeks to design, implement and evaluate such broad prevention efforts needs to be equipped with varied skills, including multicultural competence, knowledge of unique ethical challenges, and skills in diagnosis and intervention in complex systems, among others.

This chapter presents the rationale for increased engagement in prevention, provides an overview of important issues related to prevention, and identifies the types of skills needed for competence in prevention.

---

* Corresponding author: Maureen E. Kenny. Email address: maureen.kenny@bc.edu.

INTRODUCTION

The profession of counseling is rooted historically in a commitment to fostering psychological well-being across the life span (Conyne, 2004; Romano, Koch, and Wong, 2012). Whereas the roots of clinical psychology were in the treatment of disturbed client populations in hospital settings, counselors began working in school and other community settings, such as vocational guidance centers, with a focus on building client strengths. The roots of counseling in vocational guidance were closely entwined with the prevention focus of counselors and the role of the counselor in enhancing opportunities and building skills that would equip individuals to successfully navigate their lives (Kenny, 2009; Brown, Lamp, Telander, and Hacker, 2013).

Over time the distinctions between the specialties of counseling and clinical psychology have become less clear. Counselors and counseling psychologists frequently work in hospital settings and with persons with the most serious and complex psychological difficulties (Sayette, Mayne, and Norcross, 2010). Clinical psychologists frequently work in community and work settings with individuals coping with common life stressors and adjustment issues. The current distinction between these specialties may be less about the settings in which the professionals work, but the mindsets and models in which they frame their understanding of client issues and intervention strategies. As a result of the growing use of medications for persons with mild disorders, the involvement of psychiatrists and primary care physicians in the treatment of persons coping with mild disorders has increased. At the same time, psychological specialties, such as community psychology, have established prevention as a clear hallmark of their work (Prilleltensky and Nelson, 1997). The fields of social work and public health also have a long-standing commitment and expertise in the field of prevention (Kenny, Horne, Orpinas, and Reese, 2009; Swenson, 1998).

Given the psychological and economic costs of treatment and the scope of psychological, social, and economic issues confronting persons and societies across the globe, we maintain that counselors and counseling psychologists must embrace a prevention focus. While counselors should be prepared to offer remedial treatment services, they should also be well prepared to engage with a range of psychological and other professional specialties in the design, delivery and evaluation of prevention programs. A focus on prevention is consistent with the 2010 U.S. Patient Protection and Affordable Care Act, which calls for expansion of preventive services to maximize positive health outcomes (www.healthcare.gov) as well as the U.S. National Prevention Strategy which "provides unprecedented opportunity to shift the nation from a focus on sickness and disease to one on wellness and prevention" across the lifespan (National Prevention, Health Promotion, and Public Health Council, 2011). In addition to prevention programming, a preventive focus can be integrated across other types of interventions, including individual and group counseling. Conyne (2004), for example, promotes the concept of everyday prevention, in which counselors and other mental health and health professionals help clients to develop ways to promote well-being and avert distress as part of their daily routines.

This chapter discusses the argument for the importance of prevention in counseling, offers theoretical and conceptual models to guide prevention work, provides examples of prevention programs and what is known about the outcomes of those efforts, presents ethical and practice guidelines to inform prevention practice and research, and discusses the preparation that is needed for counselors to engage effectively in prevention.

MENTAL HEALTH PREVENTION

Whereas mental health treatment or remedial therapy focuses on alleviating mental health symptoms after they are evident, prevention seeks to stop problems before they occur. This focus is most evident in what is known as primary prevention (Silverman, 2003). Caplan's (1964) classic definition also includes secondary and tertiary prevention. Secondary prevention entails intervention following evidence of early signs of a problem, such as intensive language training for young children with early signs of autism, or intervention for those at-risk (e.g., premature infants). Tertiary prevention is designed to reduce the negative impact of an existing condition, such as offering vocational counseling and job training to homeless women diagnosed with depression. Consistent with its public health roots, prevention has had a long standing focus on reducing risks, with a focus on wellness enhancement being added by community psychologists, such as Cowen (1973, 1977). Romano and Hage (2000), representatives of the Prevention Section of the Society for Counseling Psychology in the American Psychological Association, further broadened the definition of prevention to include efforts to promote public policy and legislation that will enhance health and well-being in multiple contexts and across the life span. This addition augments the already broad understanding of prevention as encompassing primary, secondary and tertiary foci, and on building strengths as well as reducing risks.

Prevention is a compelling concept for a number of reasons. First of all, if problems are stopped before they occur, extensive human suffering can be averted (Kenny and Hage, 2009). In addition, effective and well-directed prevention practice can have great impact. A popular example in prevention circles derives from "The River" or "Upstream" story. Although the origins of the story are debated, the basic parable teaches the lesson of prevention. When the townspeople discovered bodies floating downstream, they worked tirelessly to rescue drowning swimmers, but more bodies kept coming. The flow of drowning swimmers stopped only after the townspeople changed their strategy. While some citizens stayed downstream to rescue swimmers, others went upstream to discover the root of the problem, a broken bridge. They worked to repair the bridge and warned people against using the bridge until the repair was completed. The parable illustrates how prevention can diminish human suffering and curtail efforts that do not produce solutions or cures for the problem.

For these reasons, prevention can also be cost-effective. The Highscope Perry Preschool Project illustrates how an early intervention prevention program can yield benefits across the life span. The Perry Preschool offered high quality academic and family intervention from 1962 to 1967 to African American children ages 3 and 4, living in poverty. Forty years later, the preschool participants, who had been randomly assigned to the intervention, were found to have higher earnings, were more likely to hold a job, had committed fewer crimes and were more likely to have graduated from high school than the adults who did not attend preschool (Schweinhart et al.,2005). The program costs were small in comparison with the social and economic benefits reaped over many years.

A reliance on treatment is also problematic since all persons and populations do not have equivalent access to and use of effective treatment options. Psychological treatment is expensive, with access in the US often being dependent upon the quality and type of health insurance. This is particularly troubling, given continuing disparities in the incidence of health and mental health problems related to social class, and the strong association between poverty and both physical and psychological problems (Speight and Vera, 2008). Of additional concern, is the fact that comfort with and use of psychological services may vary by culture (Vera, Buhin, and Isacco, 2009). Although the 1960's cliché of the ideal therapy client as "YAVIS" (Youthful, Attractive, Verbal, Intelligent, and Successful) has been dispelled, efforts are ongoing to reduce cultural barriers that prevent some cultural groups from seeking psychotherapy and to increase the cultural competence and sensitivity of mental health providers (Reese and Vera, 2007). If prevention reaches those groups who do not have access to or avail themselves of treatment, prevention may be a key in reducting disparities.

THEORETICAL PERSPECTIVES

The prevalence of health and mental health disparities by social class and race/ethnicity not only contributes to the imperative for prevention, but has influenced the development of frameworks and theories that inform prevention work.

Although no single theoretical perspective drives prevention practice and research, the literature demonstrates that theoretically-driven interventions lead to more effective outcomes (Nation et al., 2003). Developmental contextualism (Lerner, 1986, 1991, 1992) represents one broad theoretical framework, which has been identified as offering a meaningful foundation for prevention practice and research (Kenny and Romano, 2009; Walsh, DePaul, and Park-Taylor, 2009). Developmental contextualism recognizes reciprocal and ongoing interaction between the qualities of the person and the environment. The environment is also understood as multifaceted. Consistent with the ecological perspective (Bronfenbrenner, 1979), the individual is nested in a series of systems, including the family, school, community, national, and international contexts (among others), which also interact reciprocally. For example, national public policy on educational standards influences what happens in schools, and the impact of those policies on schools shapes future policy development to some extent.

At the person level, the individual also encompasses multiple interacting domains. From a holistic perspective, the social, psychological, and biological systems of the person interact reciprocally. Quite simply, for example, the levels of emotional and social stress experienced by persons can affect their physical well-being, which in turn can impact their effectiveness in social relationships or in coping with the demands of school or work. Across the range of intrapersonal and environmental dimensions, protective strengths or assets can be identified, as well as vulnerabilities that reduce well-being or place the person at risk for mental health dysfunction.

Following from the developmental contextual framework, prevention can be directed at a variety of factors. Indeed, a careful assessment process is needed to determine areas of both strength and vulnerability at the person and environmental levels. Intervention can seek to either reduce risks or enhance strengths or both for the individual or at any level of context, ranging from family, school, community or national policy. Some interventions can be focused on redressing specific risks or problems (e.g.,, substance abuse, bullying and other forms of interpersonal violence, depression). Others might be focused on building those assets or reducing risks that relate to well-being across a variety of domains. For example, the capacity to manage and regulate one's emotions may be associated with decreased depression and heightened psychological well-being, as well as better social relationships, and greater academic and career success. Interventions that support positive development and risk reduction across multiple domains may be relevant for and desirable for broad sectors of the population, such as entire classrooms of school children, and are thus labeled as universal interventions (Gordon, 1983).

PREVENTION AND SOCIAL JUSTICE

Because of the disparities in rates of physical and psychological disorder related to social class and by race and ethnicity, prevention researchers have sought to identify risk factors that contribute to such disparities, with the hopes of targeting those for intervention. The hope that prevention serves to reduce disparities suggests that it might also be a tool for realizing social justice (Kenny et al., 2009). Although the term social justice can be understood in differing ways, we adopt the understanding of socially just systems as those that offer all persons fair and equitable access to societal resources, enabling full participation in society without physical or psychological threat (Bell, 2007; Kenny and Romano, 2009). In order to further social justice, interventions should focus on building strengths at the person and family levels, as well as reducing those broader societal and structural risks that might be considered the "causes of the cause" (Pilleltensky and Nelson, 1997, p. 88).

Attention to valuing and building personal, family and community strengths is critical in order that targeted individuals and groups are not viewed as deficient in comparison with privileged members of society. Appreciation to building individual and group strengths follows from a culturally relevant approach to prevention that is developed and delivered by culturally competent professionals, generally in collaboration with community members (Reese and Vera, 2007). Cultural relevance signifies that the intervention is consistent with the beliefs, values and hoped-for outcomes of a particular community, and cultural competence relates to the training and skill of the professional in working with that specific population (Reese and Vera, 2007). Cultural relevance is generally recognized as an important characteristic for effective prevention (Kenny and Romano, 2009; Kumpfer, Alvarado, Smith and Bellamy, 2002; Walsh et al., 2009).

With regard to targeting risks, lack of access to higher education, poor quality health care, inadequate nutrition, and exposure to neighborhood violence represent some of the environmental and other structural inequities that limit opportunities and contribute to physical and mental health problems for individuals and families. The late psychologist, George Albee (1986, 2003), was an important advocate for social justice and prevention. Albee highlighted the role of environmental factors as determinants of mental health and championed the importance of reducing environmental risks to prevent mental disorders. The incidence formula (Albee and Ryan-Finn, 1993) depicts the likelihood of developing a mental health disorder as a function of organic factors, stress and toxic social conditions that foster oppression and inequity divided by the coping resources or strengths of the individual or group to resist those threats. Albee (Albee and Ryan-Finn, 1993) also recognized that toxic social conditions are more prevalent under conditions of poverty. From a prevention perspective, the incidence formula suggests that the rate of mental health disorders can be reduced by eliminating toxic social conditions and stress or by building coping resources, such as social support.

Prilleltensky et al. (Nelson and Prilleltensky, 2005; Prilleltensky, Dokecki, Freiden, and Wang, 2007; Prilleltensky and Nelson, 1997) are contemporary advocates for prevention and social justice. Like Albee (1986, 2003), Prilleltensky and colleagues recognize the importance for prevention to reduce societal risks and to build the social, emotional, and vocational capacities of individuals and groups to allow for full participation in society. Transformative societal change that fundamentally changes the social conditions that support oppression and inequity is viewed as necessary for prevention to be realized. Prilletensky and colleagues critique much prevention work for its ameliorative focus, which reduces suffering and helps people to feel better, but does not alter the underlying conditions that lead to injustice. Most counselors will have the opportunity to engage in ameliorative preventive work, which will yield benefits for individuals, groups, and the society at large. Those who strive to foster social justice, however, need to consider ways to eliminate oppression and poverty.

PREVENTION ACROSS CONTEXTS AND ACROSS THE LIFESPAN

Counselors can engage in ameliorative and transformative prevention through work in a variety of contexts and by helping clients to integrate prevention and wellness concepts in their everyday lives (Conyne, 2004). Colleges and universities, the workplace, K-12 schools, and community centers offer opportunities for skilled counselors to engage in prevention practice. Primary prevention efforts to improve physical and psychological well-being also extend across the lifespan starting in the prenatal stages and continuing into old age. The prevention of some mental health disorders and physical ailments may specifically target children, adolescents, and adults whereas other efforts, such as public policy, target large segments of the population reaching across age, gender, race, and social class. In conjunction with interventions that seek broad societal change, school, family, and community-level factors exert direct impact on psychological well-being and can be feasible and desirable targets for successful prevention intervention.

Careful analysis is needed in deciding where to intervene and how to promote strengths and reduce risks. We focus below on obesity and depression as two areas for prevention and wellness promotion that are targeted across the lifespan. These examples highlight, in alignment with developmental contextualism, how risk and well-being manifest across social contexts and life stages and the varied contextual and developmental factors that need to be considered in effective prevention work. Related to the complex array of factors that determine physical and psychological well-being across the life span, these examples illustrate the need for effective and culturally competent intervention across multiple contexts and the range of competencies needed by counselors who engage in prevention.

Obesity. Obesity is an example of an individual risk factor that has received considerable attention over the past decade. Obesity rates have climbed drastically, particularly among low-income children and families, contributing to escalating health care costs (Bermann and Lavizzo-Mourey, 2008; Stevens, 2010). The psychological, economic, biological and social factors that have contributed to obesity are complex, requiring the attention of diverse professional disciplines, including mental health counselors. The complexity of contributing factors has defied simple solutions. Indeed, one of the greatest challenges in preventing obesity is knowing how and when to intervene. Obesity prevention starts in childhood, and the school-based prevention programs are often utilized (Cook-Cottone, Casey, and Feeley, 2009). The workplace is a site for obesity prevention and wellness promotion for adults.

School-based efforts are influenced by social policies set at the national and local levels and by the array of familial, social, economic and cultural factors that characterize the schools and neighborhoods in which they are embedded. School-based intervention has been promoted by Federal legislation, such as the Child Nutrition and WIC Reauthorization Act of 2004 and 2010, which required all educational institutions participating in federal programs to enact wellness plans. These plans include enacting nutritional guidelines, providing physical education classes, and teaching children about healthy eating (Cook- Cottone et al., 2009). A meta-analysis by Cook-Cottone et al.(2009) found that prevention programs that targeted one of these areas could be effective, but the most success was achieved through programs that focused on both individual and environmental change. Evaluation efforts reveal, for example, that interventions that change the types and quality of foods served in the school setting and that engaged children and their families in physical activity are more effective than intervention that focus only on health knowledge (Hendrie et al., 2012). The authors also found that primary prevention programs targeting the general student body were more effective than programs focusing on overweight children who were already showing obesity-related health problems.

One limitation of school-based prevention efforts is the relative neglect of cultural and socioeconomic factors that contribute to poor eating habits and sedentary behaviors. Given the high rates of obesity among racial and ethnic minority children (Stevens, 2010), evidence that prevention programs are differentially effective across racial groups is concerning (Cook-Cottone et al., 2009). Cultural messages about food and parental modeling behaviors may be one factor contributing to higher obesity rates among minority youth (Stevens, 2010). As we note elsewhere in this chapter, successful prevention efforts must take into account familial, cultural, economic, and societal risk and protective factors (Weimer-Jehle, Deuschle, and Rehaag, 2012).

The community level risk factors that influence obesity rates in children and adults have been challenging to remedy through primary prevention. Although prevention has begun to incorporate culturally relevant messages, many efforts continue to neglect critical community-level risk factors, such as neighborhood safety or the urban infrastructure (Stevens, 2010). Children and adults in low-income urban neighborhoods may lack opportunities for outdoor exercise because of unsafe neighborhoods, crowded streets, and inadequate playgrounds (Chaufan, Fox, and Hong, 2011; Weimer-Jehle et al., 2012). Socially disadvantaged neighborhoods are also more likely to have fast food restaurants and less likely to have large chain grocery stores that offer healthy foods at affordable prices. The grocery stores that offer healthy alternatives to fast food, may offer these choices at above market prices (Chaufan et al., 2011). Thus, prevention strategies that ask parents to model healthy eating habits must contend with the reality that for many families nutritious food is not available or too expensive to buy. Food cost can also undermine educational efforts in schools because children do not have the means to maintain healthy eating habits outside of the school setting. Chaufan et al. (2011) suggest that it is possible to reduce these barriers to healthy living through small-scale prevention programs that help families to access healthier food and create exercise opportunities, but ultimately policy-level intervention is needed to create large-scale, sustainable change in socially disadvantaged neighborhoods.

Policy level and structural changes are needed that not only increase consumer knowledge, but also make healthy food options available and affordable. At a broad level, obesity prevention is enacted through public policies that inform consumers of nutritional alternatives to unhealthy foods and the risks of obesity. One early policy initiative, for example, was the National Labeling and Education Act of 1990, which made nutritional information more readily accessible to consumers at the point of purchase (Chaufan et al., 2011). The premise for this Act was that knowledge of food content and calories could help consumers to make healthier, more informed decisions, which in turn would be associated in a decrease in obesity rates (Bermann and Lavizzio-Mourey, 2008). Unfortunately, this strategy has been limited in impact because it does not account for the vast number of individual, social, familial, cultural, and societal risk factors that contribute to obesity rates in the United States (Chaufan et al., 2011).

Just as the school is a site for obesity prevention among children and adolescents, the workplace has been a focus for prevention among adults. According to Goertz et al. (2010), one of the benefits of workplace prevention is the ability to reach a large group of people using a variety of methods. As with children and adolescents, the most effective interventions address both individual and environmental factors. The National Heart, Lung, and Blood Institute funded a series of studies across the United States aimed at weight control and obesity prevention in the workplace. These strategies included nutritional counseling, informational pamphlets, healthy food choices in the cafeteria and vending machines, opportunities for employees to exercise, and changes in organizational culture (Pratt, Lemon, and Fernandez, 2007). An evaluation (Goertz et al., 2010) at fourteen Dow Chemical worksites showed promising short-term and long-term findings. Employees who participated in prevention programs that offered individual services,modified the workplace environment and encouraged company leaders to commit to a healthy workplace were the healthiest in the short-term and after two years. Programs that included an organizational component were more effective than programs that did not, suggesting that sustainable change requires organizational support.

Major depression. Although the National Institute of Mental Health contended in the 1980s that major depression (MD) is not preventable related to the biological predispositions underlying the disorder, evolving views and mounting empirical research have led to more optimistic views about the effectiveness of prevention programs (Muñoz, Beardslee, and Leykin, 2012). The prevention of MD has implications for individual well-being, as well as public health and economic issues. According to the Centers for Disease Control and Prevention (2010), MD is on track to become the second largest disease burden globally by 2020, and this will be associated with billions in health care costs and lost revenue for those debilitated by the disease (Couser, 2008). As with obesity, the onset of MD is associated with a broad array of intrapersonal, interpersonal, familial, community, and societal factors that complicate prevention efforts (Muñoz et al., 2012).

The school is a desirable site for mental health prevention programs in childhood and adolescence in terms of access and cost (Muñoz et al., 2010). The Penn Resilience Program

(PRP), for example, is a 12-week program based upon the principles of cognitive behavioral theory that teaches children and adolescents about their thoughts and feelings and develops skills in coping, appraisal of situations, and social interactions (Jaycox, Reivich, Gillham, and Seligman, 1994). A meta-analysis of PRP studies indicates that the program contributed to short-term symptom reduction among at-risk adolescents, although the effectiveness of the program in the long-term prevention of MD has been less clear (Brunwasser, Gilham, and Kim, 2009).

In recognition of the importance of cultural relevance for effective prevention, the PRP, which was originally developed and tested on White middle-class samples, has been adapted for use with low-income minority adolescents (Cardemil, Reivich, and Seligman, 2002). While retaining a cognitive-behavioral theoretical basis, the content of the curriculum was modified to reflect specific contextual and cultural situations. At six month and two-year follow-ups, the adapted curriculum was successful in preventing depression for Latino adolescents, but not for African American adolescents (Cardemil, Reivich, Beevers, Seligman, and James, 2007; Cardemil et al., 2002). These efforts reveal the challenges in adapting prevention curricula for different cultural groups and the need to more fully understand the nature of MD in low-income African American youth. The program's ineffectiveness for African American youth may reflect inadequate depth in cultural adaptation or incomplete attention to family, school, community, or societal factors that add to the risks for MD.

Although cognitive-behavioral interventions have been critiqued for their inattention to the contextual determinants of mental health (Helms and Cook, 1999), they are applied across the lifespan with some success in individual, group, and self-administrated formats (Muñoz et al., 2012). Coping with Depression (CWD; Lewinsohn, Antonuccio, Breckenridge, and Teri, 1984), for example, combines cognitive-behavioral and social learning theories and strives to help participants develop social skills, cope with negative thoughts, and plan for satisfying events. Presently, most of the studies evaluating the effectiveness of CWD with adults have focused on symptom reduction, but a handful of prevention studies have shown that the program can reliably reduce the incidence of MD by up to 38% in at-risk adult populations (Cuijpers, Muñoz, Clarke, and Lewinsohn, 2009).

Among adults, the workplace has also been a site for prevention programs related to the staggering economic costs of MD in terms of lost workdays and lower employee productivity (Williams, Brenner, Helms, and Brenner, 2009). The success of workplace programs lies with identifying risk factors associated with MD that can be targeted in the work setting and have clear links to work-related behaviors. For example, work-based prevention programs can effectively target self-efficacy, social support, and work-related stress, but other known risk factors, such as genetics and co-occurring psychiatric diagnoses, are outside of the employer's control (Couser, 2008). An appropriate target for workplace prevention relates to the role of work demands in creating work-related stress (Williams et al., 2009). Coping with and controlling work-related stress is of interest for its relation to MD and to increased risk of cardiovascular disease (Couser, 2008).

As with school-based programs, workplace programs typically focus on individual factors with modest outcomes. A program designed to develop proactive and pro-social coping skills with supervisors, for example, was associated with self-reported improvement in use of coping skills and reduction in hostile attitudes towards supervisors, particularly among male employees, immediately after the program and again after two-weeks (Williams et al.,

2009). Although the effects were demonstrated across gender and racial and ethnic groups at two-weeks, the gains did not hold at a six month follow-up (Williams et al., 2009). Despite short-term benefits, participants may not have internalized these coping strategies sufficiently to sustain them over time or to apply them to a wide range of work-related events. Long-term benefits may also suffer because individually-focused prevention programs do not modify the organizational culture that contributes to work-related stress and hostile attitudes towards management. Prevention efforts aimed at organizational change have not, however, yielded consistent benefits over individual-level strategies (Couser, 2008). Despite weak empirical trends, research does indicate that structural changes in the workplace, such as decreased hours and improved social support networks, can have a positive impact on reducing work-related stress and self-reported depressive symptoms (Couser, 2008). For example, Munir, Nielsen, and Cameiro (2010) found that a transformational leadership style marked by relational support, empowerment of employees, and mentoring was associated with fewer incidents of MD cross-sectionally and longitudinally in a health care facility in the Netherlands. Findings such as these are promising and provide insight into the active ingredients of prevention programs that can create supportive worksites and contribute to employee well-being.

Although many prevention programs target the working-age adult population, recent reports indicate that MD in the elderly is a growing public health concern (Konnert, Dobson, and Stelmach, 2009). Oyama et al. (2010) found that community-based screening and psychoeducation for the general public was successful in reducing the incidence of MD and suicide rates in Japanese urban and rural samples by up to 50% over a three year period. Other prevention efforts have targeted elderly in assisted living communities, hospice settings, and nursing homes. These individuals tend to be at elevated risk compared to the general population because of debilitating medical conditions, prolonged separation from their families and loss of freedom (Muñoz et al., 2012). Konnert et al. (2009) implemented a CBT-based prevention program for individuals living in a nursing home and found that individuals who participated in the intervention reported fewer symptoms of MD than counterparts in a control condition. Despite promising results, the study had an attrition rate of 33% in the intervention condition, which warrants further investigation.

As previously noted, interventions based on cognitive behavioral and social learning theory frameworks focus on individual-level change and give limited attention to contextual factors that elevate risk for MD. Prevention of MD often neglects contextual factors, such as poverty, inadequate housing, and domestic violence, which contribute to risk for MD (Gottlieb, Waitzkin, and Miranda, 2011). Unemployment, for example, is a contextually-bound stressor that has been associated with depressive symptoms, and the potential negative impact of unemployment on well-being is exacerbated by the current economic climate domestically and abroad (Reynolds, Barry, and Gabhainn, 2010). Reynolds et al. (2010) evaluated a jobs program in Ireland designed to help participants to reenter the workforce and maintain psychological well-being. The intervention focused on increasing self-efficacy beliefs, teaching job-seeking skills, building social supports, and fostering coping skills. Compared to a control group, program participants gained employment at a significantly higher rate and reported significantly less economic hardship. However, significant differences between groups in self-reported depressive symptoms were not found at follow-up. In contrast, a U. S. study by Vinokur, Price, and Schul (1995) based upon the same intervention did find significant differences for high-risk individuals assigned to the intervention and control groups in self-reported depressive symptoms at two month and six month follow-up. This finding, however, didnot hold for low-risk individuals,which may help to explain the null findings in the Reynolds et al. (2010) study, which did not identify risk levels among participants.

Overall, research reveals that prevention can be successful in reducing the incidence of MD in individuals and small groups. Community-based public health initiatives, such as early screening and psychoeducation, have been beneficial in reducing incidence of MD in the general population (Muñoz et al., 2012). Many challenges to MD prevention through public policy and public health initiatives remain related to the complex nature of MD risk factors, high level of comorbidityand its varied presentation across developmental and sociocultural contexts (Muñoz et al. 2012). Muñoz et al. (2012) argue that prevention of MD requires a strong infrastructure and funding to develop effective, readily available prevention strategies in communities, organizations, and schools. However, successful prevention also depends on structural and systemic change that modifies the risks that are the "cause of the cause," (Prilleltensky and Nelson, 1997, p. 88). The prevention of MD, like many other forms of psychological distress, requires the creation of healthy communities and environments conducive to psychological growth and well-being (Muñoz et al., 2012).

Prevention research and program evaluation have been helpful in building a knowledge base about best practice in prevention. Effective prevention clearly requires attention to the complex array of factors that determine health and mental health outcomes. The ethical considerations involved in prevention work are also complex and not fully charted due to the multiple systems, professions, clients and contexts across which intervention takes place.

PREVENTION ETHICS AND BEST PRACTICE

A growing body of evidence has documented the effectiveness of prevention as a means to enhance human functioning and reduce psychological distress (Greenberg, Domitrovich, and Bumbarger, 2001; O'Connell, Boat, and Warner, 2009). A number of professional disciplines, such as social work, public health, and community and counseling psychology, are playing an increasing role in prevention research and practice, yet conceptualizations about best practices, especially at the environmental level, and ethical guidelines are not fully articulated. The Ethical Principles of Psychologists and Code of Conduct published by the American Psychological Association (APA 2002, 2010) do not fully address the array of unique ethical issues that may arise in prevention (Schwartz and Hage, 2009). Although ethical practice in prevention shares many underlying characteristics with intervention efforts, prevention also raises unique challenges and risks not only to individuals, but also to schools, workplaces, and communities (Pope, 1990).

Prevention work is comprised of multiple steps starting with planning and development, followed by efforts to implement and evaluate programs. Consistent with the APA code (APA 2002, 2010), researchers and practitioners must do no harm (nonmaleficence) to participants at all stages of prevention. Preventionists must be alert to unintended consequences that may have damaging effects, whether directly or indirectly (Trickett, 1998). The principle of nonmaleficence is complex across all phases of prevention because of the multiple systems involved. As we discuss further in this section, collaboration with communities and across disciplines at all stages of prevention work is important in safeguarding against unintended nonmaleficence and creating interventions that are effective and socially just (Hage et al., 2007).

Each phase of prevention work presents unique ethical issues that draw upon and challenge the existing principles developed to guide psychological practice. In the development phase, researchers and practitioners should be guided by empirical research and a sound theoretical justification, which Weed (2004) calls "evidence before action." Schwartz and Hage (2009) note that the research base may be limited in some cases, raising ethical issues about the costs and benefits of exercising primary prevention with little or inconclusive research (Weed, 2004). The precautionary principle alerts researchers, practitioners, and public health professionals to discern whether sufficient information is available to guide the development of a prevention strategy. For example, this principle may be applied in the public health domain when available data is used to determine whether to issue an evacuation order for areas threatened by extreme weather (Weed, 2004).

Although simple in definition, the application of the precautionary principle is complex. The precautionary principle is driven primarily by beneficence and maleficence, but decisions must also be guided by distributive justice, equity, and respect for autonomy (Richter and Laster, 2005). Because decision-making is inherently a value-laden process, the values of those making decisions may not reflect the values of all people affected (Pope, 1990). Policy decisions are often made to reap the greatest benefit for the greatest number of people, but the decision may disadvantage or burden some groups, often those already most vulnerable in society (Richter and Laster, 2005). This raises concerns about who has the knowledge, power, or wisdom to make such decisions (Richter and Laster, 2005). Vera and Speight (2007) propose that prevention researchers disseminate their research to the general public and to policy makers to inform more just policy decisions.

Public health policy decisions are often cited as examples of primary prevention that strives to benefit large segments of the population. Although this can be effective in some cases (e.g., seatbelt laws in the United States), such policies can have unforeseen effects when social and cultural variables are overlooked (Chavens et al., 2011; Cohen et al, 2010). Attention to social and cultural factors in program design and implementation is also critical to positive outcomes for prevention in communities, schools, and organizations, and is thus an important ethical consideration (Schwartz and Hage, 2009). Universal approaches to substance abuse prevention programs may have varied effects across racial and ethnic groups (Harthun, Dustman, Reeves, Hecht, and Marsiglia, 2009). For this reason, Harthun et al. (2009) adapted the Keepin' it REAL program (Gosin, Marsiglia, and Hecht, 2003) to combat substance abuse in a Southwestern middle school. A culturally-grounded curriculum was developed that reflected the strengths of the Latino and African American youth in the school, included culturally tailored messages, and incorporated culturally-bound values, such as family and interconnectedness. The culturally relevant curriculum was developed through a participatory framework including students and teachers, illustrating the value of participant collaboration for enhancing cultural relevance (Hage et al., 2007).

The implementation phase of primary prevention can raise ethical concerns about confidentiality and informed consent. In work with communities, there may not be a clearly identified set of participants to provide informed consent. Community members who are not direct participants and do not provide consent may still be exposed to indirect effects of a prevention program (Pope, 1990). Informed consent can be complicated by the interactions between practitioners and multiple systems and stakeholders. With the use of technology, community is no longer limited to a group of people in close geographical proximity to each other. Regardless of the scope of the prevention effort, the presence of power differentials between practitioners and participants can be manifested in the informed consent process (Trickett, 1998), and ethical implementation requires that practitioners actively work to minimize these differentials to the fullest extent possible (Schwartz and Hage, 2009).

Ethical issues related to consent and confidentiality are heightened further when groups and communities receive interventions that focus on sensitive health information or personal safety (Schwartz and Hage, 2009). The Just/Us study by Bull et al. (2011) on the use of social media to deliver a sexual health education program illustrates these complexities. Bull et al. (2011) recruited adolescents of color who had a Facebook page and asked the participants to engage in respondent-driven sampling. Although this technique can be of benefit in recruiting hard to reach populations, it can expose potential participants to risks if their personal information and health status are not properly safeguarded. In the Bull et al. (2011) study, parents were invited to review the Just/Us study Facebook page, but the decision to join the study rested with the adolescents. Although this is permissible in health promotion interventions, it can be ethically questionable if adolescents are not equipped to weigh the risks and benefits of participation. As Bull et al. (2011) concluded, social media is a promising medium for prevention work, but the continued use of sites like Facebook will call for ongoing deliberation about ethical decision-making.

Once informed consent has been secured, new challenges may emerge in implementation, including the decision of who will deliver services (Schwartz and Hage, 2009). Although the researchers and practitioners who developed the program may have expertise, non professionals may be better equipped to deliver the program in some cases (Trickett, 1998). This is illustrated in a study by Sanchez, Silva-Suarez, Serna, and De La Rosa (2012) on HIV prevention for undocumented Latino workers in Florida. The researchers enlisted and trained community members to implement a curriculum to enhance the community's knowledge of HIV and introduce risk reduction techniques. According to Sanchez et al. (2012), a benefit of having community members educate each other was that it built trust in the project, which is important for program sustainability and engaging marginalized populations who may be distrustful of outsiders (Hage et al., 2007).

With regard to evaluation, prevention efforts should be evaluated for effectiveness using research practices that are rigorous, systematic, comprehensive, and culturally competent (Pope, 1990). Researchers may also need to share ownership and draw upon the "insider knowledge" of the community (Hage et al., 2007). Effective evaluation may need to go beyond the academic outcomes and focus on practical issues, such as the feasibility of long-term implementation related to available community resources and evolving needs (Reese, 2007). Researchers should also consider whether programs studied under certain research parameters generalize to other groups and settings (Schwartz and Hage, 2009). Given that effective and ethical prevention is nested in the social context, evaluative practices should remain vigilant to the possibility that a successful prevention strategy in one context may have little effect in another context (Kenny and Hage, 2009).

Another critical issue in evaluation of primary prevention is whether the program promotes social justice and reduces health disparities. As discussed earlier in this chapter, a growing number of scholars conceptualize primary prevention as a means to reduce sources of individual suffering and dismantle oppression (Kenny and Hage, 2009). Prilleltensky

(2008) argues that ameliorative prevention efforts are necessary but can be more effective and socially meaningful if accompanied by transformative efforts. Kenny and Hage (2009) note that research on transformative prevention is limited, but a study on HIV prevention presented below speaks to its potential.

Argento et al. (2011) suggest that HIV prevention in India can only be successful if programs confront the structural, systemic, and economic inequalities that create heightened risk for the most stigmatized and marginalized members of society. The authors report on the Sonagachi Project in southern India that sought to reduce HIV infection rates among sex workers by empowering these individuals to confront social, economic, and political factors that put them at risk. The workers formed a community group called Ashodaya Samithi that provided sexual health education and worked to reduce police and community-led incidents of violence. This project was successful in part because of what Campbell and Cornish (2012) called transformative communication where the stigmatized sex workers challenged the status quo by reframing sex work as an occupational health issue instead of a moral one. They also gained political power by being formally recognized as an organization and receiving support from the local media (Campbell and Cornish, 2012). Ultimately, the development of a community-led group served ameliorative and transformative purposes that helped these women to protect their health and gain political power.

PREPARING COUNSELORS FOR PREVENTION PRACTICE AND RESEARCH

The imperative for counselors to be prepared as effective prevention practitioners and researchers is clear. As noted earlier in this chapter, economic and social justice factors favor the growth of prevention initiatives. A growing body of research evidence supports the effectiveness of prevention, but also highlights the complexity of this work. Indeed, prevention practitioners need to be equipped with knowledge of best practices and awareness of the ethical issues that are unique to prevention programming. Ethical principles demand professional competence in practice and research, such that counselors and the training programs that prepare them need to attend to developing skills for competent and ethical practice.

Despite the importance of prevention and the unique skills related to prevention, counselor training has been dominated by a focus on treatment strategies directed towards those who are already experiencing psychological symptoms (Conyne, Newmeyer, Kenny, Romano, and Matthews, 2008). Specialized courses are offered sporadically across counselor and counseling psychology training programs (Matthews, 2003), with the infusion of prevention concepts in existing courses being somewhat more common (Conyne et al., 2008). Whether through specialty courses, integration of prevention in counseling courses, cross-disciplinary courses, or professional development training, we argue that counselors must seek to acquire prevention competencies through formal training or professional development that will allow them to advance best practice in prevention.

Although a broad range of skills and competencies are required for effective prevention practice, O'Neil and Britner (2009) identified critical prevention skill areas, including (1) therapeutic, interpersonal and professional skills, (2) diversity and multicultural skills, (3) group, consultation, and collaboration skills, (4) political, organizational, and environmental assessment skills, (5) program development and marketing skills, (6) intervention skills, (7) research and evaluation skills, and (8) ethical skills. A number of these, such as therapeutic, multicultural, group, research, and ethical skills, build upon the competencies that counselors develop in most professional curriculum. As evidenced throughout this chapter, prevention often challenges the type and depth of ethical and multicultural training involved in counseling, especially as the preventionist is asked to assess and intervene at levels beyond the individual, family and school. The capacity to assess and intervene in systems at the organizational, community and broader societal level, and to understand cultural, economic, and ethical issues at those levels, extend beyond typical counselor training. Research and evaluation need to be formative as well as summative, in order that data is gathered to improve interventions over the course of implementation. To wait until a program is complete to address ineffective strategies does not serve the intent of prevention to reduce suffering. With regard to counselor skills, collaboration and consultation are as salient to prevention, as is the capacity to develop a therapeutic alliance. Because prevention is complex, practitioners and researchers need to work with a team of individuals, collaborating and consulting across professions and diverse community stakeholders.

Kenny and Medvide (2013) have also identified a number of skills that are important in prevention efforts that seek to enhance social justice. Community outreach, youth and community organizing, social action, advocacy and media relations represent skill sets that are not emphasized in most traditional counselor training, but are needed to effect change in broader systems and organizational structures. Because many of these skills are taught across professional disciplines, counselors and counselor training programs may need to reach beyond professional boundaries to enroll in courses in public health, social work, community psychology, management and other disciplines. Interdepartmental and interprofessional collaboration are important in this regard. The number of course requirements currently in place by many professions and their licensing and accreditation bodies make the addition of new course requirements challenging and expensive for students, however. Training programs need to carefully review requirements to determine how to best integrate prevention competencies through existing courses and which additional courses are vital. We reaffirm the *Call to Action* first articulated by Romano and Hage (2000) and later by Conyne et al. (2008) to better prepare multiple professions to engage in effective and ethical prevention practice and research.

CONCLUSION

Prevention is an increasingly important function for the professional counselor. Although prevention is consistent with the roots of the counseling profession, mental health professionals, including counselors, have focused mostly on treatment in recent decades. A growing body of research documents the efficacy and cost-effectiveness of prevention. The role of the counselor in prevention is also supported by a concern for eliminating human suffering, reducing health and mental health disparities by race and social class and promoting wellness and social justice. Contemporary research and program evaluation also highlight the complexity of prevention programming and research. Consistent with these findings, developmental contextual theory provides an understanding of how risk factors and protective assets across contexts interact to determine individual and group health and mental health outcomes. Across varied settings and life stages, prevention should seek to address risks and promote strengths at the individual, family, community and larger societal levels. These efforts must also recognize and be relevant to the cultural background of all participants.

Many aspects of the traditional training of the counselor are relevant to prevention work. The basic therapeutic, group, evaluation and multicultural skills of the counselor are critical for the practice of prevention. Skills in collaboration and consultation and ethical awareness must be extended to encompass concerns that are unique to prevention. Prevention also requires skills in diagnostic assessment, intervention and evaluation at the broader organizational and societal levels that are not typically part of counselor training. The fields of public health, social work and community psychology may offer a knowledge base and training through formal coursework and professional development that help to build these skills. The counselor engaged in prevention work will likely need to collaborate with professionals from the health, law, and business fields as well. Prevention offers opportunities and challenges for the counseling profession. We encourage you to embrace these challenges and to prepare for the increasingly important field of prevention.

REFERENCES

Albee, G. (1986). Toward a just society: Lessons from observations on the primary prevention of psychopathology. *American Psychologist*, 41, 891-898. doi: 1987-02131 - 00110.1037/0003 -066X.41.8.891.

Albee, G. W. (2003). The contributions of society, culture, and social class to emotional disorder. In T. P. Gullotta and M. Bloom (Eds.), *Encyclopedia of primary prevention and health promotion* (pp. 97-104). New York: Kluwer.

Albee, G. W., and Ryan-Finn, K. D. (1993). An overview of primary prevention. *Journal of Counseling and Development*, 72, 115-123.

American Psychological Association (2002). Ethical principles of psychologists and code of conduct. *American Psychologist,* 57, 1060-1073. doi: 2002-11464 -00610.1037/0003 - 066X.57.12.1060.

American Psychological Association. (2010). 2010 amendments to the 2002 "Ethical Principles of Psychologists and Code of Conduct. *American Psychologist*, 65, 493. doi: 10.1037/a0020168.

Argento, E., Reza-Paul, S., and Lorway, R., Jain, J., Bhagya, M., Fathima, M.,...O'Neil, J. (2011). Confronting structural violence in sex work: Lessons from a community-led HIV prevention project in Mysore, India. *AIDS Care*, 23(11), 69-74. doi: 10.1080/09540121. 2010.498868.

Bell, L. A. (2007). Theoretical foundations for social justice education. In M. Adams, L. A. Bell, and P. Griffin (Eds.). *Teaching for diversity and social justice* (2nd ed., pp. 3-16). New York: Routledge.

Berman, M., and Lavizzo-Mourey, R. (2008). Obesity prevention in the information age: Caloric information at the point of purchase. *The Journal of the American Medical Association*, 300(4), 433-435. doi: 2008-11287 -00210.1001/jama .300.4.433.

Bronfenbrenner, U. (1979). *The ecology of human development*. Cambridge, MA: Harvard University Press.

Brown, S. D., Lamp, K., Telander, K. J., and Hacker, J. (2013). Career development as prevention: Toward a social cognitive model of vocational hope. In E.Vera (Ed.). *The Oxford handbook of prevention in counseling psychology* (pp. 374-392). New York: Oxford University Press.

Brunwasser, S. M., Gilham, J. E., and Kim, E. S. (2009). A meta-analytic review of the Penn Resiliency Program's effectiveness on depressive symptoms. *Journal of Consulting and Clinical Psychology*, 77, 1042-1054. doi: 10.1037/a0017671.

Bull, S. S., Breslin, L. T., Wright, E. E., Black, S. R., Levine, D., and Santelli, J. S. (2011). Case study: An ethics case study of HIV prevention research on *Facebook*: The Just/Us study. *Journal of Pediatric Psychology*, 36(10), 1082-1092. doi: 10.1093/jpepsy /jsq126] [Medline: 21292724]2011-24885 -00310.1093/jpepsy /jsq126.

Campbell, C., and Cornish, F. (2012). How a community health programmes build enabling environments for transformative communication? Experiences from India and South Africa. *AIDS and Behavior*, 16(4), 847-857. doi: 10.1007/s10461-011-9966-2.

Caplan, G. (1964). *Principles of preventive psychiatry*. New York: Basic Books.

Cardemil, E. V., Reivich, K. J., Beevers, C. G., Seligman, M. E., and James, J. (2007). The prevention of depressive symptoms in low-income, minority children: Two-year follow-up. *Behaviour Research and Therapy*, 45, 313-327. doi:10.1016/j.brat .2006.03 .0101664384310.1016 /j.brat.2006.03 .0102006-22431-011.

Cardemil, E. V., Reivich, K. J., and Seligman, M. E. P. (2002). The prevention of depressive symptoms in low-income minority middle school students. *Prevention and Treatment*, 5, Article 8. doi: 2002-14077-00110 .1037/1522-3736.5.1 .58a.

Centers for Disease Control and Prevention (2010). Current depression among adults-United States, 2006 and 2008. *Morbidity and Mortality Weekly Report*, 59(38), 1230-1235. Retrieved from http://www.cdc.gov/mmwr/pdf/wk/mm5938.pdf.

Cowen, E. L. (1973). Social and community interventions. *Annual Review of Psychology*, 24, 423-472.

Cowen, E. L. (1977). Baby-steps toward primary prevention. *American Journal of Community Psychology*, 5, 1-22.

Conyne, R. K. (2004). *Preventative Counseling* (2nd ed.) New York: Brunner-Routledge.

Conyne, R. K., Newmeyer, M. D., Kenny, M. E., Romano, J. L., and Matthews, C. R. (2008). Two key strategies for teaching prevention: Specialized course and infusion. *Journal of Primary Prevention*, 29, 375-401. doi: 10.1007/s10935-008-0146-8.

Couser,G. P.(2008). Challenges and opportunities for preventing depression in the workplace: A review of the evidence supporting workplace factors and interventions. *Journal of Occupational and Environmental. Medicine*, 50, 411-427.doi: 2008-04885 - 00610.1097/JOM .0b013e318168efe2.

Chaufan, C., Fox, P., and Hong, G. H. (2011). Food for thought: Menu labeling as obesity prevention public health policy. *Critical Public Health*, 21(3), 353-358. doi: 10.1080/09581596.2010.492390.

Cook-Cottone, C., Casey, C. M., and Feeley, H. (2009). A meta-analytic review of obesity prevention in the schools: 1997-2008. *Psychology in the Schools*, 46, 695-719. doi: 2009-12824-00210 .1002/pits.20409.

Cuijpers, P., Muñoz, R., Clarke, G., and Lewinsohn, P.M. (2009). Psychoeducational treatment and prevention of depression: The "Coping with Depression" course thirty years later. *Clinical Psychology Review*, 29, 449-458.

Goetzel, R. Z., Roemer, E. C., Pei, X., et al. (2010). Second-year results of an obesity prevention program at the Dow Chemical Company. *Journal of Occupational and Environmental Medicine*, 52, 291-302. doi: 2010-06248-00510 .1097/JOM .0b013e3181d46f0b.

Gordon, R. S. (1983). An operational classification of disease prevention. *Public Health Reports*, 98, 107-109.

Gosin, M., Marsiglia, F. F., and Hecht, M. L. (2003). Keepin' it REAL: A drug resistance curriculum tailored to the strengths and needs of preadolescents of the Southwest. *Journal of Drug Education*, 33(2), 119-142. doi: 2003-05937 -00110.2190/DXB9 -1V2P-C27J-V69V.

Gottlieb, L., Waitzkin, H., and Miranda, J. (2011). Depressive symptoms and their social contexts: a qualitative systematic literature review of contextual interventions. *International Journal of Social Psychiatry*, 57, 402-417. doi: 2011-13106 -00610.1177 /0020764010362863.

Greenberg, M. T., Domitrovich, C., and Bumbarger, B. (2001). The prevention of mental disorders in school-aged children: Current state of the field. *Prevention and Treatment*, 4, 1-64.

Hage, S., Romano, J., Conyne, R., Kenny, M., Mathews, C., Schwartz, J., and Waldo, M. (2007). Best practice guidelines on prevention practice, research, training, and social advocacy for psychologists. *The Counseling Psychologist*, 35, 493-566. doi: 2007-11343 -00110.1177 /0011000006291411.

Harthun, M. L., Dustman, P. A., Reeves, L. J., Hecht, M. L., and Marsiglia, F. F. (2009). Using community-based participatory research to adapt Keepin' it REAL. *Journal of Alcohol and Drug Education*, 53, 12-38. doi: 2010-02542-003.

Helms, J. E., and Cook, D. A. (1999). *Using race and culture in counseling and psychotherapy: Theory and process*. Boston, MA: Allyn and Bacon.

Hendrie, G. A., Brindal, E., Corsini, N., Gardner, C., Baird, D., and Golley, R. K. (2012). Combined home and school obesity prevention interventions for children: What behavior change strategies and intervention characteristics are associated with effectiveness? *Health Education and Behavior*, 39(2), 159-171. doi: 2198469110 .1177 /1090198111420286.

Jaycox, L. H., Reivich, K. J., Gillham, J., and Seligman, M. E. (1994). Prevention of depressive symptoms in school children. *Behaviour Research and Therapy*, 32, 801-816. doi:10.1016/0005 -7967(94)90160 -0799332410.1016 /0005-7967(94)90160 -01995-06561-001.

Kenny, M. E. (2009). Verso l'avanzamento della prevenzione nel Counseling [Toward the advancement of prevention in counseling]. *Counseling: Giornale Itlaiano di Ricerca e applicazioni*, 2, 127-137. (Translation of an original written article).

Kenny, M. E. and Hage, S. M. (2009). The next frontier: Prevention as an instrument of social justice. *Journal of Primary Prevention*, 30, 1-10. doi: 10.1007/s10935-008-0163-7.

Kenny, M. E., Horne, A. M., Orpinas, P., and Reese, L. E. (Eds.). (2009). *Realizing social justice: The challenge of preventive interventions.* Washington, DC: American Psychological Association.

Kenny, M. E., and Medvide, M. B. (2013). In E. Vera (Ed.), Prevention in the pursuit of social justice. *The Oxford handbook of prevention in counseling psychology* .(pp. 125-140). New York: Oxford University Press.

Kenny, M. E., and Romano, J. (2009). Promoting positive development and social justice through prevention: A legacy for the future. In M. E. Kenny, A. M. Horne, P. Orpinas, and L. E. Reese (Eds.), *Realizing social Justice: The challenge of preventive interventions* (pp. 17-30). Washington, DC: American Psychological Association.

Konnert, C., Dobson, K., and Stelmach, L. (2009). The prevention of depression in nursing home residents: A randomized clinical trial of cognitive-behavioral therapy. *Aging and Mental Health*, 13, 88-99. doi: 2009 -05107-01610.1080 /13607860802380672.

Kumpfer, K., Alvarado, R. R., Smith, P. P., and Bellamy, N. N. (2002). Cultural sensitivity and adaptation in family-based prevention interventions. *Prevention Science*, 3, 21-246. doi: 10.1023/A:1019902902119.

Lerner, R. M. (1986). *Concepts and theories of human development (2nd ed.).* New York: Random House.

Lerner, R. M. (1991). Changing organism-context relations as the basic process of development: A developmental contextual perspective. *Developmental Psychology*, 27, 27-32.doi: 1991-12213 -00110.1037/0012 -1649.27.1.27.

Lerner, R. M. (1992). Dialectics, developmental contextualism, and the further enhancement of theory about puberty and psychosocial development. *Journal of Early Adolescence,* 12, 366-388. doi: 1993-36975 -00110.1177 /0272431692012004002.

Lewinsohn, P. M., Antonuccio, D. O., Breckenridge, J. S., and Teri, L. (1984). *The "Coping with Depression" Course.* Eugene, OR: Castalia.

Matthews, C. R. (2003). *Teaching counselors in prevention: How are we doing?* Unpublished manuscript.

Munir, F., Nielsen, K., and Cameiro, I. G. (2010). Transformational leadership and depressive symptoms: A prospective study. *Journal of Affective Disorders*, 120, 235-239. doi: 1939470510 .1016/j.jad.2009.03 .0202009-24124-028.

Muñoz, R. F., Beardslee, W. R., and Leykin, Y. (2012). Major depression can be prevented. *American Psychologist*, 67, 285-295. doi:10.1037/a0027666.

Nation, M., Crusto, C., Wandersman, A., Kumpfer, K., Seybolt, D., Morrissey-Kane, E., and Davino, K. (2003). What works in prevention: Principles and effective prevention programs. *American Psychologist*, 58, 449-456.

National Prevention, Health Promotion, and Public Health Council (2011). *National prevention strategy: America's plan for better health and wellness.* Washington, DC: US Department of Health and Human Services, Office of the Surgeon General. Retrieved from: http://www. healthcare.gov/center/councils/nphpphc/strategy/report.pdf.

Nelson, G., and Prilleltensky, I. (2005). *Community psychology: In pursuit of liberation and well-being.* New York: Palgrave Macmillan.

O'Connell, M. E., Boat, T., and Warner, K. E. (Eds.). (2009). *Preventing mental, emotional, and behavioral disorders among young people: Progress and possibilities.* Washington, DC: National Academies Press.

O'Neil, J. M. and Britner, P. A. (2009). Training primary preventionists to make a difference in people's lives. In M. E. Kenny, A. M. Horne, P. Orpinas, and L. E. Reese (Eds.), *Realizing social justice: The challenge of preventive interventions* (pp. 141-62). Washington, DC: American Psychological Association.

Oyama, H., Sakashita, T., and Hojo, K., Ono, Y., Watanabe, N., Takizawa, T., ...Tanaka, E. (2010). A community-based survey and screening for depression in the elderly: The short-term effect on suicide risk in Japan. *Crisis*, 31, 100-108. doi: 2041821610 .1027/0227-5910 /a0000072010-08608 -007.

Pope, K. S. (1990). Identifying and implementing ethical standards for primary prevention. *Prevention in Human Services*, 8, 43-64.

Pratt, C., Lemon, S., and Fernandez, I., Goetzel, R., Beresford, S. A., French, S. A.,...Webber, L. S. (2007). Design characteristics of worksite environmental interventions for obesity prevention. *Obesity*, 15, 2171-2180. doi: 2007-15275-00210 .1038/oby.2007.258.

Prilleltensky, I. (1997). Values, assumptions, and practices: Assessing the moral implications of psychological discourse and action. *American Psychologist*, 52, 517-535. doi: 1997-04451 -00210.1037/0003.

Prilleltensky, I. (2008). The role of power in wellness, oppression, and liberation: The promise of psychopolitical validity. *Journal of Community Psychology*, 36, 116-136. doi: 10.1002/jcop.20225.

Prilleltensky, I., Dokecki, P., Frieden, G., and Wang, V. O. (2007). Counseling for wellness and justice: Foundations and ethical dilemmas. In E. Aldarondo (Ed.), *Advancing social justice through clinical practice* (pp. 19-42). Mahwah, NJ: Erlbaum.

Prilleltensky, I., and Nelson, G. (1997). Community psychology: Reclaiming social justice. In D. Fox and I. Prilleltensky (Eds.), *Critical psychology: An introduction* (pp. 166-184). Thousand Oaks, CA: Sage.

Reese, I., F. (2007). Beyond rhetoric: The ABC's of effective prevention practice, science, and policy. *The Counseling Psychologist*, 35, 576-585. doi: 576-585.2007-11343 - 00310.1177 /0011000007301434.

Reese, L. E., and Vera, E. M. (2007). Culturally relevant prevention: The scientific and practical considerations of community-based programs. *The Counseling Psychologist*, 35, 763-778. doi: 2007-17606 -00210.1177 /0011000007304588.

Reynolds, C., Barry, M. M., and Gabhainn, S. N. (2010). Evaluating the impact of the winning jobs programme on the re-employment and mental health of a mixed profile of unemployed people. *International Journal of Mental Health Promotion*, 12, 32-41.

Richter, E. D., and Laster, R. (2004). The precautionary principle, epidemiology, and the ethics of delay. *International Journal of Occupational Medicine and Environmental Health*, 171, 9-16.

Romano, J. L., and Hage, S. M. (2000). Prevention and counseling psychology: Revitalizing commitments for the 21st century. *The Counseling Psychologist*, 28, 733-763. doi: 2000-02838 -00110.1177 /0011000000286001.

Romano, J., Koch, J., and Wong, Y. J. (2012). Prevention in counseling psychology: Promoting education, health, and well-being across the life cycle. In N. A. Fouad (Ed.). *APA Handbook of Counseling Psychology* (pp. 345-367). Washington, DC: American Psychological Association.

Sanchez, J., Silva-Suarez, G., Serna, C. A., and De La Rosa, M. (2012). The Latino migrant worker HIV prevention program: Building a community partnership through a community health worker training program. *Family and Community Health: The Journal of Health Promotion and Maintenance*, 35(2), 139-146.

Sayette, M. A., Mayne, T. J., and Norcross, J. C. (2010). *Insider's guide to graduate programs in clinical and counseling psychology*. New York: Guilford Press.

Schwartz, J. P. and Hage, S. M. (2009). Prevention: Ethics, responsibility, and commitment to public well-being. In M. E. Kenny, A. M. Horne, P. Orpinas, and L. E. Reese (Eds.), *Realizing social justice: The challenge of preventive interventions* (pp. 123-40). Washington, DC: American Psychological Association.

Schweinhart, L. J., Montie, J., Xiang, Z., Barnett, W. S., Belfield, C. R., and Nores, M. (2005). Lifetime effects: The HighScope Perry Preschool study through age 40. (*Monographs of the HighScope Educational Research Foundation*, 14). Ypsilanti, MI: HighScope Press.

Silverman, M. M. (2003). Theories of primary prevention and health promotion. In T. Gullotta and M. Bloom (Eds.), *Encyclopedia of primary prevention and health promotion* (pp.27-41). New York: Kluwer Academic/Plenum Publishers.

Speight, S. L., and Vera, E. M. (2008). Social justice and counseling psychology: A challenge to the profession. In S. D. Brown, and R. W. Lent (Eds.), *Handbook of counseling psychology* (4th ed., pp. 54-67). Hoboken, NJ: Wiley.

Stevens, C. J. (2010). Obesity preventions for middle school-age children of ethnic minority: A review of the literature. *Journal of Specialists in Pediatric Nursing*, 15(3), 233-243. doi: 10.1111/j.1744-6155.2010.00242.x.

Swenson, C. R. (1998). Clinical social work's contribution to a social justice perspective. *Social Work*, 43, 527-537.

Trickett, E. J. (1998). Toward a framework for defining and resolving ethical issues in the protection of communities involved in primary prevention projects. *Ethics and Behavior*, 8, 321-337. doi: 1998-11912 -00410.1207 /s15327019eb0804_5.

Vera, E. M., Buhin, L., and Isacco, A. (2009). The role of prevention in psychology's social justice agenda. In M. E. Kenny, A. M. Horne, P. Orpinas, and L. E. Reese (Eds.), *Realizing social justice: The challenge of preventive interventions* (pp. 79-96). Washington, DC: American Psychological Association.

Vera, E. M., and Speight, S. L. (2007). Advocacy, outreach, and prevention: Integrating social action roles in professional training. In E. Aldarondo (Ed.), *Advancing social justice through clinical practice* (pp. 373-389). Mahwah, NJ: Erlbaum.

Vinokur, A. D., Price, R. H., and Schul, Y. (1995b) Impact of the JOBS intervention on unemployed workers varying in risk for depression. *American Journal of Community Psychology*, 23(1), 39-74. doi: 1996-09746 -00110.1007 /BF02506922.

Walsh, M. E., DePaul, J., and Park-Taylor, J. (2009). Prevention as a mechanism for promoting positive development in the context of risk: Principles of best practice. In M.E. Kenny, A. M. Horne, P. Orpinas, and L. E. Reese (Eds.), *Realizing Social Justice: The Challenge of Preventive Interventions* (pp. 57-78). Washington, D.C.: American Psychological Association.

Walsh, M. E., Galassi, J. P., Murphy, J. A., and Park-Taylor, J. (2002). A conceptual framework for counseling psychologists in schools. *The Counseling Psychologist*, 30, 682-704. doi: 10.1177/0011000002305002

Weed, D. L. (2004). Precaution, prevention, and public health ethics. *Journal of Medicine and Philosophy*, 29(3), 313-332. doi:10.1080/03605310490500527.

Weimer-Jehle, W., Deuschle, J. and Rehaag, R. (2012). Familial and societal causes of juvenile obesity-A qualitative model of obesity development and prevention in socially disadvantaged children and adolescents. *Journal of Public Health*, 20(2), 11-124. doi: 10.1007/s10389-011-0473-8.

Williams, V. P., Brenner, S. L., Helms, M. J., and Williams, R. B. (2009). Coping skills training to reduce psychosocial risk factors for medical disorders: A field trial evaluating effectiveness in multiple worksites. *Journal of Occupational Health*, 51, 437-442.

In: Psychology of Counseling
Editor: Annamaria Di Fabio

ISBN: 978-1-62618-388-9
© 2013 Nova Science Publishers, Inc.

Chapter 3

Colorblind Versus Multicultural Ideologies: Implications for Mental Health and Counseling

*Jasmine M. Terwilliger, Nicholas Bach, Carli G. Bryan
and Monnica T. Williams**
Center for Mental Health Disparities, University of Louisville,
Department of Psychological and Brain Sciences, Louisville, KY, US

ABSTRACT

Americans are socialized to choose either a multicultural or colorblind approach when they interact with people from different cultural groups. Multiculturalism is the ideology that different cultural groups should be embraced while colorblindness is the ideology that cultural groups should be treated the same, without regard to attributes that make different groups unique. Although the intent for colorblindness was to create fairness, it often causes confusion and heightens prejudice between social groups. A comprehensive review of the literature indicates that multiculturalism is a psychologically healthier and more enriching ideology than colorblindness, which is correlated with negative mental health outcomes. However, many individuals adopt a colorblind ideology because it does not require learning about other cultures. It is suggested that multiculturalism should be promoted in organizations, the workplace, and in schools because of its merits. Counselors and therapists should utilize a multicultural approach in working with diverse clients to facilitate rapport and improve outcomes.

INTRODUCTION

Multiculturalism and colorblindness are two competing strategies used when Americans are faced with the common dilemma of how to interact with people from minority ethnoracial

---

* Corresponding author: Monnica T. Williams. Email address: m.williams@louisville.edu.

groups (Lewis, Chesler, and Forman, 2000). Multiculturalism is an ideology that promotes the maintenance of each distinctive ethnic group's qualities, whereas colorblindness is the ideology that all ethnic groups should be treated the same, without regard to cultural attributes that make different groups unique (Levin et al., 2011).

In the United States, multiculturalism has not been embraced and European American culture has been accepted as the norm. Even before the Civil War, any group that was not "White" (European American) was devalued. Racism was blatant, and the marginalization of anyone who was not part of the majority was legally sanctioned, as illustrated by Jim Crow Laws, to preserve the power of the dominant group (in-group). "Colored" people were expected to accept European American culture, and European immigrants were expected to assimilate. Despite large cultural shifts during the Civil Rights Era, attitudes persist that implicitly encourage the promotion of European American culture over others (Helms, 1990).

The Census Bureau reports a continued increase in the number of people who are members of ethnoracial minority groups (Humes, Jones, and Ramirez, 2011). According to projections, by 2050 America will have a higher population of minorities than the White majority (Ortman and Guarneri, 2009). With an increase in people that are not part of the European American ethnoracial group, there is a greater need for understanding the various strategies for interacting with others.

COMPETING IDEOLOGIES

Multiculturalism has been shown to reduce racial prejudice and improve racial attitudes. For example, Levin et al. (2011) discovered that multiculturalism was negatively correlated to prejudice and promoted equality in social groups. This means that as multiculturalism increases, the level of social equality will increase as well. Another study showed that lower-prejudice individuals who were encouraged by multiculturalism showed more warmth and a positive opinion toward out-group individuals (Vorauer and Sasaki, 2010). Richeson and Nussbaum (2004) studied the relative impact of multiculturalism and colorblindness on racial attitudes and found that those exposed to the colorblind perspective produced more automatic racial bias whereas those exposed to the multicultural perspective generated more positive outcomes for ethnoracial relations.

One reason that multiculturalism may not be the ideology of choice is that it can be difficult to treat everyone fairly and differently at the same time. Those who are only comfortable with their own culture are often afraid of making mistakes when conversing with or approaching people from different cultures. Understanding and using multicultural ideology calls for education about the customs of other cultural groups, as well as recognizing people for being different, and taking this knowledge into consideration when interacting with them.

Colorblindness is the converse of multiculturalism and is an increasingly popular ideology in America, particularly among European Americans (Ryan, Hunt, Weible, Peterson, and Casas, 2007). In principle, colorblindness can be seen as equalizing in nature. The idea of colorblindness was built upon a need for fairness to all groups of people. It is speculated that colorblindness is more favored because it is easier for members of the majority culture to think of treating everyone the same rather than embracing new or different cultures. Additionally, it has been shown at several universities that colorblindness is more popular than multiculturalism or assimilation when students are given the three options (Levin et al., 2011). Unfortunately, when the idea of "treating everyone the same" is proposed, it is typically from the prospective of the European American majority, implying that everyone should be treated as if they were culturally European American. The implicit message is then that European American culture is superior and minority cultures somehow deficient.

COLORBLINDNESS AND SOCIAL INTERACTIONS

It has been suggested that colorblindness is practiced because non-minorities do not want to appear prejudiced. To test this idea, Norton, Vandello, Biga, and Darley (2008) conducted a research study in which college students made hypothetical college admissions decisions among sets of equally qualified African American and European American candidates. The students were more likely to choose the African American candidates over the European American candidates. The results of the study suggest that college students are concerned about appearing non-prejudiced due to heightened norms of political correctness across most college campuses (Norton et al., 2008). However, attempts such as these to appear non-prejudiced are a reflection of confusion and anxiety about how to respond in situations involving persons from different ethnoracial groups. This can lead to avoidance or negative feelings about minorities, simply because the majority individual does not know what s/he is "supposed" to do. This typically results in negative outcomes during minority-majority interpersonal interactions (Gaertner and Dovidio, 2005).

Research shows that people who support colorblindness may focus primarily on the dominant culture (Apfelbaum, Sommers, and Norton 2008). When people refuse to recognize minority cultures in a society, value and respect for these cultures decreases, causing negative attitudes towards minorities. These negative attitudes feed racism, illustrating a connection between racism and colorblindness.

In addition to being objectionable to minorities, colorblindness can be detrimental to non-minorities. Apfelbaum et al. (2008) suspect that many of the individuals who exhibit colorblindness are well-intentioned individuals who genuinely believe that colorblindness is a culturally sensitive approach to intergroup contact and agree that people intend to use colorblind behavior to prevent prejudice. To facilitate the goal of colorblindness, individuals may avoid the subject of race during interracial interactions. Paradoxically, research has shown that when the topic of race is avoided by European Americans, this leads to negative interpersonal perceptions on the part of African American observers, who then believe that such an approach is actually indicative of *greater* racial prejudice (Apfelbaum, Sommers, and Norton, 2008). Thus when a person is unwilling to acknowledge racial differences, it makes it appear as if that person does not understand how to interact properly with people from other ethnoracial groups.

Even though there have been several studies that have shown positive outcomes from multiculturalism for cross-cultural relations (Plaut, Thomas, and Goren, 2009; Richeson and Nussbaum, 2004; Ryan et al., 2007), some European Americans perceive it as a threat to their group's core values (Morrison, Plaut, and Ybarra, 2010). This reaction is because such individuals are concerned about preserving their in-group's social identity and status (Morrison and Ybarra, 2009). A good example of this is seen among those majority group members that are identified as having greater opposition toward affirmative action; they view such measures as harming their group rather than as helping others who have been disadvantaged (Lowery, Unzueta, Knowles, and Goff, 2006). Morrison et al. (2010) further concluded that those European Americans who highly identify with their ethnicity respond to multiculturalism with an increased level of prejudice against racial and ethnic minorities, whereas those who do not identify highly with their ethnicity have lower levels of prejudice. Although incorporating multiculturalism may be difficult for someit is nonetheless important to promote the appreciation of other cultures to provide an environment that will facilitate improved ethnoracial relations.

NEGATIVE EFFECTS OF COLORBLINDNESS ON ETHNIC MINORITES

When colorblind ideology is practiced, it is more difficult to appreciate other cultures because individuals do not need to learn anything new. In one study on the impact of colorblind ideology on university students of color, minority students reported that their European Americans peers knew little, if anything about their ethnic group's histories or cultures (Lewis et al., 2000). Thus, it appears that many are unaware of the different cultures that comprise America due to colorblindness. Under the colorblind ideology, the unique features of different cultures are completely hidden. Furthermore, Lewis et al. suggests that colorblindness causes minorities to feel pressure to assimilate into European American culture while representing their own ethnic group. This can cause conflict and confusion in minority individuals, thus perpetuating a cycle of intra-ethnic negativity. Additionally, minorities are often negatively stereotyped, and using a multicultural approach instead of a colorblind approach will lead to a better understanding of minority cultures and decreased stereotyping (Lewis et al., 2000).

The direct effect of colorblindness on US ethnic minorities can be readily seen throughout the United States. For example, Tarca (2005) examined a public high school in Atlanta that had recently become populated with teenagers from an African American community. Black students at this high school were struggling largely because of the school faculty's use of colorblind ideology. When asked how students of different ethnicities were treated, the high school principal stated that "when we talk about what's driven our policies here in this building, the fact that regardless of who you are, where you're from, where you live or who your parents are, if there's an issue dealing with the school we're going to treat you based on the behavior... regardless of who or where you come from." Although the principal was trying to be fair with students, he did not take the time to consider that people from different cultures or backgrounds may act differently in certain situations. Ultimately, the faculty's lack of understanding the Black students in the community only worsened the problem.

Fryberg and Stephens' (2010) research on Native Americans noted that colorblindness allows European Americans to dismiss racial issues in society while being able to live comfortably with their apparent privilege. They point out that Native American culture is misrepresented in society and many important facets of that culture have been erased from literature, media, and history. Native Americans continue to be represented in a historical context and rarely in a contemporary one. This research suggests that in a world that does not acknowledge ethnic minorities' history and experiences, minorities feel alienated in school, workplaces, and organizations.

Colorblindness can be problematic in other contexts as well. For example, African Americans may be misdiagnosed by mental health providers when cultural differences in symptom expression are not taken into account (Whaley, 1998). Without considering adaptive responses to real experiences of racism, it is easy to misunderstand certain aspects of African American psychological development and behavior. For instance, in mental health, African Americans may be over diagnosed with psychotic disorders when only European American norms are considered (Whaley, 1998). A mistrust of European Americans, resulting from discriminatory experiences, may be misinterpreted by a medical professional as a sign of paranoid schizophrenia, contributing to incorrect treatments and the overrepresentation of African Americans in inpatient facilities (e. g., Snowden, Hastings, and Alvidrez, 2009).

ORGANIZATIONS AND WORKPLACES

It is easy to miss cultural differences when colorblindness focuses on making everyone the same, and this is particularly true in the workplace. Researchers Stevens, Plaut, and Sanchez-Burks (2008) conducted research on organizations that celebrate diversity in the workplace verses the organizations that practice a colorblind ideology. They found that multiculturalism generated more positive views than colorblindness did from participants of different ethnic and culture groups employed at the organization. When multiculturalism was practiced, minority employees and volunteers reported feeling more comfortable and more expressive at work (Stevens et al. 2008). This suggests that multiculturalism ultimately improves organizations and businesses, as employers appreciate the cultural aspects of employees and the employees perform better.

Researchers Purdie-Vaughns, Steele, Davies, Ditlmann, and Crosby (2008) conducted studies to determine cues that would trigger feelings of trust and security in African Americans in educational institutions and financial organizations. When more minorities were prominently featured in a newsletter at the institution, participants were more likely to trust the company than when fewer minorities were depicted. When few minorities were present, participants felt less comfortable in the company setting than when more minorities were represented.

This illustrates that the inclusion of varied ethnoracial groups created a sense of value for a more diverse clientele, which was not present in the colorblind condition where fewer minorities were represented (Purdie-Vaughns et al., 2008).

Happier employees are more likely to work harder due to feeling accepted and comfortable in organizations and workplaces. Researchers suggest that although colorblindness may be an easier way to run a workplace, it is not as effective as multiculturalism in achieving unity and respect amongst employees (Stevens et al. 2008). Stevens et al. (2008) introduce the concept of the All-Inclusive Multiculturalism (AIM) model in their research. The AIM model serves to promote positive and effective organizational change through the development of social capital and positive relationships at work and enables organizational members to grow to their potential. Under the AIM model, employees respond to each other better, leading to an overall more successful company with an improved capacity to grow and expand financially. This model and ones similar to it may be helpful in successfully integrating multiculturalism into the work place.

ACCULTURATION AND ACCULTURATIVE STRESS

Acculturation is one of a few different ways individuals cope or fit in after moving to a new culture. Acculturation is defined as the phenomenon that results when groups of people from different cultures come into contact, leading to changes in the original cultural patterns of either or both groups (Berry, 1997).

Although acculturation includes changes that take place in both groups, there is usually more change in one of the groups, typically the minority group (Berry, 1998; Coatsworth, Maldonado-Molina, Pantin, and Szapocznik, 2005). Cross-culturally, it is important to understand the process of acculturation because so many of the people who emigrate from different countries are choosing to acculturate.

Some people have a positive experience and do not encounter much stress when they acculturate, but this is not typical. There is usually either some difficulty or stress associated with the process of acculturating. This psychological experience is called acculturative stress. High levels of acculturative stress can lead to depression, and in some cases suicide, and research has shown that those who achieve some degree of integration into the new culture experience the least stress (Berry, 1998). This is where multiculturalism can play an important role in the lives of minority and majority groups. When people are better educated about other cultures, it is easier for new people coming to the United States to be accepted and feel comfortable in their new homes. For example, many immigrants may have different needs, attitudes, and values learned from their previous environments that are often not addressed in the United States (Vasquez, 2011). Because colorblindness ignores these distinctions, it offers no help in decreasing acculturative stress.

MULTICULTURALISM IN SCHOOLS

Multiculturalism in schools is a concept that has received attention since students from different ethnoracial groups first began integrating in schools in the 1960s. However, true integration has never been achieved, despite attempts and balancing proportions of students throughout school districts via strategies such as bussing. Minority students continue to report exclusion from interaction with majority students (Lewis et al., 2000).

One problem is that a colorblind approach helps to maintain the misperception that Whiteness is normative, and therefore minority status is somehow less-than. One of the authors (MW) teaches multicultural psychology to undergraduates, and one exercise that students do early in the semester involves completion of a questionnaire about ethnic identity. There are often puzzled looks on the faces of the European American psychology students, as many have no idea how to answer questions about their ethnic group. They feel as if they have no ethnicity – they are simply White. The students seemed surprised to learn that all people have a race and an ethnicity, including the European American student. Majority White status in the US allows European Americans to forget they belong to an ethnic group at all (McIntosh, 2003).

One problem is that not even educators understand multicultural issues, so they cannot adequately teach their students. The majority of teachers are European American, middle class individuals from suburban or rural backgrounds. Research points to the educational value of linking students' lived experiences to their classroom learning, and in order for teachers to increase learning opportunities for all students, they must become knowledgeable about the cultural backgrounds of their own students (Bales and Saffold, 2011). Providing multicultural education to teachers and integrating it into school curricula is the first step to improving understanding between ethnoracial groups. It is possible to reduce prejudice when this type of education focuses on cognitive, emotional, and behavioral components, which can result in positive ethnoracial relationships (Camicia, 2007). Increasing the multicultural education delivered to students and teachers alike is a method that has been shown to be effective in facilitating more harmonious cross-cultural interactions (Han and Thomas, 2010). It is even better to instill multicultural education to students at a young age because they will grow up with this knowledge and pass it on to others (Okoye-Johnson, 2011).

IMPLICATIONS FOR COUNSELING PSYCHOLOGY

The traditional approaches to psychotherapy and diversity are often insensitive to the unique experiences of people of color. One study that focused on race and gender in psychotherapy found that incorporating an awareness of masculinity from a multicultural perspective is particularly important in the psychological practice of men (Wester, 2008). Wester (2008) describes Male Gender Role Conflict, a condition in which socialized gender roles lead to negative consequences in the individual or others. For example, male gender roles can prevent men from accepting treatment and seeking counseling because American culture tends to ignore the emotional needs of men due to stereotypes about masculinity. Compounding this is the fact that the emotional needs of stigmatized minorities, such as African Americans, are devalued due to negative stereotypes and their lower social status. Thus, when Black males attempt to seek treatment, they may encounter difficulty, particularly when treated using a colorblind approach.

Minority patients may be sensitized to racial slights, resulting in negative attitudes toward the therapist. Additionally, African American patients often evoke more complicated reactions from the therapist than European American patients since stereotypes of African Americans make them easier targets for therapists' projections (Comas-Diaz and Jacobsen, 1991). One of the authors (MW) once observed the assessment of an African American patient by a senior psychologist who was European American. The patient was nervous, talking excessively, fidgeting, and getting in and out of his seat. At one point, the therapist said "down boy," to calm the patient, which the patient felt was degrading and made him angry. Not only were the patient's actions being compared to those of a family pet, use of the word "boy" was particularly offensive as this term has historically been used to demean African American males.

The patient's offense was interpreted by the therapist as a sign of defensiveness, which would therefore make him a poor candidate for psychotherapy, and the patient was denied treatment. The senior therapist failed to understand the layers of insult embedded into his communications due to a lack of cultural understanding. A more comprehensive understanding of these issues would have resulted in a more fair-minded psychological assessment, leading to more appropriate recommendations and better psychological outcomes in the individual. Mental health practitioners' personal biases can influence professional perspectives in psychology and counseling, leading to wrong conclusions that do not consider the qualities of one's race and culture (Delsignore et al., 2010). The chances of biased diagnosis are lower when multiculturalism is integrated in mental health practice.

In one recent study, researchers found that when counselors communicated their own cultural background and acknowledged their client's cultural values, clients were more likely to see their counselor as credible and felt more relaxed in the therapeutic process (Owen, Tao, Leach, and Rodolfa, 2011). Culturally skilled counselors are aware of how their own cultural backgrounds and experiences have influence on attitudes, values, and biases about psychological processes. When therapists recognize these they are better able to access a patient's discomfort (Delsignore et al., 2010). Multiculturalism introduces different strategies for working with diverse clients and increases the mutual understanding of attitudes, values, and beliefs, leading to a more accurate diagnosis and stronger connection between the counselors and clients.

MULTICULTURAL TRAINING

Most college students studying psychology only take one multicultural psychology course in their lives (Reynolds, 2011). Nonetheless, it was found that what the students learned in that course had a significant impact on their knowledge of multicultural psychology, and this is particularly important in the area of multicultural counseling (Reynolds, 2011). There are other benefits from multicultural coursework, such as increased awareness of cross-cultural issues and better understanding of people from other cultures (Okoye-Johnson, 2011; Reynolds, 2011). It is not always easy for instructors to properly teach this subject due to numerous difficulties, including varied multicultural competence among the students, emotional ties to material taught in the course, and unexpected resistance from students (Reynolds, 2011). Despite these difficulties, most teachers report that students developed reduced prejudicial attitudes and had an overall positive experience in the course of multicultural psychology (Reynolds, 2011).

It is recommended that counselors receive a variety of multicultural training opportunities to facilitate a better understanding of racial identity and gender role attitudes (Chao, 2012). Multicultural training can create self-exploration and self-discovery within counselors, leading to a better understanding of their own culture and also making them more culturally competent counselors and individuals (Chao, 2012).

Culturally competent counselors can help clients explore issues related to their race and ethnicity. Racial identity, the feeling of belonging and pride towards one's group, involves meaningful attachment to one's racial or ethnic group (Phinney and Ong, 2007), and is an important part of a person's identity that is not the focus of traditional Eurocentric models of psychotherapy. Racial and ethnic identity is important in every group because it offers a sense of belonging and a cultural roadmap to navigating social interactions as member of a particular group, and it is essential in its influence of one's sense of self (Phinney, 1992; Tajfel, 1981). In ethnic minorities, a strong, positive ethnoracial identity has been correlated to psychological well-being and lower levels of psychopathology (*i.e.*, Chae, Lincoln, and Jackson, 2011; Williams, Chapman, Wong, and Turkheimer, 2012). Mental health clinicians should routinely take into consideration the patient's level of ethnic identity when working with minority clients. Clinicians may encourage and support such clients in the exploration of their ethnic identities, as greater achievement of ethnic identity can improve overall psychological well-being (Williams et al., 2012). Such interventions might include discussions of what the client likes about his/her ethnic group, learning more about the achievements of the client's ethnic group to bolster a sense of ethnic pride, rejection of pathological stereotypes, and increased involvement in traditional ethnic activities (Williams, et al., 2012; Williams, Gooden, and Davis, 2012). Omitting cultural concerns from the counseling room eliminates the opportunity for growth in these areas. Minorities may even devalue their own ethnoracial group if their cultural practices are not considered important in treatment (Delsignore et al., 2010).

CONCLUSION

Multiculturalism gives ethnoracial minorities the chance to celebrate their culture while promoting acceptance in a society that has struggled with the true meaning of equality. Multiculturalism promotes diversity and insists that all cultural groups be treated with respect and as equals (Fowers and Richardson, 1996). It can create a better understanding amongst individuals working and learning together. Teachers and school authorities should incorporate multicultural education into all grades of school to reduce prejudicial attitudes (Bales and Saffold, 2011). Multiculturalism should be incorporated into counseling psychology and therapy to facilitate greater of trust from patients, ultimately leading to improved diagnosis and treatment for psychological disorders (Owen et al., 2011). New research is needed, focused on the experiences and outcomes of diverse mental health patients, comparing colorblind and multicultural approaches. An overall increased awareness of multiculturalism will be helpful to improve cross-cultural relations in organizations, the work place, schools, the media, and daily life.

It is important to understand that multiculturalism is not exclusive to non-minorities, and all persons of every culture and race should embark on the journey of becoming more culturally competent. If every person embraces a multicultural perspective it will lead to multiculturalism becoming a state of being, rather than a practice that is only used for educational and therapeutic purposes. Incorporating multiculturalism into society can be complicated when it makes European Americans uncomfortable by emphasizing on non-majority cultures (Ginges and Cairns, 2000; Verkuyten, 2006), thus explaining the preference for colorblindness.

Although multiculturalism requires effort to utilize, it is necessary and will create a better atmosphere for all cultures with less prejudice and more harmony.

REFERENCES

Apfelbaum, E. P., Sommers, S. R., and Norton, M. I. (2008). Seeing race and seeming racist? Evaluating strategic colorblindness in social interaction. *Journal of Personality and Social Psychology*, 95(4), 918-932.

Bales, B. L., and Saffold, F. (2011). A new era in the preparation of teachers for urban schools: Linking multiculturalism, disciplinary-based content, and pedagogy. *Urban Education*, 46(5), 953-974.

Berry, J. W. (1997). Immigration, acculturation, and adaptation. *Applied Psychology: An International Review*, 46(1), 5-34.

Berry, J. W. (1998). Acculturation and health: Theory and research. Chapter 2. In: S. S. Kazarian and D. R. Evans (Eds). Cultural clinical psychology: Theory, research, and practice (pp. 39-57). Oxford University Press.

Camicia, S. P. (2007). Prejudice reduction through multicultural education: Connecting multiple literatures. *Social Studies Research and Practice*, 2(2), 219-227.

Coatsworth, J., Maldonado-Molina, M., Pantin, H., and Szapocznik, J. (2005). A person-centered and ecological investigation of acculturation strategies in Hispanic immigrant youth. *Journal of Community Psychology*, 33(2), 157-174.

Chae, D. H., Lincoln, K. D., and Jackson, J. S. (2011). Discrimination, attribution, and racial group identification: Implications for psychological distress among Black Americans in the National Survey of American Life (2001–2003). *American Journal of Orthopsychiatry,* 81(4), 498-506.

Chao, R. (2012). Racial/ethnic identity, gender-role attitudes, and multicultural counseling competence: The role of multicultural counseling training. *Journal of Counseling and Development*, 90(1), 35-44.

Comas-Diaz, L., and Jacobsen, F. M. (1991). Clinical ethnocultural transference and countertransference in the therapeutic dyad. *American Journal of Orthopsychiatry,* 61(3), 392-402.

Delsignore, A., Petrova, E., Harper, A., Stowe, A. M., Mu'min, A. S., and Middleton, R. A. (2010). Critical incidents and assistance-seeking behaviors of White mental health practitioners: A transtheoretical framework for understanding multicultural counseling competency. *Cultural Diversity and Ethnic Minority Psychology*, 16(3), 352-361.

Fowers, B. J., and Richardson, F. (1996). Why is multiculturalism good? *American Psychologist*, 51(6), 609-621.

Fryberg, S. A., and Stephens, N. M. (2010). When the world is colorblind, American Indians are invisible: A diversity science approach. *Psychology Inquiry*, 21(2), 115-119.

Gaertner, S. L., and Dovidio, J. F. (2005). Understanding and Addressing Contemporary Racism: From Aversive Racism to the Common Ingroup Identity Model. *Journal of Social Issues, 61*(3), 615-639.

Ginges, J., and Cairns, D. (2000). Social representations of multiculturalism: A faceted analysis. *Journal of Applied Social Psychology*, 30(7), 1345-1370.

Han, H., and Thomas, M. (2010). No child misunderstood: Enhancing early childhood teachers' multicultural responsiveness to the social competence of diverse children. *Early Childhood Education Journal*, 37(6), 469-476.

Helms, J. E. (1990). Black and White racial identity: Theory, research, and practice. Westport, CT: Praeger.

Humes, K. R., Jones, N. A., and Ramirez R. R. (2011). *Overview of race and Hispanic origin:* 2010. 2010 Census Briefs.

Levin, S., Matthews, M., and Guimond, S., Sidanius, J., Pratto, F., Kteily, F.,...Dover, T. (2011). Assimilation, multiculturalism, and colorblindness: Mediated and moderated relationships between social dominance orientation and prejudice. *Journal of Experimental Psychology*, 48, 207-212.

Lewis, A. E., Chesler, M., and Forman, T. A. (2000). The impact of "colorblind" ideologies on students of color: Intergroup relations at a predominantly White university. *The Journal of Negro Education*, 69(1-2), 74-91.

Lowery, B. S., Unzueta, M. M., Knowles, E. D., and Goff, P. (2006). Concern for the in-group and opposition to affirmative action. *Journal of Personality and Social Psychology*, 90(6), 961-974.

McIntosh, P. (2003). White privilege: Unpacking the invisible knapsack. In: S. Plous (Ed.), Understanding prejudice and discrimination. New York, NY: McGraw-Hill.

Morrison, K. R., Plaut, V. C., and Ybarra, O. (2010). Predicting whether multiculturalism positively or negatively influences European American Americans' intergroup attitudes: The role of ethnic identification. *Personality and Social Psychology Bulletin*, 36(12), 1648-1661.

Morrison, K. R., and Ybarra, O. (2009). Symbolic threat and social dominance among liberals and conservatives: SDO reflects conformity to political values. *European Journal of Social Psychology*, 39(6), 1039-1052.

Norton, M. I., Vandello, J. A., Biga, A., and Darley, J. M. (2008). Colorblindness and diversity: Conflicting goals in decisions influenced by race. *Social Cognition*, 26(1), 102-111.

Okoye-Johnson, O. (2011). Does multicultural education improve students' racial attitudes? Implications for closing the achievement gap. *Journal of African American Studies*, 42(8), 1252-1274.

Ortman J. M., and Guarneri, C. E. (2009). United States Population Projections: 2000 to 2050. US Census Bureau. Retrieved from http://www.census.gov/population/www/ projections/analytical-document09.pdf.

Owen, J. J., Tao, K., Leach, M. M., and Rodolfa, E. (2011). Clients' perceptions of their psychotherapists' multicultural orientation. *Psychotherapy*, 48(3), 274-282.

Phinney, J. S. (1992). The Multigroup Ethnic Identity Measure: A new scale for use with adolescents and young adults from diverse groups. *Journal of Adolescent Research*, 7(2), 156-176.

Phinney, J. S., and Ong, A. D. (2007). Conceptualization and measurement of ethnic identity: Current status and future directions. *Journal of Counseling Psychology*, 54(3), 271-281. doi: 10. 1037/00220167.54.3.271

Plaut, V. C., Thomas, K. M., and Goren, M. J. (2009). Is multiculturalism or color blindness better for minorities?. *Psychological Science*, 20(4), 444-446.

Purdie-Vaughns, V., Steele, C. M., Davies, P. G., Ditlmann, R., and Crosby, J. (2008). Social identity contingencies: How diversity cues signal threat or safety for African Americans in mainstream institutions. *Journal of Personality and Social Psychology*, 94(4), 615-630.

Reynolds, A. L. (2011). Understanding the perceptions and experiences of faculty who teach multicultural counseling courses: An exploratory study. *Training and Education in Professional Psychology*, 5(3), 167-174.

Richeson, J. A., and Nussbaum, R. J. (2004). The impact of multiculturalism versus color-blindness on racial bias. *Journal of Experimental Social Psychology*, 40(3), 417-423.

Ryan, C. S., Hunt, J. S., Weible, J. A., Peterson, C. R., and Casas, J. F. (2007). Multicultural and colorblind ideology, stereotypes, and ethnocentrism among Black and White Americans. *Group Processes and Intergroup Relations*, 10(4), 617-637.

Snowden, L. R., Hastings, J. F., and Alvidrez, J. (2009). Overrepresentation of Black Americans in Psychiatric Inpatient Care. *Psychiatric Services*, 60 (6), 779-785.

Stevens, F. G., Plaut, V. C., and Sanchez-Burks, J. (2008). Unlocking the benefits of diversity: All inclusive multiculturalism and positive organizational change. *Journal of Applied Behavioral Science*, 44(1), 116-133.

Tarca, K. (2005). Colorblind in control: The risks of resisting difference amid demographic change. *American Educational Studies Association*, 38(2), 99-120.

Tajfel, H. (1981). Human groups and social categories. New York: Cambridge University Press.

Vasquez, M. (2011). Crossroads: The Psychology of Immigration in the New Century. Report of the APA Presidential Task Force on Immigration, 1-10.

Verkuyten, M. (2006). Multicultural recognition and ethnic minority rights: A social identity perspective. *European Review of Social Psychology*, 17, 148-184.

Vorauer, J. D., and Sasaki, S. J. (2010). In need of liberation or constraint? How intergroup attitudes moderate the behavioral implications of intergroup ideologies. *Journal of Experimental Social Psychology*, 46(1), 133-138.

Wester, S. R. (2008). Male gender role conflict and multiculturalism: Implications for counseling psychology. *The Counseling Psychologist*, 36(2), 294-324.

Whaley, A. L. (1998). Cross-cultural perspective on paranoia: A focus on the Black American experience. *Psychiatric Quarterly*, 69(4), 325-343.

Williams, M. T., Chapman, L. K., Wong, J., and Turkheimer, E. (2012). The role of ethnic identity in symptoms of anxiety and depression in African Americans. Psychiatry Research. doi: 10.1016/j.psychres.2012.03.049

Williams, M. T., Gooden, A. M., and Davis, D. (2012). African Americans, European Americans, and pathological stereotypes: An African-Centered perspective. In G. R. Hayes and M. H. Bryant (Eds.), Psychology of Culture, Nova Science Publishers.

In: Psychology of Counseling
Editor: Annamaria Di Fabio

ISBN: 978-1-62618-388-9
© 2013 Nova Science Publishers, Inc.

Chapter 4

Applying Emotional Intelligence in Clinical Psychology

Reuven Bar-On[*]
University of Texas Medical Branch, Galveston, TX, US[†]

ABSTRACT

The purpose of this chapter is to discuss the potential application of emotional intelligence in clinical psychology as well as in other closely associated professions such as psychiatry, social work and counseling. The first section briefly describes the traditional focus of clinical psychology, concentrating primarily on assessment, psycho-diagnostics and therapeutic intervention. This section also includes a description of emotional intelligence (EI), describing how it is defined, assessed and applied as well as its impact on various aspects of human behavior and performance. The following segment examines the key findings specifically related to the impact of EI on psychological health and well-being. Based on these findings, the author justifies the application of EI in clinical psychology and then discusses ways in which it can be used in assessment, intervention and monitoring therapeutic progress. The discussion section of the chapter summarizes the key points regarding the proposed application of EI in clinical psychology and explores what needs to be done to empirically support and strengthen the use of EI in clinical work. The author concludes by describing what he thinks will be the next big paradigm shift in psychology that will have a significant impact on clinical psychology as well as psychiatry, social work and counseling.

INTRODUCTION

This section briefly describes the traditional focus of clinical psychology, followed by a review of emotional intelligence (EI) including what it is, how it is measured and applied.

---

[*] E-mail address: reuven.baron@sbcglobal.net
[†] Bar-On, R. (2012). Applying emotional intelligence in clinical psychology. In A. Di Fabio (Ed.), *The Psychology of Counseling*. Hauppauge, NY: Nova Science Publishers.

The author then summarizes the key research findings demonstrating the impact of EI on psychological health and well-being, justifying its application in clinical psychology.

The traditional focus of clinical psychology. Although clinical psychologists are involved in a variety of different activities such as providing consultation to other professionals, conducting research, teaching students and supervising clinical interns, the primary focus of this profession remains psychological assessment, psycho-diagnostics and therapeutic intervention (Compas and Gotlib, 2002; Ludy, 2005; Plante, 2005).

Psycho-diagnostics relies on administering a combination of assessment tools and techniques. There is an extensive variety of options for the clinician to choose from including psychometric instruments that assess, for example, personality traits, cognitive intelligence, neurological functioning as well as psychopathology (Groth-Marrat, 2005).

Therapeutic interventions also encompass a very wide range of techniques, including hundreds of different types of psychotherapeutic and counseling techniques. MacLennan has categorized more than 450 such techniques (MacLennan, 1996).

These various assessment tools and therapeutic techniques are designed to help understand and relieve psychological distress as well as to promote overall subjective well-being. With respect to these objectives and in light of the plethora of existing approaches, this chapter will hopefully demonstrate that emotional intelligence can and should be integrated into clinical work in order to enhance assessment, therapy and counseling.

Defining, assessing and applying emotional intelligence. Emotional intelligence (EI) has become a major topic of interest in the scientific community as well as in the lay public since the publication of a book by the same name in 1995 (Goleman, 1995). Despite the heightened level of interest in this 'new idea' since the publication of Daniel Goleman's groundbreaking book, scholars have been studying various aspects of this construct for much of the 20th century; and the historical roots of emotional and social intelligence can be traced back to the 19th century.

The first known work in this scholarly field was published by Charles Darwin as early as 1872 and focused on the importance of *emotional expression* for survival and adaptation (Darwin, 1872/1965).

Publications began appearing in the 20th century with the work of Edward Thorndike on *social intelligence* in 1920 (Thorndike, 1920), which is closely interrelated with the emotional intelligence construct. Edgar Doll published the first instrument designed to measure *socially intelligent behavior* (Doll, 1935). Possibly influenced by Thorndike and Doll, David Wechsler included two subscales ("Comprehension" and "Picture Arrangement") in his well-known test of cognitive intelligence that appear to have been designed to measure social intelligence (Wechsler, 1955). A year after the first publication of this test in 1939, Wechsler described the influence of *non-intellective factors* on intelligent behavior which was yet another reference to this wider construct (Wechsler, 1940). In the first of a number of publications following this early description, he argued that our models of human intelligence will not be complete until we can adequately describe these factors (Wechsler, 1943).

Scholarly activity in the area of *social intelligence* continued uninterruptedly from the early 1920s and included scientific studies conducted by many prominent psychologists in this field (Cantor and Kihlstrom, 1987; Kelly, 1955; Moss and Hunt, 1927; Rogers, 1961; Rotter, 1966; Thorndike, 1920). It is important to note that early definitions of social intelligence influenced the way *emotional intelligence* was later conceptualized. Contemporary theorists like Peter Salovey and John Mayer, for example, viewed emotional intelligence as part of social intelligence (Salovey and Mayer, 1990, p. 189), which suggested that both concepts are related and may, in fact, represent interrelated components of the same construct.

In the late 1940s, scientific inquiry began to center around *alexithymia* (MacLean, 1949; Ruesch, 1948), which is essentially emotional intelligence at the pathological end of the continuum in that it focuses on the ability, or rather the inability, to recognize, understand and describe emotions (Sifneos, 1967).

Two new directions that paralleled and possibly evolved from alexithymia were *psychological mindedness* (Appelbaum, 1973) and *emotional awareness* (Lane and Schwartz, 1987). From the 1970s, many mental healthcare practitioners began evaluating the "psychological mindedness" of patients to assess their suitability for psychotherapy and ability to benefit from it. Research exploring the neural circuitry that governs "emotional awareness" (Lane, 2000), as well as additional emotional and social aspects of this concept (Bar-On, Tranel, Denburg, and Bechara, 2003, 2005; Bechara and Bar-On, 2006; Bechara, Damasio, and Bar-On, 2007; Bechara, Tranel, and Damasio, 2000; Damasio, 1994; Lane and McRae, 2004; LeDoux, 1996), has begun to provide tangible evidence of the anatomical foundations of this construct which some have prematurely and inaccurately described as "an intangible myth" (Davies, Stankov, and Roberts, 1998; Matthews, Roberts, and Zeidner, 2003; Zeidner, Matthews, and Roberts, 2001).

It is important to conclude this brief historical review of EI, which began with *social intelligence* in the 1920s and progressed to *emotional intelligence* from the 1990s, by conveying that the literature reveals compelling arguments to combine the emotional and social components of this wider construct including, among others, the work of Howard Gardner (1983), Carolyn Saarni (1990) and Reuven Bar-On (1988, 1997a, 2000). Bar-On's conceptual and psychometric model of *emotional-social intelligence* directly exemplifies these efforts (Bar-On, 2000, 2006).

Since the time of Thorndike (1920), a number of different conceptualizations of the emotional intelligence construct have appeared creating an interesting mixture of confusion, controversy and opportunity regarding how best to define and measure this construct. In an attempt to help clarify matters, the *Encyclopedia of Applied Psychology* (Spielberger, 2004) suggested that there are three basic conceptual and psychometric models: (a) the Salovey-Mayer model (Mayer and Salovey, 1997) which defines this construct as the ability to perceive, understand, manage and use emotions to facilitate thinking, measured by an ability-based measure (Mayer, Salovey, and Caruso, 2002); (b) the Goleman model (Goleman, 1998) which views this construct as a wide range of skills that drive performance, measured by multi-rater assessment (Boyatzis, Goleman, and HayGroup, 2001) and (c) the Bar-On model (Bar-On, 1988, 1997a, 2000, 2006) which describes this wider construct as an array of interrelated emotional and social competencies, skills and behaviors that impact intelligent behavior in general, measured by self-report (Bar-On, 1997a, b), multi-rater assessment and structured interviewing (Bar-On and Handley, 2003a, b, c).

From Darwin to the present, most models of emotional-social intelligence have included one or more of the following factorial components: (a) the ability to recognize, understand, express and utilize emotions and feelings; (b) the ability to understand how others feel and use this information to relate with them; (c) the ability to manage and control emotions so they work for us and not against us; (d) the ability to use input from emotions and feelings to manage change, adapt and solve problems of a personal and interpersonal nature; and (e) the ability to generate positive mood, be optimistic and to be self-motivated in order to navigate through life and cope with challenges as they arise. The Bar-On conceptual and psychometric model of emotional-social intelligence captures all these components. It is described below, in light of the fact that the present chapter relies primarily on this particular model to describe the relationship between this construct and psychological health and wellbeing.

According to the Bar-On model, emotional-social intelligence is an array of interrelated emotional and social competencies, skills and behaviors that determine how effectively we understand and express ourselves, understand others and relate with them, and cope with daily demands, problems and pressure (Bar-On, 1997a, 2000, 2006). The emotional and social competencies, skills and behaviors referred to in this conceptualization comprise the 15 factors described in the Appendix.

The Bar-On Emotional Quotient Inventory (EQ-i) was developed to assess the 15 factorial components of the Bar-On model (Bar-On, 1988, 1997a, 2000, 2006, 2004). The EQ-i is described by the author as a self-report measure of emotionally and socially intelligent behavior that provides an estimate of one's underlying emotional-social intelligence. A detailed description of how this instrument was developed, normed and validated is found elsewhere in the literature (see for example Bar-On, 1988, 1997a, 2000, 2006, 2004; Geher, 2004; Plake-Impara, 1999; Stewart-Brown and Edmunds, 2007; Van Rooy and Viswesvaran, 2007). In brief, average to above average scores on the EQ-i indicate that the respondent is effective in emotional and social functioning. The higher the scores, the more positive the prediction for effective functioning in meeting daily demands and challenges. On the other end of the continuum, significantly low scores suggest an inability to be effective as well as the possible existence of emotional, social and/or behavioral problems. The EQ-i was originally constructed as an experimental instrument designed to examine the conceptual model of emotional and social functioning that the author began developing in the early 1980s during his doctoral studies (Bar-On, 1988). At that time, he hypothesized that effective emotional and social functioning should eventually lead to a sense of psychological well-being. Bar-On coined the acronym "EQ" ("Emotional Quotient") in 1985 to describe his approach to measuring emotional and social functioning, which is described in his doctoral dissertation (Bar-On, 1988).

Based on findings obtained from applying the EQ-i in numerous studies from the early 1980s to the present, the author has continued to mold his conceptualization of this construct. In 2011, a revised version of the EQ-i -- referred to as the "EQ-i 2.0" -- was renormed. Although some of the items were reworded and others added, the 15 factorial structure of the Bar-On model was re-confirmed, for the most part, in spite of the cosmetic changes that were introduced by the publisher [www.mhs.com].

By observing what EI predicts, it can be surmised where this construct has been applied and can be applied. In a number of publications, the author has described and summarized more than 30 studies that have been conducted on over 90,000 individuals who completed the EQ-i (e.g., Bar-On, 1988, 1997a, 2000, 2004, 2005, 2006; Bar-On et al., 2003, 2005; Bar-On and Handley, 2003a; Bechara and Bar-On, 2006; Bechara et al., 2007). Additionally, a recent computerized search has revealed that the author's work has been cited in more than 2,800 articles, books, theses and dissertations. Moreover, these numerous publications shed light on the predictive validity of EI by examining its ability to impact performance in social interactions, school and in the workplace as well as its effect on self-actualization, creativity, physical health, psychological health and overall subjective well-being. The findings suggest that EI is indeed cable of predicting a number of different aspects of human functioning as well as psychological health and well-being.

The impact of emotional intelligence on psychological health and well-being. The EQ-i has been administered with various measures of psychopathology including the Beck Depression Inventory, Eysenck Personality Questionnaire, Minnesota Multiphasic Personality Inventory, Ninety Symptom Check List, Personality Assessment Inventory, Toronto Alexithymia Scale, and the Zung Self-Rating Depression Scale (Bar-On, 1997a). The findings, to date, indicate that the EQ-i significantly correlates with the following signs and symptoms of psychopathology: 1) anxiety, 2) alexithymia, 3) phobia, 4) somatization, 5) obsessive-compulsive traits, 6) depressive mood, 7) suicide thoughts, 8) mania, 9) drug abuse, 10) borderline personality trends, 11) psychopathy and anti-social tendencies, 12) paranoia, and 13) psychotic ideation. Additionally, the EQ-i correlates with the ability to benefit from intervention (Bar-On, 1997a).

In one of the first studies that directly examined the relationship between EI and psychological health, the EQ-i scores of 418 psychiatric patients were compared with matched control groups in Argentina, Israel, South Africa and the United States (Bar-On, 1997a). In addition to significant differences in overall EI, the EQ-i scores revealed differences on most of the scales between the clinical samples and the control groups confirming that emotional intelligence does impact psychological health.

In a more recent study, which included a sample of 2,514 males who completed the EQ-i at the time of their induction into the Israeli Defense Forces, the author identified 152 recruits who were eventually discharged for psychiatric reasons (Bar-On, 2006). He then randomly selected an additional group of 152, among 241, who were diagnosed with less severe psychiatric disturbances that allowed them to continue their tour of duty with relatively few limitations. The EQ-i scores of these two groups were compared with a randomly selected group of 152 recruits, within the same population sample (n = 2,514), who did not receive a psychiatric profile during the entire period of their military service. This created three groups representing three different levels of psychological health: (a) individuals who were so severely disturbed that they were incapable of serving a full tour of duty, (b) individuals who received less severe psychiatric profiles which allowed them to continue active military service until completion, and (c) individuals who completed their military service without having received a psychiatric profile. Multiple regression analysis was applied to examine the impact of EI on psychological health; and the results revealed a moderate yet significant relationship between the two (.39).

The findings from the above-mentioned studies suggest that the most powerful EI competencies, skills and behaviors that impact psychological health appear to be (a) Stress Tolerance, (b) Self-Actualization and (c) Reality-Testing. This particular constellation of findings is logical, in light of the fact that deficiencies in these specific competencies may, respectively, lead to anxiety (deficiencies in managing emotions and coping with stress), depression (perceived failure in accomplishing personal goals and leading a more meaningful life) and problems related to reality testing (an inability to objectively verify feelings and thinking). It is also interesting to note that such deficiencies, in one form or another, are pathognomic for many psychiatric disturbances (American Psychiatric Association, 1994); and if not directly pathogenic, they indirectly contribute to these disturbances and/or exacerbate them. Moreover, tranquilizers, anti-depressants and neuroleptics (anti-psychotic medication) represent three of the four major classifications of psychotropic medication that are used for treating psychiatric disturbances (Kaplan and Sadock, 1991).

The findings presented here confirm and are confirmed by results generated by other EI measures. For example, the administration of the MSCEIT (Mayer, Salovey, and Caruso, 2002) has demonstrated correlations with measures of anxiety and depression ranging from .25 to .33 (Brackett and Salovey, 2004).

There is also empirical evidence indicating that EI impacts overall psychological well-being. A study conducted in 2005 examined this specific relationship (Bar-On, 2005). In that study, a 3-factor measure of well-being constructed by Bar-On was administered to assess satisfaction with (a) one's health and oneself in general, (b) one's close interpersonal relationships and (c) one's work. This operational definition of subjective well-being comprises the key reoccurring themes used to describe this construct in the literature (Clark, 2003; Helliwell and Putnam, 2004; Oswald, 1997; Ryff, 1989). In this study, the relationship between emotional intelligence and subjective well-being was examined by conducting a multiple regression analysis of data generated by 3,385 North American adults who completed this measure of well-being concomitantly with the EQ-i. The results indicated that the two constructs are highly correlated (R=.77). In another study (Bar-On, 2005), Brackett and Mayer examined the correlation between the EQ-i and Ryff's Scale of Psychological Well-Being, which also resulted in a significant correlation between EI and well-being (.54). Additionally, an earlier study also demonstrated a significant correlation between the two constructs (.41) when the EQ-i was administered with Kirkcaldy's Quality of Life Questionnaire (Bar-On, 1997a).

The findings presented here indicate that EI clearly impacts psychological health and well-being. The key EI factors involved, according to the Bar-On model of emotional intelligence, appear to be the following: Self-Regard, Stress Tolerance, Reality-Testing, Self-Actualization, and Happiness. Based on the definitions of these EI factors appearing in the Appendix, *psychological health and overall well-being are significantly influenced by one's ability to (a) accurately perceive, understand and accept oneself, (b) effectively and constructively manage emotions, (c) objectively validate one's feelings and thinking with external reality, (d) strive to achieve personal goals and actualize one's potential, and to (e) feel content with oneself, others and life in general.*

The above findings justify the application of EI in clinical assessment, psycho-diagnostics and therapeutic intervention. According to a recent computerized search moreover, the number of entries that were generated when combining the key words "emotional intelligence" with "clinical psychology" / "psychiatry" / "social work" / "counseling" suggest that less than 1% of the time EI is associated with clinical work in contrast to its association with "parenting and education" (60%), "workplace" (23%) and "medicine and healthcare" (17%). These results confirm the need to apply EI in clinical work, which has been heretofore neglected for the most part. The failure to apply EI in this area, up until now, is somewhat peculiar for a number of reasons. In addition to EI's ability to provide valuable information about the individual's psychological health and well-being, as was demonstrated here, the author's model of emotional intelligence initially evolved from his experience as a clinical psychologist and clinical supervisor working within a psychiatric healthcare setting. He originally thought that such a model would provide clinicians with a comprehensive view of emotional and social functioning on a continuum with optimal functioning at one end and pathological functioning on the other end.

APPLYING EMOTIONAL INTELLIGENCE (EI) IN CLINICAL PSYCHOLOGY

This section offers practical suggestions for applying EI in assessment and intervention. The first segment discusses its potential use in psychological assessment and psycho-diagnostics, which is followed by recommendations for debriefing the assessee and initiating intervention as well as a method for systematically monitoring therapeutic progress.

The application of EI in assessment and psycho-diagnostics. Based on the findings presented in the previous section, the author recommends applying EI-testing in psychological assessment and psycho-diagnostics. This type of testing could easily be integrated into the assessment battery that clinical psychologists typically administer together with instruments such as the WAIS (Wechsler Adult Intelligence Scale), MMPI (Minnesota Multiphasic Personality Inventory), TAT (Thematic Apperception Test), Rorschach, Projective Drawings, and the like. Results from a comprehensive EI measure, such as the EQ-i, could be used to confirm results obtained from administering the MMPI, TAT and Rorschach for example. Additionally, EI-testing could provide a potentially deeper understanding of results generated by these other concomitantly administered tests. Based on the nature of these specific tests, the author feels that it would be best to begin with the EQ-i because its items are less clinical in nature and would, therefore, be a less threatening way to ease the assessee into the testing situation.

An additional advantage of integrating the EQ-i into the clinical psychologist's battery of assessment tools is that it is more straightforward and less time-consuming to administer, score and interpret than the other diagnostic instruments that are typically used.

In light of the fact that EI impacts psychological health and well-being, EI-testing with instruments like the EQ-i could first provide a global estimate of how well the individual is functioning emotionally and socially as well as his or her overall psychological well-being. At a deeper level, and based on the Bar-On model of emotional intelligence, the results could then highlight strengths and weaknesses in specific areas such as (1) Self-Regard [*the ability to accurately perceive, understand and accept oneself*], (2) Stress Tolerance [*the ability to effectively and constructively manage emotions and stress*], (3) Reality-Testing [*the ability to objectively validate one's feelings and thinking with external reality*], (4) Self-Actualization [*the ability to strive to achieve personal goals and actualize one's potential*], and (5) Happiness [*the ability to feel content with oneself, others and life in general*].

As was previously conveyed, the higher the EQ-i scores the more positive the prediction for effective functioning in meeting daily demands, challenges and pressures, while significantly low scores suggest the possibility of emotional, social and/or behavioral problems (Bar-On, 1997a). Significantly low scores on the EQ-i Self-Regard scale could indicate an inability to accurately perceive, understand and/or accept oneself. Such scores could mean that the individual is suffering from feelings of inadequacy and inferiority, which contribute to depressive mood and limit the ability to accomplish personal goals and enjoy life. At the other end of the continuum, excessively high scores can be problematic as well indicating possible narcissistic and egocentric tendencies. At one end of the continuum (very low scores), depression will need to be ruled out; and narcissistic personality tendencies will have to be ruled out at the other end of the continuum (very high scores). Considerably low scores on the EQ-i Stress Tolerance scale could indicate an inability to effectively and constructively manage stress. Anxiety often results when this EI factor is not functioning adequately. People who score very low on Stress Tolerance may demonstrate symptoms related to stress and anxiety such as tension, irritability, apprehension, poor concentration, difficulty in making decisions and somatic complaints at times.

Excessively low scores on the EQ-i Reality-Testing scale could indicate an inability to objectively validate one's feelings and thinking with external reality. Problems in reality testing can be catastrophic for the individual and have serious consequences at work. Severe psychiatric disturbances, such as psychosis, are associated with extreme deficiencies in this EI factor. Because of this possibility, very low scores on this scale are considered indicative of a potential risk factor and are examined more closely than low scores on other scales (Bar-On, 1997a). Substantially low scores on the EQ-i Self-Actualization scale could indicate an inability to achieve personal goals and actualize one's potential. Low levels of self-actualization are associated with frustration and difficulty in doing things that one wants to do and can do. People who receive low scores on this scale may not know what they want to achieve, because they are confused about themselves in general and what they want to do in life; or they may know what they want to accomplish in life but are unable to realize their potential for various reasons. Curtailment of personal pursuits, moreover, is one of the key symptoms of depression, which will need to be ruled out.

Very low scores on the EQ-i Happiness scale could indicate an inability to feel content with oneself, others and life in general. The inability to experience happiness and difficulties in exhibiting positive mood are often symptomatic of depression. Therefore, significantly low scores on this scale are also considered indicative of a potential risk factor and are examined with more scrutiny than low scores on other scales (Bar-On, 1997a).

In addition to the above-mentioned EQ-i scales, it is advisable to examine scores on the Impulse Control and Social Responsibility scales. Markedly low scores on these scales could suggest the existence of impulse control disturbances and psychopathic tendencies respectively. Significantly low scores on any combination of the Impulse Control, Social Responsibility, Reality Testing and Happiness scales should be scrutinized more carefully than low scales on other scales, because they represent serious risk factors that can result in severe emotional, social and/or behavioral problems (Bar-On, 1997a).

The recommended approach to review and summarize results generated by EI-testing is as follows[1]:

1. *Collect all available information on the assessee.* Collect as much available information as possible on the assessee. This might include results from other psychological testing, summaries of previous assessments, interviews with the assessee and/or significant others as well any other important information that is available and accessible. Indications of EI strengths and weaknesses, based on the information available, should be noted. In the beginning, these are "indications" and "assumptions" that need to be confirmed or refuted by additional results as they are being reviewed and summarized.

2. *Focus on the 5 key EI factors discussed in the previous segment, those factors which impact psychological health and well-being the most.* While reviewing available

---

[1] These specific suggestions are phrased in the third person plural to emphasize the practical nature of their applicability.

collateral information, focus primarily on the following 5 key EI factors among the 15 measured by the EQ-i: Self-Regard, Stress Tolerance, Reality-Testing, Self-Actualization and Happiness.

3. *Begin to identify what appear to be the individual's strongest and weakest EI competencies and skills.* As more collateral information is collected, try to see what are the assessee's strongest and weakest EI competencies and skills. Then, note which of these strengths and weaknesses are associated with the 5 EI factors that are the strongest predictors of psychological health and well-being. Determine where most of the EI strengths are clustering and where the weaknesses are clustering. Begin to consider what the apparent weaknesses might have in common and mean from an EI and clinical perspective, and what may eventually need to be addressed in therapy or counseling to enhance psychological health and well-being. Identify the most serious weaknesses. Begin to think what needs to be addressed first and what may need to be addressed later during intervention. Weaknesses in one or more of the 5 EI factors, that have a significant impact on psychological health and well-being, should be made top priority during intervention.

4. *Attempt to understand the assessee's 'story' based on what is beginning to emerge from the EI results.* View what is beginning to emerge as 'bits and pieces of valuable information' that tell something important about the assessee. It may suggest what his or her most serious weaknesses are, how well he or she is presently functioning, and where there are serious problems that might be limiting the assessee. Build the assessee's 'story' carefully by developing a diagnostic picture that emerges from the results and not based on unsubstantiated assumptions. Avoid forming rigid opinions by widening the various possibilities that might explain the assessee's current behavior, functioning and performance.

5. *Prepare for the initial debriefing session carefully.* The initial debriefing session is designed to discuss what appears to be emerging from the results, what this might mean on a personal level and to think about what needs to be addressed in therapy or counseling. Plan what you are going to say, why, how and when. Use your *cognitive intelligence* in organizing the content that has been collected and your *emotional intelligence* in planning how best to convey what you want to discuss. This initial debriefing session represents an important meeting, because it is often pivotal for the beginning of the therapeutic intervention process.

The application of EI in psychotherapy and counseling. The diagnostic picture that emerges from EI-testing can provide a *roadmap* to guide and monitor therapeutic intervention. The results will identify stronger areas that can be leveraged and weaker ones that will need to be strengthened in order to enhance psychological health and well-being. The following is a recommended approach for proceeding, which begins with the initial debriefing session and progresses toward the beginning of the intervention process[2]:

1. *Promise confidentiality.* It is not only ethically correct and essential to promise confidentiality at the beginning of the intervention process, but is a valuable way to

---

[2] These specific suggestions are phrased in the third person plural to emphasize the practical nature of their applicability.

build trust to facilitate the successful continuation of this process. If for some reason you cannot promise confidentiality, you should clearly state this from the outset as well as convey who else might view the results and for what reasons. Being honest and straightforward facilitates trust, openness and cooperation in the intervention process.

2. *Use the initial debriefing session to collect additional information that clarifies and adds to what has been emerging from summarizing the test results.* The individual's reaction to the initial session, what is said and how it is said will provide additional information that will help clarify the nature of the problems, their severity and possible causes as well as potential solutions.

3. *Explain that the debriefing session can be helpful in enhancing self-awareness.* Tell the individual that the test results represent valuable information that can be applied in therapy or counseling to help better understand problematic areas as well as strengthen psychological health and well-being. Briefly explain something about emotional intelligence and how it impacts psychological health and well-being. Then, begin to discuss the EI-testing results and explore how the individual sees his or her strengths and weaknesses in these areas.

4. *Compare the individual with himself or herself and not with others or with a normative population sample.* Individuals who have completed the EQ-i should be compared with themselves and not with others or national norms. Insight often comes from understanding the weakest EI areas in comparison with the strongest ones.

5. *Summarize what has emerged from the discussion regarding the individual's EI strengths, and progress toward those areas that need to be improved.* In order to ease the individual into the session and build cooperation, begin by discussing the strongest EI factors and what they might mean with respect to psychological health and well-being. It should be conveyed that relative weaknesses suggest "opportunities for improvement." The individual should be made to feel that this is an *opportunity* to learn more about himself or herself.

6. *Ask how it was to discuss the results and if the individual learned something new about himself or herself.* Asking how easy or difficult it was to discuss the EI results often generates additional information about what the person has learned about himself/herself. This typically provides valuable input that can be used in psychotherapy or counseling.

7. *Ask what the individual wants to change, why, how and when.* To make the transition from the debriefing session to the actual therapeutic intervention and to effectively advance this process, it is important to ask what the individual would like to change based on what was discussed. To enhance personal commitment, it is important that this comes from the individual and not artificially encouraged by the person conducting the debriefing session. However, the individual should be asked (a) what exactly he or she wants to change and (b) why, (c) how he or she wants to achieve these goals and (d) when to begin in order to achieve a greater sense of well-being. The responses to these important questions provide potentially helpful content for designing, guiding and monitoring the intervention.

8. *Mobilize as much commitment for change as possible, and ask why that would be important for the individual.* It is important to elicit as much commitment as possible

from the individual in order to set the stage for successful intervention. To facilitate this, it is important for the individual to verbalize why the expressed need for change is important for him or her personally and at this time. Then, begin to develop an approach designed to facilitate change through intervention.

9. *If and when the individual agrees, the intervention process should begin by discussing attainable goals and a reasonable timeframe for achieving those goals.* It is counter-productive to create grandiose expectations, which should not be encouraged by the therapist or counselor. Do convey, however, that the individual's overall sense of well-being is expected to improve should emotional intelligence improve as a result of the intervention.

10. *Therapeutic intervention should attempt to facilitate the process of understanding and strengthening the individual's weakest EI factors.* In addition to understanding and strengthening these factors, therapeutic progress can be evaluated by accomplishing agreed upon goals, attaining better daily functioning and achieving a greater sense of well-being.

The application of EI in monitoring and evaluating therapeutic progress. EI-testing, with instruments such as the EQ-i, can be applied (a) during the intervention process to monitor progress being made as well as (b) upon completing the intervention to help evaluate its success. After completing the intervention, it is advisable that the individual undergo EI-testing a second time. By comparing pre- and post-intervention EQ-i test scores, it is relatively straightforward to identify which EI competencies, skills and behaviors have improved and to what extent. This process also pinpoints which EI factors might still need to be addressed. If the testing is done during the intervention to evaluate progress made, therapeutic goals can be modified and agreed upon together with a new timeframe in which to accomplish those goals. When comparing pre- and post-intervention EQ-i scores, it is important to first observe the degree to which the individual's overall emotional intelligence has increased.

Then, it is essential to examine the differences between the pre- and post-intervention scores on the following scales in particular: (1) Self-Regard, (2) Stress Tolerance, (3) Reality-Testing, (4) Self-Actualization, and (5) Happiness. Differences between pre- and post-intervention scores on the Impulse Control and Social Responsibility scales should be examined as well, which is especially important if there were significantly low scores on one or both of these scales prior to intervention. The results need to be discussed with the individual, in a final debriefing session, to help summarize and evaluate what was achieved as a result of the intervention process. Should the individual express a desire to continue therapy or counseling at some later time, this will need to be discussed as well; and such a discussion could also be facilitated by EI-testing.

DISCUSSION

This section summarizes the major points regarding the proposed application of emotional intelligence (EI) in clinical psychology, and concludes by exploring what needs to be done to empirically support and strengthen the use of EI in clinical work.

The application of EI in clinical psychology, as well as in psychiatry, social work and counseling, is justified in that it has been demonstrated that this construct has a significant impact on psychological health and well-being based on the studies summarized in the present chapter. It was shown that the key EI factors involved are the following:

- The ability to perceive, understand and accept one's emotions, feelings and oneself
- The ability to effectively and constructively manage emotions and stress
- The ability to objectively validate one's feelings with external reality
- The ability to set goals and the drive to achieve them in order to actualize one's potential
- The ability to generate positive mood and feel content with oneself, others and one's life

It was shown how EI-testing and assessment, focusing on the above EI factors in particular, can be seamlessly integrated into the assessment battery administered by clinical psychologists.

Moreover, it was explained that this type of testing can provide valuable information in psycho-diagnostics to confirm or refute results generated by other assessment methods. It was also shown how the findings provided by EI-testing can facilitate the development of a *diagnostic picture* to help identify what needs to be focused upon in psychotherapy and counseling.

This picture provides a *roadmap* for guiding therapeutic intervention as well as monitoring the progress achieved as a result of the intervention. What needs to be done to support and strengthen the use of EI in clinical work is to conduct additional research to empirically demonstrate that the results of EI-testing correlate with those of other diagnostic tools and measures of well-being. Additionally, it would be important to examine the *EI profile* of various diagnostic groups and to study the differences between them from an emotional intelligence perspective. It would also be valuable to examine EI differences between individuals who benefit more and those who benefit less from various types of psycho-therapeutic techniques.

The author would like to close by describing what he thinks will be the next big paradigm shift in psychology that will have an impact on clinical psychology, psychiatry, social work and counseling.

This shift is emerging from the need to create more comprehensive, robust and accurate predictive models that will be based on combining emotional and social intelligence with other predictors of performance, health and well-being. These multi-factorial models will be designed to assess and enhance EI as well as the physical, cognitive, moral, spiritual and motivational aspects of human behavior and daily performance. They will, hopefully, enhance our ability to better describe, assess and treat psychological health issues, as well as to help individuals thrive psychologically rather than merely survive.

The author is currently involved in developing such a multi-factorial model of behavior, performance and well-being.

APPENDIX

The Factorial Components of the Bar-On Model of Emotional Intelligence

EI Factors	Definitions of the EI Factors Comprising the Bar-On Model
INTRA-PERSONAL:	
Self-Regard	*To accurately perceive, understand and accept oneself.*
Emotional Self-Awareness	*To be aware of and understand one's emotions.*
Assertiveness (and Emotional Expression)	*To effectively and constructively express one's emotions and oneself.*
Independence	*To be self-reliant and free of emotional dependency on others.*
Stress Tolerance	*To effectively and constructively manage emotions.*
Impulse Control	*To effectively and constructively control emotions.*
Reality-Testing	*To objectively validate one's feelings and thinking with external reality.*
Flexibility	*To adapt and adjust one's feelings and thinking to new situations.*
Problem-Solving	*To effectively solve problems of a personal and interpersonal nature.*
INTER-PERSONAL:	
Empathy	*To be aware of and understand how others feel.*
Social Responsibility	*To identify with one's social group and cooperate with others.*
Interpersonal Relationship	*To establish mutually satisfying relationships and relate well with others.*
MOTIVATIONAL:	
Self-Actualization	*To strive to achieve personal goals and actualize one's potential.*
Optimism	*To be positive and look at the brighter side of life.*
Happiness (Well-Being)	*To feel content with oneself, others and life in general.*

REFERENCES

American Psychiatric Association (1994). Diagnostic and statistical manual of mental disorders, (4th ed., DSM-IV). Washington, DC: American Psychiatric Association.

Appelbaum, S. A. (1973). Psychological mindedness: Word, concept, and essence. *International Journal of Psycho-Analysis*, 54, 35-46.

Bar-On, R. (1988). The development of a concept of psychological well-being. Unpublished doctoral dissertation, Rhodes University, South Africa.

Bar-On, R. (1997a). The Emotional Quotient Inventory (EQ-i): Technical manual. Toronto, Canada: Multi-Health Systems, Inc.

Bar-On, R. (1997b). The Emotional Quotient Inventory (EQ-i): A test of emotional intelligence. Toronto, Canada: Multi-Health Systems, Inc.

Bar-On, R. (2000). Emotional and social intelligence: Insights from the Emotional Quotient Inventory (EQ-i). In R. Bar-On and J. D. A. Parker (Eds.), Handbook of emotional intelligence (pp. 363-388). San Francisco: Jossey-Bass.

Bar-On, R. (2004). The Bar-On Emotional Quotient Inventory (EQ-i): Rationale, description, and summary of psychometric properties. In G. Geher (Ed.), Measuring emotional intelligence: Common ground and controversy (pp. 111-142). Hauppauge, NY: Nova Science Publishers.

Bar-On, R. (2005). The impact of emotional intelligence on subjective well-being. *Perspectives in Education*, 23(2), 41-61.

Bar-On, R. (2006). The Bar-On model of emotional-social intelligence (ESI). *Psicothema*, 18, supl., 13-25.

Bar-On, R., and Handley, R. (2003a). The Bar-On EQ-360. Toronto, Canada: Multi-Health Systems.

Bar-On, R., and Handley, R. (2003b). The Bar-On EQ-360: Technical manual. Toronto, Canada: Multi-Health Systems.

Bar-On, R., and Handley, R. (2003c). The Bar-On Emotional Quotient Interview (EQ-interview). Toronto, Canada: Multi-Health Systems.

Bar-On, R., Tranel, D., Denburg, N. L., and Bechara, A. (2003). Exploring the neurological substrate of emotional and social intelligence. *Brain*, 126, 1790-1800.

Bar-On, R., Tranel, D., Denburg, N. L., and Bechara, A. (2005). Exploring the neurological substrate of emotional and social intelligence. In J. T. Cacioppo and G. G. Bernston (Eds.), Key readings in social psychology: Social neuroscience (pp. 223-237). New York, NY: Psychology Press.

Bechara, A., and Bar-On, R. (2006). Neurological substrates of emotional and social intelligence: Evidence from patients with focal brain lesions. In J. T. Cacioppo, P. S. Visser, and G. L. Pickett (Eds.), Social neuroscience: People thinking about thinking people (pp. 13-40). Cambridge, MA: MIT Press.

Bechara, A., Damasio, A., and Bar-On, R. (2007). The anatomy of emotional intelligence and the implications for educating people to be emotionally intelligent. In R. Bar-On, J. G. Maree, and M. Elias (Eds.), Educating people to be emotionally intelligent (pp. 273-290). Westport, CT: Praeger.

Bechara, A., Tranel, D., and Damasio, R. (2000). Poor judgment in spite of high intellect: Neurological evidence for emotional intelligence. In R. Bar-On and J. D. A. Parker (Eds.), Handbook of emotional intelligence (pp. 192-214). San Francisco: Jossey-Bass.

Boyatzis, R. E., Goleman, D., and HayGroup (2001). The Emotional Competence Inventory *(ECI)*. Boston: HayGroup.

Brackett, M. A., and Salovey, P. (2004). Measuring emotional intelligence with the Mayer-Salovey-Caruso Emotional Intelligence Test (MSCEIT). In G. Geher (Ed.), Measuring emotional intelligence: Common ground and controversy (pp. 181-196). Hauppauge, NY: Nova Science Publishers.

Cantor, N., and Kihlstrom, J. (1987). Personality and social intelligence. Englewood Cliffs, NJ: Erlbaum.

Clark, A. E. (2003). Unemployment as a social norm: Psychological evidence from panel data. *Journal of Labor Economics*, 21, 323-351.

Compas, B., and Gotlib, I. (2002). Introduction to clinical psychology. New York, NY: McGraw-Hill Higher Education.

Damasio, A. R. (1994). Descartes' error: Emotion, reason, and the human brain. New York: Grosset/Putnam.

Darwin, C. (1872/1965). The expression of the emotions in man and animals. Chicago: University of Chicago Press.

Davies, M., Stankov, L., and Roberts, R. D. (1998). Emotional intelligence: In search of an elusive construct. *Journal of Personality and Social Psychology*, 75, 989-1015.

Doll, E. A. (1935). A generic scale of social maturity. *American Journal of Orthopsychiatry*, 5, 180-188.

Gardner, H. (1983). Frames of mind. New York: Basic Books.

Geher, G. (Ed.) (2004). Measuring emotional intelligence: Common ground and controversy. Hauppauge, NY: Nova Science Publishers.

Goleman, D. (1995). Emotional intelligence. New York: Bantam Books.

Goleman, D. (1998). Working with emotional intelligence. New York: Bantam Books.

Groth-Marrat, G. (2009). Handbook of psychological assessment (5th ed.). Hoboken, NJ: John Wiley and Sons.

Helliwell, J. F., and Putnam, R. D. (2004). The social context of well-being. Philosophical Transactions of the Royal Society of London: *Biological Sciences*, 359, 1435-1446.

Kaplan, H. I., and Sadock, B. J. (1991). *Synopsis of psychiatry (6th ed.)*. Baltimore, MD: Williams and Wilkins.

Kelly, G. A. (1955). A theory of personality: The psychology of personal constructs. New York: Norton.

Lane, R. D. (2000). Levels of emotional awareness: Neurological, psychological and social perspectives. In R. Bar-On and J. D. A. Parker (Eds.), Handbook of emotional intelligence (pp. 171-191). San Francisco: Jossey-Bass.

Lane, R. D., and McRae, K. (2004). Neural substrates of conscious emotional experience: A cognitive-neuroscientific perspective. In B. M. Amsterdam and J. Benjamins (Eds.), Consciousness, emotional self-regulation and the brain (pp. 87-122). Amsterdam: John Benjamin.

Lane, R. D., and Schwartz, G. E. (1987). Levels of emotional awareness: A cognitive-developmental theory and its application to psychopathology. *American Journal of Psychiatry*, 144, 133-143.

LeDoux, J. (1996). The emotional brain: The mysterious underpinnings of emotional life. New York: Simon and Schuster.

Ludy, B. (2005). A history of clinical psychology as a profession in America (and a glimpse at its future). *Annual Review of Clinical Psychology*, 1, 1-30.

MacLennan, N. (1996). Counselling for managers. Brookfield, VT: Gower Publishing Company.

MacLean, P. D. (1949). Psychosomatic disease and the visceral brain: Recent developments bearing on the Papez theory of emotion. *Psychosomatic Medicine*, II, 338-353.

Matthews, G., Roberts, R. D., and Zeidner, M. (2003). Development of emotional intelligence: A sceptical – but not dismissive – perspective. *Human Development*, 46, 109-114.

Mayer, J. D., and Salovey, P. (1997). What is emotional intelligence: In P. Salovey and D. Sluyter (Eds.). Emotional development and emotional intelligence: Implications for educators (pp. 3-31). New York: Basic Books.

Mayer, J. D., Salovey, P., and Caruso, D. R. (2002). Mayer-Salovey-Caruso Emotional Intelligence Test (MSCEIT). Toronto, Canada: Multi-Health Systems, Inc.

Moss, F. A., and Hunt, T. (1927). Are you socially intelligent? *Scientific American*, 137, 108-110.

Oswald, A. J. (1997). Happiness and economic performance. *Economic Journal*, 107, 1815-1831.

Plake, B. S., and Impara, J. C. (Eds.). (1999). Supplement to the thirteenth mental measurement yearbook. Lincoln, NE: Buros Institute for Mental Measurement.

Plante, T. (2005). Contemporary clinical psychology. New York, NY: Wiley and Sons.

Rogers, C. R. (1961). On becoming a person (2nd ed.). Boston: Houghton Mifflin.

Rotter, J. B. (1966). Generalized expectancies for internal versus external control of reinforcement. *Psychological Monographs*, 80, 1-28.

Ruesch, J. (1948). The infantile personality. *Psychosomatic Medicine*, 10, 134-144.

Ryff, C. D. (1989). Happiness is everything, or is it? Explorations on the meaning of psychological well-being. *Journal of Personality and Social Psychology*, 57, 1069-1081.

Saarni, C. (1990). Emotional competence: How emotions and relationships become integrated. In R. A. Thompson (Ed.), Socioemotional development. Nebraska symposium on motivation (Vol. 36, pp. 115-182). Lincoln, NE: University of Nebraska Press.

Salovey, P., and Mayer, J. D. (1990). Emotional intelligence. *Imagination, Cognition, and Personality*, 9, 185-211.

Sifneos, P. E. (1967). Clinical observations on some patients suffering from a variety of psychosomatic diseases. *Acta Medicina Psychosomatica*, 21, 133-136.

Spielberger, C. (Ed.) (2004). Encyclopedia of Applied Psychology. Academic Press.

Stewart-Brown, S., and Edmunds, L. (2007). Assessing emotional intelligence in children: A review of existing measures of emotional and social competence. In R. Bar-On, J. G. Maree, and M. Elias (Eds.), Educating people to be emotionally intelligent (pp. 241-257). Westport, CT: Praeger.

Thorndike, E. L. (1920). Intelligence and its uses. *Harper's Magazine*, 1(40), 227-235.

Van Rooy, D. L., and Viswesvaran, C. (2007). Assessing emotional intelligence in adults: A review of the most popular measures. In R. Bar-On, J. G. Maree, and M. Elias (Eds.), Educating people to be emotionally intelligent (pp. 259-272). Westport, CT: Praeger.

Wechsler, D. (1940). Nonintellective factors in general intelligence. *Psychological Bulletin*, 37, 444-445.

Wechsler, D. (1943). Nonintellective factors in general intelligence. *Journal of Abnormal Social Psychology*, 38, 100-104.

Wechsler, D. (1955). Manual for the Wechsler Adult Intelligence Scale. New York, NY: The Psychological Corporation.

Zeidner, M., Matthews, G., and Roberts, R. D. (2001). Slow down, you move too fast: Emotional intelligence remains an "elusive" intelligence. *Emotion*, 1(3), 265-275.

In: Psychology of Counseling
Editor: Annamaria Di Fabio

ISBN: 978-1-62618-388-9
© 2013 Nova Science Publishers, Inc.

Chapter 5

Family of Origin and Career Development

Terri Duck[1], Jay Middleton[1], Deborah Simpson[1],
*Jennifer Thibodeaux[1], Janelle McDaniel and Walter Buboltz***
Louisiana Tech University, Russton. LA, US
[1]Denotes equal contribution, presented in alphabetical order

ABSTRACT

It has long been held that an individual's family environment and relationships, particularly relationships with parents, can influence career expectations and development. However, research in this area remained scant and evidence to support the importance of family variables in career development has only begun to develop recently. Data has been emerging indicating several family of origin variables can impact overall career development as well as specific aspects of career development. Of particular interest are family variables such as parental education, parental career choice and satisfaction, socioeconomic status of the family, family dynamics, culture of origin and parenting styles.

These factors appear to have influence on a range of career variables such as vocational identity, career self-efficacy, career exploration and career aspirations. Interestingly, the influence of these family variables seem to have a definite developmental aspect, in that the family is more obviously important at different ages, but is strongly present throughout the development periods in which when one is receiving primary and secondary education.

Thus it can be expected that family of origin may have a long-lasting impact on an individual's approach to their career and potentially their overall lifespan satisfaction with career. This chapter reviews the current state of the literature in relation to relevant family of origin variables and their impact on various career development outcomes. As career choice can so strongly influence all aspects of life, understanding the impact of the family on career development is paramount to assist individuals in achieving a satisfying career and life.

* Corresponding author: Walter Buboltz. E-mail address: buboltz@latech.edu.

INTRODUCTION

The family that one is raised in plays a critical role in many areas of development for family members and especially for children and adolescents. One area that parents and the family unit influence is the career development of its members. Despite this believe, research in this area remained scant and evidence to support the importance of family in career development has only begun to emerge.

Numerous career theorists have eluded to the importance of the family unit in career development over the years (Blustein, Wallbridge, Friedlander, and Palladino, 1991). For example, Super (1957) noted that an important developmental task of adolescences was the exploration of career aspirations and that these aspirations were influenced by parents because of the reliance on parents at this time of development. Vondracek, Lerner, and Schulenberg (1986) argue that the best way to view career development is from a relational context which focuses on the developing individual within a changing context. Within this framework various approaches to understanding the family and the family unit have been posited to potentially impact the career development of its members. Research has been accumulating over the past few decades on the relations between several family of origin variables and various career outcomes. This chapter provides a review of many of the more important family aspects in relation to a variety of career outcomes.

In relation to family of origin variables some theorists and researchers have examined how parenting styles or approaches are related to a variety of career development outcomes, while others have looked at features of the family unit such as conflict, cohesion and expressiveness in relation to career development outcomes. Others have examined the relationships between family members, especially attachment and how the attachment between family members influences career outcomes. Along this vein, other research has examined more demographic aspects of the family in relation to career development outcomes such as family socioeconomic status, parental education and age. Finally, research has examined the impact that culture of the family has on career development outcomes.

Within the career development context several variables have received attention as potentially being related to family of origin variables. Vocational identity has emerged as a variable of interest as well as career aspirations of young family members. Additionally, research has examined the impact of the family on career decision-making and career decision-making self-efficacy. Also, research has examined the relationship between family of origin variables and the development of vocational interests and educational expectations.

With this in mind this chapter reviews the current state of the literature in relation to relevant family of origin variables and their impact on various career development outcomes.

CAREER OUTCOME VARIABLES

Vocational Identity

Career theorists and researchers have assumed for years that an individual's family of origin plays an important role in the career development of family members (Herr and Lear, 1984). Within this area, research has focused on a number of family variables (socioeconomic status, family interaction patterns, system variables, etc.) and career outcomes (career decision-making self-efficacy, career indecision, etc.). A career variable that has received some attention in this realm is the idea of identity and how the family of origin environment influences or relates to the individual identity development of younger family members. Vocational identity as it is often called refers to the development of "the possession of a clear and stable picture of one's goals, interests, and talents" (Holland, Goffredson, and Power, 1980, p. 1191). However, before an examination of the literature pertaining to family of origin variables and vocational identity can be undertaken a brief review of identity development is warranted. This will be followed by a brief review of the relationship between family and career development and finally the current state of the literature the relationship or influence of family of origin variables on vocational identity.

Identity Development

Erikson is the most notable figure when it comes to identity development and his theory has laid the groundwork for almost all work on identity development. Erikson (1968) posited development as occurring in stages and that resolution of the current stage of development was dependent on successful resolution of the previous stages of development. According to his theory, each stage unfolds in a predetermined order and each stage is marked by a pivotal crisis. The resolution of the crisis of each stage can have either positive or negative effects on future development. Within this framework of development the crisis of the adolescent years is identity versus identity confusion. Erikson (1968) believed the natural progression was for individuals to move toward a strong and stable sense of identity through personal exploration in the areas of politics, religion, the interpersonal domain and careers. Through this exploration and resolving the crisis the individual should emerge with a stable ego identity. In his writings, Erikson eluded to the development of an occupational identity as a critical aspect of overall identity development.

Despite the tremendous development of Erikson's theory, his theory is more descriptive and thus difficult to test and research. Due to this shortcoming, other researchers (Blustein, 1994; Grotevant, 1987; Marcia, 1988) have expanded on the work of Erikson. Marcia (1966) operationalized the identity versus identity confusion developmental task of Erikson by examining how adolescents develop an inner sense of identity. To study this construct, Marcia used the ideas of crisis and commitment as organizing principles. For Marcia, crisis is a decision-making point where options and alternatives are explored and possible new ways of life are being imagined or tried. Commitment involves making a decision on a new way of life and incorporating a self-definition. Marcia believed that whether the crisis or commitment was accomplished or both were accomplished would indicate the extent of the resolution of the identity crisis. The intersection of crisis and commitment provides four possible identity types or status: diffusion, foreclosure, moratorium and achievement. For the identity diffusion status no crisis or commitment has been experienced and accomplished. Thus, these individuals tend to have a poorly organized sense of self. For the foreclosure identity status the individual has made a commitment but has not gone through the crisis aspect. These individuals tend to not have a strong internal sense of identity, but rather have based their identity on external factors and forces. Moratorium refers to the identity status or type of individuals who are currently experiencing a crisis but have not made a commitment. These individuals have a sense of wanting a sense of direction or identity but not actually having one. Finally, for the identity achieved status individuals have both experienced and accomplished a crisis and made a commitment. These individuals tend to have a strong sense of self or identity and have committed to who they will be in the future.

Career Theories, Identity and the Family

The influence of the family of origin on the career outcomes of individuals has been alluded to in numerous theories of career development and decision-making (Blustein, et al, 1991). Super (1957) suggested that family variables can influence the development of an individual's self-concept and career choice. Roe's (1957) theory focused on genetic factors and the interaction between the genetic factors and different child rearing practices that can influence vocational outcomes for children. Krumboltz (1979), in his social learning theory of career decision-making, pointed out the potential influences of the family, as family members provide learning experiences for their members and can thus influence career development and career choice by positively reinforcing or punishing behaviors that can encourage or discourage the development of certain abilities or interests. Crites (1962) indicated that identification with a parent or parental figure and their career may be seen in the interest development of their children and the potential careers they pursue. In her theory of circumscription and compromise Gottfredson (1981) indicated how family mediated sex typing can influence the career choice of younger family members. More recent theorizing and research which has been built on previous theoretical foundations has focused on the role the family unit plays in the career development process of individual family members (Carr, 2000). Social cognitive career theory posits a more integrative framework for career development. The social cognitive model examines the contextual and unique support afforded by the family in the career development process. Additionally, not only do many of the career development theories allude to or specify that the family of origin can influence and impact career development, they also include identity development as an important component within their theories. Super (1980) incorporates the development of a self-concept into his theory. Super proposed that the self-concept emerged as the result of children's observations of and identifications with adults at work. Holland (1985) incorporated the idea of vocational identity as one of the four primary tenets of his theory. In his theory, Holland looked at parental influence as providing a particular environment that exerts an influence on the development of characteristics of their children and leads to the development of vocational identity and the selection of particular career environments. Krumboltz (1979) included the idea of self-observation generalizations as part of his theory of career decision making. Accordingly, these self-observation generalizations are developed over time as an individual learns about themselves through the learning experiences they encounter in life. As can be seen, some form of identity development appears to hold a central role in many of the major theories of career development. Thus, it appears evident that based on theory, both the family and identity may important aspects of career development. However, despite this apparent connection the examination of the influence of the family of origin on career outcomes, especially vocational identity has received limited empirical investigation over the years (Arbona, 2000). Thus, this review of the literature on family factors or processes that are related to or influence vocational identity development will hopefully spur much needed research in this area.

Family Variables and Vocational Identity

Vocational identity has been one of the vocational process variables receiving some attention in the empirical literature related to family of origin variables but clearly further research is needed. Vocational identity can be broadly defined as an overall measure of career development, which signifies an individual's clarity of interests, attitudes, values and goals for the future. Although as noted above several theories have eluded to some sort of identity development as part of the career development process, Holland (1980) is the only major career theorist and researcher to develop an instrument to measure vocational identity, which is called My Vocational Situation (MVS). The development of this instrument and inclusion of the identity concept into theories of career development lead to some research examining vocational identity development and how it relates to other pertinent career variables. Although vocational identity has been examined in relation to several other variables (career decision-making self-efficacy, career indecision, etc.) this review is limited to family of origin variables influence or relationship to vocational identity.

In general the research that has examined family of origin variables in relation to vocational identity has tended to focus on systemic or relational variables within the family. Although limited, some studies have demonstrated empirical support for the relationship between family interaction patterns and vocational identity. Lopez (1989) examined the linkage between psychological separation (conflictual and emotional attachments to parents), marital conflict and vocational identity in college students. Results showed that psychological separation from parents was significantly different for male and female students. Examination of the relationship between psychological separation and marital conflict showed that the family variables accounted for roughly 13% of the variance for men. More specifically, conflictual independence from mother and conflictual independence from father as well as marital conflict were significant predictors of vocational identity for males. However, for females the family variables accounted for roughly 14% of the variance in vocational identity, but this was primarily due to conflictual independence from the father as this was the only significant predictor for females.

In a similar vein, Penick and Jepsen (1992) explored family relationship factors and family system maintenance variables in the prediction of vocational identity of adolescent students. The family relationship variables in this study were cohesion, expressiveness, conflict, sociability, idealization and disengagement and the family maintenance factors were organization, locus of control, democratic, enmeshment, laissez faire and authoritarian family styles. They found that the maintenance factors of democratic and authoritarian family style were the primary predictors of vocational identity. To a lesser extent the family relationship variables of expressiveness and conflict were also significant predictors of vocational identity. Jowdy (1994) explored the influence of family structure and separation from parents on vocational identity development. In this research, family cohesion and adaptability and healthy and unhealthy separation were believed to be related to the ego-identity statuses as outlined by Marcia (1966) which then in turn would be associated with career/vocational identity. Models were developed for each of the four ego-identity status to examine these relationships. For the achieved ego-identity status, healthy separation from parents was significantly related to achieved ego-identity, while family cohesion and adaptability and unhealthy separation from parents were not significantly related to achieved ego-identity status. Within this model there was also a significant positive relationship between achieve ego-identity and career identity. For this model, results indicate that healthy separation is related to general identity development which is then associated with career identity. For the moratorium identity status, there were significant negative relationships between healthy separation from parents and moratorium identity status and between family cohesion and the moratorium identity status. A positive significant relationship was found between unhealthy separation from parents and the moratorium identity status and no relationship was found between family adaptability and the moratorium identity status. Further examination of the model showed that there was a significant negative relationship between the moratorium identity status and career identity. For this model, separation from parents and family cohesion were significant predictors of the moratorium identity status and in turn career identity. For the foreclosed ego identity status significant positive relationships were found between family cohesion and unhealthy separation from parents and the foreclosed identity status. No relationship was found between family adaptability and healthy separation from parents and the foreclosed identity status. However, further examination showed that there was not a significant relationship between the foreclosed identity status and career identity. The results indicate that family cohesion and unhealthy separation from parents relate to identity development, but do not relate to more specific career identity. Finally, for the diffused identity status a significant negative relationship was found between healthy separation from parents and family cohesion and the diffused identity status. There was a significant positive relationship between unhealthy separation from parents and diffused identity and no significant relationship was found between family adaptability and the diffused identity status. Further examination of this model showed that the diffused identity status was significantly negatively related to career identity. These models taken together generally show that family of origin variables are related to general identity development and that this in turn relates to the more specific aspect of identity development, namely vocational/career identity.

Puffer (1998) examined family activities in relation to vocational identity in a large sample of undergraduate students. Results of canonical analysis showed that none of the family variables were significantly related to vocational identity for males. However, for females canonical analysis showed that in general, high levels of cohesion, low levels of achievement orientation, strong attachment to parents and high commitment to encouraging autonomy and independence by parents were associated with a clear and stable vocational identity. Following along this line of research, Johnson, Buboltz and Nichols (1999) examined the relationship between vocational identity development and the quality of family relationships for college students from intact and divorced families. First, results showed that there were not any significant differences between college students from divorced or intact families or between male and female students. In terms of the relationship between family variables and vocational identity, results showed that family expressiveness was positively associated with vocational identity, but the amount of variance accounted for was very small. These results indicate that students from both intact and divorced families who view their families as having open expression within the family of information and emotions tend to have higher vocational identity. In a study of college students Dodge (2001) found that personal authority and peer individuation within the family of origin was significantly related to vocational identity, while expressiveness, conflict and cohesion in the family of origin were not significantly related to vocational identity. Additionally, Dodge found that conflict and the organizational dimensions of the family origin were also not significantly related to vocational identity.

Hargrove, Creagh and Burgess (2002) examined the relationship between perceived family of origin interactional patterns and vocational identity development of college students. Hargrove et al., (2002) examined several family interactional variables using the Family Environment Scale (Moos, 1989). This instrument breaks family of origin interactions along three basic dimensions: Relationship Aspects, Personal Growth Aspects and System Maintenance Aspects. Consistent with previous studies the authors did not find any significant differences between males and females. Further regression analysis showed that all of the family variables taken together significantly predicted vocational identity with the family variables accounting for 14% of the variance in vocational identity. These results indicate that students with higher vocational identity tended to come from families that they viewed as emphasizing achievement in school and work. However, closer examination indicates that only achievement orientation, which falls within the personal growth domain within the family of origin, was a significant predictor of vocational identity. These results appear to be somewhat in conflict with previous studies which have shown that significant relationships exist between vocational identity and family of origin relationship variables.

Hartung, Lewis, May and Niles (2002) examined how family interactional patterns, namely family adaptability and cohesion, related to vocational identity. In their study of 172 undergraduate students they found that male and female students significantly differed on views of family cohesion but the magnitude of the difference was small and thus the authors collapsed the gender variable. Results showed family adaptability and cohesion was not significantly related to vocational identity. These findings tend to be in conflict with previous research which has shown that certain family interactional patterns are related to vocational identity.

The relationship between family of origin environment (family relationships, family goal-orientation and degree of organization and control within the family) and vocational identity were examined in high school students by Hargrove, Inman and Crane (2005). The use of high school students makes this a unique study as most previous research employed college students. The researchers used the three primary dimensions and the corresponding subscales of the Family Environment Scale (Moos, 1989) to make their study consistent with some of the prior research conducted in this area. Results indicated that male and female students differed on several of the family environment scales with one of these the scales being expressiveness in the family. However, males and females did not differ on their level of vocational identity. Despite these significant gender differences the authors did not analyze their data separately based on gender. A regression analysis incorporating all of the family variable scales was not significant indicating that family of origin variables do not significantly relate to vocational identity. These results are consistent with some of the previous research (Hartung, et al, 2002) on family of origin variables and vocational identity, but in contrast to other research (Hargrove et al., 2002; Johnson, Buboltz and Nichols, 1999; Penick and Jepsen, 1992) which has shown that a relationship exists between family of origin variables and vocational identity. Finally, Villarreal (2007) examined family of origin dynamics in relation to vocational identity for women in three different cultures. Results showed first that Caucasian college women exhibited higher vocational identity than Hispanic women, but no differences were found between Caucasian and African American women. Regression analysis revealed that high cohesion within the family of origin and participation in recreational activities within the family was associated with higher levels of vocational identity.

Taken together the results of these studies would tend to indicate that at least to some extent certain aspects of the family of origin or at least perceptions of the family of origin are related to vocational identity. These results would lend some support to the idea that the family of origin and interactions within the family play a role in vocational identity and this would be consistent with the career theories that elude to the importance of the family in career development. However, it should be noted that some of the studies did not find significant relationships between family variables and vocational identity while other studies found relationships that were inconsistent with previous research findings. A possible explanation for the inconsistent findings is that several of the studies reviewed were based on different family development theories and also that instruments employed to operationalize the family of origin variables varied from study to study. A second possible explanation for some of the inconsistent findings is that the majority of the studies are somewhat retrospective in that individuals are asked to answer questions about the family environment not only presently but in the past. In conclusion, results would tend to point to the importance of the family in vocational identity but clearly further research is warranted in this area to ferret out the most important aspects of the family involved in vocational identity development and the strength of these relationships.

Career Indecision

In the same way that certain family factors can promote career decision-making and career development in individuals as they mature, others can hinder this developmental process. The career decision making process is most visibly observed as individuals enter post-secondary educational programs and are confronted with the decision of which major they should choose and which career path they wish to follow. Therefore, most of the research that focuses on career indecision is conducted with college students amidst this vocational identity crisis. Feldman (2003) defines career indecision as "the inability to formulate initial career goals and experience commitment to initial vocational choices" (p. 500). Cognitively, career indecision involves a lack of career goals, direction, and self-insight, while the affective components include anxiety, ambivalence, and frustration. However, there is some disagreement as to the utility and functionality of early career indecision. If early career indecision leads to young adults discovering their true vocational interests and abilities, then it can be viewed as advantageous (Hall, 1994). Opinions on the utility of career indecision often rely on the duration of the indecision which determines if it is developmental or chronic. Chronic indecision is "driven by anxiety and fear of commitment," tends to be mostly affective and stable within individuals over time, and is viewed as more problematic than developmental indecision (Feldman, 2003, p. 502). In contrast, developmental career indecision is fueled by a lack of information and usually lessens over time as individuals gain greater self-insight and begin to receive feedback from their environment.

Kelly and Pulver (2003) conducted a study to replicate and refine career indecision types indentified in previous research, the result of which was the emergence of four indecision types. Type one – the well-adjusted information seeker – applies to someone who would be considered developmentally undecided. The second type, labeled neurotic indecisive information seekers, refers to individuals who possess both the cognitive and affective components of career indecision as well as personality characteristics that hinder the career decision-making process. The third type – low ability information seekers – have a strong need for career information related to their low verbal and math ability, and tend to score high on Extraversion and low on Openness. The fourth and final type was labeled uncommitted extraverts, and these individuals are distinguished from the other groups in that they are closed to new sources of self-knowledge because they have usually made a decision about an academic major without committing to one and are not in need of any substantial career counseling intervention. However, types one and two – the neurotic indecisive and low ability information seekers are the most in need of intervention. Thus, a distinction is made within the undecided population as to which individuals need to be identified and differentially diagnosed as undecided or indecisive (Barak and Friedkos, 1982; Fuqua and Hartman, 1983; Lopez and Andrews, 1987; Salomone, 1982).

Many factors contribute to early career indecision such as early work experience, vocational interests and abilities, and personality variables. However, here we are concerned with the influence of family environment. Feldman (2003) discusses how parents' income, parents' job insecurity, and parents' involvement in career planning activities impacts their children's indecision. Of those whose parents earned less than $20,000, only 37% completed a bachelor's degree within 5 years of high school graduation, as opposed to 61% of children from families making $60,000 or more (National Center for Education Statistics, 1999). Job insecurity experienced by parents also has an impact on the degree of career indecision their children experience. When parents have employment problems, their children are likely to be distracted from vocational pursuits and may develop unfavorable attitudes towards work in general (Feldman, 2003). Furthermore, parents' involvement in the career planning of their children builds self-efficacy in the children for seeking more career-related information and employment opportunities. It has been shown that teenagers whose parents participate in career planning with them demonstrate more career certainty, more career salience, and less career indecision than control groups (Kush and Cochran, 1993). Because of the importance of parental engagement in the career decision making process, efforts such as The Partners Program (Palmer and Cochran, 1988) have been developed to help parents find ways to engage in career guidance with their children. It consists of three workbooks: a self-exploration workbook that identifies interests, strengths and values; a career grid workbook that helps the individual choose from viable options and make a tentative decision; and a planning workbook to encourage planning toward a vocational goal. Through use of the four phases of career counseling – self-awareness, career awareness, deliberation and decision, and planning – this program inspires confidence and aids parents in building a stronger sense of career-related agency in their children.

Eigen, Hartman, and Hartman (1987) proposed that family interaction patterns affect resolution of the life-adjustment task of making a career decision. Using Olson et al.'s (1979) family systems model, they extracted two dimensions of family dynamics that discriminate functional and dysfunctional family interactions – cohesion and adaptability. Family cohesion was viewed as emotional bonding within the family and adaptability measured the family's capacity for change. Therefore, well functioning families maintain balanced levels of these two dimensions, while midrange families are balanced on one but extreme on the other, and dysfunctional families are extreme on both dimensions. While their hypotheses about the impact of interaction patterns on career indecision were not supported by their findings, they theorized that family interaction patterns that foster early, stable decision making may have a flexible structure with strong emotional attachments or a more authoritarian structure with a bonding pattern that allows for more individual freedom.

Kinnier, Brigman, and Noble (1990) examined the relationship between family enmeshment and career indecision, finding weak support for the belief that those who are enmeshed in their families of origin are more likely than those not enmeshed to experience difficulty making career decisions. Whitson (1996) found that women who reported high levels of organization and control in their families-of-origin also reported needing less support in making career decisions and having less feelings of confusion or diffusion about making a career decision. Meanwhile, Lopez and Andrews (1987) proposed that problems with identity formation during adolescence lead to role confusion and difficulties in choosing a career because these individuals lack psychological separation from their parents. They found that college students experiencing career indecision tend to report an over involvement of parents and the student over career and educational matters, implicating weak parent-child boundaries. Another theorized basis for career indecision is that the indecision provides a vehicle for delaying the young adult's separation from the parents, thus maintaining the family's equilibrium at the expense of career decision-making (Lopez and Andrews, 1987). Therefore it is important to remember that career decision making requires appropriate development, but also can be considered a component of the transition from adolescence to adulthood.

Career Decision Making

One main task of counseling psychology is assisting individuals in their career decision making. In order to assist individuals in their career development, counselors must be aware of how individuals decide on a career and the variables that influence this decision. Many models for explaining the career decision-making process are based on decision theory (Gati, Landman, Davidovitch, Asulin-Perez, and Gadassi, 2010; Jepsen and Dilley, 1974). When individuals are faced with a decision, they examine all information available and choose between two or more alternative options. The choice that is made is also affected by the anticipated consequences of their decision, which includes the examination of the probability of occurrence and how much the anticipated consequence is valued (Jepsen and Dilley, 1974).

In terms of the process of career decision making, career decisions occur throughout our life span (Super, 1980) and are influenced by the interaction between our individual characteristics, such as decision making styles (Harren, 1979) and/or personality traits (Holland, 1959), and external sources, such as family and economics (Vondracek, Lerner, and Schulenberg, 1983). In applying decision theory to career decision making, vocational choice is determined by the amount of occupational information that the individual is knowledgeable on and the amount of self-insight the individual has regarding his or her personal characteristics (Holland, 1959; Jepsen and Dilley, 1974; Peterson, Sampson, Reardon, and Lenz, 1996). For example, individuals are more likely to commit to a career choice if they are familiar with what the career will entail (occupational information) and if they know this career is something that they will enjoy (personal characteristics). The opposite is true when individuals have limited information about the career choices available and are unsure of what interests them. Many theoretical models have concentrated separately on the cognitive and developmental processes of career decision making (e.g. Holland, 1959; Super, 1980), while others have focused on the interplay between individual and contextual variables (e.g. Vondracek, et al, 1983). These theoretical models have helped establish valuable self-report measures that provide individuals with the necessary information about particular occupations and their personal characteristics, which better allows career counselors to assist individuals during their career decision-making process.

Family and Career Decision Making

Many variables affect the career path that an individual chooses, including personal and environmental factors, but one influential predictor variable that is present from the start of the decision making process is the individual's family. Roe (1957) first discussed the role that family plays in influencing career decision making as one of many variables that affect vocational choice. Roe hypothesized that a child's vocational choice is related to the desire to satisfy an unmet need, which is influenced by early parental interaction patterns and parental attitudes towards their children. Specifically, Roe proposed individuals who grew up in a household where they were the center of attention would choose a career different from someone who grew up in a household in which they were accepted or emotionally avoided by their parents. Similarly, one who grew up in a household where their emotional needs or other needs were left unfulfilled will choose a career that is different from someone who was the center of their parent's attention or accepted by their parents. There has been little evidence to suggest that Roe's theory is accurate (Roe and Lunneborg, 1990), but her priming of the importance of family on career choice opened a new realm of research for career decision making.

Bratcher (1982) elaborated on Roe's hypotheses of parental attitudes influencing career choice by identifying several components of the family systems theory that also contribute to an individual's career selection. He explained that our family's boundaries, rules, and values/traditions influence our decisions. Specifically, a family with inflexible boundaries imposed by the parental unit would limit the geographical area of where children would work, in comparison to a family with flexible boundaries. Additionally, Bratcher proposed that a family who emphasizes conformity to rules rather than freethinking hinders the ease in which career decisions are made by limiting the available options of potential occupations because of a lack of fit with the rules set within the family. The final influence that Bratcher proposed the family to have on career decision making is the strength of a family's traditions, noting that some traditions dictate which occupation one is expected to assume regardless of the individual's opinion on the matter.

One of the family systems theories that Bratcher (1982) touches upon is Bowen's theory of family dynamics. The Bowenian family systems theory explains the relationship between individuals and their family as being mediated by anxiety (Larson and Wilson, 1998), which controls the level of closeness experienced in a family system. Individuals in families that are not emotionally close experience greater anxiety because of the underlying fear of not being accepted and loved by their family. Similarly, individuals in families that are too close also experience greater anxiety, but it is because of the underlying fear of the inability to be independent. When a parent-child relationship has features of fusion (dependent attachment), triangulation (focus of attention), and intimidation (strict rules), the child is unable to gain self-insight and has little experience in making their own decisions. This inexperience leads the child to rely on either on parental guidance or the innate desire to decrease anxiety in making important life decisions, one of which is career choice. Therefore, it is assumed that the level of closeness experienced within a family also affects career decision making.

Bowlby's widely accepted attachment theory also increased the focus of family influence on personal and career development by directing attention to the relationships of significant others and the effect this relationship has on the ease of decision making (Chope, 2001). Blustein, Prezioso, and Schultheiss (1995) theorized Bowlby's attachment theory as an added explanation to the process of career decision making in the context of individuals feeling secure enough to venture from their parental unit to explore their surroundings and take risks. Similar to Larson and Wilson (1998), they acknowledge that deciding on a career involves taking particular anxiety inducing risks. They proposed that individuals who have a secure attachment to a significant other (e.g. parents, spouse, and guardian) will be more willing to take risks associated with deciding on a particular career as opposed to someone with an insecure attachment who will be more willing to avoid taking risks due to fear. Specifically, if an individual were faced with deciding whether to commit to a specific career with the possibility of later regret, someone who felt secure would be more willing to take a risk and see it as a possible learning experience rather than someone who lacked this security and instead would lean towards inaction.

Family of Origin Influences Career Decision Making

There is a growing body of literature that provides evidence of a family of origin's influence on career decision making (e.g., Larson and Wilson, 1998; Lease and Dahlbeck, 2009; Penick and Jepsen, 1992; Peterson, Stivers, and Peters, 1986; Scott and Church, 2001).While some researchers have focused on theorizing the relationship between family and career decision-making, others have tested the validity to these claims. A meta-analysis conducted by Whiston and Keller (2004) compiled evidence of research that studied the effect of family on career development, which included family effects on career decision making across the developmental life span, from the time period of 1980 to 2002. The findings indicate that one's family of origin influences five factors in career decision making: career planning behavior, career decidedness, commitment to a career choice, vocational exploration, and confidence in choosing a career.

Peterson, et al. (1986) conducted a longitudinal study that demonstrated parental influence on a child's vocational planning during childhood and early adulthood. Specifically, children rely more on their parent's knowledge to guide them in making decisions about which career would be the best fit for them rather than seeking assistance from their peers or other extended family members. Peterson et al.'s study indicate that parents played as large a role for adolescents' career decision making as was found during childhood and early adulthood. However, Penick and Jepsen (1992) have found evidence that family interaction patterns play a prominent role in career decision making throughout an individual's development. They assessed the effect of family functioning of intact families on career development of adolescents. Results of the study revealed that the system maintenance factors of Locus of Control, Democratic Family Functioning, and Enmeshment perceived by adolescents significantly predicted career decision-making behavior. Specifically, adolescents who perceive their family systems as being governed democratically by rules performed higher on scales measuring career planning involvement. These results contribute evidence to the hypothesis made by Bratcher (1982) that families whose systems are flexible in establishing and implementing rules, as demonstrated in a democratic family that values the input of all family members, produce an environment that aids in career decision making. These results also contribute evidence to the Bowenian systems theory of career decision-making in that a family's level of closeness is applicable in the prediction of career planning behavior.

Evidence that family dynamics influences career decidedness comes from a study conducted by Larson and Wilson (1998), in which they examined the parent-child relationship factors of fusion, triangulation, and intimidation and the effects they had on career decision making. Their results confirmed that a family's level of closeness (fusion and intimidation specifically) mediated by anxiety affected career decision making. Specifically, anxious individuals who came from closely enmeshed families and placed high importance on not disappointing their parents had more problems in career decision making.

There is evidence that demonstrates the effect of family attachment styles on career commitment (e.g., Blustein, Waldbridge, Friedlander, and Palladino, 1991; Scott and Church, 2001). A study conducted by Blustein et al. (1991) examined the relationship between young adult's attachment to parents and the phase in career decision making in which young adults are faced with committing to a particular career. Blustein et al. (1991) found that the combination of psychological separation and perceived attachment to parents formed a significant positive relationship with commitment to a career decision for both males and females, but the findings indicated slightly different patterns of this relationship when comparing male and female responding. Specifically, they identified that the combined variables of psychological separation and parental attachment to both parents significantly influenced females' ability to decide on a career; however, for males, career decision making was associated more with the psychological separation and parental attachment to their fathers, along with a negative association with having unique attitudes from their fathers. In other words, females were equally influenced by their relationship with both parents, but males were more influenced by their relationship with their fathers.

Research also demonstrates that family attachment styles affect vocational exploration in addition to career commitment. A longitudinal study conducted by Germeijs and Verschueren (2009) revealed that perceived attachment to parents affects the career decision-making and vocational exploration and that these effects are cross-cultural. Participants in their study were Belgium adolescents who were in their final year of high school. Germeijs and Verschueren (2009) described this time to be particularly stressful for students because they are forced to decide on their career path prior to graduating high school. Because of this stressful time, Germeijs and Verschueren (2009) explored whether perceived secure attachments to parents would influence an adolescent's career decision-making. Results indicated that perceived secure attachment to the mother was associated with an adolescent's career decision-making but no correlation was found between perceived attachment to the father and career decision-making. Similar to Blustein et al.'s (1995) assertions of Bowlby's attachment theory, Germeijs and Verschueren (2009) found that adolescents who had a secure attachment to their mother were more open to self-exploration and environmental exploration. Additionally, the findings suggest that adolescents who have a secure attachment with their mother recognize the importance of career exploration and decision-making; however, attachment security was not predictive of career choice or commitment.

Family interaction patterns were also found to be influential on career decision making self-efficacy (Hargrove et al., 2002; Lease and Dahlbeck, 2009; Nawaz and Gilani, 2011; Nota, Ferrari, Solberg, and Soresi, 2007). Hargrove et al. (2002) evaluated the predictive capability of family interaction pattern with vocational identity and career decision making self-efficacy. Their findings revealed that the combined factors of a family's level of closeness, supportiveness, organization, and rules predicted career decision making self-efficacy in college students. Regarding problem solving confidence in particular, individuals who came from homes with a high level of family conflict demonstrated a lower level of problem solving confidence. Another study conducted by Lease and Dahlbeck (2009) revealed that career decision making self-efficacy was influenced by parental attachment and parenting style for females but not males.

Career Expectations

Career and Education Expectations and Aspirations

Rowjewski (2005) defines career aspirations as a person's articulated career related goals. Expectations can be defined as what careers we view as realistic and accessible to us. What we expect and aspire to throughout our childhood, adolescence, and young adulthood regarding our career and education are influenced by many factors, including our family. Schulenber, Vondracek, and Crouter (1984) suggest, based on their review of literature, that career development has two dimensions. The first dimension involves opportunities given by the family which could include financial or educational resources. The second dimension involves family processes such as socialization and the interaction between parent and child. Rowjewski (2005) lists the following as being a hindrance to career expectations and aspirations: an individual lacking confidence in their ability to succeed at the career would like to aspire to; believing that they do not have the resources that are needed to reach the educational or other requirements that may be required for the job; family and friends are not supportive of their career aspirations; and believing that there are socictal or community barriers that make them less likely to reach their career goals. This section examines what research has found regarding these positive and negative factors that influence career aspirations and expectations, specifically in the context of family.

Career Theories integrating Career Goals and Expectations

Before discussing the research that has been done in this area, it is important to be familiar with some of the theories that are associated with career goals. Although there are no specific family theories that address the issues of career expectations and aspirations, there are career theories that hypothesize how people develop these aspirations and expectations. General career theories that address the development of career aspirations and expectations include: Super's Self-Concept Developmental Theory, Social Cognitive Career Theory, Theory of Career Circumscription and Compromise, and Status Attainment Theory. Super's Self-Concept Developmental Theory sees the development of career aspirations as tasks that are completed in a predictable sequence (Rowjewski, 2005). These tasks are: growth, exploration, establishment, maintenance, and disengagement; with exploration being the task that is very influential in career aspirations. The exploration task usually begins around age 14; during this stage the individual begins to assess their career options, eventually leading to a final decision about career (Rowjewski, 2005). In the exploration stage this final decision about career is established through: thinking about different occupational fields, establishing tentative career choices, and making the decision to obtain the education or training that will be needed for the occupation (Ochs and Roessler, 2004). Social Cognitive Career Theory states that career behavior, including career aspirations, are influenced by the interaction of self-efficacy, outcome expectations, and personal goals (Rowjewski, 2005). According to this theory, self-efficacy, expectations, and goals, are influenced by environmental factors and socialization patterns like gender, race/ethnicity, or socioeconomic status. This idea is related to Gottfredson's theory of circumscription and compromise which states that aspirations are developed through circumscription and compromise. Compromise involves letting go of idealistic aspirations and developing more realistic ones (Rowjewski, 2005). Circumscription involves an individual examining what career options are available and how those options fit the concept they have of themselves (Rowjewski, 2005).

Gottfredson (1981) discussed four stages in the development of their career aspirations. The first stage is called orientation to size and power, and occurs between the ages of 3-5. In this stage, the child moves from magical thinking about careers to viewing career aspirations as adult roles. In the second stage, orientation to sex roles, which occurs at ages 6-8, the child's orientation is to sex roles; they begin to understand the concept of sex role. Occupational aspirations are then focused on what they view as appropriate for their sex. Once children have developed a sense of what careers are acceptable for each sex and that once established, these ideas of acceptable gendered careers can be hard to change and can significantly impact career choices (Coogan and Chen, 2007). The third state, orientation to social valuation, occurs between the ages of 9-13. During this stage, the child begins to think about prestige level when deciding on a career. According to Gottfredson (1981), they will look to their peer group and social expectations, values, etc when deciding on the prestige level of a certain career. The last stage discussed by Gottfredson (1981) is the orientation to the internal, unique self, which begins at age 14 and continues on from there. During this stage, the adolescent and young adult begins to develop a personal identity and chooses a career aspiration that is consistent with that identity.

The Status Attainment Model says that when an individual is choosing a career, social forces are the most important factor (Rowjewski, 2005). Blau and Duncan discussed variables that are important in career aspirations: antecedent variables such as fathers education and occupation and intervening variables such as a person's own educational attainment or their first job (as cited in Rowjewski, 2005, p. 138). Later on, other variables were added to this theory as also being important to career aspirations. These variables include: significant others; academic ability or performance; and individual aspirations (Rowjewski, 2005).

Vocational Interests

Circumscription and Narrowing of Career Interests during Childhood

Gottfredson (1981) developed a theory of occupational interest and choice with four stages of development adapted from Van den Daele's (1968) descriptions of cognitive development in conjunction with the formation of ego-ideals in children. The four stages are arranged according to age: orientation to size and power (ages 3-5 years), orientation to sex roles (ages 6-8 years), orientation to social valuation (9-13 years), and orientation to the internal, unique self (beginning around age 14 years). According to Gottfredson, the main role of childhood in the career decision-making process is to eliminate occupations based on age-specific themes. This process may be greatly influenced by cognitive development in conjunction with factors of the individual's social environment. The most vocationally relevant factors are gender, socioeconomic background, intelligence, and the interplay of vocational interests with competencies and values. Initially, children have a generally positive view of all the occupations with which they are aware; however, this changes as they age and develop self-concepts that can be used to critically assess job-self compatibility (Gottfredson, 1981).

As children mature, they develop more differentiated and specific views of themselves in relation to the social world and a narrower, conscripted view of acceptable occupational alternatives. Ruled out first are occupations deemed inappropriate for their sex, followed by those of unacceptably low prestige in comparison to the child's concept of his or her social class. Next, interests are ruled out based on the child's view of his or her abilities. Finally, in adolescence, vocational choice is further pared down based on personal interests, values, and capacities. Therefore, the list of available choices in later adolescence is determined by what was considered congruent in earlier stages based on visible characteristics (Gottfredson, 1981). This notion is echoed by Lent, Brown, and Hackett (1996) who posit that individuals prematurely foreclose on certain career pursuits because their environments restrict their range of efficacy-building experiences or because their environment leads them to develop inaccurate beliefs about their career-related self-efficacy and occupational outcome expectations. They believe that career development interventions for children should focus on ensuring that their self-efficacy beliefs are congruent with their developing abilities so that their range of acceptable choices is not limited by misinformation or misperceptions of personal capabilities.

Vocational Interest in Childhood

Research with pre-adolescent children has shown that they use their personal interests, beliefs and values to tentatively explore the world-of-work and begin to develop initial interests (Hartung, Porfeli, and Vondracek, 2005). These personal ideas about work are shaped and influenced by the social, cultural, and physical aspects of their environment as they progress developmentally. The physical environment interacts with genetic variations and predispositions. Although it may be difficult to recognize a biological aspect to career choice, behavior-genetics research has been employed to investigate the influence of genetic and biological factors on the vocational interests of children. Monozygotic and dizygotic twin studies have shown repeatedly shown that 35-50% of the variance in vocational interests can be attributed to genetic influence (Betsworth et al., 1994; Lykken, Bouchard, McGue, and Tellegen, 1993; Moloney, Bouchard, and Segal, 1991). Primarily, recent research has focused on the environmental influences that shape vocational interests in early childhood.

Vocational Interest in Adolescence

Vocational interest in adolescence is differentiated from that of childhood by the emerging development of abstract reasoning and the greater influence of peers over that of parents and other adults. Adolescence is a critical time of burgeoning interests and development in many areas that is most often facilitated by those whom the adolescent deems to be most influential. Some have theorized that interests emerge and are evaluated as the individuals are exposed to new activities and tasks. As they engage in these new activities, adolescents either experience success or failure which leads to the development of self-efficacy and outcome expectancies. Lent, Brown, and Hackett (1994) theorized that either interests were reflective of beliefs of self-efficacy and outcome expectancy or that self-efficacy acted as a moderator for the relationship between interests and abilities. Lent et al.'s (1994) research on this relationship led to the formulation of a social-cognitive theory – later modified by career theorists into social-cognitive career theory (SCCT). SCCT, as proposed by Lent, Brown, and Hackett (1996), hypothesizes that general cognitive ability and academic/work skills that individuals develop through past experiences influence performance via self-efficacy beliefs.

The relationship between dimensions of parenting and occupational aspirations has also been studied in adolescents (Jodl, Michael, Malanchuk, Eccles, and Sameroff, 2001). Jodl et al. (2001) were interested in how parental values, beliefs, and behaviors affect their children's vision of themselves and thus their career development. They acknowledged the importance of the parent-child relationship as an indicator of parental identification; the strength of the bond between child and parent (i.e. secure versus insecure attachment) impacts the internalization of parental values and beliefs. Jodl et al. found that parents' values and beliefs directly predicted youths' values and beliefs. They also found that higher maternal perceptions of children's academic abilities were associated with higher academic self-concept in adolescents and that mothers' educational expectations and aspirations for their children were positively correlated with higher levels of educational aspirations among youth.

Echoing the findings of Jodl et al.(2001), a survey of high school juniors assessing youth perceptions of parental influence on their career development found that parental and youth values, aspirations, and plans are highly correlated (Otto, 2000). Mothers were found to be the primary source of influence on youths' career development as the participants reported talking most seriously with their mothers about what occupation they wanted to enter (81%). Over fifty percent of respondents said that their mothers were most aware of their career interests and abilities, followed by fathers and friends. Turner, Steward, and Lapan (2004) also examined the influence of parental support and family structure on adolescents' academic self-efficacy, particularly math self-efficacy. Their results showed that both mother's and father's support positively affected the adolescents' math self-efficacy, while adolescents from single-parent families reported significantly less math self-efficacy than those from two-parent intact families.

Vocational Interest in Young Adults

Research in the area of career development has often involved samples from college students in introductory psychology classes. Therefore, there is no dearth of information about career and vocational development at this level, even though one would expect some career-related differences between those enrolled in college and those not enrolled in college. The decision to enroll in college results from a different career development pathway, and perhaps different family influences, than the decision not to enroll in college. In either case, as individuals reach young adulthood, they are continually influenced by the same family variables that influenced them during their childhood and adolescence, albeit in different ways. Young, Friesen, and Borycki (1994) retrospectively examined parental influences through narratives of young adults and identified five ways in which this occurs. These five types of narratives were 1) progressive narrative with a dramatic turning point, 2) progressive narrative within a positive evaluation frame, 3) progressive narrative with negatively evaluated stages, 4) anticipated regressive narrative, and 5) the sad narrative. These five types refer to the variety of parental influences, both positive and negative, that impinge upon career development. Three of the five groups represent progressive narratives and this reflects the "need for individuals to construct their lives as success stories. This need is intensified by the socially constructed developmental tasks expected of older adolescents and young adults such as entering an occupation, finding a life partner and living independently of parents" (Young, Friesen, and Borycki, 1994, p. 188). During this stage of development, individuals progressing into young adulthood look back on the influences of their parents as either hindering them or encouraging them in their path to vocational identity. The third type, progressive narrative with negatively evaluated stages, was utilized by those who felt they had made progress in their career without being influenced one way or the other by their parents. The fourth type, anticipated regressive narrative, was characterized by a sense of inevitable failure in relation to the career expectations of their parents. The final group, the sad narrative, characterized individuals who have lost a sense of hope, control, and self-esteem partly because they lacked sufficient parental assistance. This study highlights the overwhelmingly influential nature of early parental assistance, or lack thereof, on career development even into young adulthood.

FAMILY VARIABLES

Family, Self-Efficacy and Career Development

Self-Efficacy

Self-efficacy can be defined as a person's belief in his or her abilities (Bandura, 1997). Further, self-efficacy can influence in behavior in a number of ways. First, those with strong self-efficacy beliefs are likely to have cognitions which encourage accepting and completing difficult tasks. Motivation also tends to be stronger in those with high levels of self-efficacy because they believe that they can successfully accomplish a task. Moreover, such individuals tend to be good planers and are able to anticipate problems and possible solutions. Those with high levels of self-efficacy also tend to have more positive and stable moods for several reasons. Those with high self-efficacy will tend to believe that they are better able to cope with stress, and they also tend to reduce the amount of environmental stressors. Further, such individuals are able to ignore negative thoughts and avoid ruminating behaviors. Finally, self-efficacy influences physical health for several reasons. As already noted, levels of stress will likely be lower in people with strong self-efficacy. Another reason for this relationship is that such people tend to monitor their health habits more than those with reduced self-efficacy.

Family, Career Self-efficacy and Career Interaction

The interaction of self-efficacy, family, and career choices can be traced back to childhood, however, the relationship between these variables is somewhat complex (Bandura, Barbaranelli, Vittorio-Caprara, and Pastorelli, 2001). For example, path analysis revealed a child's self-efficacy towards careers may be domain specific. One child may have a strong self-efficacy in towards science and technology, but a lower self-efficacy towards literacy and art. Unsurprisingly, domain strengths tend to be areas in which child have occupational preference. Further, these domain specific self-efficacies appear to be influenced by a child's overall academic self-efficacy. Variables, such as socioeconomic status and parent's academic aspirations influence children's career aspirations only by affect overall academic efficacy, aspirations, achievement.

Self-efficacy has also been implicated in influencing the engagement of women in nontraditional careers. For example, Nevill and Schlecker (1988) found that women with high self-efficacy were more likely to engage in nontraditional career related activities. One could argue that having high levels of self-efficacy gives women the confidence needed to explore career options that may socially be unacceptable. Further, research by Scott and Mallinckrodt (2005) found that female college students who had higher science self-efficacy were more likely to major in science than those with lower self-efficacy. Moreover, such women were less likely to have fathers who were controlling. However, not all studies have found a relationship between high levels of self-efficacy and nontraditional career orientation (Mathieu, Sowa, and Niles, 1993).

Family also appears to influence self-efficacy with regards to career decision making as noted in a study conducted by Nawaz and Gilani (2011). In their study they surveyed 550 adolescents and young adults attending a number of post-secondary schools in Pakistan. The participants completed measures on parental and peer attachment as well as a survey on career decision making self-efficacy. Researchers found that both stronger parental and peer attachment led to greater career decision self-efficacy ($r = .29$ and $.23$ respectfully). When dividing the sample based on gender the results were similar, with both males and females reporting that increased levels of career decision making self-efficacy were correlated with stronger parental and peer attachment. Further, regression analysis revealed that 9% of career decision self-efficacy could be accounted for by attachment with one's parents. Similarly, Germeijs and Verschueren (2009) sampled 281 12th grade students, and three different completion stages, and found that the perception of relationship security with either the mother or father increased career decision-making self-efficacy. Moreover, the relationship between career decision-making self-efficacy and parental security appeared to be stable across all three stages of 12th grade. Stringer and Kerpelman (2010) explored the influence of parental support on career choices on career decision self-efficacy by surveying 345 college students. Using structural equation modeling, researchers found that parental support led the greater career decision self-efficacy in students. Specifically, higher levels of emotional, verbal, and instrumental support coincided with higher levels of career problem solving, planning and goal selection. Furthermore, both increased levels of parental support and career decision making led to a better understanding of career identity.

However, the effect of self-efficacy and family may be more complicated in terms of their effects on career decision making. For example, Nota et al., (2007) surveyed 253 Italian youth about family support, career search self-efficacy, and career indecision. Italian students in a technical training high school indicated that they had lower family support than those in an arts or math and science preparation school. For males, but not females, those with more family support tended to have less career indecision. However, the most interesting finding is that self-efficacy mediated the relationship between family support and career indecision for males. For females, since no relationship existed between family support and career indecision self-efficacy could not severe as a mediator, but greater family support did led to greater self-efficacy and stronger self-efficacy reduced career indecision. This study replicated previous research which had also found a relationship between parental support and self-efficacy (Ryan, Solberg, and Brown, 1996).

Such findings also appear to apply to students from diverse ethnic backgrounds. Turner and Lapan (2002) surveyed 139 adolescents which comprised of a significant number of Asian Americans, Hispanics, African Americans, and foreign nationals. Their results revealed that the perception of parental support increased self-efficacy across all six of Holland's dimensions, (with the variance accounting for anywhere from 29% to 43%), but did not have an effect on vocational interest. Research has also been conducted solely on African American youth and the influence of parental support on career self-efficacy (Alliman-Brissett, Turner, and Skovholt, 2004). Researchers surveyed 162 African-American adolescents and found that for that instrumental assistance and emotional support predicted their self-efficacy in knowing one's self in various career and education situations, but not self-efficacy for career planning and discovery.

However, self-efficacy for career planning and exploration, as well as career decision-making efficacy, was predicted by parental career modeling. Parental career modeling includes such behaviors as parents taking their children to work or showing them how they do their job. For girls, parental modeling and emotional support promote self-efficacy in transitioning from school to work. Similarly, parental emotional support, but not parental modeling, predicted expectations of career choice outcomes and self-efficacy of knowing one's self. However, research has also found that ethnic differences do not influence the role of self-efficacy (Gushue and Whitson, 2006). Researchers did find that greater parental support did lead to greater career decision making self-efficacy, but that ethnicity was not a factor. Overall, it appears that self-efficacy is influenced by family regardless of one's ethnicity.

One researcher studied the family environment and its relationship with career decision-making self-efficacy (Whiston, 1996). The researcher hypothesized that high levels of family conflict would be related to increased trouble making career decisions. Two hundred and fourteen undergraduates completed surveys on family environment and career decision making.

The only support found for the original hypothesis was that high levels of family control and organization tended to have poor career decision-making self-efficacy for women. First, considering this study did not engage in experimental manipulation, there may be a third variable influencing both career decision making and self-efficacy. Another possibility is that high levels of organization and control in a family undermines a women's ability to develop her sense of ability.

There is some research supporting this possibility. In a study of 834 college students researchers explored the relationship between parental and peer control, parental and peer autonomy support, career decision-making self-efficacy and career indecision (Guay, Sencal, Gauthier, and Fernet, 2003). Factor analysis found that as both parental and peer autonomy support increased so did career decision making autonomy and self-efficacy. Also, greater parental and peer control led to decreased abilities in career decision making self-efficacy and autonomy. Greater control also led to increases in career indecision. The researchers also conducted SEM and found that paths of all of the previous relationships were supported with the exception of parental control on career decision-making self-efficacy and autonomy. Therefore, while parental control does appear to influence self-efficacy, it may not be a direct relationship.

Parenting Styles/Approaches and Career Outcomes

Parenting

During young childhood, parents tend to exert a stronger influence over developing interests than school or peers. Research suggests that the acquisition of knowledge about occupations occurs in childhood and early adolescence, when parents are the primary source of information for their children. There are many variables associated with parenting that can potentially contribute to vocational outcomes such as vocational interest. Bryant, Zvonkovic, and Reynolds (2006) attempted to organize these variables into three domains, one of which consists of the development of exploratory processes in relation to interest development. This developmental process occurs within the ongoing, dynamic and bi-directional context of family and parenting and is dependent upon many factors, including ease of communication and availability of parents.

Attachment theory (Bowlby, 1969) which emphasizes the role of parental responsiveness to a child's needs and the way this leads to exploration and the establishment of a secure parent-child relationship (Bryant et al., 2006) has been applied to the importance of parent child interactions in career decision making. Bowlby (1982) asserted that consistency in caregiver interactions provides children with a sense of security that affords them the comfort needed to explore the world around them. In time, individuals develop internal working models of attachment that provide an enduring experience of security as they mature and develop attachment relationships with significant others (Blustein et al., 1995). The connection between attachment and the development of vocational interests is maintained through the fostering of exploratory behavior in children. Children with a secure attachment to their mothers are more curious and more likely to engage in exploration of their environments, leading to the development of positive relationships with teachers and comfort with seeking help from others (Bryant et al., 2006). Exploration occurs throughout the life span and is a behavior that promotes learning and skills development as individuals begin to relate to the outside world. Likewise, the level of attachment between a child and caregiver/parent will affect the modeling of vocational interests and values. While initially established in early childhood, parent-child attachment exerts greater influence as individuals progress through the career development process.

Other parenting variables, such as autonomy granting, also contribute to a child's willingness for exploration. Diana Baumrind (1966) developed three distinct categories or styles of parenting: authoritarian, permissive, and authoritative. In her initial descriptions of authoritative parenting, Baumrind detailed the way authoritative parents value "autonomous self-will and disciplined conformity" (p. 891), while exerting control that does not confine the child with restrictions. A study by Steinberg, Elmen, and Mounts (1989) evaluated the relationship between aspects of authoritative parenting (acceptance, psychological autonomy, and behavioral control) and school achievement. Their findings implicated authoritative parenting in the facilitation of academic success, while also indicating that each element of this style acts independently. Authoritative parenting is also a predictor of children's self-esteem and success in school, as well as lower levels of stress in parents and children (Brand, Hatzinger, Beck, and Holsboer-Trachsler, 2009; Heaven and Ciarrochi, 2008; Steinberg, Lamborn, Dornbusch, and Darling, 1992).

Parental encouragement, a factor prominent in the authoritative style, has been associated with an intrinsic motivational style and higher academic performance in children. Ginsburg and Bronstein (1993) examined the three familial factors of surveillance of homework, reaction to grades, and general family style. They found that higher surveillance, negative control following reactions to grades, uninvolvement, and over or undercontrolling family styles were related to the development of an extrinsic motivational style and poorer academic performance. Meanwhile, parental encouragement and autonomy-supporting family styles were correlated with intrinsic motivation and higher academic performance in children. Steinberg et al. (1992) found the dimensions of parental involvement and educational encouragement that exist in authoritative parenting to be a positive influence on school performance and engagement. Thus, it follows that a style of parenting that fosters autonomy and intrinsic motivation would also lead children to develop interests earlier.

Parental Education and Parents Occupation

One's parent's education plays a role on our own career and educational expectations and aspirations. Research has found this to be the case across variables such as gender, age, ethnic groups, and socioeconomic status. Addington (2005) looked at this relationship by examining the role that maternal education plays on adolescents' college plans. This study found that mother's education is significantly related to the college aspirations of adolescents of both sexes. Interestingly, Addington (2005) found that as the level of maternal education increases, the odds that her children will plan to graduate from college also increases. For example, she found that if a child's mother is a college graduate, the odds increase by 5.09 that their children will plan to attend some sort of post-secondary education as compared to those mothers that do not have a high school education. Overall, they found this across all levels of maternal education; as mother's education increases, so do the odds that their children will aspire to higher education. Ojeda and Flores (2008) also looked at the influence of parental education on educational aspirations of Mexican American high school students. They found that parental education was a significant predictor of educational aspirations. Fisher and Padmawidjaja (1999) found that parents in their study encouraged their children to exceed their own education and occupation level; so in their study, having parents with a limited education did not decrease adolescents' expectations to attend college or to obtain a professional occupation.

Research has also been conducted examining the career aspirations of younger age groups of children. Trice and Knapp (1992) examined the career aspirations of 5th and 8th grade children and how they relate to their parent's occupations. In both grades and both genders, there was a greater match with the mother's occupations then with the father's. Similarity to the mother's occupation was somewhat higher among rural children than children from an urban environment. Interestingly, boys reported to aspire to their mother's occupation at a higher rate than their father's when their parents' career status was equal or when their mother had a higher career status. The authors suggested two possible reasons for children looking to their mother's career for their early career aspirations. The first explanation given is that women's jobs are becoming more interesting and diverse as compared to previous decades. The second reason is that children may know more about their mother's jobs than their fathers; in fact, the children surveyed were more likely to give accurate information about their mother's job. Smith (1989) also found differences when examining the influences parents have on educational expectations and aspirations. They found that maternal education positively influenced students' ideal educational aspirations, realistic educational expectations, and school grades. Paternal education only had an effect on realistic educational expectations. They suggest that the mother may have this stronger influence because mothers traditionally give the children more time and attention, therefore, they may be a more influential role model. Trice (1991a) gathered a sample of 422 11-year old children from a rural and an urban school in Virginia. The purpose of their study was to look at the stability of the children's career aspirations and how similar their aspirations were to the careers of their parents. They found, throughout their interviews with the children, that their career plans were relatively stable and that the plans were strongly related to the career of their parents' and other careers they had been exposed to in their communities. This was especially true of the rural children, which the authors suggest is perhaps reflecting the fact that the rural children are exposed to less variation in careers. Trice (1991b) found that when questioning adults (mean age 46.4) about their childhood and adolescent aspirations were and their current adult occupation, that 41% of the childhood aspirations matched the classification category of their father's occupation; when looking at adolescent aspirations, this match percentage went down to 23%. This pattern was found in both males and females. When looking at mothers' occupations, the match between childhood and adolescence aspirations was below the chance level. Interestingly, Trice also found that if in childhood, the career aspirations were similar to their father's, the individual was more likely to continue in that career category than if their childhood aspirations differed from their father's. Other research has looked at how children rate their parents' job satisfaction. Trice and Tillapaugh (1991) asked 3rd and 5th grade children to rate their parents' satisfaction with their job. They found that the children were able to predict their parents' satisfaction significantly and if the children thought their parents' were satisfied with their jobs, they were more likely to aspire to that occupation.

When examining the career aspirations and expectations, the question arises whether children's career aspirations predict the occupations that they choose in adulthood. Trice and McClellan (1993) examined this question by using a sample of 271 students from the Terman longitudinal study of gifted children gathered in 1926; the children in this sample ranged from age 6 to 17 years. Trice and McClellan examined the aspirations these children had during the Terman study and what their actual career was fifteen years later. They compared exact matches between career aspirations and occupation and aspirations and occupational theme. Occupational theme were based on Holland's six occupational themes, which include the categories: Realistic (trades), Investigative (scientific occupations), Artistic, Social (helping professions), Enterprising (person-oriented business professionals), or Conventional (data-oriented business professions) (Spokane and Cruza-Guet, 2005). It was found that matches based on occupational themes were much higher than exact matches between aspirations and occupation.

For example, for boys aged 6 to 9 years, the exact matches for career aspirations and their occupation 15 years later was 26% but that percentage increased to 54% in this age group when looking at matches based on occupational theme. This pattern was also seen in girls, for example, girls aged 10 to 13 years had a match percentage of 31% when examining their childhood career aspirations and their actual occupation. This percentage jumped to 69% when examining the matches based on occupational theme. In general, the researchers found higher match rates for adults who, as children, had aspirations based on the occupational themes of Realistic, Investigative, Social, and Artistic.

Parental Expectations for Family Members

Parental expectations are thought to have an important influence on career aspirations. Paa and McWhirter (2000) looked at various factors that influence the career expectations of high school students and found that girls ranked their mother's influence high as it related to their expectations; parents were found to be one of three top influences in their environment. When researching the post-secondary education plans of 10th and 12th graders and the influential people they felt had expectations of them, Mau, Hitchcock, and Calvert (1998) found that students perceived their mothers as having higher expectations than their fathers when it related to them attending college. Females reported higher levels of these parental expectations then males. Adragna (2009) also examined the influence of parental expectations on career. Adragna found that mothers had a significant influence on their sons' future career aspirations and that students surveyed were aspiring to a slightly higher level of prestige than their parents. Parents can also directly tell their children what their expectations are for them by suggesting careers that they should aspire to. Trice, McClellan, and Hughes (1992) examined 576 children in kindergarten, Grades 2, 4, and 6, and examined direct suggestions made to them by significant people in their lives about future careers. They found that suggestions made to these children about what job they should have when they grow up increased with age. For example, only 9% of kindergarten students but 24% of 6th graders reported that people in their lives had suggested possible occupations. Although there was an increase in suggestions made with age, the percentage of children that reported a suggested occupation as a career they aspire to decreased with age. For example, 83% of kindergarten students reported the suggested career as a possible career choice; that percentage decreased to 57% when questioning 6th graders.

The majority of suggestions were made by parents; followed by grandparents, siblings, and teachers. Also interesting is that half of the suggestions that were made by the children's parents' were for their own professions, although few of the children gave their parent's career as the occupation they would like.

Parental Support and Career Aspirations of Family Members

The amount of parental support in career aspirations among students of different ethnicities has also been shown to vary (Hill, Ramirez, and Dumka, 2003). Researchers interviewed 31 adolescents from a variety of ethnic backgrounds, including Caucasian, African American, Mexican American, and Mexican Immigrants. Those from a Mexican American or Mexican Immigrant background reported having either supportive or very supportive families. Comparatively, Caucasian and African American adolescents reported their families as unsupportive or very unsupportive. The lack of parental support had a pair of negative effects.

First, all of the adolescents who claimed their parents were either unsupportive or very unsupportive did not have clearly defined career goals. Moreover, adolescents who believed that there were social barriers, such as income, citizenship status, and English language skills, preventing them from achieving their goals more often reported not having parental support. The researchers suggested that parental support may buffer against the perception of social barriers.

Family Dynamics

Family Systems

The family systems approach to career development proposes that the degree to which individuals explore career interests is directly influenced by the quality of family interactions. Penick and Jepsen (1992) tested family systems propositions as applied to career development and found that family members' perceptions of family interactions explained more variance in vocational identity than achievement, gender, and socio-economic status. Using Moos' (1989) Family Environment Scale, Hargrove, et al., (2002) operationalized family functioning into the following three family dimensions: quality of family relationships, family-supported goal orientations, and degree of control and organization. Hargrove et al. found the family-supported goal of achievement orientation to account for a significant portion of the variance in vocational identity. They also found family supported goals of achievement, intellectual-cultural, and moral-religious emphasis orientations to be related to the degree of family conflict and expressiveness. Additional research (Hargrove et al., 2005) examined the interactions between family dynamics and vocational identity. The perceived quality of family relationships, defined as the degree to which family members are encouraged to express feelings and problems, played a small but significant role in predicting career planning attitudes of adolescents. Additionally, perceived quality of relationship factors in the family was related to career planning activities, lending support to the role of family in adolescents' degree of curiosity about and exploration of careers.

In an examination of how family culture affects career development, Bryant et al. (2006) proposed a model including parenting variables as well as financial, human, and social capital, among other variables. Parenting is viewed as occurring in a bidirectional manner, within a larger multilayered system, on an ongoing basis. Financial capital is described by Bryant et al. as wealth or income, whereas human capital consists of "skills and capabilities that parents can parlay into parental beliefs of self-efficacy to help their children master skills needed for future vocational success" (p. 152). Finally, social capital refers to the functions of obligations, expectations, and trustworthiness within social structures between two or more individuals. Parents develop social capital with their children which develops into mutually felt obligations, expectations, and trust. A major way that parents build social capital with their children is through engaging in shared parent-child activities. Such experiences during middle childhood are linked to occupational exploration during adolescence. Schmitt-Rodermund and Vondracek (1999) found parental behaviors, such as encouragement of these joint activities, to be an influence on the scope of childhood exploration of interests, leading to greater adolescent exploration, vocational exploration, and career planning during high school.

Birth Order and Family Structure

Adlerian vocational psychology posits that family variables such as birth order and family constellation affect career development and behavior. Parents usually place different demands on and have different expectations for older versus younger children. Savickas (1988) and Watkins (1984) reported that birth order significantly affects the type of interactional/environmental events that children experience which in turn influence their vocational behavior through differing personality styles, vocational interests, and values. Leong, Hartung, Goh, and Gaylor (2001) found that children exist in psychologically different family configurations based on perceived birth order, as well as sibling group size and spacing between siblings. They also found that psychological birth order influences patterns of vocational interest.

White, Campbell, Stewart, Davies, and Pilkington (1997) also examined the relationship between psychological birth order and career interests by administering the UNIACT Interest Inventory and the White-Campbell Psychological Birth Order Inventory (PBOI). They found that oldest child scores on the PBOI were significantly related to the social and business areas; thus the need to strive for perfection and please others is related to an interest in socially oriented careers requiring interpersonal abilities. Conversely, higher scores on the youngest child scales were negatively correlated with the science and technical dimensions of the Interest Inventory. Finally, White et al. found that higher scores on the oldest and only child scales appear to be related to interest in data-driven and conventional fields. They conclude that it is not the birth order itself that affects vocational interest, but, rather, the pattern of behaviors and attitudes that emerge from family experiences – namely, psychological birth order.

Apart from their differential treatment by parents, siblings also affect one another's career development by acting as role models and sources of relational influence and support. Schultheiss, Palma, Predragovich, and Glasscock (2002) examined the nature of sibling influence on career exploration and decision making. The following seven categories of influence existed between siblings: emotional support, social integration, esteem support, information support, positive role model, negative role model, and personality and ideology. Schultheiss et al.'s (2002) findings highlighted the role of social support as an important factor in career development. Their research also underscored the fact that many young adults learn about world of work from siblings who provide a source of information.

Parental Identification, Connectedness, and Separateness in the Family

Progression into adulthood is also marked by the assumption of adult roles often modeled after that of the individual's parents. Steele and Barling (1996) investigated the influence of maternal gender-role beliefs and role satisfaction on daughters' vocational interests. Female undergraduate students and their parents were surveyed to identify the students' career choices, gender-role ideologies, identification with parents, and perceptions of parents' gender-role ideologies and role satisfaction, as well as the parents' reported gender-role ideology and role satisfaction. They found that actual and perceived maternal attitudes influence the gender-role ideologies of daughters, which then influence the gender stereotyped nature of daughters' career choices. This coincides with social learning theory which states that people are more inclined to learn from models similar to themselves, i.e. daughters and their mothers. Also consistent with this theory was the additional finding that daughters' maternal identification is a moderator of the relationship between perceived maternal gender-role ideology and the daughters' own ideology. Therefore, the amount of identification between children and their parents is a strong predictor of the strength of parental influence.

A similar study by Li and Kerpelman (2007) conducted with female undergraduates examined the correlation between mother-daughter and father-daughter relationships and young women's certainty about their career aspirations. The authors approached this subject from the perspective of identity control theory which places the process of identity-shaping within the day-to-day interactions between adolescents and their parents. These interactions, and the feedback that individuals receive, either support or challenge their existing identity and in turn affect their future aspirations. Li and Kerpelman found that parent-daughter connectedness predicted the young women's anticipated distress and subsequent willingness to change to fit their parents' views when there was disagreement about career aspirations. The father's education level and a history of having career discussions with the father were positively related to the daughter's willingness to change to her father's view. Through the lens of identity control theory, these results indicate that daughters experience identity disruption when their parents view their career aspirations differently than they do. This disruption is predicted by feeling connected to one's parents and it is mediated by parent-child connectedness and willingness to change.

The concepts of connectedness and separateness can also be addressed from a family systems perspective to analyze their effects on occupational identity. Within family systems it is theorized that well differentiated families will be able to balance these two constructs by supporting a healthy exchange of feedback and promoting clear identity standards (Kerpelman, Pitman, and Lamke, 1997). Berríos-Allison (2005) analyzed family emotional environment and identity control processes to assess their influence on occupational identity status among college students. Occupational identity is categorized into four groups – diffusion, moratorium, foreclosure, and achievement – based on the level of exploration and commitment individuals experience with occupational choices within the process of ego identity development. Identity foreclosure as it relates to occupation means that the individual has made a commitment to a career (or college major) without engaging in exploration. Moratorium occurs when students are actively exploring majors or careers without having made a commitment. Diffusion indicates a lack of career exploration and a lack of commitment. The final category, occupational identity achievement, involves students committing to a career or major subsequent to the exploration process (Marcia, 1966).

Berríos-Allison (2005) was interested in how a family's tolerance for connectedness and separateness would affect individuals' scores for the four identity statuses. The study demonstrated a relationship between family tolerance for connectedness and students' achievement, in that supportive families encouraged occupational exploration and commitment. In contrast, intrusive families were more likely to lead individuals to have a status of moratorium. Families that were both controlling and supportive were associated with individuals in the foreclosure identity status. Berríos-Allison explains this by implying that these students "sense an emotional environment conducive to premature decision making," while being "dependent on their parents to make decisions" (p. 242). Finally, diffused students in this sample were found to be from families that were intrusive and controlling, a mixture that led to confusion and disengaged career decision making. The study results suggest that family dynamics are an essential component to understanding the occupational issues with which college students struggle.

Family Characteristics

Socioeconomic Status

Diemer and Hsien (2008) examined the role that sociopolitical development has on the aspiration-expectation discrepancy among lower socioeconomic status adolescents. They found that sociopolitical development was associated with lower SES adolescents having higher career expectations. Specific variables that were found to be associated with these higher expectations were helping others in the community and discussing current events with parents and guardians. In a study on the educational plans and career expectations of Mexican American females in high school, it was found that coming from a family with a higher socioeconomic status was predictive of the students perceiving that they had more support from their parents, higher levels of acculturation, fewer barriers, and stronger commitment from their family (McWhirter, Hackett, and Bandalos, 1998). When looking at the factor of SES, they also found that it was an indirect influence on educational plans and career expectations. Khallad (2000) found SES to be positively related to educational but not career aspirations when looking at Palestinian and U.S. youth. Kenkel and Gage (1983) examined the career aspirations of low income women.

The found low income girls: 1) were likely to aspire to careers that traditionally are considered feminine; 2) range of occupations was small; and, 3) there was some change in what careers they girls aspired to between grade school and high school. In contrast to what some other studies have found, Sellers, Satcher, and Comas (1999) found that children from different SES group did not differ in their choice of traditional or nontraditional occupations. Titus (2006) used national survey data to examine college completion in students coming from low socioeconomic backgrounds. He found that college students coming from low SES are less likely to complete a bachelor's degree and suggests that the value and norm differences in SES groups may contribute to the higher percentage of students from higher SES completing their degree.

Gender and Gender Role Stereotyping

Li and Kerpelmen (2007) examined parental influence the certainty that young women had about their careers aspirations. They found that the degree of closeness felt in the parent/child relationship impact this. Specifically, they found that if a young woman was close to her parents, she was more distressed if her parents did not agree with her career aspirations and would strive to make career decisions that were consistent with the views of her parents. Jacobs, Chin, and Bleeker (2006) studied the effect of parent's gender-typed occupational expectations on their children's occupational expectations longitudinally. Occupations were divided into male-typed, female-typed, and neutral. They found that parental expectations regarding gender-typed occupations when their adolescents were 15 years were related to the adolescent's own gender typed occupational expectations at age 17 years. With regards to parental and adolescent gender; they found that father's expectations were related to daughter's occupational expectations but not to son's. On the other hand, mother's occupational expectations were relevant to both genders' own expectations. This changed when the researchers examined the relationship of parents and young adult child's gender typed occupational expectations 11 years later. At this time, father's gender typed occupational expectations significantly predicted both daughters' and sons' job choices; however, mother's expectations were only predictive of daughter's job choice. Bona, Kelly, and Jung (2010) examined internal and external factors that influence career aspirations in college female students. They categorized these career aspirations into male-dominated, female-dominated, or neutral. The researchers found that women who were pursuing male-dominated careers had more interest and confidence in the areas of math and science. They also found that gender role attitudes did not differ between groups.

However, they did find that women who were pursuing more female-dominated careers were more likely to have parents who modeled traditional gender roles. Jacob et al. (2006) also looked at the job satisfaction of young adults depending on the gendered nature of their jobs. They found that overall, females had more job satisfaction than males. Females in gender-nontraditional jobs had more satisfaction than females in gender neutral jobs. Males had less satisfaction in gender nontraditional jobs than females; and males in gender traditional jobs had higher levels of satisfaction than those in nontraditional or gender neutral jobs. Maranta and Mansfield (1977) also looked at children's sex role stereotypes regarding careers. Specifically, they were interested in examining the impact of maternal occupation on this stereotyping. They found that mother's occupation did influence the career choices made by their children. For example, if a mother had a traditionally female occupation, the child was more likely to choose a similar career as compared to those who had nontraditional careers. Interestedly, although this pattern was seen in choosing careers, when examining aspirations, only 16% of the girls aspired to the careers of their mothers. This stereotyping of roles lessened as the children got older. Mendez and Crawford (2002) examined the career aspirations of adolescent girls and boys who were considered gifted. They found that the girls in their study perceived that they had a larger range of career options available to them. Related to this, the girls also were more flexible with regards to gender roles when aspiring to careers.

The boys in the study were more likely to aspire to careers that would require more education and were more prestigious. Interestedly, the researchers found that adolescent girls were more likely to express interest in careers that required more education, were more prestigious, and were traditionally male dominated if they perceived themselves as being more internally motivated toward achievement.

Traditionality

Social and cultural aspects of an individual's environment include the family in the broader social context of socioeconomic status and cultural identity, structural features of the family, and process-oriented features such as family dynamics and parenting variables (Schulenberg, Vondracek, and Crouter, 1984). Vocational interests often develop through interactions with significant others, and usually the most significant influence in a child's life is that of his or her parents.

The beliefs and attitudes of parents impact the subsequent beliefs and attitudes of their children. Of particular interest to career choice is the traditionality of beliefs and attitudes regarding occupations. Evidence suggests that the traditionality of the mother's occupation had a significant relationship to the traditionality of the child's interests (Barak, Feldman, and Noy, 1991). Further studies into the shaping ability of parental traditionality for children's occupational aspirations underscore the importance of the mother's traditionality (Fulcher, 2011). Mothers' gender-role flexibility and non-traditional attitudes were associated with children's occupational aspirations. Mothers with more traditional occupations and attitudes were shown to have children with more traditional aspirations and more efficacy in traditional domains. Thus, environmental factors play an important role in shaping the interests of children.

Parental Influence, Race, and Ethnicity

Parental influence appears to vary by race and ethnicity. In one study researchers interviewed 94 African American and 208 Caucasian high school students about the influence of parents on career decisions (Otto, 2000). Major differences arose in how parents influence each group of students. For example, 46% of African American students discuss occupational choices with their fathers, which is considerably less than the Caucasian students (68%). Caucasian students noted that father were second, only after mothers, in discussing career choices. Like Caucasians, African American students ranked mothers first, however, fathers were also ranked after school peers, adult peers, and adult relatives. Once differences between the influence of fathers is accounted for, the number of similarities between the two groups increases. For example, about half of both groups discussed trade school with their parents in the past year, and both African Americans (86%) and Caucasians students discussed with their parents career training other than a four-year university.

Research has also examined career expectations and aspirations among different ethnic and racial groups. Chang, Chen, Greenberger, Dooley, and Heckhausen (2006) examined life goals and educational and occupational disparities across ethnicities in high school seniors. They studied six ethnic groups: White; African, Mexican, Other Latino, Filipino, and East/Southeast Asian Americans. Their results found that educational and occupational goals were the highest priority across all ethnic groups; and that the average long term educational aspiration was to attend a 4-year college. They did find ethnic differences in the group when looking at expectations to finish college. When looking at expectation to complete college, Latino students had relatively lower long-term educational aspirations. Booth and Myers (2011) examined career aspirations between African American and Caucasian female college students. They found that African American women had higher career commitment than Caucasian women and were also more motivated to move up in the careers. When looking at types of careers, they found that African American women aspired to more traditional careers than Caucasian women. Khallad (2000) examined the career and educational aspirations of Palestinian and U.S. youth. He found that 71% of Palestinian youth and 76% of U.S. youth aspired to a bachelor's, master's, or doctoral degree. He also found that 84% of Palestinian youth but only 65% of U.S. youth aspired to high status careers such as a physician or engineer.

Cultural Influences

Appalachian

Some specific populations have been studied in-depth because of the strength of the impact of culture on career aspirations or decision making, such as the Appalachian culture. Appalachians are people who are born within the area of the Appalachian Mountains which include portions of 13 states (Tang and Russ, 2007). Historically, Appalachians come from low SES communities that are isolated from other one another. The result of such isolation has lead to an increased reliance on family and community. Due to an increased reliance on family, individuals from these cultures place greater weight on their advice when making education and career choices (Fisher, 1993). The importance of family has been explored in a number of areas, such as health behaviors (Denham, Meyer, and Toborg, 2004; Meyer, Toborg, Denham, and Mande, 2008) and adolescent peer choices (Templeton, Bush, Lash,

Robinson, and Gale, 2008). The influence of family is so great that career choices may be forsaken based on such guidance (Fisher, 1993). Moreover, there is often a tremendous deal of pressure on children to assist with financial support if one of the parents dies. Unfortunately, parental influence is not limited to directives: parental neglect may also lead to less interest in education attainment (Brown, Rehkopf, Copeland, Costello, and Worthman, 2009). Research has also found that strong levels of parental support increase self-efficacy in Appalachian students (Ali and Saunders, 2006). In fact, in determining the life choices of Appalachian youth, "family circumstances trump the influence of standard proxy indicators of social experience such as gender, race-ethnicity, or cultural group" (Brown et al., p. 238).

The importance that family plays in occupational decision making may be problematic for career counselors (Tang and Russ, 2007). Goals that focus on individual achievement and desire over that of the family may be reacted to in a hostile manner. Tang and Russ (2007) proposed the Career Intervention Model for People of Appalachian Culture (CIMPAC) which places an emphasis on cultural and contextual factors. Based on both ecological and social cognitive career theory, the CIMPAC makes a number of recommendations when providing career counseling for those from Appalachia. Developing a foundation of trust is a critical first step. Next, the counselor should appraise the social and economic barriers the individual faces. Only after accomplishing these steps should a counselor try to increase career self-efficacy in a client. Increasing career self-efficacy will help the client become more confident and assertive in exploring occupational opportunities. Attempts to increase self-efficacy are benefited by understanding the background and history of the client. Finally, the counselor should try to incorporate both family and social resources to aid the client.

Asian and Asian-American

Another group of particular interest is Asian-American children because of the two vastly different cultural influences experienced by these children. Okubo, Yeh, Lin, Fujita, and Shea (2007) researched Chinese youth in the United States and the effects of having two different cultural expectations on career decision making. They found that parents of these Chinese youth had high expectations. The youth reported the expectations included pursuing careers valued highly in the Chinese culture such as becoming a doctor, teacher, or engineer. The youth also reported experiencing a struggle between Chinese culture and the American culture with regards to their career dreams and the actual career they were pursuing. Other studies have found that English language fluency and career related support from parents predicted higher career and educational aspirations and plans to college when looking at Chinese immigrant youth (Ma and Yeh, 2010). Career related support included the parents teaching job related skills and giving verbal encouragement. Kim (2002) examined the relationship between parental involvement and expectations in Korean immigrant families. They noted that all the parents in the study had very high expectations regarding their children's educational achievement; these high expectations were more likely if the children came from lower income families. As previous research has stated, Kim (2002) also found that parents' education level was found to have a significant, positive effect on the educational achievement of their children. This study also looked at other factors in the family, and found that for this group of individuals, the factors of communication, homework checking, TV rules and going-out rules were also statistically significant for educational achievement. Leung, Ivey, and Suzuki (1994) examined the differences between Asian American and Caucasian students in career aspirations. When looking at the type of careers that these groups were interested in, they found that the Asian American students were more attracted to careers that were logical, analytical, and non-personal and less attracted to those careers that involved forceful communication and interpersonal influencing. The authors suggest that the prestige of the career is a factor that needs to be examined when attempting to explain the findings as Asian American students were more likely than the Caucasian students to consider occupations with higher prestige. Based on their results, the researchers also suggest that their findings show that Asian American men are more likely than Caucasian men to consider careers that are traditionally male occupations. In contrast, they suggest that Asian American females are more likely than Caucasian females to consider nontraditional female occupations.

Qualitative research conducted by Fouad et al. (2008) stressed the strong role that family plays in career choice for Asian-Americans. They conducted a semi-structured interview of 12 Asian-Americans, who worked in a wide range of fields such as accounting, chemistry, education, and business. The subjects also varied greatly in age, ranging from early twenties to 80. There was also a range of ethnic differences in this sample, with those of Chinese, Southeast Asian, and Japanese descent represented. Fouad et al. (2008) found that family, culture, external influence, career goals, role models, work values, and self identity were all important factors leading to career selection. However, of the seven, family was the only one listed by all 12 subjects. The domain of family was divided into a number of subcategories. Family expectations, which included expectations of success in both work and school, were found to be important to all of the participants. Economic obligations were also a strong motivator, with many of the subjects reporting that they were expected to help support their family. However, family obligations were not limited to monetary assistance but also included emotional support. The majority of the sample felt obligated to take care of aging family members. Similarly, family expectations have been found to be a critical factor for British South Asian women teachers, with many of them reporting pursing such a career because it was an acceptable choice for their family (Butt, MacKenzie, and Manning, 2010). However, gender appears to play a role as well since British South Asian men reported that their family preferred them to go into another field such as engineering rather than teaching.

Considering how important family can be to those of Asian descent, it is unsurprising to learn that family conflict can have a devastating effect on career decisions (Ma and Yeh, 2005). The researchers recruited one hundred and twenty-nine Chinese Americans ranging from 14 to 21, the majority of whom reported that Chinese was their first language. All of the participants were recruited from a neighborhood youth employment center. Among the measures the participants completed were the Career Decision Scale, which includes subscales on career certainty and indecision, the Asian American Family Conflicts Scale, and the Relational-Interdependent Self-Construal Scale (RISC). The RISC measures how a person's self-construal is intrinsically related to others. The results revealed that high levels of intergenerational conflict lead to greater career indecision. Moreover, Chinese youth whose definition of themselves was attached to being close to others were more likely to feel certain in occupational choices. However, other research indicated that, in Asian Americans, high levels of psychological distress lead to occupational indecision, which in turn leads to increased perceptions of family conflict (Constantine and Flores, 2006). Therefore, the relationship between career indecision may be bidirectional in Asian Americans. Further evidence of the importance of family can be seen in the choice to pursue a career in medicine (Amin, Tani, Eng, Samareskara, and Huak, 2009). Researchers surveyed 192 ethnic Chinese medical students in Singapore about their motivations to pursue a career in medicine. Family expectations were ranked third after finding a challenging job and finding a job that pays well. Further, over two-thirds (67.2%) of the sample would have preferred to have studied abroad, however nearly a third (28.1%) of this group cited "distance from home" as a reason they did not. Finally, research indicates that Asian-American and Chinese students prefer Investigative, a Holland subtype, occupations more than Caucasian students (Tang, 2002). However, when researchers asked what careers participants would choose if there were no limitations the differences between groups disappears. The discrepancy between realistic and idea career aspirations could exist for a number of reasons, however, researchers believe that one factor influencing Asian-American and Chinese students is parental pressure.

For those from a Chinese background the importance of family can be explained by a combination of religious and historical factors. First, Chinese culture is heavily influenced by Confucianism which promotes social order via hierarchical affiliation (Yue and Ng, 1999). Further, within Confucianism there is a strong emphasis placed on a patriarchal model of family. Males are often expected to help look after family members as they age. It is likely that Confucianism is an important reason why China, along with most other Asian countries, is a collectivistic culture. Further, this supports the notion that Confucianism ideas and collectivist traits are related to one another (Robertson and Hoffman, 2000). While the Cultural Revolution initially limited the use of private land, economic reforms in the 1970's allowed families to farm in land (Esherick, 2006). Such economic reforms led to further interdependence of families member since children become a source of labor, and therefore as a means of economic improvement.

Greek

Some research has also been conducted on Greek students and career decision making (Koumoundourou, Tsaousis, and Kounenou, 2011). Researchers had 289 Greek junior high school students complete surveys which measured career decision making, parental authority style, family cohesion, and self-evaluation.

The self-evaluation measure contained questions on self esteem, self-efficacy, locus of control, and neuroticism. Results indicated that male students whose parents had permissive or authoritarian parenting styles reported more difficulty in deciding on a career. Further, male students who reported greater family cohesion had fewer problems with career decision making. For female Greek students, only an authoritarian parenting style had a negative influence on career decision making, with self-evaluation mediating the relationship. Parental education and occupation appear to influence career aspirations in Greek youth (Gouvias and Vitsilakis-Soroniatis, 2005). Researchers surveyed Greek adolescents in 1995 and from 2000-2001 and found a number of results which reveal the strong influential nature of parental characteristics.

For example, in the 2000-2001 sample, the higher the level of education of the father, the higher the career aspiration of the student. Regression analysis revealed that when the father completed some form of higher education, the child was nearly twice as likely to desire a professional career ($\beta = .06$, $p = .001$). However, parental education did not impact the student confidence of success in their desired field. Similarly, students whose parents worked in well-regarded fields show a strong desire to follow a similar career path.

African American

Research has also explored the relationship between African American siblings and similarities in career income earnings (Conley and Glauber, 2007). First, African American siblings were similar to that of their Caucasian counterparts in terms of choosing careers of similar prestige. However, Caucasian siblings had more similar incomes than African American siblings. The differences in African American sibling income converge as they grow older and eventually resemble that of their Caucasian counterparts. The researchers argued that these differences occur for two reasons. One reason is that African Americans experience greater volatile life experiences in childhood. The other reason is African Americans often come from lower socioeconomic status backgrounds; therefore, they have less protection to prevent and cope with negative events that influence career choice.

CONCLUSION

Although this review of literature is not exhaustive, there are some tentative conclusions that can be made. Research shows that parent's occupation and education do affect children and adolescent's career aspirations and that there is some evidence that career aspirations in childhood can continue to influence future occupational choices. In general, parental expectations are influential when it comes to career aspirations and expectations, but the perceived expectations can differ based on the gender of the parent. The influence of parents' on career also seems to differ depending on the gender of the child their developmental level. Ethnicity appears to be an important factor when looking at career aspirations and expectations and is an area that career counselors need to be aware when working with different ethnic and racial groups. Socioeconomic status also appears to be a factor in college or educational aspirations but not as influential in career aspirations and expectations. The multitude of research demonstrating the influences of family of origin on career development and career decision making is impressive, but the examination of the influences of nontraditional families (e.g. same sex parents) on career decision making is sparse (e.g. Scott and Church, 2001). There has been research regarding lesbian and gay individuals seeking career counseling (e.g., Elliot, 1993; Hetherington and Orzek, 1989; Pope et al., 2004) but little to no research investigating the influence of same sex parents on career decision making. Also, with the rise of increasing technology and globalization of the economy, it will become more critical to assess career decision making in the evolving world of work. The Theory of Career Construction (Savickas, 2005) presents a model for understanding career development across the life-span and may provide a useful framework for understanding careers and lives in the new world economy. While family of origin may vary in its impact on final career choice as the job market changes, it will always play a vital role in the development of the individual and their interactions with society and workplace.

Career Counseling: The Counselor, the Individual, and the Family

Traditionally, the majority of career counseling has focused on the individual in the process of making a career choice or adjusting to work. Few approaches take the family of origin into account in the process of career counseling despite research that has demonstrated that the family can play an important role in the career development of individuals. For example, Whiston and Keller (2004) note that many individuals who seek career counseling are struggling with career decision making and research shows that one main caveat to this struggle is the influence of one's family. Even though family of origin is evidenced to mediate career decision making, it receives little attention in the counseling process (Chope, 2001). To address this caveat, counselors may want to discuss the roles that an individual's family has played in past decision making scenarios. This may provide valuable information to the career counselor for an individual's current hesitancy, such as how involved the family was in making these past decisions and whether this involvement was welcomed by the individual (Chope, 2001).

Additionally, Zingaro (1983) suggested that family therapy techniques would be useful in career counseling settings. For individuals who are having difficulty deciding on a career, he suggests that these individuals may be undifferentiated from their family, and as a result, they may experience anxiety at the prospect of being responsible for creating their career identity. Suggested therapeutic techniques to help the client differentiate from his or her family include educating the client about family systems theory, have the client create a family genogram to see his or her family dynamics, and help the client identify emotional reactions that are generated by family interactions to minimize future emotional reactions. While these techniques may be helpful to individuals whose career decision making difficulties stem from family dynamics, it is important to differentiate whether the problem stems from the inability to decide on a career or an inability to make decisions (Osipow, 1999).

Another aspect of the family that has not been incorporated into the counseling process is the impact of parenting style and attachment on career development. It would appear that providing a child or adolescent with a firm, structured environment in which they can express feelings and assume autonomy during development may be an optimal strategy for facilitating the child's later achievement of his or her career goals. Counselors working within schools and younger clients may want to also work with their parents to help the parents learn to strike such a balance in their interactions with their children and adolescents. For counselors working with older clients, the counselors should explore the previous interactions between their client and their parents to determine the impact of those interactions on development and to ascertain if accurate conclusions were drawn and the impact of these conclusions on current career development.

Without a proper understanding of the implications of parenting style and differentiation of self for one's career search, a counselor may direct interventions toward excessive career assessment or mistake the client for being under motivated, when in fact they are experiencing difficulties or problems in the parental relationship. This review points to the need for career counselors to conduct a thorough developmental history before and during the career intervention process, and perhaps to engage the client's parents in his or her course of therapy. Such inducement would assist the counselor and client in identifying areas for improvement in the parental relationship which may strengthen one's pursuit of his or her career goals.

Finally, the career counselors must examine the family characteristics of the client's family of origin and determine the impact that these factors may be having on their career development and career decision making. For example, what is the parental educational and status level and how that influences the development of the client and is impacting their current struggles. How has the family socioeconomic status and culture of the family impacted vocational interest development? Clearly, counselors need to examine all aspects of the family of origin and how those different variables have and are currently influencing the client. Due to the vast number of family factors that need to be examined and the individuals differences of each client, it would behoove counselors to take a more holistic approach to career counseling. Savickas et al., (2009) provide a useful paradigm to understanding career development in the current world economy that may be useful for many career counselors.

REFERENCES

Addington, L. A. (2005). Following in her footsteps: Revisiting the role of maternaleducation on adolescents' college plans. *Gender Issues*, 22(2), 31-44.

Adragna, D. (2009). Influences on career choice during adolescence. *Psi Chi Journal of Undergraduate Research*, 14(1), 3-7.

Ali, S. B., and Saunders, J. L. (2009). The career aspirations of rural Appalachian high school students. *Journal of Career Assessment*, 17, 172-188.

Alliman-Brissett, A. E., Turner, S. L., and Skovholt, T. M. (2004). Parent support and African American adolescents' career self-efficacy. *Professional School Counseling*, 7, 124-132.

Amin, Z., Tani, M., Eng, K. H., Samaresekara, D. D., and Huak, C. Y. (2009). Motivation, study habits, and expectations of medical students in Singapore. *Medical Teacher*, 31, 560-569.

Arbona, C. (2000). Annual review: Practice and research in career counseling and development. *Career Development Quarterly*, 49, 98-134.

Bandura, A. (1997). *Self*-efficacy: The exercise of control. New York: W. H. Freeman.

Bandura, A., Barbaranelli, C., Caprara, V. G., and Pastorelli, C. (2001). Self-efficacy beliefs as shapers of children's aspirations and career trajectories. *Child Development*, 72, 187-206.

Barak, A., Feldman, S., and Noy, A. (1991). Traditionality of children's interests as related to their parents' gender stereotypes and traditionality of occupations. *Sex Roles*, 24(7/8), 511-524.

Barak, A., and Friedkos, R. (1982). The mediating effects of career indecision subtypes on career-counseling effectiveness. *Journal of Vocational Behavior*, 20, 120-128.

Baumrind, D. (1966). Effects of authoritative parental control on child behavior. *Child Development*, 37(4), 887-908.

Berríos-Allison, A. C. (2005). Family influences on college students' occupational identity. *Journal of Career Assessment*, 13(2), 233-247.

Betsworth, D. G., Bouchard, T. J. Jr., Cooper, C. R., Grotevant, H. D., Hansen, J. C., Scarr, S., and Weinberg, R. A. (1994). Genetic and environmental influences on vocational interests assessed using adoptive and biological families and twins reared apart and together. *Journal of Vocational Behavior*, 44, 263-278.

Blustein, D. L. (1994). "Who am I?": The role of self and identity in career development. In M. Savickas and R. Lent (Eds.). Convergence in career development theories: Implications for science and practice (pp. 139-154). Palo Alto, CA: CPP Books.

Blustein, D. L., Prezioso, M. S., and Schultheiss, D. P. (1995). Attachment theory and career development: Current status and future directions. *The Counseling Psychologist*, 23, 416-432.

Blustein, D. L., Walbridge, M. M., Friedlander, M. L., and Palladino, D. E. (1991). Contributions of psychological separation and parental attachment to the career development process. *Journal of Counseling Psychology*, 38(1), 39-50.

Bona, L., Kelly, A., and Jung, M. (2010). Exploring factors contributing to women's nontraditional career aspirations. *Psi Chi Journal of Undergraduate Research*, 15(3), 123-129.

Booth, C. S., and Myers, J. E., (2011). Differences in career and life planning between African American and Caucasian undergraduate women. *Journal of Multicultural Counseling and Development*, 39, 14-23.

Bowlby, J. (1969). Attachment and Loss: Vol. 1. Attachment. New York: Basic Books.

Bowlby, J. (1982). Attachment and loss: Retrospect and prospect. *American Journal of Orthopsychiatry*, 52(4), 664-678.

Brand, S., Hatzinger, M., Beck, J., and Holsboer-Trachsler, E. (2009). Perceived parenting styles, personality traits and sleep patterns in adolescents. *Journal of Adolescence*, 32, 1189-1207.

Bratcher, W. E. (1982). The influence of the family on career selection: A family systems perspective. *The Personnel and Guidance Journal*, 61(2), 87-91.

Brown, R. A., Rehkopf, D. H., Copeland, W. E., Costello, J. E., and Worthman, C. M. (2009). Lifecourse priorities among Appalachian emerging adults: Revisiting Wallace's organization of diversity. *Ethos*, 37, 225-242.

Bryant, K. B., Zvonkovic, A. M., and Reynolds, P. (2006). Parenting in relation to child and adolescent vocational development. *Journal of Vocational Behavior*, 69, 149-175.

Butt, G., Mackenzie, L., and Manning, R. (2010). Influences on British South Asian women's choice of teaching as a career: "You're either a career person or a family person; teaching kind of fits in the middle". *Educational Review*, 62, 69-83.

Carr, A. (2000). Family therapy: Concepts, process and practice. New York: Wiley.

Chang, E. S., Chen, C., Greenberger, E., Dooley, D., and Heckhausen, J. (2006). What do they want in life?: The life goals of a multi-ethnic, multi-generational sample of high school seniors. *Journal of Youth and Adolescence*, 35(3), 321-332.

Chope, R. C. (2001). Influence of the family in career decision making: Identity development, career path, and life planning. *Career Planning and Adult Development*, 17, 54-64.

Conley, D., and Glauber, R. (2007). Family background, race, and labor market inequality. *Annals of the American Academy of Political and Social Science*, 609, 134-152.

Constantine, M. G., and Flores, L. Y. (2006). Psychological distress, perceived family conflict, and career development issues in college students of color. *Journal of Career Assessment*, 14, 354-369.

Coogan, P. A. and Chen, C. P. (2007). Career development and counseling for women: Connecting theories to practice. *Counselling Psychology Quarterly*, 20(2), 191-204.

Crites, J. O. (1962). Parental identification in relation to vocational interest development. *Journal of Educational Psychology*, 53, 262-270.

Denham, S. A., Meyer, M. G., and Toborg, M. A. (2004). Tobacco cessation in adolescent females in Appalachian communities. *Family and Community Health: The Journal of Health Promotion and Maintenance*, 27, 170-181.

Diemer, M. A. and Hsieh, C. (2008). Sociopolitical development and vocational expectations among lower socioeconomic status adolescents of color. *The Career Development Quarterly*, 56, 257-267.

Dodge, T. (2001). An investigation of the relationship between family of origin and selected career development outcomes (Doctoral dissertation). Louisiana Tech University, Ruston, LA.

Eigen, C. A., Hartman, B. W., and Hartman, P. T. (1987). Relations between family interaction patterns and career indecision. *Psychological Reports*, 60, 87-94.

Elliot, J. E. (1993). Career development with lesbian and gay clients. *The Career Development Quarterly*, 41(3), 210-226.

Erikson, E. H. (1968). Identity: Youth and crisis. New York: Norton.

Esherick, J. (2006). The Chinese Cultural Revolution as history. Stanford, CA: Stanford University Press.

Feldman, D. C. (2003). The antecedents and consequences of early career indecision among young adults. *Human Resource Management Review*, 13, 499-531.

Fisher, S. L. (Ed). (1993). Fighting back in Appalachia: Traditions of resistance and change. Philadelphia: Temple UP.

Fisher, T. A. and Padmawidjaja, I. (1999). Parental influences on career development perceived by African American and Mexican American college students. *Journal of Multicultural Counseling and Development*, 27(3), 136-154.

Fouad, N. A., Kantamneni, N., Smothers, M. K., Chen, Y., Fitzpatrick, M., and Terry, S. (2008). Asian American career development: A qualitative analysis. *Journal of Vocational Behavior*, 72, 43-59.

Fulcher, M. (2011). Individual differences in children's occupational aspirations as a function of parental traditionality. *Sex Roles*, 64, 117-131.

Fuqua, D. R., and Hartman, B. W. (1983). Differential diagnosis and treatment of career indecision. *Personnel and Guidance Journal*, 62, 27-29.

Gati, I., Landman, S., Davidovitch, S., Asulin-Perez, L., and Gadassi, R. (2010). From career decision-making styles to career decision-making profiles: A multidimensional approach. *Journal of Vocational Behavior*, 76(2), 277- 291.

Germeijs, V., and Vershueren, K. (2009). Adolescents' career decision-making process: Related to quality of attachment to parents? *Journal of Research on Adolescence*, 19, 459-483.

Ginsburg, G. S., and Bronstein, P. (1993). Family factors related to children's intrinsic/ extrinsic motivational orientation and academic performance. *Child Development*, 64, 1461-1474.

Gottfredson, L. S. (1981). Circumscription and compromise: A developmental theory of occupational aspirations. *Journal of Counseling Psychology Monograph*, 28(6), 545-579.

Gouvias, D., and Vitslakis-Soroniatis, C (2005). Student employment and parental influences on educational and occupational aspirations of Greek adolescents. *Journal of Education and Work*, 18, 421-449.

Grotevant, H. D. (1983). The contribution of the family to the facilitation of identity Formation in early adolescence. *Journal of Early Adolescence*, 3, 225-237.

Guay, F., Senecal, C., Gauthier, L., and Fernet, C. (2003). Predicting career indecision: A self-determination theory perspective. *Journal of Counseling Psychology*, 50, 165-177.

Gushue, G. V., and Whitson, M. L. (2006). The relationship among support, ethnic identity, career decision self-efficacy, and outcome expectations in African-American high School students: Applying social cognitive career theory. *Journal of Career Development*, 33, 112-124.

Hall, D. T. (1994). Psychological success and the boundaryless career. *Journal of Organizational Behavior*, 15, 365-380.

Hargrove, B., Creagh, M., and Burgess, B. (2002). Family interaction patterns as predictors of vocational identity and career decision-making self-efficacy. *Journal of Vocational Behavior*, 61, 185-201.

Hargrove, B. K., Inman, A. G., and Crane, R. L. (2005). Family interaction patterns, career planning attitudes, and vocational identity of high school adolescents. *Journal of Career Development*, 31(4), 263-278.

Harren, V. A. (1979). A model of career decision making for college students. *Journal of Vocational Behavior*, 14(2), 119-133.

Hartung, P., Lewis, D., May, K., and Niles, S. (2002). Family interaction patterns and college student career development. *Journal of Career Assessment*, 10, 78-90.

Hartung, P. J., Porfeli, E. J., and Vondracek, F. W. (2005). Child vocational development: A review and reconsideration. *Journal of Vocational Behavior*, 66, 385-419.

Heaven, P., and Ciarrochi, J. (2008). Parental styles, gender and the development of hope and self-esteem. *European Journal of Personality*, 22, 707-724.

Herr, E. L., and Lear, P. B. (1984). The family as an influence on career development. *Family Therapy Collections*, 10, 1-15.

Hetherington, C. and Orzek, A. (1989). Career counseling and life planning with lesbian women. *Journal of Counseling and Development*, 68(1), 52-57.

Hill, N. E., Ramirez, C., and Dumka, L. E. (2003). Early adolescents' career aspirations: A qualitative study of perceived barriers and family support among low-income ethnically diverse adolescents. *Journal of Family Issues*, 24, 934-959.

Holland, J. L. (1959). A theory of occupational choice. *Journal of Counseling Psychology*, 6, 35-45.

Holland, J. L. (1980). My vocational situation: An experimental diagnostic form. Palo Alto, CA: Consulting Psychologist Press.

Holland, J. L. (1985). The psychology of vocational choice: A theory of personality types and model environments. Oxford, England: Blaisdell.

Holland, J. L., Gottfredson, D. C., and Power, P. G. (1980). Some diagnostic scales for research in decision making and personality. *Journal of Personality and Social Psychology*, 39, 1191-1200.

Jacobs, J. E., Chhin, C. S., and Bleeker, M. M. (2006). Enduring links: Parents' expectations And their young adult children's gender-typed occupational choices. *Educational Research and Evaluation*, 12(4), 395-407.

Jepsen, D. and Dilley, J. (1974). Vocational decision-making models: A review and comparative analysis. *Review of Educational Research*, 44(3), 331-349.

Jodl, K. M., Michael, A., Malanchuk, O., Eccles, J. S., and Sameroff, A. (2001). Parents' roles in shaping early adolescents' occupational aspirations. *Child Development*, 72(4), 1247-1265.

Johnson, P., Buboltz, W., and Nichols, C. (1999). Parental divorce, family functioning, and vocational identity of college students. *Journal of Career Development*, 26, 137-146.

Jowdy, D. (1994). The influence of family structure, separation from parents, and ego identity formation on career identity development and career exploration (Doctoral dissertation). Virginia Commonwealth University, Richmond, VA.

Kelly, K. R., and Pulver, C. A. (2003). Refining measurement of career indecision types: A validity study. *Journal of Counseling and Development*, 81, 445-454.

Kenkel, W. F. and Gage, B. A. (1983). The restricted and gender-typed occupational aspirations of young women: Can they be modified. *Family Relations*, 32, 129-138.

Kerpelman, J. L., Pitman, J. F., and Lamke, L. K. (1997). Toward a microprocess perspective on adolescent identity development: An identity control theory approach. *Journal of Adolescent Research*, 12, 325-346.

Khallad, Y. (2000). Education and career aspirations of Palestinian and U.S. youth. *The Journal of Social Psychology*, 140(6), 789-791.

Kim, E. (2002). The relationship between parental involvement and children's educational achievement in the Korean immigrant family. *Journal of Comparative Family Studies*, 33(4), 529-540.

Kinnier, R. T., Brigman, L., and Noble, F. C. (1990). Career indecision and family enmeshment. *Journal of Counseling and Development*, 68, 309-312.

Koumoundourou, G., Tsaousis, I., and Koenenou, K. (2011). Parental influences on Greek adolescents' career decision-making difficulties: The mediating role of core self-evaluations. *Journal of Career Assessment*, 19, 165-182.

Krumboltz, J. D. (1979). A social leaning theory of career decision making. In A. M. Mitchell, G. B. Jones, and J. D. Krumboltz (Eds.). Social learning and career decision making (pp. 19-49). Rhode Island. Carroll Press.

Kush, K., and Cochran, L. (1993). Enhancing a sense of agency through career planning. *Journal of Counseling Psychology*, 40, 434-439.

Larson, J. H., and Wilson, S. M. (1998). Family of origin influences on young adult career Decision problems: A test of bowenian theory. *The American Journal of Family Therapy*, 26(1), 39-53.

Lease, S. H., and Dahlbeck, D. T. (1999). Parental influences, career decision-making attributions, and self-efficacy: Differences for men and women? *Journal of Career Development*, 36(2), 95-113.

Lent, R. W., Brown, S. D., and Hackett, G. (1994). Toward a unifying social cognitive theory of career and academic interest, choice, and performance. *Journal of Vocational Behavior*, 45, 79-122.

Lent, R. W., Brown, S. D., and Hackett, G. (1996). Career development from a social cognitive perspective. In D. Brown and L. Brooks (Eds.), Career choice and development (3rd ed.). San Francisco: Jossey-Bass.

Leong, F. T. L., Hartung, P. J., Goh, D., and Gaylor, M. (2001). Appraising birth order in career assessment: Linkages to Holland's and Super's models. *Journal of Career Assessment*, 9(1), 25-39.

Leung, S. A., Ivey, D., and Suzuki, L. (1994). Factors affecting the career aspirations of Asian Americans. *Journal of Counseling and Development*, 72, 165-178.

Li, C., and Kerpelman, J. (2007). Parental influences on young women's certainty about their career aspirations. *Sex Roles*, 56, 105-115.

Lopez, F. G. (1989). Current family dynamics, trait anxiety, and academic adjustment: Test of a family based model of vocational identity. *Journal of Vocational Behavior*, 35, 76-87.

Lopez, F. G., and Andrews, S. (1987). Career indecision: A family systems perspective. *Journal of Counseling and Development*, 65, 304-307.

Lykken, D. T., Bouchard, T. J., McGue, M., and Tellegen, A. (1993). Heritability of interests: A twin study. *Journal of Applied Psychology*, 78, 649-661.

Ma, P. W., and Yeh, C. J. (2005). Factors influencing the career decision status of Chinese American youth. *The Career Development Quarterly*, 53, 337-347.

Ma, P. W. and Yeh, C. J. (2010). Individual and familial factors influencing the educational and career plans of Chinese immigrant youth. *The Career Development Quarterly*, 58, 230-245.

Maranta, S. A, and Mansfield, A. F. (1977). Maternal employment and the development of sex-role stereotyping in five- to eleven-year-old girls. *Child Development*, 48, 668-673.

Marcia, J. (1966). Development and validation of the occupational identity scale. *Journal of Personality and Social Psychology*, 3, 551-558.

Marcia, J. (1988). Ego identity, cognitive/moral development and individuation. In D. K. Lapsley and F. Clark (Eds.), *Self, ego, and identity* (pp. 211-225). New York: Springer.

Mathieu, P., Sowa, C., and Niles, S. (1993). Differences in career self-efficacy among women. *Journal of Career Development*, 19, 187-196.

Mau, W., Hitchcock, R., Calvert, C. (1998). High school students' career plans: The influence of others' expectations. *Professional School Counseling*, 2(2), 161-167.

McWhirter, E. H., Hackett, G., Bandalos, D. L. (1998). A causal model of the educational plans and career expectations of Mexican American high school girls. *Journal of Counseling Psychology*, 45(2), 166-181.

Mendez, L. M. R., and Crawford, K. M. (2002). Gender-role stereotyping and career aspirations: A   comparison of gifted early adolescent boys and girls. *The Journal of Secondary Gifted Education*, 13(3), 96-107.

Meyer, M. G., Toborg, M. A., Denham, S. A., and Mande, M. J. (2008). Cultural perspectives concerning adolescent use of tobacco and alcohol in the Appalachian mountain region. *The Journal of Rural Health*, 24, 67-74.

Moloney, D. P, Bouchard, T. J. Jr., and Segal, N. L. (1991). A genetic and environmental analysis of the vocational interests of monozygotic and dizygotic twins reared apart. *Journal of Vocational Behavior*, 39, 76-109.

Moos, R. (1989). Family environment scale Form R. Palo Alto, CA: Consulting Psychologists Press.

National Center for Education Statistics (1999, June). Report No. 155: Life after college. Washington, DC: U.S. Department of Education.

Nawaz, S., and Gilani, N. (2011). Relationship of parental and peer attachment bonds with career decision-making self-efficacy among adolescents and post-adolescents. *Journal of Behavioral Science*, 21, 33-48.

Nevill, D. D., and Schlecker, D. (1988). The relation of self- efficacy and assertiveness to willingness to engage in traditional/nontraditional career activities. *Psychology of Women Quarterly*, 12, 91-98.

Nota, L., Ferrari, L., Solberg, V. S. H., and Soresi, S. (2007). Career search self-efficacy, family support, and career indecision with Italian youth. *Journal of Career Assessment*, 15, 181-193.

Ochs, L. A., and Roessler, R. T. (2004). Predictors of career exploration intentions: A social cognitive career theory perspective. *Rehabilitation Counseling Bulletin*, 47(4), 224-233.

Ojeda, L., and Flores, L. Y. (2008). The influence of gender, generation level, parents' education level, and perceived barriers on the educational aspirations of Mexican American high school students. *The Career Development Quartely*, 57, 84-95.

Okubo, Y., Yeh, C. J., Lin, P., Fujita, K., and Shea. J. M. (2007). The career decision-making process of Chinese American youth. *Journal of Counseling and Development*, 85, 440-449.

Olson, D. H., Sprenkle, D. H., and Russell, C. R. (1979). Circumplex model of marital and family systems: I. Cohesion and adaptability dimensions, family types, and clinical applications. *Family Process*, *18*, 3-28.

Osipow, S. H. (1999). Assessing career indecision. *Journal of Vocational Behavior*, 55, 147–154.

Otto, L. B. (2000). Youth perspectives on parental career influence. *Journal of Career Development*, 27(2), 111-118.

Paa, H. K., and McWhirter, E. H. (2000). Perceived influences on high school students' current career expectations. *The Career Development Quarterly*, 49, 29-49.

Palmer, S., and Cochran, L. (1988). Parents as agents of career development. *Journal of Counseling Psychology*, 35, 71-76.

Penick, N. I., and Jepsen, D. A. (1992). Family functioning and adolescent career development. *Career Development Quarterly*, 40, 208-222.

Peterson, G. W., Sampson, J. P., Jr., Reardon, R. C., and Lenz, J. G. (1996). A cognitive information processing approach to career problem solving and decision making. In D. Brown, L. Brooks, and Associates (Eds.), Career Choice and Development (3rd ed., pp. 423 475). San Francisco, CA. Jossey – Bass Publishers.

Peterson, G. W., Stivers, M. E., and Peters, D. F. (1986). Family versus nonfamily significant others for the career decisions of low-income youth. *Family Relations*, 35, 417-424.

Pope, M., Barret, B., Szymanski, D. M., Chung, Y. B., Singaravelu, H., McLean, R., and Sanabria, S. (2004). Culturally appropriate career counseling with gay and lesbian clients. *The Career Development Quarterly*, 53(2), 158-177.

Puffer, K. (1998). A study of collegians' family activities, roles and interpersonal relations and their vocational identity, career choice commitment and decision making: An application of the developmental contextual framework (Doctoral dissertation). Purdue University, West Lafayette, IN.

Robertson, C. J. and Hoffman, J. J. (2000). How different are we? An investigation of Confucian values in the United States. *Journal of Managerial Issues*, 12, 34-47.

Roe, A. (1957). Early determinants of vocational choice. *Journal of Counseling Psychology*, 4(3), 212-217.

Roe, A. and Lunneborg, P. W. (1990). Personality and development choice. In D. Brown, L. Brooks, and Associates (Eds.), Career Choice and Development (2nd ed., pp. 68-101). San Francisco, CA: Jossey – Bass Publishers.

Rowjewski, J. W. (2005). Occupational aspirations: Constructs, meaning, and application. In S. D. Brown and R. W. Lent (Eds.), Career Development and Counseling (pp. 131-154). New Jersey: Wiley.

Ryan, N. E., Solberg, V. S., and Brown, S. D. (1996). Family dysfunction, parental attachment, and career search self-efficacy among community college students. *Journal of Counseling Psychology*, 43, 84-89.

Salomone, P. R. (1982). Difficult cases in career counseling: II – The indecisive client. *Personnel and Guidance Journal*, 60, 496-500.

Savickas, M. L. (1988). An Adlerian view of the Publican's pilgrimage. *Career Development Quarterly*, 36, 211-217.

Savickas, M. L. (2005). The theory and practice of career construction. In S. D. Brown and R. W. Lent (Eds.), Career development and counseling: Putting theory and reasearch to work (pp. 42-70). Hoboken, NJ: Wiley.

Savickas, M. L., Nota, L., and Rossier, J., Dauwalder, J., Duarte, M., Guicharad, J.,... Van Vianen, A. (2009). Life Design: A paradigm for career construction in the 21st century. *Journal of Vocational Behavior*, 75, 239-250.

Schmitt-Rodermund, E., and Vondracek, F. W. (1999). Breadth of interests, exploration, and identity development in adolescence. *Journal of Vocational Behavior*, 55, 298-317.

Schulenberg, J., Vondracek, F., and Crouter, A. C. (1984). The influence of the family on vocational development. *Journal of Marriage and the Family*, 46, 129-143.

Schultheiss, D. E. P., Palma, T. V., Predragovich, K. S., and Glasscock, J. M. J. (2002). Relational influences on career paths: Siblings in context. *Journal of Counseling Psychology*, 49(3), 302-310.

Scott, D. J. and Church, A.T. (2001). Separation/attachment theory and career decidedness and commitment: Effects of parental divorce. *Journal of Vocational Behavior*, 58(3), 328-347.

Scott, A. B., and Mallinckrodt, B. (2005). Parental emotional support, science self-efficacy, and choice of science major in undergraduate women. *The Career Development Quarterly*, 53, 263-273.

Sellers, N., Satcher, J., and Comas, R. (1999). Children's occupational aspirations and comparisons by gender, gender role identity, and socioeconomic status. *Professional School Counseling*, 2(4), 314-318.

Smith, T. E. (1989). Mother-father differences in parental influence on school grades and educational goals. *Sociological Inquiry*, 59(1), 88-98.

Spokane, A. R. and Cruza-Guet, M. C. (2005). Holland's theory of vocational personalities in work environment. In S. D. Brown and R. W. Lent (Eds.), Career Development and Counseling (24-41). New Jersey: Wiley.

Steele, J., and Barling, J. (1996). Influence of maternal gender-role beliefs and role satisfaction on daughters' vocational interests. *Sex Roles*, 34 (9/10), 637-648.

Steinberg, L., Elmen, J. D., and Mounts, N. S. (1989). Authoritative parenting, psychosocial maturity, and academic success among adolescents. *Child Development*, 60, 1424-1436.

Steinberg, L., Lamborn, S. D., Dornbusch, S. M., and Darling, N. (1992). Impact of parenting practices on adolescent achievement: Authoritative parenting, school involvement, and encouragement to succeed. *Child Development*, 63, 1266-1281.

Stringer, K. J., and Kerpelman, J. L. (2010). Career identity development in college students: Decision making, parental support, and work experience. *Identity: An International Journal of Theory and Research*, 13, 181-200.

Super, D. (1957). *The psychology of careers*. New York: Harper and Row.

Super, D. (1980). A life-span, life-space approach to career development. *Journal of Vocational Behavior*, 16, 282-298.

Tang, M. (2002). A comparison of Asian American, Caucasian American, and Chinese college students: An initial report. *Journal of Multicultural Counseling and Development*, *30*, 124-134.

Tang, M., and Russ, K. (2007). Understanding and facilitating career development of people of Appalachian culture: An integrated approach. *The Career Development Quarterly*, 56, 34-36.

Templeton, G. B., Bush, K. R., Lash, S. B., Robinson, V., and Gale, J. (2008). Adolescent socialization in rural Appalachia: The perspectives of teens, parents, and significant adults. *Marriage and Family Review*, *44*, 52-80.

Titus, M. A. (2006). Understanding college degree completion of students with low socioeconomic status: The influence of the institutional financial context. *Research in Higher Educatioon*, 47(4), 371-398.

Trice, A. D. (1991a). Stability of children's career aspirations. *The Journal of Genetic Psychology: Research and Theory on Human Development*, 152(1), 137-139.

Trice, A. D. (1991b). A retrospective study of career development: I. relationship among first aspirations, parental occupations, and current occupations. *Psychological Reports*, 86, 287-290.

Trice, A. D. and Knapp, L. (1992). Relationship of children's career aspirations to parents' occupations. *The Journal of Genetic Psychology*, 153(3), 355-357.

Trice, A. D., and McClellan, N. (1993). Do children's career aspirations predict adult occupations? An answer from a secondary analysis of a longitudinal study. *Psychological Reports*, 72, 368-370.

Trice, A. D., McClellan, N., and Hughes, M. A. (1992). Origins of children's career aspirations: II. Direct suggestions as a method of transmitting occupational preferences. *Psychological Reports*, 71, 253-254.

Trice, A. D., and Tillapaugh, P. (1991). Children's estimates of their parents' job satisfaction. *Psychological Reports*, 69, 63-66.

Turner, S., and Lapan, R. T. (2002). Career self-efficacy and perceptions of parent support in adolescent career development. *The Career Development Quarterly*, *51*, 44-55.

Turner, S. L., Steward, J. C., and Lapan, R. T. (2004). Family factors associated with sixth-grade adolescents' math and science career interests. *The Career Development Quarterly*, 53, 41-52.

Van den Daele, L. (1968). A developmental study of the ego-ideal. *Genetic Psychology Monographs*, *78*, 191-256.

Villarreal, A. (2007). Career development in a relational context: An examination of family of origins dynamics, relational health, ethnic identity and career development in diverse college women (Doctoral dissertation). Texas Woman's University, Denton, TX.

Vondracek, F. W., Lerner, R. M., and Schulenberg, J. E. (1983). The concept of development in vocational theory and intervention. *Journal of Vocational Behavior*, 23, 179-202.

Vondracek, F. W., Lerner, R. M., and Schulenberg, J. E. (1986). Career development: A life-span approach. Hillsdale, New Jersey: Lawerence Erlbaum.

Watkins, C. E., Jr. (1984). The individual psychology of Alfred Adler: Toward an Adlerian vocational theory. *Journal of Vocational Behavior*, 24, 28-47.

Whiston, S. C. (1996). The relationship among family interaction patterns and career indecision and career decision-making self-efficacy. *Journal of Career Development*, 23(2), 137-149.

Whiston, S. C. and Keller, B. K. (2004). The influences of the family of origin on career development: A review and analysis. *The Counseling Psychologist*, 32(4), 493-568.

White, J., Campbell, L., Stewart, A., Davies, M., and Pilkington, L. (1997). The relationship of psychological birth order to career interests. *Individual Psychology*, 53(1), 89-104.

Young, R. A., Friesen, J. D., and Borycki, B. (1994). Narrative structure and parental influence in career development. *Journal of Adolescence*, 17, 173-191.

Yue, X., and Ng, S. H. (1999). Filial obligations and expectations in China: Current views from young and old people in Beijing. *Asian Journal of Social Psychology*, 2, 215-226.

Zingaro, J. C. (1983). A family systems approach for the career counselor. *The Personnel and Guidance Journal*, 62, 24-27.

In: Psychology of Counseling
Editor: Annamaria Di Fabio

ISBN: 978-1-62618-388-9
© 2013 Nova Science Publishers, Inc.

Chapter 6

Adaptive Counseling Theory: A New Perspective for Career Counseling

Jean-Luc Bernaud[*]
INETOP-CNAM, Paris, France

ABSTRACT

Interventions in counseling psychology aim to accompany various issues and clients that, moreover, change during the intervention. This chapter aims to present the adaptive counseling theory (ACT), which provides frameworks for caring various career issues but also for considering the evolution of clients during counseling sessions.

Taking the term "adaptive counseling" initially proposed by Howard in psychotherapy and by Tracey and Anderson in career counseling, this chapter presents the theoretical foundations in three stages: (1) the differential approach of clients allows to understand the career issues, (2) the characteristic-treatment interaction model is illustrated by recent research, (3) the adaptive counseling model is presented in terms of interventions. A new conception of individualized and adaptive counseling conceiving it as an "engineering" that takes into account the characteristics of clients and their evolution is also exposed.

INTRODUCTION

Development and dissemination of career counseling theories is a major challenge. A century after the work of Frank Parsons (1909), the reference models have diversified, but in practice, recent theoretical approaches are few employed by practitioners in favor of empirical and no theoretical procedures, of practices centered on the use of instruments or of quite old model. This distance of practitioners towards counseling theories is explained in

---

[*] E-mail address: jeanluc.bernaud@cnam.fr.

different ways. It can be noted a lack of unity of psychological counseling field which must meet very diverse professional goals and which, in some countries like France, is still in search of identity (Bernaud, Cohen-Scali, and Guichard, 2007). It is also noted (Fielding, 2000) a gap between theories viewed as monolithic, epistemologically correct but practically blurred in their applications, and the reality of social demands required to meet some specific objectives such as helping to employability, improving psychological well-being or managing a career transition.

To be considered effective and lasting, a counseling theory must meet certain criteria. One of its main objectives is to provide a framework for thinking about the act of counseling, with a view to determine the best operational postures for intervention of practitioner. It is important that practices emerge relying on the five following key points:

- a body of research demonstrated the soundness and the validity of the theoretical approach;
- a model respecting counseling legal and ethical deontology, with particular emphasis on respect for promised performances, confidentiality of results and a no-directive relationship towards client;
- the availability of evaluative research on the effectiveness and effects of counseling intervention;
- a possible application of the model to a variety of clients in terms of level, age, professional or academic specialty, culture, and psychological and vocational characteristics;
- the fact that the theoretical model can be easily transmitted and taught for easy ownership among young professionals in particular.

The objective of this chapter is to describe a theoretical model of career counseling that is designed to meet these different criteria. The Adaptive Counseling Theory (ACT) presented below is a reformulation and extension of the theory proposed originally by Howard, Nance, and Myers (1986) in the counseling field. According to this approach, it is providing an universal framework for thinking counseling activity taking into account two fundamental parameters: (1) the adaptation of counseling methods and approaches to diversity of issues and clients and (2) the adaptation of the posture of counselor following the evolution dynamic of client during counseling.

In this chapter, we discuss first the differential approach of career counseling that permits to understand the differences between clients; then the aptitude-treatment interaction model will be developed in order to provide tailored interventions, finally the individualization and adaptation of counseling will be exposed.

INDIVIDUAL DIFFERENCES IN CAREER COUNSELING

"If I differ from you, away from you harm, I will rise" Saint Exupéry, Letter to an hostage.

Differences between individuals constitute one of basic data - perhaps most important - in any approach to counseling. Clients are facing counselor with a variety of issues, demands and expectations in relation to their taking in charge. Career counseling needs effective models for understanding client, client's problem and request, in order to adapt then the intervention to the described situation. To do this, it is important that the singularities of individuals are seen as an opportunity (Tomkiewicz, 1996) and not as a constraint. A first challenge of counseling is to answer the following questions: what is the essence of the problem presented by the client? Does the analysis of client's psychological cognitive or emotional functioning enlighten us for the modalities of client's taking in charge? How to take into account the constraints and resources of the person in the dynamics of counseling? Answering these different questions requires the necessity to examine works in this field. Research relative to counseling differential approach focused on preferences about methods, the role of career indecision or a set of constructs and finally, on the differentiated evolution of participants who follow a career counseling.

Bernaud and Caron (2004) sought to understand the structure of preferences towards career counseling devices. To do this, participants rated the attractiveness of 24 help scenarios and they filled in measures of career interests, career indecision and family social capital. The structure of attractiveness was examined with multidimensional scaling and the analysis permitted to identify three dimensions close to the model by Shivy and Koehly (2002). Dimension I distinguishes scenarios oriented towards the discovery of professional life, of more "scholastic" activities, based on a search for information through career counselors or new technologies. Dimension II distinguishes forms of informal and brief help (discussion with parents, friends, but also personal research on the Internet), more involved forms of help, conducted with a professional and focused on self-knowledge. Dimension III distinguishes for its part, recreational help scenarios (discover his/her personality, share with friends, watch a video) more "applied" scenarios (go to an open day, participate in a group career counseling). For explaining the students' preferences, multiple regressions showed that some variables are predictive of the attraction for the scenarios: profiles of social and enterprising interests, corresponding to the attraction for people, are related to scenarios of career counseling with a relationship to others, confirming the observations of this research field (Boyd and Cramer, 1995). Different dimensions of career indecision are predictors: the need for information about themselves for the fact of administering tests, the anxiety relative to choice for dialogue with the relatives and need for professional information regarding professional activities. Finally, it is observed that people with a broad social network show an ability to invest help scenarios that develop the network and they seem ready to mobilize for individualized approaches that are potentially more effective. These different data show that clients are not neutral in relation to career counseling devices. They emit an opinion which depends on their perception of the usefulness of methods and the effort required to achieve certain goals. Participants' vocational characteristics and social context where they are placed orientate their preferences to certain counseling approaches. Thus, this research contributes to understand the involvement and adaptation of clients in the proposed tasks.

Other studies focused on the typological analysis of people engaged in career counseling. The objective was to identify the most common problems among clients. Part of this research involves the concept of career indecision. According to Brown and Krane (2000), typological analysis of patterns of indecision suggests three types of clients: those who are simply looking for specific information without the need for assistance in the choice; those expressing a problem of career choice and are anxious; finally, those who have multiple problems associated with the choice (diffuse identity, low self-esteem, etc.).

Other researches take into account multidimensional data. Multon, Wood, Heppner, and Gysbers (2007) sought to characterize the career problems expressed by clients. Through a cluster analysis, four groups of issues have been identified. Participants in cluster 1 (32%) express a positive mental health and are ready for a transition. They need information about themselves and the world of work. They tend to be undecided deal with situations where have to decide. These are balanced individuals who express an accompaniment focused on the exploration of possibilities, comparisons of these possibilities, and decision making. Individualized career counseling devices seem well adapted to their problems. Participants in cluster 2 (16%) also have good mental health and are ready for transition. However, they seem more determined and less waiting for information that subjects in the previous cluster. The desirability of a short career counseling, focused on the confirmation of considered options, as could be the most appropriate intervention. Participants in cluster 3, which represent 18% have psychological problems, are unstable in their objectives, dependent on others in the process of transition and need help to clarify their interests. These are participants who need a care focused on career and on improving their condition, where psychological support is central. Finally, participants in cluster 4 (34%) also have psychological difficulties, high levels of indecision, they also lack information, but are more willing to confront situations of transition, with a certain level of autonomy. Their problems are closer to those of participants in cluster 3, but with the need to a less intense care in terms of psychological support. Using a different protocol, Ruchlen, Milburn, and Hill (2004) identified two groups: one is characterized by high anxiety, a fear of the consequences of counseling, a clear self-image while the other consists of stable individuals. These last seem to benefit at best of the proposed intervention, which is a sole counseling interview. This research confirms partly the previous, which suggests that the management of emotional states is an important differentiating criterion.

In a study conducted among jobseekers Guénolé, Bernaud, and Boudrias (in press) studied their vocational problems starting from measures chosen according to the literature on employability. Then, they were taken into account: career decision self-efficacy, employability (Van der Heijde and Van der Heijden, 2006), resources to face career transitions, career indecision, self-esteem, psychological distress, and social support. Cluster analysis to process data identified three groups. The first (43% of the sample) is characterized by a mean level in the following areas: career development, self-efficacy, self-esteem, employability, indecision, depression. Participants in cluster 2 (21%) have a high level of psychological distress, a very low self-efficacy, low self-esteem, and a fairly high level of indecision. Cluster 3 (35%) consists of individuals with good levels of skills, expertise, ready for a career transition, with a good level of self-efficacy. They don't have depressive disorders, and feel good about themselves. This differentiation of the three groups provides interesting tracks for designing tailored interventions.

Observation of individual differences in career counseling may also involve different patterns of evolution shown during an interview. Covali, Bernaud, and Di Fabio (2011) studied, using three variables (work alliance, career decision self-efficacy and career development), the evolution of clients during individual sessions of career counseling. Cluster analysis revealed a typology of evolutions in three times of intervention: before entering the device, after the feedback of career counseling tools, after the last individual interview for helping in the construction of project. Results show that the three groups of clients are differentiated: those who benefit greatly from the intervention, those who benefit moderate and finally those who are not progressing. Blatantly, this research shows the presence of differential effects, career counseling intervention used in this research as an individual career counseling, being particularly effective in a proportion of clients between 20 and 30%.

Presentation of previous studies leads to a fundamental observation: participants in an activity of counseling have not the same problems, they don't evaluate different services in the same way and they react differently to the same career counseling device. Therefore it is possible to conclude that these studies open the way to a reflection about what would be a counseling service tailored to the needs and demands of clients.

CHOOSE AN ADAPTIVE COUNSELING SERVICE: THE APTITUDE-TREATMENT INTERACTION MODEL

Heppner and Heppner (2003) consider that taking into account the characteristics of the beneficiaries is a key element for the development of new research on career counseling process. In this perspective, the study of the characteristics of the subjects is not considered as such, but in its interaction with intervention modalities: it is an Aptitude Treatment Interaction (ATI). This notion permits depending on the case to moderate the effects or make an hidden effect to appear.

The ATI concept was developed by Cronbach and Snow (1977) and highlights treatments more or less effective depending on client characteristics. According to Snow (1991), aptitude is any measurable individual characteristic: aptitude, attitude, behavior style, etc. Treatment regards any situational variable: intervention modalities, used material, individual versus collective sessions, characteristics of professional, etc. Finally interaction occurs when the effect of treatment depends on the characteristics of clients. Aptitude-treatment interaction belongs to the moderating effects, different from mediating effects (Frazier, Tix, and Barron, 2004). These works experience two election areas.

The first is the influence of cognitive styles on learning situations, a perspective developed by Cronbach and Snow (1977) and recovery in many studies. The second was studied in depth in the field of psychotherapy (Shoham-Salomon and Hannah, 1991): it aims to determine the type of intervention (analytic, cognitive, systemic - familiar, Rogerian, etc.) which best suits to psychopathology and problems of the patient. In addition, a number of studies were developed in the field of career counseling. There are researches highlighting the role of demographic variables such as subjects' gender or their cultural background. Interpretation of these data is sometimes difficult to establish, by the presence of multiple associated variables: their interest is more convenient, for example to optimize career counseling for international students.

Other works were inspired by the approach of vocational interests. Kivlighan, Hageseth, Tipon and McGovern (1981) showed the existence of a link between the Holland's type and the feedback format. Procedure consisted of two feedbacks of an interests inventory, one involving exchanges between participants, the other requiring an individual resolution of the career choice problem; participants were also characterized by two orientations, one towards people (social or enterprising), the other towards tasks (realistic or investigator).

Results showed a significant interaction that occurs at a level of vocational maturity evolution: task-oriented subjects evolved more favorably in the individual condition and those oriented towards people had the same outcome in the collective condition. In addition, the perception of the group varied in the same direction: it was more favorable when subjects were confronted with good match. In a similar paradigm, Kivlighan and Shapiro (1987) studied the relationship between Holland's types and the evolution of vocational identity in subjects participating in a structured approach of an interests inventory, which required working independently with a printed booklet. Results showed in essence that three types moderated changes in vocational identity: conventional, investigative and realistic. A more structured and empowering approach seems appropriate for task-oriented participants. Bernaud and Loss (1995) showed, for their part, that investigative, artistic and social subjects benefited most (in terms of vocational maturity evolution) of a collective and structured feedback session of an interests inventory. Investigative subjects, in particular, are characterized by a very strong evolution in terms of ownership of Holland's typology.

Eden and Aviram (1993) proposed an original help device for job search based on Bandura's self-efficacy theory. To do this, they built exercises whose function is to develop one of the causes of self-efficacy. Results showed an effect of counseling on proactive job search behaviors, but it is much more important for participants who initially had low self-efficacy. It is therefore an interaction effect ATI type.

Massoudi, Masdonati, Clot-Siegrist, Franz, and Rossier (2008) identified that the best predictor of career counseling effectiveness (evaluated from satisfaction and reducing indecision) was the work alliance; against moderators inherent to factorial personality dimensions had no effect for clients.

An illustration of aptitude-treatment interaction was also proposed by Carrein and Bernaud (2010). In this research, authors used an experiment device to assess how participants responded to different levels of non-verbal self-disclosure of counselor. The situation was a filmed counseling interview, in which were integrated, depending on experimental conditions, information on personality of counselor (personal taste and family status). Participants were asked to rate the level of professionalism of the counselor and parallel filled in a scale about fear of intimacy. Results clearly showed an aptitude-treatment interaction: situations of self-disclosure of counselors lead to a lower assessment of their skills when the participant feared intimate situations.

In summary, the aptitude-treatment interaction offers new perspectives to understand what types of interventions are most relevant for some participants, but also raises issues of vigilance that focus on participants' sensitivity to some bias in evaluation or counseling.

These research data - which are to strengthen in favor of more comprehensive approaches in counseling - leading the way in developing an adaptive to person counseling. This vision is now fairly shared in the design of devices (Barak and Friedkes, 1982).

NEW PERSPECTIVES IN CAREER COUNSELING: INDIVIDUALIZED AND ADAPTIVE COUNSELING

A large number of observations converge on the need for an individualization of counseling. Thus Walsh (2003, p. 459), ask the following question: "Have the interaction between different career counseling and specificities of clients have really been analyzed? Is it not possible that the effects of career counseling varies depending on the personality of the clients?". Two points can be raised about this issue: the adaptation of counseling process to the problem presented by the client at the beginning of sessions (individualized counseling) and the adaptation of the counseling process in response to changes of client (adaptive counseling).

Regarding the first point, individualized counseling, it is possible to be inspired on what was developed in the field of training. According to Trollat and Masson (2009, p. 89) individualized training is

> "training that recognizes and takes into account the singularity of the subject: his/her needs, his/her paths, his/her experience, his/her achievements, his/her constraints, his/her resources, his/her self-direction skills, his/her strategies; a training which takes into account the social dimension of learning in an empowering and identity construction perspective; a co-constructed training, negotiated between the involved parties which concretize the interaction between a project of instituted training and individual training projects. This co-constructed training has an impact on the role of actors and of organization, it is regulated and evolves over time".

However, individualization should not be confused with individualism. Instead, the logic of individualization is to increase equality between learners, seeking to maximize the effectiveness of learning for everyone. The parallelism between training and counseling is supported by the fact that in the conceptualization of counseling, there is not a work of expertise but face a work of training to develop career skills. In this context, the development of client autonomy and reasoning become fundamental educational objectives. Betz and Taylor (2001) developed a model and a measuring instrument that detected career skills and was used in several research protocols. The model consists of five dimensions: the ability for self-assessment, the ability to find information on educational and professional environments, the definition of objectives, the ability to make projects for the future and to plan, the ability to solve career problems.

Build an individualized counseling path involves answering two levels. The first level is the adaptation relative to the format of counseling process. This level depends on the customer's request but also on psychological functioning, physical or medical constraints and intrinsic needs. For example, one of the major points in individualized counseling is the linguistic or cognitive adaptation to client. Depending on the level of vocabulary, counselors must be able to adapt their language to the latter understandable and useful to client, they make good performances to understand client's career problems and to engage in constructive decisions. Sometimes, when client has cognitive disorders, uncertain mastery of the language, or simply a poor vocabulary, counselors must be able to develop intervention strategies in slowing the rate of speech, choosing a simple vocabulary, using techniques such as metaphors or using more simple media, more pictures, or requiring less cognitive complexity. This professional adaptation is most often empirical, at the discretion of counselor, because there are few models of intervention and also little research on the theme of the role of language counselor (Meara, Shannon, and Pepinsky, 1979). However we know that some metaphors are more effective than others: the narrative analogies of mean level of complexity are those that produce the best estimation of clients. It is also possible that some clients appreciate more complex interventions and the use of metaphors adapted to these clients represents a field of heuristic research (Lyddon, Clay, and Sparks, 2001). Similarly, the interpretive framework of theories on learning styles is able to provide a better understanding of what is right to focus on to promote the processes of change in clients (Fortin, Chevrier, and Amyot, 2002).

The issue of format also arises regarding the structuring of counseling methods. Counselor is faced with the choice of a variety of intervention formats that must be thought in function of each client: individual format or collective format of intervention, how to work with the client (by leaving great deal of autonomy or guiding), the ergonomics of materials (an issue that can be applied in the presence of motor or sensory disabilities), the choice of tools (in terms of number and diversity), the format of feedback (which can, for example, rely on nomothetic or constructivist methodologies; Bernaud, Danet, and Dinar, 2009). The choice of a strategy for counseling arises from the demand analysis conducted during the first interviews to better understand the constraints, obstacles, aspirations and skills of client. This implies, on the part of counselor, the establishment of an engineering intervention in the form of a chip shuttle, involving a co-construction and summarizing selected options and their motivations.

The second level focuses on comprehensive intervention strategy which must take into account the psychological and career problems of clients. This implies, as we noted above, rely on a typology. As reported Multon et al. (2007, p. 82) "this type of empirically validated taxonomy is fundamental to conduct research to analyze processes and outcomes of careers of beneficiaries and the different types of interventions". In career counseling interventions, based on a synthesis of works on individual differences, it seems that three scenarios appear repeatedly, with different shades and degrees. The first group consists of individuals who don't have psychological disorders, are relatively autonomous and close to a decision for their career or their employability. Counseling is preferred then to reassure them, to help them to confirm and specify the considered options. Several methodologies seem appropriate for these career issues: short sessions (between 2 and 7 hours), including an information work and an accompaniment for operational implementation of the professional project, possibly together with a support so that can deal obstacles and resolve different types of problems that will inevitably arise. The second group consists of people who face a consisting career problem, having multiple determinants: difficulty identifying their work values and their professional competences, lack of information on possible career opportunities, deficit in the establishment of a professional operational strategy. This type of situation, fairly classic, requires a longer treatment (15 to 25 hours) accompanied by more sophisticated methods of self-knowledge and knowledge of the labor market and the development of a support for decision making. Individual interventions face to face with the counselor are generally more appropriate in this case. The third group generally presents multiple difficulties, psychological but also vocational, which in some cases can be associated with medical and/or social problems. For facing with these difficulties where causes are complex, the issue of career support needs to be asked. An acute decompensation, for example, is not compatible with career counseling. On the other side, it is in a number of cases in which psychological disorders are a consequence and not a cause of career difficulties (Paul and Moser, 2009). In this case, it is important to treat the source in the same manner as for the second group in matching of strengthening psychological support and/or a change in social conditions in which the person lives. Psychological accompaniment can be delegated, for avoiding confusion of role, to an exterior psychotherapist. In some cases, the use of exercises inspired by positive psychology (Seligman and Csikszentmihalyi, 2000), development of self-efficacy (Eden and Aviram,

1993), test feedback (Poston and Hanson, 2010) Rogerian type emotional support can help to improve self-esteem of clients and help them to overcome their psychological problems.

Obviously, these three groups are a pretty rough cut of the issue of demand analysis, each client is unique and approaching more or less of each group. The construction of an individualized path can also base on a theory of the determinants of career indecision, which strengthens some aspects depending on posed problem: more or less looking for information about themselves, dealing with conflicts between different types of information, realizing a cognitive method of decision support, managing external conflicts, etc. (Kelly and Lee, 2002).

In summary, support for different people requires both individualization and personalization of counseling. Individualization means that professional architecture counseling activity in a modular fashion, with a path that each client can follow depending on the issues raises and the constraints presents. Personalization goes even further: it corresponds to a "tailored" approach which considers questions on a case by case basis and assumes from counselor to elaborate a specific program and to develop appropriate behaviors.

A second important point concerns management of evolution of client during counseling. An useful model in this field was proposed by George Howard and his colleagues in psychotherapy (Howard et al., 1986). This author proposed to adapt, depending on the maturity level of clients, the level of directivity and support by counselor. Directional behaviors are characterized by the fact of presenting objectives, conducting specific exercises that shape the intervention. Support behaviors are defined by an explanation of quality of relationship, developing empathic attitudes and a concern of counselor for client. The combination of these two behaviors - directivity and support - provides four styles of therapeutic intervention described as: supporting, teaching, delegating and supervising.

Counselor, according to this theory, should choose the form of intervention that correspond to the level of maturity of client. It has been observed in research in psychotherapy and career counseling (Anderson and Tracey, 1995) a negative correlation between the level of development of clients and their degree of preference for a directive intervention and an inverted U correlation between their level of development and their preference for a counselor who supports.

If this model fits into the framework of approaches of individualization of counseling, it helps to think to extensions in terms of changes in client during counseling. Indeed, the development of career maturity of client is a natural phenomenon and specific in career counseling. Thus it is possible to suppose that the adaptive counseling theory can also apply to postural adjustment of counselor during counseling. A general model of intervention that results from previous observations is that the attitude of counselor can not be uniform throughout interviews. Counselor can probe the evolution of clients and their attitudes in function of what is observed. Thus, a probable configuration is a decrease in directivity with the advancement of exchanges: first interviews have a function of framing explaining the objectives, providing the materials to be treated, recalling the temporality and exchange rules. Gradually the need for development of clients autonomy implies a more flexible framework to enable them to set their own guidelines, steps and goals. In the last interviews, clients define themselves the structure to observe and counselor occurs only very little, mainly for the invite to be attentive to possible obstacles or competences to acquire. The supportive attitudes seem more useful for intermediate levels of vocational maturity. Therefore, the first and last phases of intervention are more technical: they aim to inform, frame, give exploration exercises and planning. Against by the intermediate phases, or face different options in order to make a decision, require more support. This is justified by the anxiety in the future that arouse decision making, potential conflicts with the environment that it generates and the fear felt by the client face change and challenge oneself.

The adaptive counseling theory therefore requires relying on a new concept: the competence to generate adaptive flow depending on the likely evolution and actual client. This implies in counselors the ability to regulate their behavior through standard procedures but also through their ability to cope with unpredictable and sometimes chaotic changes (Pryor and Bright, 2007). In this sense, it is necessary great finesse to analyze and act when resistance to change suddenly appears during intervention, when clients begins to doubt seriously and without reasons about their competences, or when unforeseen event (illness, unemployment, meeting, etc.) tainted the well-organized pattern of counseling intervention. This implies, in counselor, to have a sense of discernment to understand what is at stake and to propose the intervention modalities that are most useful for client.

CONCLUSION

This chapter has set an ambitious goal: to formalize a new direction through the adaptive counseling theory. It observed that the choice of interventions in relation to the concerns and needs of clients is one of the most common questions in research in counseling. Faurie (in press) also arrives at this conclusion: "Different observations incite to encourage a differential approach of accompaniment devices to the project for adapting them to the diversity of student profiles rather than a uniform approach, the same device for all students".

Adjust practices to the needs of clients and their evolution during the interviews requires new skills for the recruitment and training of counselors. These should be primarily adaptive for a specific elaboration (individualized or personalized) of counseling and the ability to cope with changes or unexpected situations. Learning these new skills should be able to do from case studies or role-playing games, taking into account, in particular, dynamic models and models of adaptive competences (Pulakos et al., 2002).

Moreover, the adaptive counseling theory raises research issues and business challenges. For research, the challenges are to find ways to improve the effectiveness of career counseling. Indeed, meta-analyzes (Whiston, Sexton, and Lasoff, 1998) show that the effects are moderate and that a means to obtain significant effect size is to individualize intervention. It is therefore necessary to encourage research that reflect the types of clients and that use the characteristic-treatment interaction model to better understand the effectiveness of interventions. It is also necessary to have research highlighting the dynamic processes involved in counseling and defining why adaptive regulations made by counselor are factors of progress.

In terms of practical modalities, the adaptive counseling theory implies new training modules for students in counseling and providing new tools for intervention. It involves a structured model of demand analysis to understand how to shape the intervention. From this point of view, it seems essential to accurately assess, at the beginning of career development intervention, indecision and psychological disorders. It also requires thinking about counseling intervention as engineering, which means designing individualized and/or personalized paths, which are negotiated with client and adjusted by stage points throughout the intervention.

Finally, the adaptive counseling theory assumes that practitioners are familiar with techniques for individual evaluation of counseling interviews to foster reflection on research and to adjust their own practices.

REFERENCES

Anderson, M. Z., and Tracey, T. J. (1995). Application of adaptive counseling and therapy to career counseling. *Journal of Career Assessment, 3*(1), 75-88.

Barak, A., and Friedkes, R. (1982). The mediating effects of career indecision subtypes on career-counseling effectiveness. *Journal of Vocational Behavior, 20,* 1-3.

Bernaud, J.-L., and Caron, M. (2004). Un modèle différentiel des préférences vis-à-vis de la relation d'aide en orientation professionnelle [A differential model for career counseling preferences in relation to vocational guidance support]. *L'Orientation Scolaire et Professionnelle, 33,* 103-123.

Bernaud, J.-L., Cohen-Scali, V., and Guichard, J. (2007). Counseling psychology in France: A paradoxical situation. *Applied Psychology: An International Review,* 56, 131-151.

Bernaud, J.-L., Danet, L., and Dinar, M. (2009). Comparaison des effets de trois modes de restitution de questionnaires vocationnels: Nomothétique, constructiviste et intégré [Effects of three interpretation styles for interests inventories: Nomothetic, constructivist and integrated]. *L'Orientation Scolaire et Professionnelle, 38,* 135-160.

Bernaud, J.-L., and Loss, I. (1995). Evaluation expérimentale des effets d'une méthode de restitution de questionnaires d'intérêts [Experimental evaluation of the effects of an interest questionnaire method of explanation]. *L'Orientation Scolaire et Professionnelle, 24,* 99-113.

Betz, N. E., and Taylor, K. M. (2001). *Manual for the career decision self-efficacy scale and CDMSE - short form.* Colombus, OH: The Ohio State University.

Boyd, C. J., and Cramer, S. H. (1995). Relationship between Holland high-point code and client preferences for selected vocational counseling strategies. *Journal of Career Development, 21,* 213-221.

Brown, S. D., and Krane, N. E. R. (2000). Four (or five) sessions and a cloud of dust: Old assumptions and new observations about career counseling. In S. D. Brown and R. W. Lent (Eds.), *Handbook of Counseling Psychology* (3rd ed., pp. 740-766). New York: Wiley.

Carrein, C., and Bernaud, J. L. (2010). Counselor's non-verbal self-disclosure and fear of intimacy during employment counseling: An aptitude-treatment interaction illustration. *Journal of Employment Counseling, 47,* 134-144.

Covali, T., Bernaud, J.-L., and Di Fabio, A. (2011). Processus de changement et variabilité individuelle au cours des consultations d'orientation. *Swiss Journal of Psychology, 70*(3), 175-183.

Cronbach, L. J., and Snow, R. E. (1977). *Aptitude and instructionnal methods.* New York: John Wiley.

Eden, D., and Aviram, A. (1993). Self-efficacy training to speed reemployment: Helping people to help themselves. *Journal of Applied Psychology*, *78*(3), 352-360.

Faurie, I. (2012). Sentiments d'efficacité personnelle et dynamique du projet professionnel [Self-efficacy and dynamic of professional project]. *Psychologie du Travail et des Organisations*, *18*, 37-60.

Fielding, A. J. (2000). Pourquoi le praticiens disent-ils que la théorie n'est pas utile à la pratique? Une proposition pour adapter la pratique aux exigences du 21° siècle [Why do practitioners say that theory is not useful to practice? A proposal to adapt the practice to the needs of 21th century]. *L'Orientation Scolaire et Professionnelle*, 29, 79-90.

Fortin, G., Chevrier, J., and Amyot, E. (2002). Relation entre la stratégie d'intervention de l'aidant en formation et son style d'apprentissage [Relationship between the counselling process and learning style]. *Canadian Psychology*, *43*, 91-105.

Frazier, P. A., Tix, A. P., and Barron, K. E. (2004). Testing moderator and mediator effects in counseling psychology research. *Journal of Counseling Psychology*, *51*, 115-134.

Guénolé, N., Bernaud, J.-L., and Boudrias, J.-S. (in press). Problematiques vocationnelles chez les beneficiaires d'un accompagnement a la recherche d'emploi: Une approche typologique [Vocational problems among beneficiaries of an accompanying to job search: A typological approach]. *Risorso Uomo*.

Heppner, M. J., and Heppner, P. P. (2003). Identifying process variables in career counseling: A research agenda. *Journal of Vocational Behavior*, *62*, 429-452.

Howard, G. S., Nance, D. W., and Myers, P. (1986). Further thoughts on the development of adaptive counseling and therapy. *The Counseling Psychologist*, *14*(4), 587-591.

Kelly, K. R., and Lee, W. C. (2002). Mapping the domain of career decision problems. *Journal of Vocational Behavior*, *61*, 302-326.

Kivlighan, D. M., Hageseth, J. A., Tipton, R. M., and McGovern, T. V. (1981). Effect of matching treatment approaches and personality types in group vocational counseling. *Journal of Counseling Psychology*, *26*, 315-320.

Kivlighan, D. M., and Shapiro, R. M. (1987). Holland type as a predictor of benefit from self-help career counseling. *Journal of Counseling Psychology*, *34*, 326-329.

Lyddon, W. J., Clay, A. L., and Sparks, C. L. (2001). Metaphor and change in counseling. *Journal of Counseling and Development*, *79*(3), 269-274.

Massoudi, K., Masdonati, J., Clot-Siegrist, E., Franz-Pousaz, S., and Rossier, J. (2008). Évaluation des effets du counseling d'orientation: Influence de l'alliance de travail et des caractéristiques individuelles [Assessing the effects of career counseling: The influence of working alliance and individual characteristics]. *Pratiques Psychologiques*, *14*(2), 117-136.

Meara, N. M., Shannon, J. W., and Pepinsky, H. B. (1979). Comparison of the stylistic complexity of the language of counselor and client across three theoretical orientations. *Journal of Counseling Psychology*, *26*(3), 181-189.

Multon, K. D., Wood, R., Heppner, M. J., and Gysbers, N. C. (2007). A cluster-analytic investigation of subtypes of adult career counseling clients: Toward a taxonomy of career problems. *Journal of Career Assessment*, *15*, 66-86.

Parsons, F. (1909). *Choosing a vocation*. Boston: Houghton Mifflin.

Paul, K. I., and Moser, K. (2009). Unemployment impairs mental health: Meta-analyses. *Journal of Vocational Behavior*, *74*(3), 264-282.

Poston, J. M., and Hanson, W. E. (2010). Meta-analysis of psychological assessment as a therapeutic intervention. *Psychological Assessment, 22*, 203-212.

Pryor, R. G. L., and Bright J. E. H. (2007). Applying chaos theory to careers: Attraction and attractors. *Journal of Vocational Behavior, 71*(3), 375-400.

Pulakos, E. D., Schmitt, N., Dorsey, D. W., Arad, S., Hedge, J., and Borman, W. C. (2002). Predicting adaptive performance: Further tests of a model of adaptability. *Human Performance, 15*(4), 299-323.

Rochlen, A. B., Milburn, L., and Hill, C. E. (2004). Examining the process and outcome of career counseling for different types of career counseling clients. *Journal of Career Development, 30*, 263-275.

Seligman, M. E., and Csikszentmihalyi, M. (2000). Positive psychology: An introduction. *American Psychologist, 55*, 5-14.

Shivy, V. A., and Koehly, L. M. (2002). Client perceptions of and preferences for university based career services. *Journal of Vocational Behavior, 60*, 40-60.

Shoham-Salomon, V., and Hannah, M. T. (1991). Client-treatment interactions in the study of differential change process. *Journal of Consulting and Clinical Psychology, 59*, 217-225.

Snow, R. E. (1991). Aptitude-treatment interaction as a framework for research on individual differences in psychotherapy. *Journal of Consulting and Clinical Psychology, 59*, 205-216.

Tomkiewicz, S. (1996). Apologie de la différence [Apology of the difference]. *Pratiques Psychologiques, 1*, 3-12.

Trollat, A.-F., and Masson, C. (2009). La formation individualisée. Conférence de consensus [Individual training. Consensus conference]. Dijon: Educagri éditions.

Van der Heijde, C. M., and Van der Heijden, B. I. J. M. (2006). A competence-based and multi-dimensional operationalization and measurement of employability. *Human Resource Management, 45*, 449-476.

Walsh, W. B. (2003). Diversity, flexibility, and career interventions. *Journal of Vocational Behavior, 62*(3), 459-463.

Whiston, S. C., Sexton, T. L., and Lasoff, D. L. (1998). Career-intervention outcome: A replication and extension of Oliver and Spokane. *Journal of Counseling Psychology, 45*, 150-165.

Research and Intervention:
Expanding the Horizons

In: Psychology of Counseling
Editor: Annamaria Di Fabio

ISBN: 978-1-62618-388-9
© 2013 Nova Science Publishers, Inc.

Chapter 7

A Longitudinal Study of Adolescent Perceptions of the Role That Education Plays in Their Self-Definition

*Janet Usinger**
University of Nevada, Reno. NV, US

ABSTRACT

In the past several decades there has been a steady parade of efforts to improve education and counsel students to continue their education beyond high school. Yet despite concerted efforts to improve the educational attainment of young people, concern continues in the United States about low college-going rates. A federally funded State Gaining Early Awareness and Readiness for Undergraduate Programs (GEAR UP) project provided an opportunity to add to our understanding of how adolescents themselves understand and interpret the role that education plays in their own personal development.

The qualitative study followed a cohort of 60 students who lived in economically disadvantaged urban and rural communities from seventh grade to twelfth grade, using an interview approach to data collection. Five interconnected themes were identified in the data: (a) determination to succeed; (b) things happen magically; (c) school is a place of happiness; (d) I can show my pride; and (e) learning is secondary to more important things. Beyond the themes identified, the overwhelming majority of the students clustered into the following four categories: (a) I'm capable; (b) I'm smart, but frustrated; (c) I feel stuck; and (d) a relational self-definition. For a few, school was incompatible with their self-definition, the last cluster. Although the research was not designed to empirically test self-determination theory, this theory proved to be an appropriate analytic filter. How the three fundamental needs associated with self-determination theory, autonomy, competence, and relatedness, were presented in the clusters is explored. Implications for practice are presented.

---

* correspondence Author: Janet Usinger, Educational Leadership, Mail Stop 283, University of Nevada, Reno, Reno, NV 89557, USA. Fax: +1-775-784-6766.
Email address: usingerj@unr.edu.

INTRODUCTION

It is well understood that individuals who achieve higher levels of education tend to be more successful in complex global economies. Levin, Belfield, Meunnig, and Rouse (2007) reported that, when considering lifetime earnings, the difference between a male high school dropout and a male college graduate was between $950,000 and $1,387,000. Indeed, as individuals attain higher levels of education, their life chances improve in terms of employment, income, health status, and housing. These benefits are not only personal; a more educated populace translates into the development of more sophisticated and high technology industries, higher government revenues, and lower government spending.

In the past several decades there has been a steady parade of efforts to improve education in the United States and counsel students to continue their education beyond high school. Increasingly, school reform efforts have been designed to ensure that all students leave the K-12 educational system college and career ready. The federal government, state governments, and philanthropic foundations have developed media campaigns to increase the college-going rate. Wide varieties of programs have been developed to guide and support students who are the first in their family to pursue postsecondary education. Need-based, merit-based, and specialized scholarships and other financial aid sources abound. Surveys repeatedly indicate that students aspire to a good education and a successful career.

Yet despite these concerted efforts and collective desires to improve the educational attainment of young people, concern continues in the United States about high rates of school dropout and low college-going rates. Much research has been conducted to examine the role that student demographics, school related factors, policy, and community differences play in educational outcome. A State Gaining Early Awareness and Readiness for Undergraduate Programs (GEAR UP) project has provided an opportunity to add to our understanding of how adolescents themselves understand and interpret the role that education plays in their own personal development.

This study was conducted as part of a larger study, the purpose of which was to explore how adolescents socially construct their career aspirations and the role that education plays in that process. The study included a cohort of 60 students who were followed longitudinally from seventh grade to twelfth grade, using an interview approach to data collection. The career construction findings of the study are found in greater detail in Usinger and Smith (2010). This portion of the study is an exploration of how adolescents perceived school in their lives. The following describes the participants, the qualitative design of the research, and the data analysis. This is followed by the research results, discussion of the findings, conclusions, and implications for practice.

METHOD

Participants

GEAR UP is a federally funded project that provides support to first generation college-going students so they may pursue postsecondary education. The program's general design included academic enrichment, college preparation activities, and college counseling for a cohort of seventh grade students, who lived in economically disadvantaged communities. Services were provided from middle school through high school. The GEAR UP project represented in this study also included a scholarship for eligible students to attend a community college or university in the state where the project was implemented (Nevada Department of Education, 2001).

The qualitative study presented drew from a GEAR UP cohort of approximately 2,500 students; 60 students volunteered to participate in this study. Under the auspices of the university Institutional Review Board (IRB), the criteria and process for selecting the students were established in advance. A cross-section of adolescents representing a continuum of students who were succeeding to those who were struggling socially and/or academically was sought. Of equal importance was the desire to recruit *under-the-radar* students (i.e., students who did not stand out or take center stage for one reason or another). The most important goal was to recruit a cross-section of students because it was believed that students would change over time. For example, introverted seventh grade students identified as under-the-radar may excel in high school. Likewise, students who did well in seventh grade could struggle in later years. Additionally, because of the longitudinal nature of the study, another criterion was the likelihood that the student would be available to participate for the six year duration of the study.

To provide a representative sample, seventh grade students were recruited from each of the 13 GEAR UP middle schools that were part of the statewide project. The cohorts of seventh grade classes ranged from five students in the smallest rural schools to over 400 in the largest urban schools, complicating the selection process. The principal investigator of the study (author of this chapter) spent a great deal of time with the cooperating schools to achieve the desired goals of recruiting a cross-section of students. In the rural schools, recruitment presentations were made to the entire class; students were allowed to volunteer. In the large urban schools, school counselors were asked to consider the inclusion criteria of the study and assist in finding a manageable group of students from which to recruit. Because of their position in the school, counselors were able to suggest students who were succeeding or struggling; the challenge was to identify the under-the-radar students at the large urban schools. Based upon their relationships with students and knowledge of their status, counselors brought together a manageable cross-section of students for recruitment. In the same manner as in the rural schools, the principal investigator presented the study to the urban student groups and allowed students to volunteer to participate. All students who volunteered signed assent documents; informed consent was also obtained from parents or guardians for the student's participation.

The 60 students who volunteered to participate in the study self-identified as: 24 Caucasian; 16 Native American; 10 Latino/a; 8 African American; and 2 Pacific Islanders. Twenty-four students attended urban schools, each of which could be described as *inner-city*; 36 students attended rural schools, frequently located in remote, isolated communities. Rural students were over-represented as all of the students in the two very small (i.e., class sizes of 4-6 students) rural schools were needed to provide the required cross-section. All of the schools had over 70% free and reduced priced lunch (FRL) rates.

Recruitment efforts resulted in the desired cross-section of students. Thirty-nine of the students graduated high school with a regular or advanced diploma. One student received an adjusted diploma (met the requirements for the student's Individualized Education Plan [IEP]). Six were awarded certificates of attendance (sufficient credits, but failed one of the high school exit exams). Two did not graduate with their class (insufficient credits). Six were expelled or dropped out of school. Six moved out of state during the course of the study: two as the result of (parent reported) discrimination at school, three due to custody issues, and one family moved.

Students were affected by a wide variety of life circumstances over the course of the study. Reflective of families who live in economically disadvantaged communities, more of their experiences were negative than positive. For example, six experienced the death of a parent during the course of the study: three from automobile accidents; two from chronic illnesses; and one murder. Many family members (and three students) experienced serious legal troubles. Family instability was common, including two students who experienced homelessness for a period of time. There were three pregnancies and one student fathered a child.

Data Collection

Semi-structured interviews were conducted twice a year, once in the fall and once in the spring, for a period of six years, from the time the students were in seventh grade through their senior year in high school. All interviews were face-to-face by one person, principal investigator and author of this chapter. This was done to establish continuity and trust with the youth. The length of the interviews changed over time. At the beginning, interviews lasted 20-30 minutes; by the end of the study, interviews generally lasted one class period, 50 minutes, or longer. Interviews were audio-recorded for verbatim transcription. Most of the interviews were conducted at the school in a semi-private location, such as a conference room, empty classroom, or empty office. A few interviews were conducted at the student's home, initially at the request of the parent and later out of habit. The interviews conducted in homes were conducted away from other family members to maintain privacy.

Field notes were written and included the various issues occurring at the school or in the community. Artifacts relevant to the students' lives were collected. Memoing was conducted to capture reflections about how the students changed over time. These memos were critical to keep the running story that was unfolding about each student.

Every effort was made to maintain contact with the students during the course of the study. If a student was absent for one of the interviews, the subsequent interview included key questions from the previous interview to ensure that a complete set of responses to questions was obtained from each student. A complete set of responses to 12 interviews was obtained for 50 students. A partial set of interviews was conducted with 10 students: one left the state and two were expelled from school after eighth grade, resulting in a set of responses to four interviews; two left the state after the ninth grade, resulting in a set of responses to six interviews; three left the state during the tenth grade, resulting in a set of responses to seven or eight interviews; two dropped out of school during the spring semester of the eleventh grade, resulting in a set of responses to 10 interviews. Two other students dropped out during the spring semester of their senior year; a complete set of responses was collected for these two students. Even if their interviews did not constitute a complete set, data from all 60 students was included in the analysis because of the desire for a cross-section of students representing the spectrum of life circumstances.

The investigator entered into the relationship with each student as an adult interested in understanding how the student thought about his or her future. Establishing and building trust with the student was essential; a conversational partnership as described by Rubin and Rubin (2005) was employed. All interviews were conducted from the stance that statements made by the students represented their interpretation of the truth. No attempt was made to verify or validate their statements. The focus was always on how the student represented him or herself and the student's interpretation of his or her unique world.

The interviews during seventh grade were designed to get to know students, particularly their interests both in and out of school, as well as to make sure they were comfortable with the research process. Starting in eighth grade, interviews included three primary components: (a) a portion of the interview built on the running story of each student; (b) a set of interview protocol questions was followed to focus on specific themes and ideas (e.g., relationships with teachers, grades and tests, leadership, personal expectations, influential people, anticipated and actual transition from middle to high school to postsecondary education/work, as well as anticipated futures); and (c) all interviews included questions about the classes the students were taking, the classes that students liked and did not like, and an exploration of their current thinking regarding their career ideations, including the factors that were contributing to their thinking. Questions were designed to elicit beliefs and attitudes about themselves and the world around them, as well as personal characteristics such as self-esteem, self-efficacy, and locus of control. In addition, school, family, peer, and community related factors were explored through many of the questions and probes. One of the goals of these lines of questioning was to understand how the student interpreted and coped with the many situations encountered over the life of the study.

Preparing the Data for Analysis

Because of the longitudinal nature of the study and the increasingly large dataset, a log was kept to identify which interviews had been conducted and on what date. All field notes and memoing were dated and coded so as to be linked with the appropriate adolescent. Audio-recordings were transcribed verbatim, primarily by one undergraduate student. Because she had conducted the interviews, the investigator transcribed some of the interviews, particularly if the student was hard to understand due to an accent and/or challenging speech pattern. All interview recordings and written documents were organized in two ways. De-identified recordings and transcripts, as well as artifacts, field notes, and memos directly associated with the student were physically filed chronologically in a segmented file folder labeled with the participant's code number. The transcribed interviews resulted in 546 documents of analyzable material. Interviews ranged in length from 5 to 20 pages. Earlier interviews were shorter; by the end of the study, they averaged 15 pages.

All interviews were also imported into NVivo software. Software was used because of the size and complexity of the dataset. The data were filed both by year and into a case which represented an individual student. This initial organization allowed for the data to be analyzed either by time or by adolescent. Data could also be examined electronically for additional coding as data analysis progressed. Upon importation into NVivo, interviews were auto-coded in reference to the specific question or topic covered by the interview question. Auto-coding was conducted for two reasons. First, some of the questions were asked during more than one interview and other questions were asked only once. This initial auto-coding allowed for the questions repeated in more than one interview to be connected. Second, coding to specific questions or topics was an essential organizational process due to the very large data set that was developing.

Data Analysis

The purpose of the qualitative analysis was to allow the data to reveal the common themes found in the interviews. This process, described below, used three primary strategies to establish validity of the themes: (a) negative or discrepant information was purposefully sought; (b) peer debriefing; and (c) selective member checking (Creswell, 2003). The investigator had primary responsibility for the data analysis; she had conducted all of the interviews and thus was familiar with the data. To gain additional perspective about the data, extensive conversations were held with the undergraduate student who transcribed the interviews. These conversations provided the opportunity to test preliminary themes for face validity. In addition, five graduate students analyzed different portions of the interviews for class assignments. In these situations, an open dialogue was fostered so different interpretations of the data were welcome in establishing content validity. When differences in interpretation surfaced, they were openly discussed, and the data were revisited and discussed collectively until a consensus was reached. Interpretation of the data was member checked with several of the students in the study who were accessible.

Consistent with constructivist grounded theory as described by Charmaz (2006), a four-phase analytic approach was used. All of the interviews had been thoroughly reviewed and analyzed to explore the process that the adolescents undertook to socially construct their career aspirations (see Usinger and Smith, 2010). Building upon this familiarity with the data, during the second phase of analysis, all interviews and memos for each student were again read chronologically for references to the students' educational experiences. This holistic analysis resulted in the identification of overarching themes, which were entered into NVivo as free nodes (i.e., codes that stand independently). During the third phase, interviews were reviewed again, using a line-by-line approach to more fully elaborate and illuminate the themes that had been identified during the second, holistic phase. At this point, adjustments were made to the descriptions of the themes, sub-themes were identified, and interview sections were appropriately coded. A constant comparative method within and between adolescents was also employed (Glaser and Strauss, 1967). Finally, focused coding was undertaken to provide analytic direction to the line-by-line coding. This focused coding allowed for synthesis and explanation of the data. Free nodes were organized into tree nodes (i.e., codes that form a hierarchy based upon commonality) to provide a more complete understanding of the themes. Throughout the process, extensive memos were written about the themes and additional reflections about the students. Memos were linked to statements found in the transcripts.

A model was created to depict how the themes were revealed in each student. The model reflects: (A) what school represented to the student; (B) the student's revealed self-definition in relation to education; (C) significant relationships; (D) type(s) of interaction with significant relationships; (E) the student's revealed envisioned future self; and (F) process to attain goals (Figure 1).

Coded sections of the transcripts were reviewed again to find explicit support for the model. It was only at this point that the research question was used as a filter in the analysis. As such, although the role that education plays in career ideation was the intent of the study, no attempt was made to force statements into a predetermined theoretical coding structure.

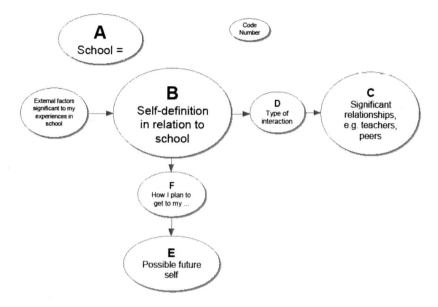

Figure 1. Model developed and used to depict revealed themes. A profile was created for each student. All students exhibited a self-definition in relation to school and believed that school equaled something specific. Almost all students engaged in significant relationships. Only some students revealed a possible future self. Only a few students had external factors that affected their experiences in school.

RESULTS

Themes

Five interconnected themes were identified in the data: (a) determination to succeed; (b) things happen magically; (c) school is a place of happiness; (d) I can show my pride; and (e) learning is secondary to more important things.

Determination to succeed. This theme was clearly present early in the interview process. Indeed, indications of determination were found in the first interview and memos of many students in the seventh grade. Determination took two general directions. For some students, the sense of determination was *toward* something – to be somebody important, special, or notable. For others, the determination was *away* from something – to be different from their past.

Some students indicated a specific goal which remained fairly consistent throughout the study. The goal often related to a specific career, for example meteorologist, accountant, astronaut, or fighter pilot; or the goal was more nebulous, for example to do something important or to be somebody. Of note, some fretted because they could not *name* their career aspiration. Nevertheless, each of these adolescents knew they wanted to be in control of and define their future. Fundamentally their statement was *I am determined to succeed.*

Determination could also be related to something the student did not want, most frequently to be different from other family members and/or the student's own background. Perhaps because all of the students in the study lived in economically disadvantaged communities, the desire to *not be poor* was the strongest statement in this sub-theme. Indeed, throughout the course of the study, many indicated that they were determined to have financial stability and, more often, financial success, which had eluded their parents. For instance, one girl stated, "I don't want to end up like my parents. Well not my parents, my dad. Like, my dad, he lives in a trailer, and I don't know, he barely gets by and everything." Some students whose families did not have stellar reputations in the community wanted to take a different path in their lives. One stated this quite clearly,

> My parents think I'm just a dumb retard, but I know that I'm not gonna drink, I'm not gonna do drugs, I'm not gonna do any of that stuff, because I've seen what it's done to my family and I'm not that dumb. I'm not one of those people who like, 'Oh, okay, well my brother does it, so it's cool.' No. I see what's not cool about it, so… People just judge me, 'Oh, well you're just another drunk [family name].' No, I'm not.

Within the determination theme, school was understood to be a place to hone the skills the adolescents felt necessary to reach their goals. For some, this consisted of learning everything possible. This group tended to take advantage of every learning opportunity provided, although some were more obvious in their approach than others. Some unequivocally stated they were taking particular classes or taking advantage of specific opportunities in order to reach their goals. Others described similar activities, but did not explicitly connect their actions to their goals; they simply described the activities as part of their everyday living. Students who revealed this sense of determination often expressed frustration when they did not believe a particular teacher was effective. If these students did not feel they were adequately learning, they found fault with the teacher's abilities.

For others who reflected the theme of determination, school was a place where they could hone their negotiation skills. This group used the various people at the school (e.g., teachers, administrators, fellow students) to perfect their ability to read others, understand power structures, and network to advance their goals. For instance, when one boy was asked about emerging as a leader at his school, he stated, "Always, every time. And somehow, I can do it, and either I get picked to be the leader or voted to be the leader. Even people I don't know. …" Another boy stated, "… I can understand situations; I can read people's face motions better than normal people could …"

Things happen magically. The second theme was the notion of magic, which revealed itself in two ways. The first was that things should just happen without effort, as if by magic. For example, students stated that grades should always be good and credits just happen; no effort should be required to achieve their desires. In some instances, external forces (e.g., teachers, administrators, prayer) were understood to solve the student's problems or provide answers, as if with the wave of a magic wand.

The other idea was that education would magically change the students' lives. Students envisioned themselves as different people in the future – after getting an education. The analogy is a caterpillar undergoing a metamorphosis into a butterfly. As adolescents, these students perceived themselves to be like a caterpillar, just crawling along. Once they obtained an education they anticipated becoming a beautiful butterfly. However, the biological processes that occur during the *cocoon* stage (in this situation, personal development and learning) were not part of their reasoning. For these students, education was represented by symbols (e.g., a diploma, grades) as if they were saying; *once I am in possession of an education [as evidenced by my diploma] I will be ok.*

School is a place for happiness. Within this third theme, school was a place of accomplishment, discovery, and joy. For many, learning new things represented happiness. There was exuberance in the students' descriptions about what they were learning. Challenges could also be framed as happiness, often because the student was able to navigate his or her way through the difficulty: "[My teacher] always challenges me, always, and I like that." In these situations, the students recognized and valued the strategies they had taken to overcome obstacles.

For others, school provided the opportunity to meet new people, a source of joy. Many students prided themselves on their ability to get along with different types of people; they attributed attendance at their particular school to their developing tolerance and acceptance of people different from them. When asked about the best thing in high school, one student who attended a high school with one of the most notorious reputations in the city stated,

> The people. They're really nice and funny, and even if you're not like them, like you have the people who hang out in the lower quad who are like gothic and they're punkers and you've got the cheerleaders. The cheerleaders will be nice to you, even if you're a punker. I know half the cheerleading squad. They're all my friends.

School was also a place where students could be with others who provided positive reinforcement, which made the student feel accepted. Reinforcement could come from friends, but teachers were more frequently referenced. The most joyous reinforcement cited by students was when the teacher recognized the personal trials and tribulations the students had experienced. "Like, I'd stay after school and I would talk to her and she'd just listen to my problems and she'd give me really good advice ... she just cared about me." Some even valued the teacher's role in keeping the student *in line.* This is perhaps best captured by one student, "... what I do to keep me going straight is like, I kinda build a family at school, so if I do something wrong they would like put me straight." As the students made these statements, school was portrayed as a haven.

I can show my pride. This theme was directly related to happiness, but was self-directed. This theme also took two distinct directions. One was pride in accomplishments, closely related to happiness. Students were proud of their successes, both academic and extracurricular. Equally, some students were very reflective of their personal development over the course of the study; many described their increasing confidence and abilities relative to previous years.

The second type of pride was in self; when this subtheme was revealed, the students were proud of themselves as individuals. They were proud of their attributes or characteristics that allowed them to feel successful. For instance, they were proud of their intellectual prowess or their ability to lead others, "It makes me feel good to see that people recognize that I have a leadership spirit and I can get the job done. ..." Significantly, school was not the source of their pride; rather the school setting allowed these students the opportunity to display their innate talents.

Learning is secondary to more important things. Although each of the themes identified above were readily found in the data, a more ubiquitous theme throughout the course of the study was the idea that learning was secondary to more important things. When asked if going to school was important, one girl nonchalantly stated, "Yes, it's probably the second or third most important thing to me." Line-by-line analysis revealed that this theme is best described on a continuum. At one end, statements indicated *I recognize that I have to go to school and I accept that, but things other than learning motivate me to get up the morning and go to school.* At the other extreme, statements indicated *school is a complete waste of my time and I would rather be doing ANYTHING else.*

For some, relationships were paramount. There was an array of important relationships for the students. For many students, family issues, needs, and obligations shaped their thinking. Family relationships ranged from activities the students enjoyed doing (e.g., travel, camping, hobbies, just being together) to serious concerns (e.g., death of a family member, legal issues, and financial crises). Additionally, many students were very mindful of the expectations their parents or guardians held regarding the student's future. Pleasing their parents was not necessarily the focus of these statements; rather, being able to navigate parental expectations was the more common direction. As the study progressed and students approached high school graduation, balancing parental expectations with their own goals and desires tipped in favor of the adolescent.

Some students found school acceptable because it allowed them to be with their friends – their first priority. Often indistinguishable from statements about being with friends, the desire to play sports and engage in extracurricular activities dominated their thinking about school. When asked the best memory of middle school, one boy stated, "Uh, like just sitting there with all my friends and stuff and doing sports ..." It must be noted that some students went to school to play sports, others played sports as part of their educational experience. At both ends of this particular continuum, however, students placed friends, sports, and other extracurricular activities high on their list of reasons to go to school.

Relationships with teachers were found in several themes, including this one. Almost all students had difficulties with teachers. However, unlike the situations described under the determination theme, whereby students were frustrated if they were not learning, students reflected in this theme were perpetually in conflict with almost all of their teachers. Every interview for the six years of the study included multiple statements about fighting with teachers. Over time, it became increasingly clear that the *fight* was very meaningful to the adolescent. Indeed, the conflict appeared to represent an exploration of power relationships; the content of these statements was often how teachers treated the student, in comparison with how the adolescent perceived the teacher treated other students. As such, fighting provided an opportunity for the adolescent to stand up for him or herself, which was more important than learning the content of the course. It was as if these students valued the engagement, albeit negative, in order to establish their autonomy.

In addition, many students indicated that teachers were responsible for their learning. If the student did not understand the course content or received poor grades, responsibility was assigned to the teacher. Sometimes the students added that the teacher did not like them, "... I don't like him 'cause he's too hard. He doesn't like me, so we don't really get along and it feels like he kinda grades harder on me than he does everybody else ..."

For some, education consisted of the symbols of learning (e.g., grades, credits, a diploma). They spoke of education as something one *gets* as if purchased at a store and put on the shelf. For instance, when talking about finishing high school, one boy stated, "I'd rather get my diploma than my GED. ... I want to show everybody that I passed high school." Or, in response to a question about keeping her grades up, one girl responded,

> So that when I come in next year, I have [a] good, strong source of my grades and I just keep that the rest of the year so that when I go to college, I can look at my grades and see that I kept them up.

These statements were frequently cast as if obtaining this tangible thing (i.e., *my* education) would be available upon demand; *it's something I can get when I need it.* When asked if education provides a road to a better life, one student stated,

> You don't need an education, then, you just need to have, you know, you just need to have to want. I mean, if you want to succeed, then you write it out that you're gonna succeed, and you do all this stuff. Then, yeah, education can only help, it's not the key."

For many students, the actual process of learning was problematic. For some, the technical aspects of learning (e.g., grammar, algebraic formula, scientific processes, etc.) were difficult. However, relatively early in the data collection, one girl responded to a question about why she liked working (bussing tables) and didn't like going to school. The expected response was that she liked earning money or she liked the independence. Her response, however, was "because I don't like to think." The idea of not liking to think was revealed by several adolescents. It appeared that for many students, learning was considered hard work that required autonomous concentration on abstract ideas and/or the need to cogently defend their thinking. Although no one stated it explicitly, it was as if these students were saying, *learning requires an investment and I don't want to make that particular investment.* One boy summed it up in this interview exchange:

Q. You hate writing?
R. With a vengeance.
Q. Why?
R. Because I hate putting ideas to paper. Ideas are fine in my head, but ideas to paper, no thanks.
Q. What's wrong with putting them on paper?
R. Too much thought process. You have the general idea, notion, idea in your head (pause)
Q. But when you write it down, it has to be specific?
R. Yup.
Q. So it's the process you don't really like.
R. Nope. Hate it.

Similarly, many students stated that learning was problematic because teaching wasn't on the students' *terms.* These statements were quite different from statements that the student was not able to learn from the teacher; rather, these statements indicated that the student wanted to design his or her own education, otherwise it would be discounted. When asked about a principal, one girl stated "cause I don't like her dumb rules." Another girl was perpetually in a battle with her various science teachers:

> I don't like scientists because they always want to over-analyze everything. They can't just leave things be. ... They gotta go into everything and find out the meaning of everything and some things don't have an explanation. ... I don't know, some things I just feel like I don't need to know and that [some things] should just be left well enough alone.

Another boy had indicated over the years that he wanted to be an architect, engineer, or own his own business; his academic record suggested that his goal was realistic. However, when discussing his postsecondary plans, he stated,

> Technical schools don't worry about all the stuff that colleges worry about. If you go to college and you were to study to be an automotive technician, you've got to go there for two years, as opposed to one year. You've got to go there and you've got to enroll in math courses, science courses, English courses, all this other stuff. Technical school, you can go in there for twelve months, run through the entire program, and you don't have to worry about talking correctly or writing down exactly how you feel about it.

When asked about how she learns, one girl stated, "It's all summed up, depending on what kind of day it is. If I have attitude, I'm not gonna do very well listening or writing, I'm just not gonna do it."

Likewise, for some students having a "short" career (i.e., one that did not require a long educational preparation) was important. Even for students who expressed a strong desire to go to college during the first part of the study, as they approached high school graduation and college, their thinking changed. They started questioning whether the time required to complete college was worth it. Earning money (often for the family) was a higher priority than pursuing their education.

The closer the students got to high school graduation, the more clearly many of the students expressed a desire to be *done* with school, although it must be noted that some expressed this earlier in their high school experience. Often students who had experienced repeated academic struggle increasingly gave up on their education. Many talked about college, but their statements were vague and unformulated, as if the adolescent knew what he or she was supposed to say, but did not really believe it. Other statements appeared to justify or rationalize why an education was not important for their future. Although some students simply wanted to be on their own, another common thought was captured by one student,

> I don't think anybody [in my family] has been to college. But they, some of them, some of the jobs are like, they really like it and they get, they still get paid pretty well. And they have fun in their lives ... some people can find some ways, like certain jobs and certain things that they do that don't require college and they can just go through life being happy and everything.

As students approached graduation, most wanted to receive their diplomas, but parallel statements increasingly suggested that the students found education irrelevant to their *real* life, although real could not be defined. As these students expressed a desire to end their education, it tended to be in order to escape various activities, not necessarily to move toward something. Statements tended to reflect what they did not want to do rather than what they wanted to do.

Student Clusters

Each of the five themes identified above contained subthemes, often revealing dichotomous or contradictory perspectives of the overarching theme. Therefore, how the subthemes were revealed in each student was explored. A model (see Figure 1) was created; the specific manner in which each theme and/or subtheme was portrayed in each student was included in the model. For instance, the subthemes found in the theme *determination to succeed* became components of (B) self-definition in relation to school and (E) possible future self. The theme *things happen magically* was integral to (F) how I plan to get to my ...; it also contributed to (E) possible future self. The themes *school is a place of happiness* and *I can show my pride* were components of all parts of the model: some students found happiness in relationships (C); others found either happiness or pride in the processes associated with relationships (D), as well as future self (F); yet other students indicated that school (A) equaled happiness or a place to display their pride in self. The theme *learning is secondary to more important things* often contributed to (A) school is ..., as well as significant relationships (C).

Once a model was completed for each adolescent, attempts were made to logically group the students. At first, students were grouped based upon their possible future self (E), but other aspects of the model did not align. Students were then grouped based upon what school represented to them (A); again there was lack of alignment. The grouping that reflected the greatest fit was based upon student self-definition in relation to education (B); students tended to cluster into five different profiles based upon their self-definition as it related to their experiences in school. All students understood that school was part of their daily activities. The overwhelming majority of the students clustered into the following four categories: (a) I'm capable; (b) I'm smart, but frustrated; (c) I feel stuck; and (d) a relational self-definition. For a few, school was incompatible with their self-definition, the last cluster. It must be noted that some students fell into different categories during the course of the study, an expected situation when considering normal adolescent development. The numerical descriptions found immediately after each title reflect the cluster with which the student aligned at the end of the study.

I'm capable. (15 students; 9 female, 6 male; 6 Native American, 5 Caucasian, 3 Latino, 1 African American; 12 rural, 3 urban) This group of students was purposefully focused on their future and what they needed to do to achieve their goals. Determination for this group tended to be directed and realistic. Their goals could either be specific (e.g., an accountant or naval pilot) or general (e.g., to be successful or make a difference). In general, they saw their futures as an extension of the present and modified their goals to reflect their developing abilities and interests. For all of these students, school was a means to achieve their personal goals.

All believed that personal effort was part of the process. What was noteworthy was that although they recognized that work was required for their success, work was not associated with drudgery or sacrifice – it was simply part of the process and the students believed they were capable of doing the work. Because they accepted responsibility for their learning, they focused inward to find direction and solutions when confronted with obstacles or problems. Two explicitly stated that they wanted to work hard now, so it would be easier later.

No one in this group ever stated that they considered themselves smart; indeed, when interview probes focused on being smart, these students either denied it or were visibly uncomfortable with the designation. Their explanation for their success was that they paid attention, worked hard, or that the work was related either to their interests or personal goals. Indeed, some were emphatic that they were not academically inclined, including the desire to pursue a vocational trade.

Some in this cluster were not particularly engaged in academics, but knew they had to do well in school to achieve their goals. For instance, one boy expressed a determination to enter the military from the first interview in seventh grade. Indeed, he indicated that he felt compelled to be a fighter pilot since he could remember, and aspired to attend the Naval Academy. As he moved through high school, he explicitly stated that the high school he attended was not a particularly good "fit" for him and at times his grades suffered. He continually adjusted his thinking about his aspirations to reflect the reality of his grades. Ultimately he joined the Army and was assigned to work in the Unmanned Aircraft System (i.e., drone) program, which for him was consistent with his desire to fly a fighter jet.

Some were informed by their hobbies. For instance, one girl who self-identified as an artist appeared to have learned the process of constant improvement through perfecting her artistic abilities. Another loved playing the base; her orchestral training appeared to inform her sense of quality and the need to practice.

For some, a sense of capability became evident during the course of the study. One student in particular stands out, although the pattern was found in other students. In this situation, her mother was ill with diabetes and kidney problems that required dialysis; the mother ultimately died during the timeframe of the study. During the first half of the interviews, the student was completely dedicated to her mother's needs. As her mother's illnesses became more severe, the student became conflicted between her mother's needs and her own future after her mother's inevitable death. At one point, the daughter appeared to just want to *run away* from her situation. Shortly after her mother's death, she began to articulate goals "for my mother." These goals and aspirations ultimately became her own.

In general, the students in this group liked their teachers and the classes they were taking, but could easily find fault in a teacher who was not teaching effectively. They clearly identified teachers who they felt were not living up to their teaching responsibilities. On the other hand, they valued teachers who they believed supported their personal and budding professional development. They also tended to be frustrated with peer students who did not share their aspirations and interfered with their work. These students were focused on themselves and their future.

Thirteen of the students in this group graduated with a standard or advanced diploma; one student graduated with a certificate of attendance (sufficient credits, but did not pass one or more of the high school exit exams); one student moved out of state during high school. Twelve (including the student who received a certificate of attendance) enrolled in a postsecondary institution immediately following high school and either have or are on track to graduate from college as of this publication. The student whose mother died during the course of the study attempted college, dropped out, but returned to college one year later and is on track to graduate. One enlisted in the military. It is unknown what happened to the student who moved out of state midway through the study.

I'm smarter than ... / superior to ..., but frustrated. (14 students; 9 males, 5 females; 8 Caucasians, 4 African Americans, 1 Latino, 1 Native American; 8 urban, 6 rural) This group of 14 students perceived themselves to be smart and/or superior to others. Because of their perceived natural abilities, they felt they were *above* the need to study or practice. Unless forced, most students in this group tended to take the easiest route available to them; when work was involved, it was considered drudgery or sacrifice. When asked to explain why her grades improved, one girl stated with distain, "I cancelled out my social life."

At the same time, all expressed perpetual frustration because they did not feel in control of their destiny. Their frustration escalated as they approached the end of high school, in large part because their progress in school, as measured by grades and credits earned, did not always match their self-definition. They tended to either not trust or not believe in the *system* (educational system, economic system, and social structure) because in their estimation, *if the system(s) were running fairly, good things should be happening to me because of my natural abilities.*

All of the students in this group were determined to do something significant in their future. Their future selves frequently reflected fame and fortune. In order to achieve their aspirations, they adopted three distinct strategies. It must be noted that students did not adopt one strategy exclusively; some students utilized all of the following strategies. First, some intentionally used school to make contacts with people who they thought would give them an advantage in the system. For these students, making the right contacts through school was believed critical to the student's future success. Statements of "sucking up to the teacher" because he or she could make it "easier for me" were common. One girl "toughed" it out in an academically challenging magnet program because she believed that people would see that she had graduated from the "best school in the state, and I think the third best school in the country," giving her an advantage in her future. She also believed she could make contacts at the school that could help her in her future. Another boy always seemed to be in some type of dilemma. As an example, he wasn't able to get into the magnet school of his choice. He invested a great deal of time and energy persuading the principal of his middle school to intervene. He could do this because he had cultivated what he described as a strong personal relationship with the principal during the two years he was in middle school. Later, when he was at risk for being removed from the same magnet program because of poor grades, he again focused all of his attention on the administrators at the high school to intervene on his behalf. His focus always seemed to be to engage with people who held power so he could tap into an established relationship when necessary.

The second strategy was to use their perceived superiority to manipulate or *outsmart* the system in some way. For instance one student had an individualized education plan (IEP) for a learning disability. He did not believe he needed it, but stated that he found it quite convenient when he hadn't studied or wanted "a bit more help." Another believed that if he observed something, he would understand it. He held a job for a short period of time and was intent upon watching his boss to learn and mimic his boss's strategies so he (the student) could become wealthy. For this group, school represented a place to hone the students' skills to outwit people who hold power.

The third strategy was to become angry and resort to confrontation and/or discount the power structure of the school (i.e., teachers and administrators). It must be noted that many of the students who adopted the strategies listed above resorted to anger at the people they perceived held power over them. However five students in this cluster never tried to cajole or influence people in power. These students simply believed they were smarter or superior to others and became angry when a teacher, counselor, or administrator did not value their abilities. For the students who resorted to this strategy, school represented an opportunity to engage in conflict. These students often sought out and/or capitalized on situations through which they could demonstrate being *right* at the (usually public) expense of the teacher, counselor, or administrator. At the same time, they constantly stated that they had no choice but to acquiesce to individuals they perceived to be the power brokers at the school, creating a vicious cycle of increasing frustration.

Eleven of the students in this group graduated high school; two dropped out, one in her junior year after giving birth and the other in her senior year having repeatedly not passed the high school exit exam; and one did not graduate (insufficient credits). Seven enrolled in college immediately after high school. Of these seven, one received an associate's degree, two have persisted in college or university, three did not persist into their second year, and one did not persist beyond the fall semester of the second year. Two of the eleven students who graduated high school enlisted in the military; one immediately following high school and the other after working construction and attending community college part time. One of the eleven students who graduated high school immediately entered the workforce. The other student of the eleven was arrested for armed robbery during the summer after high school graduation.

I feel stuck. (14 students; 10 female, 4 male; 6 Caucasian, 4 Latino, 2 Native American, 1 African American, 1 Pacific Islander; 8 rural, 6 urban) This group of students all wanted to succeed and tried, but nothing seemed to *click* and they did not feel successful in school. Of note, none indicated that they *were* incapable; rather they *felt* incapable and the feelings of inadequacy increased with repeated failed attempts. They frequently talked of others who they believed were smart, but the students in this cluster frequently could not figure out why the other students were successful. The theme magic was very strong; they repeatedly stated that others were just able to *do* something. They tended to believe that someone else (usually the teacher) was responsible for their learning. This group also tended to lack an imagined future; their thoughts were more in the present.

Several of the students in this cluster were identified as "I'm capable" during the initial, holistic analysis of the data. Their identification was based upon their statements of determination; they had strong statements of goals and aspirations. However, during the line-by-line analysis, the statements were always couched in "I'm trying" to do something or "if" I do something (e.g., go to college). Definitive statements of what they were planning or actually doing were absent.

Most of the students in this cluster believed themselves to be capable in middle school and were proud of their relationships, particularly with teachers who they believed liked them and supported them as individuals. As they moved into high school and experienced more complex curricula, they tried to keep up, but frequently could not. Their initial reaction was confusion; they could not understand why their experiences were different in high school compared to middle school. Confusion often became frustration. Some expressed their frustration by blaming others (e.g., teachers, family situations) for their lack of success; others came to accept not "getting it."

Despite experiencing academic setbacks, some students continued to hold the same career aspirations throughout their middle and high school years. For instance, one boy continued to aspire to be an astronaut, despite failing math and being removed from the aviation magnet program. Another continued to aspire to being a doctor, again despite struggling with math (beginning with algebra); she also struggled with science. For these students, the reality of academic struggle did not cause them to rethink their future selves; it was as if magically they would become the person they envisioned.

Their internal struggle of wanting to succeed, but not being able to achieve what they perceived as success was frequently resolved by finding an alternative means of feeling good about themselves. Two found satisfaction when they felt successful in jobs they obtained. Indeed, one repeatedly stated he felt more like a "man" when he worked and was able to be financially independent – and help his mother with her bills. He didn't dislike school, but his sense of self was derived from work and he did not graduate high school with his class. Another boy turned to drugs as a way of escaping his feeling of frustration.

Others focused on the needs of family members. One girl in particular stands out. Her mother died of cancer during the course of the study and her father had numerous medical complications when she was in high school. The more she struggled in school, the more she found meaning in helping her parents with their medical needs. She always talked about moving out of the isolated rural community where she lived with her father. Nevertheless, her statements about her father needing her were said in such a manner to suggest that helping her family was how she found personal meaning.

In other instances, their internal struggle was portrayed through blaming teachers and/or confrontation with other students and, often, teachers. This was quite different from the conflicts with teachers expressed by the "I'm smart" cluster. When students felt stuck, there was no sense of a *game of power* being played; frustration and confusion was the basis of conflict for these students.

Of the fourteen students, seven graduated high school; four received a certificate of attendance (sufficient credits, but did not pass one of the high school exit exams); one did not graduate (insufficient credits); and two dropped out of school. Of the students who graduated, one completed a bachelor's degree and is now seeking an advanced degree; three started college or university, but did not persist into the second year. Of the students who received a certificate of attendance, it is known that two entered the workforce and one has been in and out of jail.

Relational self-definition. (9 students: 5 female, 4 male; 4 Caucasian, 2 African American, 2 Latino, 1 Native American; 5 urban, 4 rural) This group of students really liked to be at school because school sustained their need for relationships with others. Doing well academically was considered part of the process; these students worked hard to maintain their grades and were reasonably successful. However, learning was not their primary motivation for getting up in the morning and going to school.

For some, friends were paramount. School represented a place where they could interact with friends. One was an avid basketball player; although he clearly loved the sport, line-by-line examination of the data revealed his actual enjoyment was being with his teammates. Another was in the International Baccalaureate (IB) program and struggled. However, she felt that as long as "we are all in this together" and will "make it together" she could endure.

For others, being part of clubs and school activities was important. One was in the IB program during middle school, but decided to not pursue IB in high school and attended a comprehensive high school with a notorious reputation for gang and other illicit activities. She described herself as the "bridge" between various rival groups in the school and strongly valued her connection to so many people. Another girl moved from a school where she had struggled academically and socially with both teachers and peers. When she moved to a new school, she became active in school activities and came to enjoy school tremendously.

For others, relationships with teachers and other adults were very important. One boy who experienced homelessness (i.e., was a *couch-surfer*) during his senior year in high school created a family from people at school. He described his basketball coach as "my coaches, they always be a father figure to me" and many of his teachers "like my mother." He repeatedly stated that these relationships were important to ensure that he remain on track to succeed academically.

Of the nine students, eight graduated high school, one with an adjusted diploma (student with individualized learning plan [IEP]); one received a certificate of attendance (sufficient credits, but did not pass one or more of the high school exit exams). Three entered college or university immediately after high school and have persisted. One entered university, but did not persist through the first year. One worked for a year and then entered community college.

Education is incompatible with my self-definition. (8 students: 6 male, 2 female; 6 Native American, 1 Caucasian, 1 Pacific Islander; 6 rural, 2 urban) Five of the students in this group envisioned themselves in the future, but none believed that education was necessary for their future. For the most part, they attended school, but there was no real interest in what was happening at school. One boy envisioned himself breaking horses; another just wanted to play sports. A girl wanted to get married and have children; she definitely did not want to work. Two had interests in middle school, but lost their interests and did not find new ones. The disposition of these students was not favorable. One graduated high school and entered the workforce. One was expelled. Three moved out of state; one of these students is known to have dropped out of school.

It is difficult to ascertain the self-definition of three of the students in this group, all Native American: two male, one female; one urban, two rural. During middle school, and for one student into the first year of high school, these students were disconnected from the activities of school, much like the other students in this group. The difference, however, was that the parents took these students out of the public school system. It was reported that all three students transferred to tribal schools out of state. It is unknown whether these students actively engaged in their new schools.

DISCUSSION

The overwhelming majority (87%) of the students in this study rationally grasped the importance of education and found some form of meaning in attending middle and/or high school. Some students were focused on their future and used the various opportunities available in the school setting to advance their goals. Many were focused on the interactions and relationships inherent in a school setting.

Race and ethnicity did not appear to be an appropriate indicator for how students (who found meaning in school) clustered relative to their understanding of the role that education played in their personal development. Students of each race/ethnicity were proportionately represented in four of the five clusters. This was similar to the findings of how these same students developed their career aspirations (Usinger and Smith, 2010).

In addition to race/ethnicity, academic ability was not a particularly salient indicator of how students clustered either. Most of the students in the "I'm capable" cluster performed well academically, but some did not consider themselves academically inclined and some students had an IEP based upon a learning disability. The same pattern was found in the "I'm smart, but frustrated" cluster. Some students excelled academically, but others did not and one of the students had an IEP as well. Perhaps most significantly, several students in the "I feel stuck" and "education is incompatible with my self-definition" clusters showed academic promise, but they could not connect with the process of learning as designed at their schools.

In contrast, trends for urban/rural and male/female were found. Rural students were overrepresented in both the "I'm capable" and "education is incompatible with my self-definition" clusters; however, it must be noted that the overall sample of students in the study consisted of more rural than urban adolescents. More significantly, males (particularly Native American males) were overrepresented in the "education is incompatible with my self-definition" cluster and parents of three of the eight students in this group removed their son or daughter from their local public school and enrolled them in tribal schools out of state. Long-term data was not collected from students who left the state; therefore, it is unknown whether they connected to their new schools. One Native American girl who remained in the study might provide some insight, however. When asked about taking history quizzes, she responded, "… the only part I keep in my head is what she says about Native Americans. But whatever else she talks about, I don't remember."

One theory that provides insight into the findings of this study is self-determination theory (SDT), an approach to human motivation and personality which includes the conditions or environments that either facilitate or forestall these growth-oriented processes in people (Ryan and Deci, 2000). Self-determination theory differentiates between intrinsic motivation, the state of doing an activity out of interest and inherent satisfaction, and extrinsic motivation, which is externally regulated. In addition, SDT includes amotivation, or the state of lacking the intention to act. The theory is based upon the assumption that three basic psychological needs are necessary for growth and well-being of an individual's personality and cognitive structure: competence, relatedness, and autonomy (Ryan and Deci, 2000, 2002).

Ryan and Deci (2000) argued that feelings of competence do not enhance intrinsic motivation unless accompanied by a sense of autonomy. The students in the "I'm capable" cluster clearly revealed the synergy of these two psychological needs, competence and autonomy. Each student in this cluster either possessed or developed a sense of personal agency during the course of the study. This was complemented by their belief in their capacity to persevere in diverse, and often challenging, circumstances. Furthermore, they did not perceive work (e.g., school work or practicing to perfect a skill) in a particularly negative way; it was something that was necessary for achievement and they were capable of doing it. Although acknowledging their challenges, these students focused inwardly on what they could do to direct and be in control of their futures.

Relatedness is the third cognitive structure, according to Ryan and Deci (2000). Self-definition theory includes the hypothesis that intrinsic motivation is more likely to flourish in contexts characterized by a sense of security and relatedness. For the "I'm capable" cluster, relatedness was in evidence, but secondary to their sense of autonomy. For this cluster, relationships held value primarily when they supported the student's sense of autonomy and competence. Figure 2 illustrates the relationship between the three psychological needs of SDT found in this cluster.

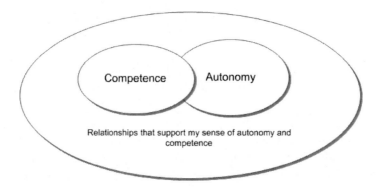

Figure 2. Relationship of the "I'm capable" cluster to the three psychological needs associated with SDT. All three basic needs were revealed in this cluster of students.

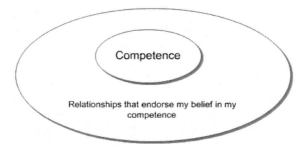

Figure 3. Relationship of the "I'm smart, but frustrated" cluster to the three psychological needs associated with SDT. Only two basic needs were revealed in this cluster of students; relatedness suggested relationships that bolstered the student's sense of competence, rather than belongingness.

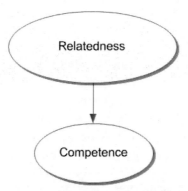

Figure 4. Relationship of "relational self-definition" cluster to the three psychological needs associated with SDT. Although only two basic needs were revealed, relatedness (i.e., belonging) contributed to the student's sense of competence.

The "I'm smart, but frustrated" cluster displayed a different orientation of these three psychological needs. Each student believed in his or her competence, the feeling of effectiveness in one's ongoing interaction with the social environment and experiencing opportunities to exercise or express one's capabilities (Ryan and Deci, 2000). However, students in this group did not exhibit a corresponding sense of personal agency or autonomy; rather their frustrations were born from the belief that others held sway over their destiny. As such, it was essential that adolescents in this cluster control relationships with others, particularly individuals the students perceived as holding power. Anger with the power structure (and those in it) was pervasive, but some students worked to cajole or outwit others to ensure that their capabilities were acknowledged. Relatedness for this group appeared to be strategic power games to feel competent. See Figure 3.

For the "relational self-definition" cluster, relatedness was a central need. Ryan and Deci (2002) described relatedness as the tendency to connect with and be integral to and accepted by others; in other words, belongingness. Unlike the students in the "I'm smart, but frustrated" cluster, however, relatedness for these students contributed to their sense of competence. They persevered because of their sense of belonging. At the same time, autonomy did not appear to hold great value. See Figure 4.

The "I feel stuck" cluster revealed a pattern of *desire* for relatedness and *desire* for competence. Relatedness was intermittently satisfied in the school setting; however, an actual sense of competence mostly eluded these students. Particularly in middle school, students in this cluster related well to teachers who the students felt understood their personal struggles or praised the student for his or her abilities. As the student progressed through the educational system into high school, two conditions changed. First, courses became more complex and the students frequently struggled academically. Additionally, urban high schools were considerably larger than the middle schools the students had attended. At this point, students could not rely upon the types of relationships with teachers that had been trusted in middle school; relationships ceased to be personal. Often students could not figure out how to bolster their competence as it related to schoolwork and became increasingly frustrated with their inability to realize meaning through academics. Some turned away from school to find a sense of competence.

For instance, some found meaning in work; others found meaning in tending to family members in need. Some continued to go through the motions associated with school work, but increasingly displayed feelings of defeat. At the extreme, some entered the "education is incompatible with my self-definition" cluster and found no meaning in school or their education. Regardless, autonomy was either weak, non-existent, or sought through others. See Figure 5.

Figure 5. Relationship of "I feel stuck" cluster to the three psychological needs associated with SDT. In addition to a lack of a sense of autonomy, students in this cluster increasingly lacked a sense of competence following unsuccessful attempts. Relatedness was more aptly defined as seeking a friendship than belonging.

In an exploration of the development of learning enjoyment, Hagenauer and Hascher (2010) hypothesized that learning enjoyment would be positively linked to the fulfillment of the three SDT psychological needs of autonomy, competence, and relatedness. In addition to finding that learning enjoyment decreased between sixth and seventh grade, Hagenauer and Hascher also found that an autonomy-supporting school environment proved to be the weakest factor to positively affect students' self-efficacy and learning enjoyment compared to caring teachers and instructional quality, which were much stronger factors. Diaries completed by students in the study lacked references to the importance of autonomy as a factor affecting their actual learning enjoyment (Hagenauer and Hascher, 2010). The findings from this study were somewhat similar. Only the "I'm capable" group, or 25% of the students, revealed a sense of autonomy. For this group, personal agency was very important and appeared to drive their actions. However, for the students in the "I'm smart, but frustrated", "I feel stuck", and the relational self-definition clusters, representing over two thirds of the students in the study, relatedness as represented by interactions with others was far more important than their desire for autonomy. For the relational self-definition cluster, competence was found through relatedness. The "I'm smart, but frustrated" group needed others to enable their sense of competence. Most in the "I feel stuck" group were seeking friendship and wanted others to be responsible for their learning. In these three groups, autonomy was either weak, not in evidence, or not identified as important.

While relatedness was most strongly expressed in the students of this study, it was revealed in a unique manner as well. In a study of the ecological factors on adolescent perceptions of school connectedness, Waters, Cross, and Shaw (2010) assessed the outcome variable, connectedness to school, through five statements: 'I feel part of this school'; 'I feel close to people at this school'; 'I am happy to be at this school'; 'teachers treat students fairly'; and 'I feel safe at this school.' Each of these statements suggests a positive orientation to the school. Although this positive construct was found in many of the students in the study presented, there was an additional subset of students in both the "I'm smart, but frustrated" and "I feel stuck" groups who expressed their frustrations through anger and fighting with teachers, administrators, and often peers. These students frequently made statements about not liking school or believing that the teachers were not fair; nevertheless, there was a sense of pride in their statements about the battles in which they engaged at school. Furthermore, unlike other students who held specific reasons for not liking a teacher (e.g., the student was not learning from the particular teacher) these students picked fights with almost every teacher and/or administrator. Additionally, unlike other students who believed education to be inconsistent with their self-definition, these students rarely missed a day of school. It was as if they needed to *do battle* for their own reasons and the school environment provided the perfect opportunity for these students to express themselves. As such, they were strongly connected to school, but in a rather perverse way.

Ryan and Deci (2000) further described self-determination on a continuum, from nonself-determination or amotivation, to self-determination or intrinsic motivation. In between these two extremes is extrinsic motivation, which is regulated through four distinct mechanisms. *External* regulation is the least autonomous form of extrinsic motivation and is reflective of classic operant theory, most famously connected to B.F. Skinner (1953). *Introjected* regulation involves adaptation that has been internalized, but not accepted as one's own; behaviors are performed as an ego-enhancer or to avoid guilt or shame. *Identified* regulation is more self-determined and involves a conscious valuing of the goal or an acceptance of the behavior, including a high degree of perceived autonomy. *Integrated* regulation provides the basis for the most autonomous form of extrinsically regulated behavior; behaviors are congruent with personally endorsed values, goals, and needs. Integrated regulation shares many of the qualities with intrinsic motivation, but they have a separable outcome (Ryan and Deci, 2000).

In a study of upper elementary (fourth through sixth) grade students, Ryan and Connell (1989) found that the process of internalizing a value or behavioral regulation was more likely to occur if one had adopted the belief that the relevant outcomes were potentially under ones control. Specifically, they reported that perceived internal control was most strongly correlated with the two middle subscales of identification and introjection. Koestner and Losier (2002) further contended that internalizing the value of school participation was more important to psychological growth and development than whether students were intrinsically motivated about school. In this study, the "I'm capable" cluster was the only group that fit the identification model of perceived internal control, coupled with holding the value of the process of learning over symbols of education.

The introjection category of external regulation whereby motivation is derived from "internal, esteem-based pressures to act, such as avoidance of guilt and shame or concerns about self- and other-approval" (Ryan and Connell, 1989, p. 750) is of particular interest in this study. Our findings suggested a slightly nuanced interpretation of this regulation by the students who appeared to exhibit behaviors most consistent with introjection – the "I'm smart, but frustrated" group. Students in this cluster were definitely focused on self- and other-approval, they also did not accept the expectations and regulations of the school as their own. Indeed, they tended to not trust systems in general. Yet, for the most part, their acts were not born out of guilt or shame. These students were proud of what they perceived to be their innate abilities, but felt that teachers and others in power were either holding them back or held the key to possible advancement. In some instances, the students in this group contended that teachers were simply jealous because the student was smarter or more talented than the teacher. Others were frustrated because their innate talents were not being appropriately recognized. It must be noted that several in this group talked about having to "buckle down because my grandmother will kill me" or "I'll get grounded if I don't pull my grades up" or other statements indicating a degree of guilt or anxiety. However, these arguments appeared to be more of a deflection away from their more consistent and internalized belief that the system simply was not conforming to the students' expectations and desires.

As discussed by Anderman and Maehr (1994), the students in the "I'm smart, but frustrated" group also believed that their abilities were fixed traits that they possessed. However, their reluctance to put forth an effort and potentially fail was not because of a concern of looking "dumb" (Anderman and Maehr, 1994, p. 290), rather it was because they thought that they did not have to work because their perceived innate abilities should be sufficient. Only once in the duration of the study did two students express feelings of embarrassment by poor grades. One student was represented in the "I'm smart, but frustrated" cluster; the other was represented in the "I'm capable" cluster.

Self-determination theory may also illuminate the one demographic trend that was found in the data. Boys are at greater risk for not completing their education than girls (Wilson, Zozula and Grove, 2011) and the disposition of the students in this study reflected these statistics. Ryan and Deci (2002) described amotivation as the "state of lacking the intention to act" (p. 17). Amotivation was revealed by students in both the "I feel stuck" and "education is inconsistent with my self-definition" clusters, but for different reasons. Ryan and Deci cited lack of competence, or self-efficacy as described by Bandura (1997) as one reason for amotivation. As many of the students in the "I feel stuck" cluster became increasingly frustrated about their ability to succeed academically, they made statements about wanting to do well in school and continue their education past high school, but their statements lacked conviction and appeared to be more an expected response to a question they had heard repeatedly. In essence, they increasingly gave up on their education because of a decreasing sense of competence and self-efficacy.

Ryan and Deci (2002) also indicated that one of the reasons for amotivation is that the individual does not value the activity or outcomes of the activity. This description was more characteristic of the "education is inconsistent with my self-definition" cluster, which was dominated by boys, Native Americans, and rural students. During the course of the study, several students made what appeared to be a conscious decision that their futures were not dependent upon, or even connected to, formal education. Unlike students in other clusters, these students did not display any emotion (positive or negative) about this decision; they simply made it.

As indicated, students did not necessarily remain in the same cluster for the entire length of the study. Several students would have been placed in the "I feel stuck" cluster if the timeframe of the study had been different. For instance, one girl struggled both academically and socially at the beginning of the study. She moved during her second year of high school to another community. Because she remained in the state where the study was conducted, interviews continued to be conducted with her. After adjusting to the move, she found meaning through her relationships at her new school and ended up in the relational self-definition cluster. Other students made the decision to take control of their lives during the course of the study and ended up in the "I'm capable" group. Likewise, some appeared to have lost their sense of direction and struggled to find meaning in school – and other societal structures. These students became part of the "I feel stuck" group at the end of the study; one made the decision that "education is inconsistent with my self-definition."

CONCLUSION

The purpose of this study was to explore how adolescents understand the role that education plays in their lives. It was part of a larger qualitative study to explore how adolescents socially construct their career aspirations and the role that education plays in that process. Although the research was not designed to empirically test self-determination theory (SDT) (Ryan and Deci, 2000), this theory proved to be an appropriate analytic filter because of the manner in which the themes revealed themselves in the 60 adolescents (see Figure 1). Self-definition related to education was the concept that provided alignment of the other concepts revealed in the data.

Ryan and Deci (2002) argued that among the three fundamental needs (i.e., autonomy, competence, and relatedness) SDT posits that satisfaction of the need for autonomy is the most salient to the person's growth. Results of this study suggest that autonomy served as the *glue* that provided balance to competence and relatedness. The "I'm capable" cluster exhibited all three psychological needs. Students in this group were best able to navigate challenges and focus on what was necessary for their growth and development. Their focus was on their future and what they needed to do to get there.

Likewise, the "education is inconsistent with my self-definition" group also reflected a strong sense of autonomy. They made the decision to disengage from the educational system and each student appeared to *own* that decision. However, because education was the focus of the analysis, it is impossible to speculate about how other concerns, more relevant to the adolescents, would have revealed competence and relatedness.

When autonomy was either weak or non-existent, students tended to struggle in a variety of ways. It must be noted that the disposition of the students who lacked a sense of autonomy was often positive, but *getting there* was frequently challenging. For the students in the "I'm smart, but frustrated" cluster, the lack of autonomy created a rather perverse interaction between the needs of relatedness and competence. Although these students argued vociferously about their own competence, they needed others to endorse their belief, suggesting a lack of internalization of their belief in their own competence. Additionally, students in this cluster tended to engage in transactional relationships with others rather than relationships reflective of interpersonal trust.

The weakness or lack of autonomy associated with the "I feel stuck" cluster created even more challenges because it was coupled with a lack of a sense of competence and a desire for relatedness. It must be noted that many of the students in this group demonstrated competence; however, they were unable to acknowledge, let alone embrace, their own strengths and abilities. Furthermore, the relationships these students sought from adults in the school setting were based upon the desire for friendship; therefore, they did not seek the type of guidance that would endorse a sense of competence, making it even more difficult for those students to engage in self-determination.

The one exception to the idea that autonomy is central to self-determination was the relational self-definition cluster. This group of students did not necessarily value autonomy. Rather it was through relatedness that they found competence.

In summary, all of the students in this study rationally knew that education was important for their future. They repeatedly stated that in order to have a bright future and good job, education was important. Yet only a portion embraced the idea in a manner that made it integral to their personal reality. As the students who did not internalize education as a personal value approached the end of their education, they increasingly convinced themselves that education was not as important for their futures as they had once believed.

Two limitations of this study must be noted. First, only a partial data set was collected from 10 of the 60 students who agreed to be part of the original study: six students left the state where the study was conducted; two students were expelled and left the community; two students dropped out of school and their locations became unknown. As a result, their specific thinking over time regarding their future and the role that education plays in shaping that future was not captured. When these 10 students left the study, each was on a negative path (i.e. were in the "I feel stuck" or "education is inconsistent with my self-definition" cluster); however, some or all of them may have decided to take control over their lives, as some of the students who remained in the study did.

Second, the study was designed to explore the thoughts and ideas that the students had about their personal development and future self; it was not to examine the various activities in which the students were engaged. Students talked about various academic support and extracurricular activities, but there was no intent to gather details about the activities.

Therefore, it is difficult to make specific recommendations for strategies to more fully engage students in the learning process.

Future analysis using this dataset will explore how the students changed over time. For some students the change was maturation and development within the same self-definition. However, other students made personal decisions that caused their thinking to change rather dramatically. In some instances, the change was that the student decided to take control over his or her life; in other instances, life circumstances caused the student to become overwhelmed. Future analysis will explore the factors that contributed to the changes noted.

It is also recommended that future research more fully explore the role of relatedness for adolescents. In this study, relationships with adults were more important and helped shape student thinking more than autonomy and competence. Understanding the subtleties of these relationships and the concept of relatedness could provide important insight into how to guide students as they transition into adulthood.

IMPLICATION FOR PRACTICE

According to the functional theory of education, formal education assists in facilitating the smooth functioning of a society. The assumption is that stability is created through the interrelationship between each part of society (i.e., family, education, political and economic systems, health, and religion). Each societal component has its own unique role; the specific functions of education are: (a) socialization of children to be productive members of society; (b) personal and social development; (c) selection and training of individuals for positions in the society; and (d) promoting change and innovation (Ballantine and Spade, 2008). As the economic system has become increasingly globalized and based upon harnessing knowledge and information, the educational system has been impacted. One of the principal pressures that economic globalization has had on the educational system is the demand by policy-makers, business leaders, and the general public to increase the average level of education (Carnoy and Rhoten 2008). Two primary means of affecting change in the educational system in the United States have been through legislative mandates such as No Child Left Behind (NCLB) and competitive funding such as Race to the Top. The NCLB legislation imposes sanctions on schools that do not make Adequate Yearly Progress (AYP). If a school does not make AYP for several years, changes in school leadership and the teaching staff can be imposed. Race to the Top does not necessarily impose sanctions, but a requirement for this highly competitive funding is that schools be able to demonstrate improvements in academic achievement in a very short timeframe.

Niemiec and Ryan (2009) argued that student autonomy can be supported by minimizing evaluative pressure and any sense of coercion in the classroom. The challenge, of course, is that when schools are under serious pressure, it is difficult for teachers and school leaders to focus on anything beyond a fairly narrow version of accountability demands – get student scores up fast! Anything that might be interpreted as diverting attention from the academic curriculum is circumspect. As such, counselors, teachers, and school leaders must find ways to explore the principles of SDT so as to understand how they contribute to academic achievement. Results of this study support the basic premise of SDT that when students' basic needs for autonomy, competence, and relatedness are supported in the classroom, students are more likely to internalize their motivation to learn and be more engaged in their studies (Niemiec and Ryan, 2009). Indeed, the "I'm capable" cluster exhibited all three psychological needs and were the most engaged in both the learning process and how education was directly connected to their futures. However, this cluster represented only a quarter of the students in the study. Although it is recognized that the students changed over time, at the end of the six year study, when students exited high school, two-thirds of the students did not exhibit a strong sense of autonomy; rather they were far more focused on the relatedness aspect of SDT.

Niemiec and Ryan (2009) argued that students who feel competent, but not autonomous, do not maintain an intrinsic motivation for learning. This description fit the "I'm smart, but frustrated" cluster. Yet promoting more self-directed and autonomous behavior could be challenging with students who reflect this profile, at least based upon the findings of this study. These frustrated students thought they did not have to work to be successful. Bird and Markle (2012) recommended that schools can foster subjective well-being, a concept similar to SDT, by incorporating personal goal setting as a regular part of the curriculum and ensuring that students choose realistic, but meaningful goals to pursue. Because it is a regular part of the curriculum, this approach has the potential of redirecting students away from attempting to exert power over teachers in order to gain a feeling of autonomy as they work toward personal goals. As teachers are frequently focused on the content of their courses, counselors can play a critical role in this effort. Indeed, they are in the position to provide leadership in helping students identify and work toward realistic goals. They can also work in collaboration with teachers to integrate student goals with the curriculum.

A more deliberate approach to personal goal setting would also help students better understand the relationship between their education and their futures. Even though future-oriented questions were intentionally asked during each interview session, many of the students were not focused on their futures; or their futures were imagined abstractly or magically; or it was cast in terms of fame and fortune. Counselors can serve in the essential role of assisting students who have budding interests align their personal goals with the opportunities available at the school or in the community. Counselors can further guide students to set aspirational, but realistic goals, as well as monitor progress and celebrate milestones toward the students' goals. The "I feel stuck" cluster exhibited neither competence nor autonomy. During their middle school years, many in this group felt competent, but increasingly lost that feeling in high school as coursework became harder and more complex. Niemiec and Ryan's (2009) suggestion that teachers approach relatedness by the teacher genuinely liking, respecting, and valuing the student requires a cautionary note. This was the type of relationship (i.e., personal friendship) that the students in this cluster valued in middle school and sought in high school. The problem, however, was that this approach did not translate into a feeling of competence by these students. To foster a sense of competency in these types of students, the suggestion is to follow Niemiec and Ryan's recommendation that counselors and teachers provide students with the appropriate tools and feedback to promote success and feelings of efficacy. In this way, students can engage and personally value activities that they can actually understand, but more importantly, master. The distinction between these two approaches to relatedness is critical. In addition to interviewing students, this study also included interviews with school personnel for contextual understanding. It was not uncommon for teachers to describe ways that they were attempting to support both autonomy and competency. Because the study included several students at the same school (particularly rural schools), it was possible to explore how different students reacted to the teachers' statements. Some students (primarily in the "I'm capable" and relatedness self-definition clusters) interpreted messages of autonomy and competence as supportive; others interpreted the messages very differently. The "I'm smart, but frustrated" cluster tended to not trust encouragement from school personnel, perhaps because these students were primarily engaged in power struggles with authority figures. The students in the "I feel stuck" cluster sought personal validation and did not focus on statements that promoted autonomy and competency. Indeed, each student had a somewhat unique interpretation of the same message delivered by the same teacher, counselor, or principal. Bird and Markle (2012) argued that effective mentoring requires substantial training in cognitive behavioral, solution-focused coaching strategies; results from this study support that recommendation. Counselors have the academic preparation as well as professional experiences to take the leadership in designing appropriate mentoring programs. They could provide professional development and ongoing support for teachers as well.

Finally, school personnel can foster the three psychological needs, autonomy, competence, and relatedness, by partnering with youth serving community-based organizations. It is recommended, however, that non-formal or out-of-school activities be based upon the principals of positive youth development (PYD), as described by Lerner, Almerigi, Theokas, and Lerner (2005). This strength-based approach to youth development promotes the Five Cs of PYD, competence, confidence, character, connection, and caring. Working in partnership, schools and youth-serving organizations can support young people to express their individualities and their potentials in a manner that contributes to their personal well-being and the well-being of society. Many students, particularly those from the relational self-definition group, thrived from their extracurricular activities. Collaborating with organizations and encouraging extracurricular activities may help students become more competent and autonomous both in and out of the school setting.

In summary, the findings of this study portray the complexity of how adolescents use the school setting and the process of education to find meaning, as well as realize their aspirations. Many students articulated the importance of education in providing for their future stability and prosperity; however, meaning was often derived from relationships that did not necessarily support their envisioned ambitions. Counselors have the skills and can play an important role in assisting students as they navigate a multitude of influences toward adulthood.

AUTHOR NOTE

This research was supported by the US Department of Education, Office of Postsecondary Education, P223S010009. The author is indebted to numerous colleagues, including Stephanie Woolf and Jafeth Sanchez who contributed to this research; and particularly to Kathleen Hill for her help with this chapter. Special thanks for comments on drafts of this chapter go to Rita Laden, Charlotte Curtis, and Marilyn Smith.

REFERENCES

Anderman, E. M., and Maehr, M. L. (1994). Motivation and schooling in middle grades. *Review of Educational Research*, 64, 287-309. doi:10.3102/00346543064002287.

Bandura, A. (1997). Self-efficacy:The exercise of control. New York: W.H. Freeman.

Bird, J. M., and Markle, R. S. (2012). Subjective well-being in school environments: Promoting positive youth development through evidence-based assessment and intervention. *American Journal of Orthopsychiatry*, 82(1), 61-66. doi:10.1111/j.1939-0025.2011.01127.x.

Carnoy, M., and Rhoten, D. (2008). What does globalization mean for educational change? In J. H. Ballantine and J. Z. Spade (Eds.), Schools and Society, (pp. 486-490). Thousand Oaks, CA: Sage Publ., Inc.

Charmaz, K. (2006). Constructing grounded theory: A practical guide through qualitative analysis. Thousand Oaks, CA: Sage Publ., Inc.

Creswell, J. W. (2003). Research design: Qualitative, quantitative, and mixed method approaches (2nd ed.). Thousand Oaks, CA: Sage Publ., Inc.

Glaser, B. G., and Strauss, A. L. (1967). Discovery of grounded theory. Chicago: Aldine.

Hagenauer, G., and Hascher, T. (2010). Learning enjoyment in early adolescence. *Educational Research and Evaluation*, 16(6), 495-516. doi:10.1080/13803611.2010.550499.

Koestner, R. and Losier, G. F. (2002). Distinguishing three ways of being internally motivated: A closer look at introjection, identification, and intrinsic motivation. In E. L. Deci and R. M. Ryan (Eds.), *Handbook of self-determination research* (pp. 101-121). Rochester, NY: University of Rochester Press.

Lerner, R. M., Almerigi, J. B., Theokas, C., and Lerner, J.V. (2005). Positive youth development: A view of the issues. *Journal of Early Adolescence*, 25(1), 10-16. doi:10.1177/027243604273211.

Levin, H., Belfield, C., Meunnig, P., and Rouse, C. (2007). The costs and benefits of an excellent education for all of America's children. New York: Center for Benefit-Cost Studies of Education at Teachers College, Columbia University.

Nevada Department of Education (2001). State of Nevada GEAR UP state application. Nevada: Governor's Office.

Niemiec, C. P., and Ryan, R. M. (2009). Autonomy, competence, and relatedness in the classroom: Applying self-determination theory to educational practice. *Theory and Research in Education*, 7(2), 133-144. doi:10.1177/1477878509104318.

Rubin, H. J. and Rubin, J.S. (2005). Qualitative interviewing: The art of hearing data (2nd ed.). Thousand Oaks, CA: Sage Publ., Inc.

Ryan, R. M., and Connell, J. P. (1989). Perceived locus of causality and internalization: Examining reasons for acting in two domains. *Journal of Personality and Social Psychology*, 57(5), 749-761. doi:0022-3514/89/500.75.

Ryan, R. M., and Deci, E. L. (2000). Self-determination theory and the facilitation of intrinsic motivation, social development, and well-being. *American Psychologist*, 55(1), 68-78. doi:10.1037/0003-066X.55.1.68.

Ryan, R. M., and Deci, E. L. (2002). Overview of self-determination theory: An organismic dialectical perspective. In E. L. Deci and R. M. Ryan (Eds.), Handbook of self-determination research (pp. 3-33). Rochester, NY: University of Rochester Press.

Skinner, B. F. (1953). Science and human behavior. New York: Macmillan.

Usinger, J., and Smith, M. (2010). Career development in the context of self-construction during adolescence. *Journal of Vocational Behavior*, 76, 580-591. doi:10.1016/j.jvb.2010.01.010.

Waters, S., Cross, D., and Shaw, T. (2010). Does the nature of schools matter? An exploration of selected school ecology factors on adolescent perceptions of school connectedness. *British Journal of Educational Psychology*, 80, 381-402. doi:10.1348/000709909 X484479.

Wilson, J. A., Zozula, C., and Grove, W. R. (2011). Age, period, cohort, and educational attainment: The importance of considering gender. *Social Science Research*, 40(1), 136-149.

In: Psychology of Counseling
Editor: Annamaria Di Fabio

ISBN: 978-1-62618-388-9
© 2013 Nova Science Publishers, Inc.

Chapter 8

Racial Identity Profile Patterns of White Mental Health Practitioners: Implications for Multicultural Counseling Competency in Research and Practice

*Renée A. Middleton[1], Bengü Ergüner-Tekinalp[2],
Elena A. Petrova[3], Natalie F. Williams[1]
and Thomandra Sam[4]*

[1]Ohio University, Athens, OH, US
[2]Drake University, Des Moines, IA, US
[3]University of Wisconsin Oshkosh, Oshkosh, WI, US
[4]Western Carolina University, Asheville, NC, US

ABSTRACT

Researchers used a mixed-methods approach to increase understanding of the racial identity development of White mental health practitioners and its bearing on the therapeutic dyad. This is the fourth and final product embedded within a larger program of study (DelSignore et al., 2010; Middleton et al., 2005; Middleton et al., 2011). Qualitative data drawn from mental health practitioners' self-reported critical incidents was linked to racial identity profile patterns. The methodology for the quantitative component was modeled after research conducted by Carter, Helms, and Juby (2004). The data yielded predominantly blended triumvirate and quadripartite racial identity profile patterns. The most common profile yielded a blended triumvirate profile formulation of Disintegration, Reintegration and Contact (D-R-C). Implications of findings are discussed along with recommendations for future research and practice.

RACIAL IDENTITY PROFILE PATTERNS OF WHITE MENTAL HEALTH PRACTITIONERS: IMPLICATIONS FOR MULTICULTURAL COUNSELING COMPETENCY IN RESEARCH AND PRACTICE

Over the last 40 years, scholars and researchers have studied the importance of multicultural counseling in clinical practice, research, and training as an essential requirement for all psychologists and counselors (Carter and Qureshi, 1995; Nwachuku and Ivey, 1991; Parker, Bingham, and Fukuyama, 1985; Pope-Davis and Ottavi, 1994b; Sue, Arredondo, and McDavis, 1992; Wrenn, 1962). Beginning in the 1960s, racial identity development (RID) has been theoretically linked with multicultural counseling. As psychologists and counselors of color questioned the applicability of traditional Eurocentric theories and practices (Sue et al., 1982; Pope-Davis and Ottavi, 1994a; Vontress, 1967; Vontress, 1971; Wrenn, 1962), researchers also began to examine the concept of culturally encapsulated counselors and racial bias (Wrenn, 1962).

The contemporary movement to examine RID began in the 1990s (Helms, 1990, 1995). Helms (1990), Sabnani, Ponterotto, and Borodovsky (1991) believed understanding RID of White counselors and clients was perhaps the single most significant advancement in multicultural counseling — setting a new course for training, research, and practice. Sabnani et al. (1991) integrated the work of multicultural counseling competencies (MCC), racial identity theory (RIT), and multicultural training to present a comprehensive model to increase multicultural counseling sensitivity and competency. As empirical research on minority identity models advanced, this model enhanced previous work to include an intentional focus on White Racial Identity Development (WRID). Sabnani et al. (1991) and others (Helms, 1990, 1995; Ponterotto and Mallinckrodt, 2007) have called for continued research on WRID and recommended that such research incorporate both quantitative and qualitative methodologies.

The major theoretical and practical tenets of RIT/D stem from research conducted primarily on graduate students, early in their mental health training experience (Neville, Heppner, Louie, Thompson, Brooks, and Baker, 1996; Ottavi, Pope-Davis, and Dings, 1994; Parker, Moore, and Neimeyer, 1998; Pope-Davis, and Ottavi, 1994b). This study compiles national data on a sample of White mental health practitioners in the United States. Since the majority of psychologists, professional counselors, and trainees are White middle-class individuals (Pedersen, 1991; Ponterotto, 1988; Sue and Sue, 2003), this current study considers how White racial identity may emerge within the therapeutic dyad.

The research in this article is based on a transtheoretical framework we call *Person(al)-As-Professional (P-A-P)*. Prior to describing the model several terms used in this study bear defining. *Multicultural counseling* focuses on counseling practice among individuals from different backgrounds based on race, ethnicity, and culture (Arredondo et al., 1996). *Multicultural counseling competency* (MCC) takes into account the worldview of the practitioner and its influence on the client and includes factors such as attitudes/beliefs, knowledge, skills, and relationships (Sue et al., 1982). *Multiculturalism,* in the clinical setting is defined as the existence of a prevailing and vitalizing environment originating from effective intra- and intercultural exchanges. The exchanges include individuals who respect, value, and learn from one another, creating a synergistic environment that is both dynamic and productive (Middleton, Flowers, and Zawaiza, 1996; Middleton, Rollins, and Harley, 1999).

THE PERSON(AL)-AS-PROFESSION(AL) (PAP) TRANSTHEORETICAL FRAMEWORK

The underlying premise of the P-A-P transtheoretical framework is that one's personal attributes and identity are not mutually exclusive from one's professional perspective or identity as a mental health practitioner. We use the prefix *trans-* to indicate the biological, environmental, cognitive, and psychosocial components of the model which equally contribute to the development of the personal and professional identity of a mental health practitioner. Personal Aspects, WRID, MCC, and Interpersonal Schemata (see Figure 1) are the four core dimensions depicted in this framework.

Person(al) Aspects. Race, ethnicity, gender, age, sexual orientation, physical ability, and socioeconomic status are personal aspects in the framework. The dimensions in this model are not fully descriptive of what holistically constitutes the P-A-P; other aspects may also be considered. In our framework, the individual's personal aspects and experiences shape professional practice and competency, and thereby the profession. *Race* is used here as a sociopolitical construct, not as a biological reality (Smedley and Smedley, 2005).

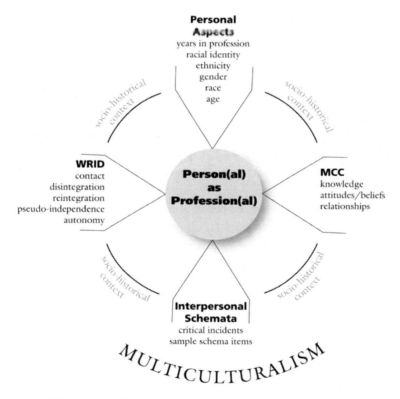

Figure 1. The Person(al)-As-Profession(al) (P-A-P) Transtheoretical Framework. WRID = White Racial Identity Development, MCC = Multicultural Counseling Competencies.

Although RID is a personal aspect, we separate WRID as a dimension distinct from the Personal dimension because of its relationship to MCC and its overall significance to the P-A-P transtheoretical framework (DelSignore et al., 2010; Middleton et al., 2005; Middleton, Ergüner-Tekinalp, Williams, Stadler, Dow, 2011). Multiculturalism frames the P-A-P transtheoretical framework because attaining multiculturalism is vital to the maintenance of MCC.

The socio-historical context refers to the lived experiences of the mental health practitioner, including, but not limited to, values and upbringing of family of origin; exposure to cultural diversity in the work, social, educational, and living environment; experiences of discrimination and victimization; access to societal resources (jobs, housing, education, medical care, etc.); social movements in a particular historical era; political climate; and religious affiliation. A detailed description of the three primary dimensions examined in this study—*WRID, MCC* and *Interpersonal Schemata*—are provided in the section that follows.

The *White Racial Identity Development (WRID)* dimension depicts one's ego status in the development of one's own identity as a racial being. The *Contact* status is marked by satisfaction with racial status quo and either one's obliviousness to or participation in racism. The *Disintegration* status is represented by disorientation and anxiety provoked by unresolved racial moral dilemmas that force one to choose between own-group loyalty and humanism. *Reintegration* is a reversal or regression to the idealization of one's socioracial group, as well as the denigration and intolerance for other groups. In this status, racial factors may strongly influence life decisions. *Pseudo-Independence* is characterized by an intellectualized commitment to one's own socioracial group and deceptive tolerance of other groups. The *Immersion/Emersion* status is represented by a search for understanding of one's personal meaning of racism and the ways in which one benefits from White privilege. At this status, a redefinition of Whiteness occurs and life choices may incorporate racial activism. The last status, *Autonomy,* is represented by an informed positive socioracial group commitment, use of internal standards for self-definition, and a capacity to relinquish the privileges of racism.

Helms (1996) states that profiles constellations are a more accurate reflection of the complex nature of RID, than any one single status. Racial identity profiles are descriptive manifestations of an individual's racial identity attitude (Carter, Helms, and Juby, 2004). Each profile pattern has accompanying information-processing strategies (IPS) used to avoid or assuage anxiety and discomfort around issues of race (Helms, 1995). The IPS used at each accompanying status are a) Contact—denial, obliviousness, or avoidance of anxiety-evoking racial information; b) Disintegration—disorientation, confusion, and suppression of information; c) Reintegration—distortion of information in an own-group enhancing manner; d) Pseudo-Independence—reshaping racial stimuli to fit one's own societal framework; e) Immersion-Emersion—reeducating and searching for internally defined racial standards; and f) Autonomy—flexible analyses and responses to racial stimuli.

Carter, Helms, and Juby (2004) established a formula to analyze responses to the WRIAS subscales, providing a more accurate reflection of the participants' racial identity status. This method of analysis offered a window into the practitioners' racial attitudes and beliefs and allowed researchers to group individuals with similar profile patterns. In delineating the limitations of their study, Carter et al. (2004) recommended future studies examine the characteristics of specific profile types.

Multicultural counseling competence (MCC) encompasses attitudes/beliefs, knowledge, skills, and relationship (Sodowsky, Taffe, Gutkin, and Wise, 1994). In this study, we focused specifically on *attitudes/beliefs* as a component of MCC to gain insight into practitioner cognition. The *Interpersonal Schemata* dimension of the P-A-P transtheoretical framework is represented by the verbatim responses of the participants to an open-ended question. The question was designed to provide insight into how one uses cognitive and psychodynamic processes to conceptualize racial dynamics within interpersonal interactions. A *schema of the other* is any person perceived as not possessing membership to the same reference group as the participant. This differs from the WRID dimension, where the focus is on self as a racial being. These cognitive representations of interpersonal events shape one's interpretation of a situation, event, or experience (Horowitz, 1991; Safran, 1990). In this study, these events are described as critical incidents.

PURPOSE OF THE STUDY

There is a lack of empirical research regarding practitioners' RID and its influence on MCC. The data reported in the current study is embedded within a larger program of study in which both quantitative and qualitative data were collected simultaneously (DelSignore et al., 2010; Middleton et al., 2005; Middleton et al., 2011). The current study is a concurrent mixed-methods approach, weighted toward quantitative analysis, with nested qualitative narratives (Creswell, 2003). The quantitative feature of this study reports the predominant constellations of RID profiles of White mental health practitioners.

The critical incidents were matched with the individual's RID profile to make meaning of the interpersonal schemata. The criticality of the incident is based on the justification, significance, and meaning given to it by the individual (DelSignore et al., 2010). These critical incidents served as indicators of developmental shifts in attitudes/beliefs that inform the professional perspective of the mental health practitioner (Arredondo et al., 1996). Critical incidents inquiry has been used to collect and analyze qualitative research data (Angelides, 2001; Skovholt and McCarthy, 1988) in psychology and counseling (Cormier, 1988; Fukuyama, 1994; Furr and Carroll, 2003; Leong and Kim, 1991; Mwaba and Pedersen, 1990).

The primary purpose of this study is to gain insight into the racial identity attitudes and representative schemata among a sample of White mental health practitioners. Specifically, we examine three dimensions of our P-A-P transtheoretical framework: MCC, Interpersonal Schemata, and WRID.

The research questions posed are:

1. What are the racial identity profiles of a sample of White mental health practitioners?
2. What is the association between the quantitatively derived racial identity profiles of White mental health professionals and a component of their MCC (attitudes and beliefs) expressed qualitatively via a sample of cognitive interpersonal schemata items (critical incidents)?

METHOD

Participants

As an extended analysis of data presented in Middleton et al. (2005), the sample demographics, instrumentation, and data collection procedures in the current investigation are the same. The population of study in Middleton et al. (2005) and the current embedded study was White mental health practitioners working in the field. Participants were selected based on the following criteria: a) doctoral and/or master's degrees only, b) clinical and counseling subfields only, c) certified practitioners only, d) self-identified as White, and e) work in a geographic region of the United States. There was a total response rate of 11%, however, the researchers excluded surveys from individuals who did not self identify as white, resulting in 412 surveys. Participants ranged in age from 23 to 81 years of age, with a mean age of 47.99 years (SD = 10.59). Of the 412 participants, 265 were female (64%) and 146 were male (35%); one participant did not report gender. Participation in the study was both anonymous and voluntary. Subjects surveyed in this study were obtained from the membership rosters of the American Psychological Association (APA) and the American Counseling Association (ACA) (APA, N = 55,218; ACA, N = 61,905). It is quite possible that participants held memberships with both the APA and ACA; however, for data analysis and interpretation purposes, the professional group identity of the participant was most important. Of those responding, 51% (n = 211) were members of APA and 49% (n = 201) were members of ACA. On a demographic questionnaire, participants were asked to self-identify based on one of the following professional groups: counseling psychologists, clinical psychologists, or professional counselors.

Potential respondents identified by APA consisted of 3,000 members, of whom 2,603 (87%) were White Americans. Of the 2,603 surveyed, 54% were male and 46% were female. Surveys were mailed to all regions: New England (11%), Middle Atlantic (19%), East/West North Central (22%), South Atlantic (15%), East/West South Central (10%), Mountain (6%), and Pacific (17%). Employment characteristics of APA members were independent practice, 55%; hospital, 13%; clinic, 6%; university settings, 6%; and other human services, 20%. Our sample of APA respondents (n = 211) was 44% male and 54% female with an average of 20 years in the profession (SD = 8.43). More specifically, among counseling psychologists, 53% were male and 47% were female; 88% reported having a doctoral degree, while 11% reported a master's degree as their terminal degree. Among clinical psychologists, 39% of respondents were male, while 62% were female; 98% reported having a doctoral degree.

Ethnic/racial demographic information from ACA was not available at the time of this study. However, the regional breakdown of the pool of 3,000 was New England, 8%; Middle Atlantic, 12%; East/West North Central, 22%; South Atlantic, 23%; East/West South Central, 15%; Mountain, 10%; and Pacific, 9%. Employment characteristics for ACA members in this study were as follows: private counseling centers, 31%; school setting, 21%; university setting, 17%; and community agency, 16%. The remaining 15% worked in government agencies, rehabilitation agencies, colleges, or business settings. ACA's membership is 71% female and 29% male. In our sample of ACA respondents (n = 201), 74% were female and 26% were male; 83% of the counselors reported having a master's degree as their terminal degree. Average number of years in the profession was 10 years (SD = 8.78). Profile constellations with fewer than 5 members were not included in our discussions. Therefore, 77 participants were not included in the final discussions, leaving the final sample size at 387.

Instruments

White Racial Identity Attitude Scale (WRIAS)

The 50 self-report items of the WRIAS (Helms and Carter, 1990) were used to assess the 5 racial identity attitude statuses proposed by Helms (1984): (1) Contact, (2) Disintegration, (3) Reintegration, (4) Pseudo-Independent, and (5) Autonomy. Internal consistency reliability coefficients in an initial investigation of the WRIAS by Helms and Carter (1990) achieved Cronbach alphas of .55, .77, .80, .71, and .67 for the WRIAS Contact, Disintegration, Reintegration, P-I, and Autonomy scales, respectively. In our study, coefficient alpha reliabilities calculated for test scores of the 5 WRIAS scales were .60, .77, .74, .83, and .79 for the Contact, Disintegration, Reintegration, P-I, and Autonomy scales, respectively.

Survey of Demographic/Training Data and Operationalization of Multicultural Competencies (DTD-OMC)

The demographic questionnaire elicited participants' age, gender, highest degree earned, year highest degree earned, professional identity, and racial-ethnic origin. Only the data related to White Americans was analyzed. The survey was used to gather qualitative data regarding the self-identified critical incidents of the mental health practitioners in the sample of this study. The critical incidents question was developed based on recommendations made by Arredondo et al. (1996) for operationalizing MCC in the domains of Attitudes/Beliefs, Knowledge, and Skills.

Research Design and Procedure

We developed an open-ended question to operationalize (Arredondo et al., 1996) a subcomponent of MCC - attitudes/beliefs. The question focused on examining a critical incident occurring in the life of the practitioner. Critical incidents are defined as some event or situation that marked a significant turning point or change in the life of a person (Tripp, 1993). We asked participants to describe incidents that were "critical," conceivably requiring them to engage in cognitive processes, recalling and interpreting their experiences as such. The question related to critical incidents read, *"What critical incidents in your history have influenced your professional perspective on cultural diversity?"* These critical incidents are viewed as marking significant paradigmatic shifts in the construction of the P-A-P perspective of the *person* as *professional*.

The qualitative data provides insight into the psychological and/or cognitive schema of the practitioner, while the quantitative data provides information at a different level of analysis (Tashakkori and Teedlie, 1998). The quantitative data is helpful in conceptualizing the various constellations of the WRID profiles.

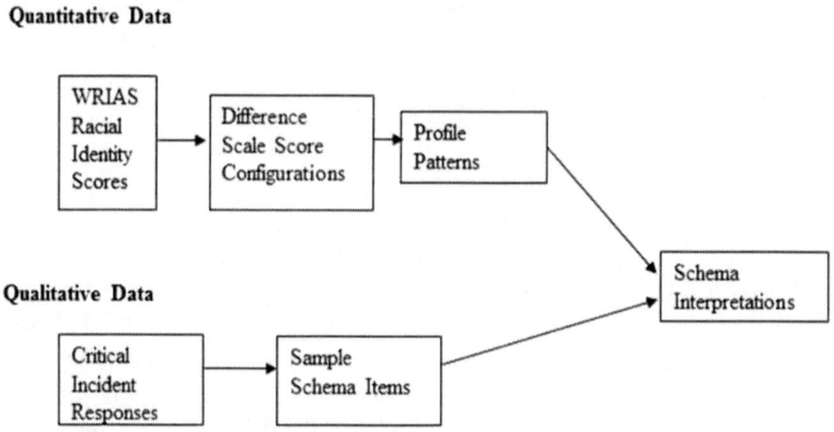

Quantitative Data

Figure 2. Visual depiction of the integration of qualitative and quantitative data.

The data resides side-by-side as two different pictures that collectively illustrate various predominate profile patterns of White mental health practitioners (Creswell, 2009). The mixed-methods approach in this study integrated a collection of both qualitative and quantitative data at different stages in the analysis (Hanson, Creswell, Plano Clark, and Creswell, 2005). We gave weighted significance to the quantitative data in the study; the data was integrated for the purpose of identifying and interpreting the racial identity profile constellations of White mental health practitioners (see Figure 2).

As Figure 2 illustrates, the quantitative data used to establish the racial identity profile patterns were derived via use of the WRIAS scores. Each score was compared with the adjacent subscale score producing difference scale score configurations. Profile patterns were then established based on these comparisons (Carter et al., 2004). The qualitative data was collected from the first open-ended question of the DTD-OMC survey assessing critical incidents. The responses provide examples (*Sample Schema Items*) for the racial identity constellations (*Profile Patterns*) established through the quantitative analysis. Together, these data were integrated to form the basis of the analysis for the sample of White mental health practitioners in this study. *Profile Patterns, Sample Schema Items,* and *Schema Interpretations* were derived. Figure 2 illustrates the process of integrating qualitative and quantitative data that led to the development of *Schema Interpretations*. What follows is a detailed description of the scoring approach and procedures used to create the profiles, sample items, and interpretations.

Creation of the Profiles

To create the profile patterns, the WRIAS subscale scores were calculated for each participant. The standard error of difference bands were calculated to find the significant differences between theoretically adjoining subscales (e.g., Contact vs. Disintegration, Disintegration vs. Reintegration, Reintegration vs. Pseudo-Independence, Pseudo-Independence vs. Autonomy, and Autonomy vs. Contact). The formula used to calculate the standard error of difference bands, as suggested by Helms (1996) and Carter et al. (2004) is:

$$SE_{dif} = SD \sqrt{2 - r_{xx} - r_{yy}} \times 1.96$$

In the above formula, *SD* represents the average standard deviation of the subscales in each comparison. The r_{xx} and r_{yy} are the reliabilities for the subscales compared. Based on this formula, we derived our significance band intervals for our sample population (see Table 1). Using these significance bands, participants' subscale scores were compared with their adjacent subscale scores. Three possibilities existed in determining whether the subscale scores in each comparison differed significantly: (a) less than one standard error difference between two subscales was considered as having no significant difference, and was labeled as *equal*; (b) one or greater than one standard error difference between two subscales was considered as *high* in the direction of the higher score; or (c) two or greater than two standard error difference between two subscales was considered as *very high* in the direction of higher score (Carter et al., 2004). Consequently, there were 5 options available in comparing the strength of endorsement for each pair of comparisons. For example, in comparing the subscales of Autonomy and Contact, possible options were: (a) very high Autonomy, (b) high Autonomy, (c) equal or no significant difference between Autonomy and Contact, (d) high Contact, and (e) very high Contact.

Of the possible 5^5 (or 3,125) combinations available, 80 profiles were present in this data set. Of the 80 profiles, 64 occurred in fewer than 5 participants, of which 43 were single participant profiles. Profile formulations of less than 5, while considered important from an individual perspective, were not included in our analysis of grouped profile patterns.

From these differential scale score configurations, we have identified a total of 58 profile variations that we have categorized under 7 major profile formulations (DRC, DRPC, DR, DRAC, DRA, RC, DRP) from our sample of respondents (see Table 2). The percentages reported for the profile constellations were rounded up.

Sample Schema Items Drawn from Critical Incidents

The critical incidents question from the DTD-OMC yielded responses that were used to create *Sample Schema Items*. First, lists were created of individual cases, divided by the different quantitatively derived profile patterns. After obtaining the different lists of WRID profile patterns, four of the authors of this manuscript collected the list of quotes from participants with the 7 primary Profile Patterns presented in this study.

The four authors evaluated the different groups of responses independently; selecting three quotes per profile pattern for which interrater agreement was highest. Neuendorf (2002) defines interrater reliability as the amount of correspondence among two or more raters in agreement on the values assigned to a variable. High agreement among the authors assured high interrater reliability.

Table 1. Point Values for Determining Statistical Significance of White Racial Identity Attitude Scale Subscale Comparisons

	1	2	3	4	5
1. Contact	–	0.311	0.308	0.386	0.370
2. Disintegration	–	–	0.230	0.327	0.308
3. Reintegration	–	–	–	0.324	0.305
4. Pseudo-Independence	–	–	–	–	0.384
5. Autonomy	–	–	–	–	–

After selecting the highest endorsed quotes (with either three (75%) or four (100%) of the authors agreeing) on the highest rated responses, the three authors focused on selecting one quote per profile pattern that would best illustrate each of the 7 primary profile pattern presented in this study. Thus, the sample schema items were selected. For examples of other critical incidents drawn from the sample in this study that may be used to create other sample schemata items, see DelSignore et al. (2010).

Determining Schema Interpretations

Three of the authors provided an interpretation to each of the selected sample schemas. The authors acknowledge a potential for bias in the selection of the *Sample Schema Items* and the development of the *Schema Interpretations* based on the RID of each author. To minimize this effect, all three authors viewed the responses independently. Following this, a consensus for inclusion was established. It should also be noted that sample schema items chosen for the purpose of this study might have been affected by interactional influences emerging from the group process.

RESULTS

Prior to beginning the quantitative analysis, the distribution was examined to determine normality of scores for each racial identity status. Skew analysis showed that the Disintegration and Reintegration subscales were slightly positively skewed. Log transformations were applied to remove skew and improve normality. These new values were used to generate profiles for these subscales. There were no differences in the profiles generated using the log transformations; however, to simplify our reporting, we report the profiles generated by the log transformations (see Table 2).

In the first research question posed, "What are the racial identity profiles of a sample of White mental health practitioners?" and the results yielded predominantly blended profiles (Helms, 1996). The profiles in Table 2 were grouped based on various like profile constellations, resulting in 7 major profile formulations. For example, there were 12 like formulations of the D-R-C profile and 13 like formulations of D-R-A profile. The second research question posed in this study was, "Is there an association between the racial identity profiles of the professionals and a component of MCC (attitudes and beliefs) expressed as interpersonal schema (critical incidents)?" Results for the 7 major profile formulations are discussed below, and are accompanied by a representational sample schema item and the interpretation.

Group 1

Profile Pattern: Very High D/Very High R and High to Very High C Profile (N = 213 or 60%)

In this D-R-C profile, Disintegration scores were very high in relation to Contact, Reintegration scores were very high in relation to Pseudo-Independence scores, and Contact scores ranged from high to very high in relation to Autonomy scores.

Table 2. White Racial Identity Development Frequencies and Combinations of Profile Patterns (N= 355)

Profile Frequencies	C vs D	D vs R	R vs P	P vs A	A vs C
DRC					
(*n* = 213 or 60%)					
n = 110	D	=	R*	=	C*
n = 35	D*	R	R*	=	C*
n = 26	D*	=	R*	=	C*
n = 25	D*	D	R*	=	C*
n = 5	D	=	R*	=	C
n = 4	D	=	R*	=	C*
n = 2	D	D	R*	=	C*
n = 2	D	R	R*	=	C*
n = 1	D*	=	R*	=	C*
n = 1	D	D	R	=	C
n = 1	D	R*	R*	=	C
n = 1	D	R*	R*	=	C*
DRPC					
(*n* = 51 or 14%)					
n = 21	D*	=	R*	P	C*
n = 12	D*	=	R*	P*	C
n = 4	D*	=	R*	P	C*
n = 4	D*	D	R*	P	C*
n = 3	D*	R	R*	P	C*
n = 3	D	=	R*	P	C*
n = 2	D*	R	R*	P*	C
n = 1	D*	D*	R*	P	C
n = 1	D*	R*	R*	P	C
DR					
(*n* = 28 or 8%)					
n = 17	D*	=	R*	=	=
n = 1	D*	R	R*	=	=
n = 4	D*	D	R*	=	=
n = 2	D*	D*	R*	=	=
n = 1	D*	R*	R*	=	=
n = 1	D	=	R	=	=
n = 1	D	D	R	=	=
n = 1	D	R	R*	=	=
DRAC					
(*n* = 28 or 8%)					
n = 10	D*	=	R	A	C*
n = 6	D*	=	R*	A	C
n = 4	D*	=	R*	A*	C
n = 4	D	R	R*	A	C
n = 2	D*	R	R*	A*	C
n = 1	D*	R*	R*	A	C

Table 2. (Continued)

Profile Frequencies	C vs D	D vs R	R vs P	P vs A	A vs C
DRAC continued					
$n = 1$	D	R*	R*	A	C
DRA					
($n = 23$ or 6%)					
$n = 6$	D*	=	R*	=	A
$n = 3$	D*	D	R*	A	=
$n = 2$	D*	D	R*	A*	=
$n = 2$	D*	R*	R*	A	A
$n = 2$	D*	R*	R*	A	=
$n = 1$	D*	=	R*	=	A
$n = 1$	D*	=	R*	=	A*
$n = 1$	D*	=	R*	A*	A
$n = 1$	D*	=	R*	R*	A*
$n = 1$	D*	R	R*	A	=
$n = 1$	D	=	R*	=	A
$n = 1$	D	R*	R*	A*	=
$n = 1$	D	R*	R*	A	=
RC					
($n = 6$ or 2%)					
$n = 2$	=	=	R*	=	C*
$n = 1$	=	R*	R*	=	C*
$n = 1$	=	R	R*	=	C*
$n = 1$	C	=	R	=	C
$n = 1$	=	R	R*	=	C
DRP					
($n = 6$ or 2%)					
$n = 3$	D*	R*	R*	P*	
$n = 1$	D*	=	R*	=	P
$n = 1$	D*	D*	R*	P*	
$n = 1$	D*	R*	R*	P	=

This triumvirate-type profile was by far the most dominant schema, representing 60% of the sample respondents in this study. The very high D-R-C schema relative to other subscales scores suggests that these practitioners use a combination of IPS strategies, as described by Helms (1995), including obliviousness, suppression and out-group distortion to cope with racial information.

Sample Schema Item

I grew up in a family where I was taught that African Americans were not my equals; there are 2 groups of African Americans (1. Blacks, 2. Niggers) and we belonged to a country club that did not allow Blacks and Jewish people to be members. After taking a multicultural counseling class and gaining greater exposure to people of difference (racially, sexually, religious, age, etc.) I refused to attend the country club any more and began to challenge my family on their views of different people. In the process, I started and continue to work on my own cultural biases and strive to improve my multicultural competencies.

Schema Interpretation

The Contact status is reflected in the schema item above. At the core of this individual's upbringing is a cognitive accessible schema that accepts societal-imposed racial characterizations and rules. Disorientation occurs at the status of Disintegration as the ego is exposed to new information via a multicultural counseling class. This causes a racial moral dilemma as the individual seeks to incorporate the new information into the existing accessible cognitive schema. The Reintegration status is evidenced by the respondent's admission that he/she must continue to work on biases, which implies idealization of one's own racial group.

Group 2

Profile Pattern: Very High D-R/High P and High to Very High C Profile (N = 51 or 14%)

This D-R-P-C quadripartite profile was observed where Disintegration scores were very high in relation to Contact Scores, Reintegration scores were very high in relation to Pseudo-Independence, Pseudo-Independence was high in relation to Autonomy, and Contact scores ranged from high to very high in relation to Autonomy. Individuals with this profile type utilize a variety of IPS strategies (ambivalence, negative out-group distortion, selective perception, or denial of the differential significance of Whiteness) to assuage anxiety and discomfort around the issue of race. Pseudo-Independence present within the ego contributes to what may be viewed on the surface as a professed liberalism toward other groups.

Sample Schema Item

When I was a youngster, my mom and I lived in public housing in the NYC area. THE PROJECTS were filled with many cultures. I was welcomed and frequently visited and played with kids of a black family on my floor.

Schema Interpretation

The Reintegration status is evidenced by the statement "I was welcomed." When referring to living in New York City public housing, it reflects that this individual saw himself or herself as not belonging in the projects. The individual was part of the projects but saw himself or herself as different from others in the community. There is an out-group distortion implied by the fact that others belong but the respondent does not. The Contact status may be evidenced by the fact that the individual does not view or acknowledge the self or others as racial beings. There is obliviousness to race and the individual would rather focus on culture than race. The Disintegration status may be evidenced by disorientation resulting from living in public housing as a White American. This poses a conflict or racial moral dilemma; the individual must ask, "Why am I here?" The Pseudo-Independent status is evidenced by the individual's assumed liberalism and deceptive tolerance of others by playing with kids of Black families.

Group 3

Profile Pattern: Very High D/Very High R Profile (N = 28 or 8%)

In the D-R profile, Disintegration scores were very high in relation to Contact and Reintegration was very high in relation to Pseudo-Independence. The participants appeared to rely on dual combinations of Disintegration and Reintegration as their dominant racial identity schemata. Here, IPS strategies are disorientation, suppression, minimization, selective perception, or out-group distortion.

Sample Schema Item

I grew up and still live in rural New England. Therefore most of my exposure to others has been all White. However, as a result I have always had an interest in other cultures and races.

Schema Interpretation

The Reintegration status of this individual is evidenced by the idealization of his or her socio-racial group reflected by the decision to isolate exposure to other racial beings. The Disintegration status is evidenced by the respondent's "interest" in other cultures but lack of investment in changing behavior, state of isolation, or environment. Thus, the individual's state of dissonance remains unresolved.

Group 4

Profile Pattern: Very High D-R/High A and High to Very High C Profile (N = 28 or 8%)

The D-R-A-C profile was the second quadripartite profile observed in our sample of respondents. Disintegration scores were very high in relation to Contact scores, Reintegration scores were very high in relation to Pseudo-Independence, Autonomy was high in relation to Pseudo-Independence, and Contact scores ranged from high to very high in relation to Autonomy. Even though Autonomy was weakly expressed relative to other schemata, it was relatively accessible. Thus, IPS strategies of strong denial or failure to acknowledge privilege, selective perception and avoidance are present, as well coexisting with elements of flexibility and informed positive socioracial group commitment.

Sample Schema Item

1950s being criticized for singing with Black people in a park by customers I waited on in my after-school job. Worshiping with a Black congregation. Living as a student in France (1970) and in China (1979). Intimacy with individuals from different cultures. Being born again by the Spirit of God (which is not a White spirit or a female spirit or an

American spirit or a Baptist spirit, etc.) the ground is absolutely level at the foot of the cross.

Schema Interpretation

Disorientation is indicative of the status of Disintegration. For this individual, disorientation occurred from being criticized for singing with Black people. The individual faced a racial moral dilemma of either continuing with the behavior or complying with the expected norms of his or her own racial group. Autonomy may be evidenced by the individual's decision not to comply, but continuing to use an internal standard for self-definition. The Contact status remains accessible to the individual as there continues to be naiveté and denial that race and racism run counter to the ideals of spirituality. It is reasonable to assume that an individual operating at the status of Contact and Autonomy would also have passed through the status of Reintegration.

Group 5

Profile Pattern: Very High D-R/High A (N = 23 or 6%)

The D-R-A profile was the second triumvirate-type profile observed in this sample of respondents. Disintegration scores were very high in relation to Contact scores, Reintegration scores were very high in relation to Pseudo-Independence and Autonomy was high in relation to Pseudo-Independence. Practitioners with this profile-type seemed to operate more strongly from a dual schema of Disintegration and Reintegration; however, Autonomy is an accessible status under the right circumstances. Here, IPS strategies are the ability to exhibit flexible analyses and responses to racial stimuli as well as the other IPS strategies listed above in the D-R profile.

Sample Schema Item

I grew up in a family that did not encourage racial diversity. Attending college was the most critical incident for me, because I experienced a variety of cultural interactions and relationships that continues to change my perspective to this day.

Schema Interpretation

Because of this individual's family history, the status of Disintegration remains accessible to the ego. Nevertheless, consistent with the status of Autonomy, the individual is able to use flexible standards for perceiving and interacting with other racial or cultural groups. However, the individual's Reintegration status is evident by the acknowledgment that there is a need to continue to change his or her perspective of other racial groups.

Group 6

Profile Pattern: High to Very High R/ High to Very High C (N = 6 or 2%)

In this R-C profile, Reintegration scores were high to very high in relation to Disintegration; Contact was very high in relation to Autonomy. This dual profile type was a rare occurrence representing only 2% of our sample population. IPS strategies included selective perception and out-group distortion, as well as obliviousness to racism and one's participation in it.

Sample Schema Item

"Working with different cultures, watching them interact and react."

Schema Interpretation

The Contact status is evident through this individual's unwillingness to acknowledge race and referring to all diversity as "cultures." This individual is also unwilling or unable to specify which groups in particular he or she is watching. The individual sees him- or herself apart from the "different cultures." We would question whether this individual has selective perception as he or she is watching other cultures. Based on the person's Reintegration status, there has to be out-group distortion if this individual is not interacting with other diverse groups. In absence of interaction, distortions are bound to occur.

Group 7

Profile Pattern: Very High D/Very High R/Very High P (N = 6 or 2%)

The D-R-P profile was the third triumvirate-type profile observed in this sample of respondents. Disintegration scores were very high in comparison to Contact, Reintegration was very high in comparison to Disintegration, and Pseudo-Independence was high to very high in comparison to Reintegration scores. IPS strategies were ambivalence about racial moral dilemmas, selective perception, and out-group distortion.

Sample Schema Item

"I am Jewish and aware of anti-Semitism, have been involved in interracial relationships in the past have gay and lesbian friends, so I am aware of differences."

Schema Interpretation

This is a person who has self-identified as a majority member on the demographics survey—White American—while at the same time identifies as a minority member, Jewish. There is likely conflict between this person's racial-cultural heritages. The person may experience moral dilemmas and conflict within the self as to how he or she will navigate through the world as a culturally diverse individual. The individual can "choose" when to reveal his or her Jewish identity. Having personally experienced discrimination (anti-Semitism), the individual can address it directly. At other times the presence of Disintegration suggests that this person also may witness discrimination of self or others, but choose not to act or address it. The presence of Reintegration can be operational if the individual is aware of differences, but does not take any action to minimize discrimination of other groups. With respect to Pseudo-Independence, there is an acknowledgment or recognition of differences with respect to other groups (e.g. gay, lesbian friends); however, the individual acknowledges only the oppression of Jews, but not oppression of other groups. It is possible that a deceptive tolerance of other groups (e.g. gay, lesbian) is present.

DISCUSSION AND IMPLICATIONS

The reader should note that because the statuses in Helms' WRID model (1990) are nonlinear, the interpretations the authors provided with respect to each of the sample schema items are open to other interpretations within the framework of the complex blends identified. For example, with respect to the D-R-C profile (Group 1), the sample schema item selected— "I started and continue to work on my own cultural biases,"—also may reflect White guilt (Disintegration) rather than White superiority (i.e., Reintegration). Both interpretations fit the individual's complex racial identity schemata and are consistent with Helms' (1990) belief that there are no "pure" statuses.

The racial identity profile patterns obtained in this study produced a combination of dual, triumvirate, and quadripartite profile patterns. Although complex racial identity blends are consistent with Helms' (1990) supposition regarding the racial identity of individuals, no empirical evidence supported this theory (Helms, 1995) to this degree of complexity. Previous studies using this profile scoring system (Helms, 1996; Carter et al., 2004) identified primarily flat or undifferentiated profiles as the most frequently occurring. A flat or undifferentiated profile indicates that no single racial identity status dominates a person's profile.

In our sample of respondents, undifferentiated profile patterns were almost nonexistent. We believe the more complex patterns emerged in our study because of the composition of our sample. Our sample comprised individuals who had 10–20 years of experiencing working in the mental health field as opposed to young college-age adults. Therefore, as Carter et al. (2004) have speculated, it is conceivable that the psychological resolutions of college-aged adults have not yet fully formed or differentiated with respect to race or the processing of racial stimuli. Thus, it is reasonable to conclude that the psychological resolutions of experienced practitioners become more fully formed as a result of having significantly more opportunities for socialization with race and racial stimuli in the clinical setting when compared to college-aged practitioners-in-training.

The most prominent pattern obtained was the D-R-C triumvirate profile (n= 213 or 60%). The high frequency of the D-R-C schema relative to other racial identity profiles patterns suggests that the majority of practitioners sampled use a combination of Information-Processing Strategies (IPS) including obliviousness, ambivalence, suppression, and negative out-group distortion to cope with racial information (Helms, 1995). This study focused more on attitudes and beliefs with respect to RID and MCC rather than behavior. However, racial identity theorists (Carter, 1995; Helms, 1984; Ponterotto, 1988; Thompson and Carter, 1997) point out that whatever the profile pattern of the therapist, his or her awareness is likely to have major implications for the client and the process of psychotherapy. This belief is consistent with our P-A-P transtheoretical framework. Therefore, a White therapist with a D-R-C profile pattern can cause harm to clients. In working with clients whose racial-cultural identity differs from his or her own, the therapist may intentionally or unintentionally a) reinforce a client's feelings of racial self-hatred; b) prevent or block a dissonance client from looking at inconsistent feelings or beliefs; c) overlook, dismiss, or negate resistance; and d) perceive the autonomously aware client as having a confused self-identity (Sue and Sue, 2003).

Based on what we know about Helms' (1990) racial identity theory, we can conclude that White practitioners with the D-R-C profile have limited relational contacts with members from racial-cultural groups different from their own, especially with respect to personal or social encounters. However, relational contacts are present, causing the White person to become increasingly conscious of his or her Whiteness. Consequently, the individual may experience dissonance and conflict, resulting in feelings of guilt or anxiety. The dissonance results from having to deal with inconsistencies in the individual's own life in upholding humanistic, nonracist values and their contradictory behavior.

For example, a White person who consciously believes that he or she "treats everyone the same" suddenly experiences reservations about having African Americans or Latinos move next door or having to be supervised by or report to an African American. From a personal perspective, the practitioner may opt to resolve the dissonance by avoiding or having limited contact with other-race in their families, places of worship, neighborhoods, and social gatherings. From a professional perspective, the White practitioner may take solace or reassure him/herself that racism is not a part of their schema by providing any number of reasons to justify the absence or significant underrepresentation of Blacks or other-race persons not receiving mental health services in their practice. Practitioners working in a community agency (hospital, community mental health center, clinic, etc.) may seek reassurance by disassociating themselves from any responsibility for the significant underrepresentation of Blacks and other race persons in their agency. They may see their lack of involvement in providing services to underrepresented populations as the agency's fault for lack of effective outreach strategies. The reasons for the underrepresentation may be attributed to any number of reasons (all of which may be true), but never racism. Adopting this mindset allows White practitioners to avoid perceiving themselves as having biases and prejudices, and see themselves as colorblind. Recognizing the unequal treatment of minority groups in their personal and professional experience, practitioners possessing the D-R-C profile may have difficulty in resolving the conflict, guilt, or anxiety they are feeling and retreat into a pattern of blaming racially diverse clients for their own problems (Sue and Sue, 2003).

The next prominent profile formulation was the D-R-P-C (n= 51 or 14%) quadripartite profile pattern. Sixteen percent of practitioners sampled in this study were able to access the more advanced status of Pseudo-Independence. Examination of the sample as a whole indicates that 30% (n=108) of the practitioners showed commitment to the more advanced statuses of Pseudo-Independence and Autonomy. These advanced statuses (Pseudo-Independence and Autonomy) appear as part of a blended profile in the form of the D-R-P-C and D-R-A-C quadripartite profiles or the D-R-A and D-R-P triumvirate-type profiles. Thus, with respect to the D-R-P-C and D-R-P profiles, when we compare Pseudo-Independence to Autonomy in the differential scoring procedure developed by Helms (1996), Pseudo-Independence is strong enough to be accessible among a small sample of practitioners ($n = 57$ or 16%) of this particular sample of mental health practitioners. Autonomy was accessible in the D-R-A or the D-R-A-C profile formulations ($n = 51$ or 14%) using the comparative scoring procedure in relation to Pseudo-Independence. Clearly, the profiles and schema items derived using this new scoring procedure offer additional information beyond what one derives from using merely the untransformed mean scores of the racial identity statuses (Helms, 2007).

Some researchers (Rowe, Behrens, and Leach, 1995) have expressed concern with validating key propositions in Helms' theory and model of WRIT/D. Our research supports the validity of several essential theoretical propositions posited by Helms (1995):

1. Racial identity development occurs as racial identity statuses evolve from the effective management of and exposure to racial stimuli.
2. Statuses do not appear to be supplanted by one another; rather, earlier statuses remain accessible to the extent that they can be endorsed by and accessible to the ego in subsequent statuses under the "right" circumstances.
3. Blends of statuses are more likely to be present in the individual than are solitary statuses and dominance is determined by the statuses that most often govern the person's racial reactions.

RECOMMENDATIONS FOR FUTURE RESEARCH AND PRACTICE

The mixed-method research design presented in this manuscript represents an effort to take White racial identity theory in a new direction. Primarily, this study used critical incidents to operationalize a specific domain of MCC (attitude and beliefs) to understand how White American mental health practitioners begin the process of moving toward a nonracist White identity. Based on the totality of our findings, we offer the following recommendations:

Research

1. More empirical research is needed on specific patterns and clusters of racial identity profiles to increase understanding of the developmental process and operationalization of racial identity theory.
2. The vast majority of racial identity research has examined students in training. More research is needed to examine racial identity development among practitioners and the impact of RID/T on the therapeutic dyad.
3. Future research utilizing mixed-methods, or more complex, nonlinear statistical methodologies could enrich our understanding of racial identity theory and development.
4. Statistical methodologies for addressing complex patterns formed by interactive convergent and divergent forces in dynamic systems may be more appropriate for the improvement of our science and inquiry of racial identity theories. Methods such as cluster analysis or those associated with chaos theory may be more effective in assessing the validity and usefulness of racial identity measures and theories.
5. Racial identity development models lack an adequate integration of gender, class, sexual orientation, and other socio-demographic group identities or person(al)

aspects of the individual. Multiculturally competent scholars will begin to incorporate these personal aspects in their research.

Practice

1. Mental health practitioners are encouraged to examine the impact of their attitudes and beliefs with respect to others as socioracial beings.
2. Multiculturally competent counselors and psychologists will be prepared to apply racial identity theory to their work in order to provide culturally relevant services to their clients.

LIMITATIONS

The authors acknowledge two limitations to the findings presented in this manuscript. First, the design of the research questions in the qualitative analysis limited our understanding of the critical incidents reported by mental health practitioners. The question regarding critical incidents did not differentiate between formal or informal critical incidents. Secondly, we based our schemata interpretations on the authors' supposition of how potential linkages could be made from the qualitative responses to the White racial identity profile patterns. The authors acknowledge that the selection and interpretation of the sample schema items and schema interpretations may have been biased based on the racial identity development of each individual author, as well as by interactional influences between statuses of racial identity development.

CONCLUSION

This manuscript brought together critical incidents and White racial identity profile patterns as two important aspects of the professional and personal identity development of White American mental health practitioners. Studying these variables contributed to a better understanding of the cognitive processes involved in the development of White racial identity attitudes and MCC. The uniqueness of the mixed-methods research design described in this manuscript lies precisely in its attempt to relate psychological constructs such as WRID and MCC to concrete, measurable variables obtained through self-reports of mental health practitioners. Uniqueness of these analyses also lies in the examination of the person and how that person, shaped by personal and professional life experiences, has internalized schema to operate from a complex, unique racial identity profile pattern. The Person(al)-as-Profession(al) transtheoretical framework represents a novel approach to move the WRID and MCC literature in a new direction in understanding the constructs of WRID and MCC among practitioners in psychology and counseling.

Our findings advance the study of WRID in several important ways. First, because our sample is similar to the demographics of psychologists and professional counselors who are members of the APA and ACA, our findings offer the potential to better understand how the complex RID profiles might be distributed among mental health practitioners who are members of APA and ACA. Second, our findings support the work of Helms (1996) and Carter (1996) indicating that profile patterns and schema items provide greater and perhaps more accurate insight into the complex interplay of the racial identity statuses of the individual practitioner. Finally, we more fully examine the notion of racial identity blends discussed by Helms (1995) as an important aspect of her theory of WRID.

AUTHOR NOTE

We gratefully acknowledge the contributions of Holly A. Stadler, Dean and Professor, Roosevelt University. Please address correspondence to: Renée A. Middleton, Ph.D., Dean and Professor, Department of Counseling and Higher Education, The Gladys W. and David H. Patton College of Education, McCracken Hall 133, Athens, OH 45701, Office: 740-593-9449, Fax: 740-593-0569, Email: middletonr@ohio.edu.

REFERENCES

Angelides, P. (2001). The development of an efficient technique for collecting and analyzing qualitative data: The analysis of critical incidents. *Qualitative Studies in Education, 14*, 429–442. doi: 10.1080/09518390110029058.

Arredondo, P., Toporek, R., Brown, S., Jones, J., Locke, D., Sanchez, J., and Stadler, H. (1996). Operationalization of the multicultural counseling competencies. *Journal of Multicultural Counseling and Development, 24*(1), 42–79.

Carter, R. T. (1995). *The influence of race and racial identity in psychotherapy: Toward a racially inclusive model.* New York: John Wiley.

Carter, R. T. (1996). Exploring the complexity of racial identity attitude measures. In G. R. Sodowsky and J. C. Impara (Eds.), *Multicultural assessment in counseling and clinical psychology* (pp. 193–223). Lincoln, NE: Buros Institute of Mental Measurements.

Carter, R. T., Helms, J. E., and Juby, H. L. (2004). The relationship between racism and racial identity for white Americans: A profile analysis. *Journal of Multicultural Counseling and Development, 32*(1), 2–17.

Carter, R. T., and Qureshi, A., (1995). A typology of philosophical assumptions in multicultural counseling and training. In J. Ponterotto, M. Casas, L. Suzuki, and C. Alexander (Eds.), *Handbook of multicultural counseling* (pp. 239–262). Thousand Oaks, CA: Sage Publications.

Cormier, L. S. (1988). Critical incidents in counselor development: Themes and patterns. *Journal of Counseling and Development, 67*(2), 131–132.

DelSignore, A. M., Petrova, E., Harper, A. Stowe, A. M., Mu'min, A.S, and Middleton (2010). Critical Incidents and Assistance-Seeking Behaviors of White Mental Health Practitioners: A Transtheoretical Framework for Understanding Multicultural Counseling Competency. *Cultural Diversity and Ethnic Minority Psychology, 16*, 352-361. doi: 10.1037/a0018694.

Fukuyama, M. A. (1994). Critical incidents in multicultural counseling supervision: A phenomenological approach to supervision research. *Counselor Education and Supervision, 34*(2), 142–151.

Furr, S. R., and Carroll, J. J. (2003). Critical incidents in student counselor development. *Journal of Counseling and Development, 81*(4), 483–489.

Hanson, E. W., Creswell, W. J., Plano Clark, L. V., and Creswell, J. D. (2005). Mixed methods research designs in counseling psychology. *Journal of Counseling Psychology, 52*, 224-235. doi: 10.1037/0022-0167.52.2.22.

Helms, J. (1984). Toward a theoretical explanation of the effects of race on counseling: A black and white model. *The Counseling Psychologist, 12*, 153-165. doi: 10.1177/0011000084124013.

Helms, J. (1990). Toward a model of white racial identity development. In J. Helms (Ed.), *Black and White racial identity* (pp. 49-66). Westport, CT: Greenwood Press.

Helms, J. E. (1995). An update of Helms's white and people of color racial identity models. In J. Ponterotto, M. Casas, L. Suzuki, and C. Alexander (Ed.), *Handbook of multicultural counseling* (pp. 181–198).

Helms, J. E. (1996). Toward a methodology for measuring and assessing racial identity as distinguished from ethnic identity. In G. Sodowsky and J. Impara (Eds.), *Multicultural assessment in counseling and clinical psychology* (pp. 143–192). Lincoln, NE: Buros Institute of Mental Measurement.

Helms, J. E. (2007). Some better practices for measuring racial and ethnic identity constructs. *Journal of Counseling Psychology, 54*, 235-246. doi: 10.1037/0022-0167.54.3.23.

Helms, J. E., and Carter, R. T. (1990). Development of the white racial identity attitude scale. In J. E. Helms (Ed.), *Black and white racial identity attitudes: Theory, research, and practice* (pp. 67–80). Westport, CT: Greenwood Press.

Horowitz, M. J. (1991). Relationship schema formulation: Role-relationship models and intrapsychic conflict. *Psychiatry, 5*(3), 260–274.

Leong, F. T., and Kim, H. W. (1991). Going beyond cultural sensitivity on the road to multiculturalism: Using the intercultural sensitizer as a counselor training tool. *Journal of Counseling and Development, 70*, 112–118.

Middleton, Flowers, C. and Zawaiza, T. (1996). Affirmative action, multiculturalism, and Section 21 of the 1992 Rehabilitation Act Amendments: Fact or fiction? *Rehabilitation Counseling Bulletin,40*(1),11-30.

Middleton, Rollins, C. and Harley, D. (1999). The historical and political context of the civil rights of persons with disability: A multicultural perspective for counselors. *Journal of Multicultural Counseling and Development, 27*(2), 115-120.

Middleton, Stadler, H.A., Simpson, C., Guo, Y., Brown, M.J., Crow, G., Schuck, K., Alemu, Y., and Lazarte, A.A. (2005). Mental health practitioners: The relationship between white racial identity attitudes and self-reported multicultural counseling competencies. *Journal of Counseling and Development, 83*(1), 444-456.

Middleton, Ergüner-Tekinalp, B., Williams, N. F., Stadler, H. A., Dow, J. E. (2011). *International Journal of Psychology and Psychological Therapy, 11*(2), 121-138.

Mwaba, K., and Pedersen, P. (1990). Relative importance of intercultural, interpersonal, and psychopathological attributions in judging critical incidents by multicultural professional counselors. *Journal of Multicultural Counseling and Development, 18*(3), 106–118.

Nwachuku, U., and Ivey, A. (1991). Culture-specific counseling: An alternative training tool. *Journal of Counseling and Development, 70*(1), 106–111.

Neuendorf, A. K. (2002). *The content analysis guidebook.* Thousand Oaks, CA: Sage Publications.

Neville, H. A., Heppner, M. J., Louie, C. E., Thompson, C. E., Brooks, L., and Baker, C. E. (1996). The impact of multicultural training on white racial identity attitudes and therapy competencies. *Professional Psychology: Research and Practice, 27,* 83–89. doi: 10.1037/0735-7028.27.1.83.

Ottavi, T., Pope-Davis, D., and Dings, J. (1994). Relationship between white racial identity attitudes and self-reported multicultural counseling competencies. *Journal of Counseling Psychology, 41*(2), 149–154. doi: 10.1037//0022-0167.41.2.149.

Parker, W., Bingham, R., and Fukuyama, M. (1985). Improving cross-cultural effectiveness of counselor trainees. *Counselor Education and Supervision, 24,* 349–352.

Parker, W. M., Moore, M. A., and Neimeyer, G. J. (1998). Altering white racial identity and interracial comfort through multicultural training. *Journal of Counseling and Development, 76*(3), 302–310.

Pedersen, P. B. (1991). Introduction to the special issue. *Journal of Counseling and Development, 70*(1), 4.

Ponterotto, J. (1988). Racial consciousness development among white counselor trainees: A stage model. *Journal of Multicultural Counseling and Development, 16,* 146- 156.

Ponterotto, J. G. and Mallinckrodt, B. (2007). Introduction to the special section on racial and ethnic identity in counseling psychology: conceptual and methodological challenges and proposed solutions. *Journal of Counseling Psychology,* 54, 219-223.

Pope-Davis, D. B., and Ottavi, T. M. (1994a). The relationship between racism and racial identity among white Americans: A replication and extension. *Journal of Counseling and Development, 72,* 293–297.

Pope-Davis, D. B., and Ottavi, T. M. (1994b). The relationship between racism and racial identity among white Americans: A replication and extension. *Journal of Counseling and Development, 72*(3), 293–297.

Ridley, C. R. (1986). Diagnosis as a function of race pairing and client self-disclosure. *Journal of Cross Cultural Psychology, 17,* 337-351. doi: 10.1177/0022022186017003 006.

Rowe, W., Behrens, J. T., and Leach, M. (1995). Racial/ethnic identity and racial consciousness: Looking back and looking forward. In J. G. Ponterotto, J. M. Casas, L. Suzuki, and A. Alexander (Eds.), *Handbook of multicultural counseling* (pp. 218–235). Thousand Oaks, CA: Sage Publications.

Russell, G. L., Fujino, D. C., Sue, S., Cheung, M. K., and Snowden, L. R. (1996). The effects of the therapist-client ethnic match in the assessment of mental health functioning. *Journal of Cross-Cultural Psychology, 27,* 598-615. doi: 10.1177/0022022196275007.

Sabnani, H. B., Ponterotto, J. G., and Borodovsky, L. G. (1991). White RID and cross-cultural training: A stage model. *The Counseling Psychologist, 19,* 76–102.

Safran, J. D. (1990). Towards a refinement of cognitive therapy in light of interpersonal theory: I. Theory. *Clinical Psychology Review, 10,* 87–105. doi: 10.1016/0272-7358(90)90108-M.

Skovholt, T. M., and McCarthy, P. R. (1988). Critical incidents: Catalysts for counselor development. *Journal of Counseling and Development, 67*(2), 69–72.

Smedley, A., and Smedley, B. D. (2005). Race as biology is fiction, racism as a social problem is real: Anthropological and historical perspectives on the social construction of race. *American Psychologist*, *60*(1), 16–26.

Sodowsky, G., Taffe, R., Gutkin, T. B., and Wise, S. (1994). Development of the multicultural counseling inventory: A self-report measure of multicultural competencies. *Journal of Counseling Psychology*, *41*, 137–148. doi: 10.1037//0022-0167.41.2.137.

Sue, D. W., Arredondo, P., and McDavis, R. J. (1992). Multicultural counseling competencies and standards: A call to the profession. *Journal of Counseling and Development*, *70*(4), 477-486.

Sue, D. W., and Sue, D. (2003). *Counseling the culturally diverse: Theory and practice*. New York: John Wiley and Sons, Inc.

Sue, D. W., Bernier, J. E., Durran, A., Feinberg L., Pedersen, P B., et al. (1982). Position paper: Cross-cultural counseling competencies. *Counseling Psychologist*, *10*(2), 45–52.

Thompson, C. E., and Carter, R. T. (1997). An overview and elaboration of Helms' RID theory. In Chalmer E. Thompson and Robert T. Carter (Eds.), *Racial identity theory: Applications to individual, group, and organizational interventions* (pp. xiv and 97–107). Mahwah, NJ: Lawrence Erlbaum Associates.

Tripp, D. (1993). *Critical incidents in teaching*. London: Routledge.

Vontress, C. E. (1967). The culturally different. *Employment Science Review*, *10*, 35–36.

Vontress, C. E. (1971). Racial differences: Impediments to rapport. *Journal of Counseling Psychology*, *18*(1), 7–13.

Wrenn, C. G. (1962). The culturally encapsulated counselor. *Harvard Educational Review*, *32*, 444-449

In: Psychology of Counseling
Editor: Annamaria Di Fabio

ISBN: 978-1-62618-388-9
© 2013 Nova Science Publishers, Inc.

Chapter 9

Life Designing and the Adaptability Needs of an Unwed Pregnant Teenager: A Case Study[*]

Jacobus G. Maree[#] and Esta Hansen
University of Pretoria
Faculty of Education, University of Pretoria, Pretoria, South Africa

ABSTRACT

This chapter describes the usefulness of a life design approach in helping counsellors identify and deal with the adaptability needs of a pregnant teenager. The participant was selected purposively from among a group of undergraduate students at an institution for unwed mothers. The intervention aimed to enhance the participant's involvement in her life design process and to facilitate co-constructive conversation and occurred over a period of three months. Quantitative data were gathered using the *Myers-Briggs Type Inventory* and the *Career Adapt-Abilities Scale.* Qualitative data were gathered during in-depth (one-on-one, semi-structured) interviews and discussions with the participant and by observing her. Data collection was facilitated by administration of the *Career Interest Profile,* the life line technique, the career construction interview as well as informal questionnaires. Following the intervention, the participant seemed better equipped to confront the complexities of her life and appeared motivated to realise specific goals that could stand her in good stead in her career development. The effectiveness of using a life design counselling process to augment the design of a person's life was thus demonstrated.

The results indicate that the approach to life design counselling described in this chapter is a useful qualitative strategy in the career counselling process. It enables counsellor and client to develop awareness of clients' Self and uncover their major life

---

[*] This chapter is based on the article Maree, J. G., & Hansen, E. (2011). Identifying and dealing with the adaptability needs of an unwed pregnant teenager. *Journal of Psychology in Africa*, 21(1), 211-2. Permission was requested and granted by the Editor, Prof. Elias Mpofu, to rework the article for publication in this volume.

[#] Corresponding author: Jacobus G. Maree. Email: kobus.maree@up.ac.za.

themes and subthemes. More research, involving more participants in diverse contexts, is needed, though.

INTRODUCTION

Recognition has grown over the past 25 years and longer of the value of qualitative approaches to career counselling. The development and application of narrative intervention strategies and assessment instruments in career counselling have accordingly received increasing attention. Hartung (2011), Savickas (2011a, 2011b, 2011c), Subich (2011) and others have emphasised the need to demonstrate the efficacy of these interventions and instruments in career counselling settings. Similarly, many authors (Di Fabio and Maree, 2012; Maree, 2012; Niles, 2003; Savickas, 20011b, 2011c; Skovholt, Morgan, and Negron-Cunningham, 1989) have urged researchers and practitioners to research and report on the value and limits of narrative career counselling in private practice and in group-based contexts and, especially, in non-traditional contexts. The present study is one attempt to respond to these calls.

The advent of the fourth economic wave and the associated changes in the global economy of the 21st century have brought about significant changes to the workplace and are changing the theory and practice of career counselling globally. Savickas (2011a, p. 6) asserts that

> the applied science of vocational psychology and the profession of career counselling have been asking new questions during the first decade of the 21st century. The questions arise from the demise of jobs ... In response to the recurring transitions that they will face as they move from project to project, individuals cannot maintain their employment, so they must maintain their employability.

Savickas (2008, personal communication) believes economic developments can determine how individuals retain their sense of social identity and feeling of self-worth during repeated occupational changes in the course of their lifetimes. Savickas (1993, 2009b) accordingly suggests shifting the emphasis in career counselling from career development to self-development. Because workers are currently frequently confronted with issues of restructuring and transformation in the workplace, the workplace of today must be redesigned to enable young people in particular to adapt to changing needs, changing interests and new experiences.

In the 21st century, the youth should prepare themselves for restructuring and transformation in the workplace. Adolescents' future expectations are often negatively affected by such changes, and they need to be reminded constantly of the importance of retaining hope of eventually entering a career where they can 'live their dream', design successful lives and make social contributions. Career counsellors have the responsibility of helping adolescents meet unique challenges in choosing a career and, more importantly, in scripting career and life stories (Cochran, 2007) that will enable them to self-construct and complete life portraits (Guichard, 2009; Savickas, 2011b, 2011c). The scripting process is well suited to exploring personal meanings and helping adolescents resolve problems and find meaning in life.

Given the situation outlined above, we believe that the challenges faced by adolescents warrant close investigation. The research hiatus in this area needs swift rectification in the context of a) career counselling, including life designing, b) diversity issues, and c) dealing with disadvantaged and abandoned youths

We begin our investigation by considering the concept 'unwed'. Like other adolescents, unwed teenagers have to deal with the developmental challenges outlined earlier. Apart from having to adapt their view of themselves in the here and now to include their pregnancy and how their condition will inform decisions they have to make, they also have to adjust this view in such a way that it can encompass their future career and life decisions. In the remainder of the chapter, we will investigate the usefulness of a life design approach in helping counsellors identify and deal with the adaptability needs of an unwed pregnant teenager.

We will begin by reviewing the theory of career construction and discussing life design counselling and career adaptability. This will be followed by a description of the two theoretical models that guided the study, namely social constructivism and systems theory. We conclude by presenting verbatim data as part of the research findings.

THEORETICAL BACKGROUND

Amundson (2005) argues that some concepts related to career management theory also touch on constructivism. Such concepts are "boundaryless" (Arthur and Rousseau, 1996) and "portfolio" (Hall, 1992, 1996), which have been linked to the theory and practice of career counselling. Young and Collin (1988) call on practitioners to rethink the emphasis on and limits of positivist approaches to career counselling and career conceptualisation. Valach and Young (2004, p. 63) argue that "human actions have meaning, as does career, which is composed of human actions. In turn, the search for meaning leads us to a hermeneutical methodology", which applies not only to practice and research but also reflects a process in which people are continuously engaged in constructing and decoding meaning in action and career.

Career Construction: a Postmodern Career Counselling Theory and Model

Career construction theory (Savickas, 2005) offers a theoretical framework for understanding career behaviour, career choices and career development. It also proposes a counselling model as well as methods of assessment and intervention that can help people construct their own careers. This theory views development as adaption to the environment rather than as the maturing of internal structures (Savickas, 2005). An individual's career is seen as a central part of his or her life, and the construction of career meaning within a unique context is emphasised. Individuals thus have the opportunity to identify the manner in which they want to fit a career into their lives and not the other way round. The focus is on career choice, adaptability and development as integrated processes based on four core concepts: life structure, career personality, career adaptability and life themes (Savickas, 2005, 2009b).

A Life Design Counselling Perspective

According to Savickas (2011b), prevailing career theories neither satisfactorily explain the uncertain and fast-changing career structure nor speak to the needs of marginal workers. He argues that the social constructionist paradigm for the self and career makes available new core constructs for the study and management of 21st century work lives. Vocational psychologists who are looking beyond the positivist career narrative of personality traits and developmental stages are now formulating heuristic constructs intended to help adolescents understand and negotiate a life-course filled with transitions.

Clients are offered an opportunity during life design counselling to contribute within their unique contexts to the process of facilitation by bringing unique expectations and experiences to the process making it dynamic and life-long. Savickas (2002) contends that life design counselling enables clients to write and rewrite their career stories in order to connect their work roles with their career self-concepts. They thus focus not only on career development but also on designing lives that are experienced as satisfactory and that can be redesigned as needs, interests and life experiences change (Savickas, 1993).

Life design counselling as a co-constructive process thus draws on contributions from both counsellor and, in this case study, adolescent. The role of the counsellor as co-constructing, facilitating agent is central. The facilitator and the adolescent bring their subjective worlds of experiences, values, beliefs and personal views to the process (Maree, Bester, Lubbe, and Beck, 2001). Clark, Severy, and Sawyer (2004) maintain that the views and subjective experiences that counsellor and adolescent attach to different concepts extend the adolescent's experiential world.

Career Adaptability

Career development stages and tasks are covered in Super's (1957, 1983) career development theory. Career construction theory builds on Super's (1957, 1983) life span, life space theory (Hartung, 2007) and includes four fundamental dimensions of career behaviour, namely life structure, career adaptability, career personality and life themes. The segments of Super's theory covered by career construction are growth, exploration, establishment, management and decline. The adaptability segment of career construction theory refers to career development tasks and role transitions as well as to strategies for dealing with the challenge of working through developmental tasks and negotiating role transitions. Whereas career maturity refers to adolescents' readiness to make educational and occupational decisions (Savickas, 1995), career adaptability has a more holistic meaning that is applicable to all life span stages. Savickas (1997) asserts that in order to connect the segments of Super's theory, the concept 'career maturity' should be replaced by 'career adaptability' as the central construct in career development theory. This implies that 'career maturity' will not be applicable only to the exploration stage and that 'career adaptability' will not refer only to the establishment stage of career development and growth.

Relevance of the concept 'adaptability' to 21st century career counselling. Adaptability is a critical construct in career construction theory that helps explain career development (Hartung, Porfeli, and Vondracek, 2008). Whereas integration of the life span, life space and self-concept segments of Super's theory (1957, 1983) is facilitated by the individual's adaptability to the environment (Savickas, 1997), the theory is extended by its focus on (career) adaptability, which encourages the use of other conceptual models from other disciplines (Savickas, 1997). By stressing adaptability, career counsellors can help prepare clients to manage change (Campbell and Unger, 2004a, 2004b; Savickas, 1997). Adaptability is inevitably required by the rapid changes in technology and the economy (Savickas, 1997).

Career adaptability. This dimension of career construction theory focuses on the developmental tasks and role transitions as well as the coping strategies of individuals to negotiate the numerous crossroads, transitions and changes they encounter during the course of their lifetimes. According to Hartung (2007), career adaptability is the origin of particular attitudes, beliefs and competencies (ABCs). Each adaptability transaction should strengthen the group and improve the individual's ability to adapt (Savickas, 2003). Savickas (2005) identifies four dimensions of career adaptability: concern, control, curiosity and confidence, each referring to a specific developmental task that impacts on the way in which adolescents will be able to self-construct, design lives and complete life portraits (Guichard, 2009; Savickas, 2011b, 2011c). These dimensions represent the general adaptability resources and strategies used by individuals to manage critical tasks, transitions and traumas during the process of career construction (Hartung, 2007).

Career concern. Refers to people's concern with their own future careers (Savickas, 2005), to the belief that people have a future that is worth preparing and that such preparation will enhance their future.

Career control. Refers to people's belief that they themselves are responsible for the construction of their careers.

Career curiosity. Refers to the desire to learn more about types of occupations individuals may be interested in as well as the opportunities that accompany such occupations (Savickas, 2005). Career curiosity, according to Hartung (2007), implies productive career investigation and a realistic approach to the future.

Career confidence. This dimension has two closely related components, namely an increase in problem-solving capabilities and the belief that people can act efficiently.

(Career) Adaptability and unwed pregnant teenagers. Improved educational and occupational performance may well lessen the chance of teenagers falling pregnant. Brosch, Weigle, and Evans (2007) found a positive correlation between inadequate educational and occupational performance and the incidence of teenage pregnancy. During the adolescent developmental phase, teenagers are confronted with the tasks of exploration and decision making and of moving from dependence to relative independence and autonomy as individuals (Ackerman, 2005). These tasks reflect the dimensions of adaptability delineated above and highlight the importance of helping teenagers who are at risk of falling pregnant to work through these developmental tasks and so decrease the chances of pregnancy. In terms of the aim of this study, pregnant teenagers' educational and occupational aspirations were accordingly looked at from the perspective of their (career) adaptability needs.

Social Constructivism

Reality and knowledge are subjective, and objective neutrality is impossible (Doan, 1997). Social constructivism (the notion that all forms of construction, to a greater or a lesser extent, occur in social contexts) is grounded in the belief that people construct reality socially through the use of shared and agreed-upon meanings communicated through language, social interaction and relationships. According to Chope and Consoli (2007), language is a source of identity formation for people of all cultures, and all people acquire a sense of identity and of self (Who am I?) by using language. Watson and Kuit (2007) state that language is used to construct meaning during the process of life design when the focus shifts to the telling of a career and life story in an attempt to facilitate the design of a successful life. From a constructionist perspective, these narratives are an individual's interpretation of meaning in his or her life. Adolescent and counsellor enter into a co-constructive relationship through dialogue. The role of language in the construction of meaning and achievement and self-construction of career adaptability by unwed pregnant teenagers seems particularly vital. When an adolescent falls pregnant, she inevitably experiences major issues relating to communication. These issues include self-doubt, fear, anger, uncertainty regarding whom to talk to (or not to talk to), what to say, when to talk, where to talk and whether even to end the pregnancy. From a constructionist point of view, narratives are an unwed pregnant adolescent's interpretation of the meaning and significance of her life, which now becomes inseparably intertwined with the life of her unborn child.

Systems Theory

Phenomena are, according to this theory, best understood as a hierarchy of systems each consisting of smaller subsystems and at the same time being part of a bigger, comprehensive system (Prins and Van Niekerk, 2001). Disruption on any level of the system hierarchy will influence all other levels of the hierarchy. The theory holds that contexts cannot remain stable and that the spotlight falls on the meaning attached to the social and psychological world of the individual through social processes and interaction. The social aspect of interaction in relationships is thus dominant in social constructionism (Blustein, Palladino Schultheiss, and Flum, 2004). Stead (2004) states that social constructionism does not accept one truth but proposes, rather, the existence of many truths and multiple realities that are constructed in interaction with others in a specific context. The developmental tasks of an unwed pregnant teenager include acquiring developmental-related attitudes, beliefs and behavioural patterns (Ackerman, 2005) as well as competencies (Hartung, 2007) that impact the temporally and contextually related challenges she is experiencing. Being pregnant at a premature juncture in her life constitutes a barrier that will strongly influence her future life and career. The assignments that have to be mastered by such adolescents are significantly more burdensome than would otherwise be the case. From a systems theory perspective, an unwed pregnant adolescent should be regarded as an individual system at a time of complex change. Systems theory can be used to investigate the complex context of unwed pregnant adolescents as systems. Unless relevant support and resources can be provided to these adolescents to help them feel they can achieve their dreams, their career aspirations and goals may not be realised (Powers, Hogansen, Greenen, Powers, and Gil-Kashiwabara, 2008). Savickas (2005) states that inadequate career concern may lead to feelings of hopelessness. In this chapter, the client's career concerns will be approached against the backdrop of Savickas' comment: *In the modern era, the emphasis was on individual differences. In this day and age, the emphasis has shifted to the individual* (Savickas, 2010; personal communication with the authors).

Aim of the Study

This case study investigated the usefulness of a life design approach in helping counsellors not only identify but, more importantly, also deal with the adaptability needs of a pregnant teenager. The study sought to answer the following questions.

a. How can a life design approach be applied in the case of a young unwed pregnant girl who seeks career counselling?

b. How can career counselling facilitate a young unwed pregnant girl's reflection on her career adaptability needs in such a way that career and life counselling is promoted and the girl takes responsibility for her own actions?

METHOD

Participant and Context

The participant (Grace[1]) was a purposefully selected unwed pregnant teenager seeking career counselling (she thus met the selection criteria for the study).

Procedure: Multi-Method Data-Gathering Plan

The investigation was based on an interpretivist paradigm involving understanding and interpreting meanings revealed during interactions. The research design was qualitative in nature and comprised a case study.

Data Gathering

Psychometric instruments. The psychometric tests used in the study were the *Myers-Briggs Type Inventory (MBTI)* (Briggs and Briggs Myers, 1994) (this test was standardised in South Africa with satisfactory psychometric properties reported) and the *Career Adapt-Abilities Scale (CAAS)* (Savickas, 2009a) (the latter test's results were interpreted qualitatively only). The tests were scored by an independent person who was 'blind' to the study.

Qualitative techniques. Qualitative data were gathered during in-depth (one-on-one, semi-structured) interviews and discussions with Grace and by observing her.

The following techniques facilitated data collection: the *Collage*, the *Career Interest Profile (CIP)* (Maree, 2010), the life line technique (Cochran, 1997), the career construction interview (Hartung, 2010; Savickas, 2009c, 2009b) as well as the administration of informal questionnaires.

---

[1] A pseudonym is used in the case study.

Data Analysis

Approach. A deductive approach was followed in the data analysis in terms of which the data were evaluated and categorised according to predetermined categories found in the literature. In the analysis, the four core dimensions of adaptability identified in the *CAAS*, *concern, control, curiosity* and *confidence* (Savickas et al., 2009), were used as the predetermined themes.

The template style of data analysis depended on these four predetermined themes (Hartung, 2007; Hartung et al., 2008; Savickas, 2003, 2005). Inductive data analysis was done to identify subthemes of the four themes.

Presentation of findings. Verbatim responses by Grace will be given to confirm significant themes. The identified themes will be discussed according to the stages of the life design counselling process.

An uninterrupted text would have reflected the interconnectedness of the data and the themes more suitably, but we distinguished between the stages in order to promote easier understanding of the text and to facilitate referencing.

By discussing the data according to the different stages rather than the individual sessions, we acknowledged the interconnectedness of the themes while addressing the central theme, namely the handling of adaptability needs from a life design perspective.

Criteria for Quality Assurance

Criteria for Quality Assurance

Triangulation and crystallisation. Different quantitative and qualitative data-gathering methods were used to facilitate triangulation and crystallisation (Richardson in Janesick, 2000) in order to enhance the trustworthiness of the study.

Trustworthiness. Trustworthiness was ensured through the use of various strategies during the data collection and analysis. Issues of credibility, confirmability, transferability, dependability, triangulation and crystallisation were addressed.

Credibility. Credibility was facilitated by prolonged engagement with, and continuous observation of, Grace during the research. The data obtained, the methods used and the decisions made in the course of the research were fully documented.

Confirmability. The data obtained, the methods used and the decisions made during the research were fully documented.

Transferability. The research was based on comprehensive descriptions of the case study without any attempts at generalisation. All observations were documented in a researcher journal with detailed descriptions of Grace's personal situation and the techniques used to elicit data. Information was also provided on the context of the case to enable readers to judge the applicability of the findings to other settings.

Dependability. The data were coded independently by an external coder to enhance the accuracy of the deductive process and to ensure that the identified themes accurately represented the data.

Intervention

The intervention aimed to enhance Grace's involvement in her life design process and to facilitate co-constructive conversation (Cochran, 1997). Savickas et al. (2009) explain that life designing is based on five assumptions about people and their working lives, namely (a) contextual possibilities, (b) dynamic processes, (c) non-linear progression, (d) multiple perspectives and (e) personal patterns. Because their life design framework for career counselling incorporates Guichard's (2005) theory of self-constructing and Savickas' (2005) theory of career construction – both of which describe occupational behaviour and its development – it is structured to be life-long, holistic, contextual and preventive of inadequate self-construction. Counselling is seen as an uninterrupted, interactive process that never stands apart from emotions and feelings; a process that facilitates problem solving and decision making in the context in which people live and develop (Duarte, 2009, 2010).

Savickas and his colleagues' (2009) life design strategy comprises six steps and is informed by the idiosyncratic reality resulting from the unique experience of every person.

The six steps are: (i) defining the problem and identifying what the client hopes to achieve (construction of working alliance), (ii) exploration by counsellor and client of the client's current system of subjective identity forms2 (mapping and exploration of a system of subjective identity forms), (iii) opening perspectives by narrating the client's story and reviewing this story (discovering, rewriting, reorganising and revising life stories), (iv) placing the problem in a new story and perspective, (v) specifying and selecting activities that investigate issues surrounding identity, and (vi) conducting follow-up sessions. Life designing aims to increase clients' adaptability, narratability and activity. Adaptability concerns change while narratability concerns continuity.

Together, the ability to design a successful life and to adapt provide individuals with the flexibility and dependability of selves that enables them to engage in meaningful activities and thrive in knowledge societies. Activity, on the other hand, concerns the actual activities during which the person learns which abilities and interests he or she would prefer to exercise (Savickas et al., 2009).

Ethics

Steps were taken to ensure Grace's wellbeing throughout the study. Her informed consent was obtained, and full confidentiality was maintained. She was given feedback by the researchers during all the phases of the study, and the research findings were released in an acceptable and responsible manner.

RESULTS

Several themes (see Table 1 for a summary of the main themes and subthemes) emerged qualitatively through the course of the life design counselling process.

---

[2] A subjective identity form is the way a given individual sees him/herself and others in a particular context and how he or she relates to others and the objects in this context (Savickas et al., 2009).

Table 1. Identified themes based on the literature

Themes and subthemes identified	Source of information
Main theme: a. Concern	
Subthemes	
a.i. Concern with career future	*Collage* Idioms *CIP* (Maree, 2010)
a.ii. Positive attitude towards the future	Idioms
a.iii. Anticipation	*MBTI* (Briggs and Briggs Myers, 1994) Role models Life line
a.iv. Optimism/Hope	Role models *Collage* Idioms *CAAS* (Savickas, 2009a)
a.v. Planfulness	Idioms *CIP* (Maree, 2010)
Main theme: b. Control	
Subthemes	
b.i. Independence	Role models *Collage* Life line *CAAS* (Savickas, 2009a)
b.ii. Interpersonal autonomy	Role models *Collage* Idioms *CAAS* (Savickas, 2009a)
b.iii. Intrapersonal willpower	Life line *CAAS* (Savickas, 2009a)
b.iv. Responsibility for/Ownership of the future	Idioms Life line
Main theme: c. Curiosity	
Subthemes	
c.i. Self-knowledge	Role models *Collage* *CIP* (Maree, 2010) Life line *CAAS* (Savickas, 2009a)
c.ii. Open attitude towards new experiences	*MBTI* (Briggs and Briggs Myers, 1994) Idioms
Main theme: d. Confidence	
Subthemes	
d.i. Problem-solving abilities	*Collage* Life line
d.ii. Self-acceptance	Role models Life line
d.iii. Self-worth	Role models Life line *CAAS* (Savickas, 2009a)
d.iv. Expectation of success	*Collage* *CIP* (Maree, 2010) *CAAS* (Savickas, 2009a)

In order to realise the full potential of the co-constructive nature of interpretivist research, we did not make any interpretations of the client's narratives but, rather, presented a nuanced understanding of the participant's life design process as it emerged during the study.

Qualitative results. The themes are discussed according to the following stages: (a) constructing a working alliance, (b) mapping and exploring a system of subjective identity forms, (c) opening perspectives, and discovering, rewriting, reorganising and revising life stories, (d) placing the problem in a new story and perspective, (e) specifying and selecting activities that investigate issues surrounding identity and, lastly, (f) conducting a follow-up session.

A summary of the confirmed main themes and the subthemes that emerged during the life design counselling process, as well as the sources of information, is given in Table 1.

Construction of a Working Alliance

An important goal of life design counselling is facilitating insight and agency in the client's own context (Savickas et al., 2009). During the construction of a working alliance, attempts are consequently made to help people develop effective strategies for problem solving, plans of action and general life design (Savickas et al., 2009). It was explained to Grace in this study that she alone was the architect of her life (Campbell and Ungar, 2004a, 2004b), but that the counsellor would work with her to co-construct an ideal future and design a preferred life. Grace eventually took ownership of the process. Her answer to the question: *Can you do whatever you want to do?* was *Only when things go right* (b.iv). She then added: *Things go right only when I make them go right* (b.iv).

Grace faced several unique challenges the most important of which, according to her, was her pregnancy: *Getting pregnant while I'm at school.* Not only was her educational career seriously disrupted, she also felt disappointed by the turn her life had taken. She expressed the wish to *get on my way again, make money and make my life simpler and more manageable.* Although Grace would have preferred to pass Grade12 as soon as she could, she decided not to return to school until after the birth of her baby. Her future after the birth was particularly unsure as her family was unable to support her.

Grace's descriptions of her family revealed a history of broken and inadequate relationships. Because both her parents were alcoholics, she lived with her grandmother: *I would rather live with my magogo because my parents are alcoholics.* Grace's grandmother was unemployed, causing them to live in extreme poverty. Grace nevertheless remained optimistic and hopeful: *I will cope with things, you know, as long as I have a warm family* (a.iv). This, however, was not an outlook anchored in reality. During the process of (re-) designing her life, an important goal was to help her form a more realistic view of her family situation so that she could identify and deal with the attendant challenges. The complexity of her situation made this a sensitive and long-term process that fell outside the boundaries of the present study.

According to Duarte (2010), the counsellor should attempt to clarify the client's different roles during the establishment of a working alliance. Grace recognised that she would soon have to take on the additional role of a mother but denied that this would influence her situation: *I want to achieve everything even though I'm a mother, young girl* (d.iv). *It is nothing to worry about.* She felt optimistic about the impending change: *I will cope with it, you know* (a.iv) but could not connect this optimism to a real, carefully planned future (Hartung, 2007). A goal of life designing in the study was accordingly to clarify Grace's role as a single mother. The achievement of this goal would help Grace approach her future with planfulness and ground her optimism in reality (Savickas, 2003).

Mapping and Exploration of Subjective Identity Forms

During this stage, Grace's subjective identity forms were examined in order to determine the identity image she had constructed of herself in different contexts (Guichard, 2009). A bridge was thus built between her experiences (past and present) and future expectations. During this process, her investigation of possible selves was encouraged (Oyserman, Bybee, and Terry, 2006).

A particular challenge faced by Grace was her experience of isolation and loneliness, which applied to her school as well as family contexts. Regarding school, she observed: *I have a best friend, but she is not there at the school.* Regarding her family context, she remarked: *But they were not there, I was always alone.* Grace's isolation and resultant lack of support were evident in her having to adapt to difficult circumstances, including the real danger of rape, without any support from her parents. When Grace and *magogo* stayed with the family briefly, rape became an even greater danger, yet family members remained uninvolved and unconcerned. Notwithstanding Grace's warnings and fears, no adult family member listened to her, even when a *dangerous man* raped one of her cousins. Grace said the following about a role model of hers (Oprah Winfrey): *She knows what questions to ask. She always talks on behalf of those who have no voice.* Grace also tried to speak to *magogo* and other family members on behalf of her younger cousins (to highlight the danger of being raped in which they found themselves); a characteristic that resonated with her core self and became part of her construction of her identity image (Savickas et al., 2009). Grace's experiences at school also indicated loneliness and isolation: *Sometimes at school I am embarrassed by some people. They ask me to write on a chalk board for teacher but when I get up they call me names that embarrass me ... yet, I do it* (d.i). A more recent school experience that Grace included in her narrative was her Grade 11 failure: *I am sorry to admit that I failed grade 11* and her academic problems: *I feel very incompetent when I am expected to do class work. I don't always understand and it is difficult to find help* (c.i).

Grace's identity image at the time of the intervention reflected her situation and her hope to survive: *I will cope* (a.iv) and *I just have to cope, you know* (a.iv). This view of herself as someone who could cope with difficult situations was shaped largely by her earlier experiences of surviving rejection, loneliness and a hostile environment devoid of any support (Savickas et al., 2009). This identity image was strengthened by her favourite saying (her advice to herself): *Strive to survive* (a.iv). Grace linked her striving for survival to hope and optimism: *Do what you do with all your power and in the hope that things will change. You can survive anything* (a.iv) and *You can always like, you know, strive to do something better. You must hope your actions will make your future better. You must do what you do with hope. You must strive* (a.ii). However, she also gave some indication of her incipient realisation that her hope and optimism were not anchored in a real future or planful attitude: *Things do not always happen; others often don't know you and what you do but you have to keep on hoping to achieve* (a.iv). Her identity image of someone who could survive difficult circumstances was thus built almost exclusively on the frail foundation of hope.

A gap existed between Grace's existing identity image and her looked-for identity. Her expectations centred on:

- financial and social success – *This will be my car* [pointing at pictures in her collage] *and i-phone. I will look so beautiful and I will invite my friends to come and enjoy* (d.iv). *I want to achieve everything even though I'm a mother, a young girl* (d.iv);
- acknowledgement – *I would like it if one day, somewhere, in my career, I could be in front of many people. They will promote me for dealing with difficulty at work* (a.i);
- an end to her isolation – *I wish I could be one of them, of the team and be able to encourage others* (a.i).

Opening of Perspectives, and Discovering, Rewriting, Reorganising and Revising Life Stories

During this stage, Grace's life story was repeated and rewritten based on the information obtained during the first two stages. She was tactfully informed that pursuing her two envisaged fields of study, geology and veterinary science, as possible career paths were unrealistic options at this stage. Instead, she had to establish some normality in her life first, after which she could attempt to pursue viable career options. Care was taken to prevent Grace from seeing herself as a failure and to support her in identifying her strong points and perceiving her weak points as possible future strengths.

Grace summarised her strong points as follows:

- *Life sciences. I should pass* (c.i).
- *I can write a song and add music to it as well* (c.i).
- *Young children like to play with me* (c.i).
- *I know who I am* (self-knowledge).
- *I know that I have to think about my future* (anticipation of events).
- *Problems are there to be solved* (problem-solving skills).
  Grace also identified the following weak points.
- *I feel lonely at school. My friend was moved to another class. But I still strive* (a.iv).
- *I would like to be less self-centred* (c.i).

Although identified as a weak point, Grace's loneliness seemed to be contextual rather than pervasive. To help her establish a sense of normality, she was encouraged to deal with her feelings of loneliness. According to Savickas et al. (2009), people's self-concepts can change only through new experiences and by observing other people. The context of Grace's interactions therefore had to be widened to enable her to design a more complex identity image than her existing image, which centred on survival. During the life design counselling, Grace took part in activities that provided meaning and helped her construct a new view of herself (Duarte, 2010).

Placing of the Problem in a New Story and Perspective

During this stage, Grace reinterpreted her future expectations and possible outcomes (Duarte, 2010). The reinterpretation of her situation offered her an exciting new perspective – the affirmation of her ability to realise her preferred identity: *The sky is the limit ... I want to achieve everything even though I'm a mother, a young girl (d.iv). But it is nothing to worry about. I will still continue to strive for what I want. I will strive. I don't want to give up anything about my future* (b.iii).

Grace perceived her pregnancy as the biggest obstacle to realising her potential: *Getting pregnant while I'm at school is my biggest problem.* However, it was pointed out to her that the part of her life story involving her pregnancy had the potential to be rewritten. The paternal grandmother of Grace's baby, for instance, showed genuine concern for Grace. This relationship enabled Grace to experience support, to observe a potential role model and thus to change her self-concept in a positive way (Savickas, 2005). It would, after all, be possible for her to find her way again: *There is still a future for me. After having had the baby I can still have my life* (a.i).

Specifying and Selecting Activities that Investigate Issues Surrounding Identity

During this stage, Grace and the researchers decided on ways to actualise her co-constructed life design, which included developing her capacity to act in a more predetermined manner by thinking before acting and by learning from her mistakes. She decided to start with job analysis so that she could become more aware of the realistic educational and career choices she had to make, to anticipate possible life choices, to work perseveringly and patiently, to act in the interests of herself and her child, and to take charge of her future by considering various career alternatives. The initial goals were looked at again, and general self-reflection was facilitated.

Specific activities that Grace and the researchers decided on:

- Starting and maintaining an emotional calendar (Maree, 2008)
- Writing a letter to herself as an adult and mother of a five-year-old child
- Writing a letter to her unborn child
- Writing a letter to the father of her child
- Continuing her life line into the future
- Completing her life chapters

Follow-up Session 1

Since life design is considered a life-long process, the researchers stressed that the responsibility to actively design her life rested with Grace alone. A month after the initial sessions, Grace reported that she had started doing job analyses and volunteering at a kindergarten during the mornings. She was beginning to consider primary school teaching as a career option. She said that she was maintaining an emotional calendar but was finding it difficult always to identify the reason for the emotions she was experiencing. She reported that she had enjoyed writing the letters but admitted having as yet written only to her unborn child. She was again encouraged to write down her thoughts, even if not in letter format.

At the time of the intervention, Grace's life was focused on the birth of her baby. She said she hoped to pay more attention to her educational and occupational decisions following the birth. After a three-month period, Grace showed a willingness to accept personal responsibility for her future and also showed signs of a new hope for her future:

> The sky is still the limit … I want to achieve my dreams even though I will be a mother. I will always continue to strive for what I want because I don't want to give up anything about my future.

At the time of the intervention, Grace's life was focused primarily on the birth of her baby. She said she hoped to pay more attention to her educational and occupational decisions after the birth of her child. After a three-month period, the participant showed a willingness to accept personal responsibility for her future.

In addition, she showed signs of a new hope for her future as is evident from the following remark.

Follow-up Session 2

At the time of writing of the current chapter, two years after the intervention, Grace's daughter was one year and eight months old. Grace was doing well and confirmed that she did not have any plans to have another child in the foreseeable future. She had completed Grade 12 successfully and had applied to do a course in Nursing at the Medical University of South Africa. In her own words: *I really want to become a nurse so I can help people that are in need; people like myself when you and I worked together.* Her mother and grandmother had already agreed to look after her daughter for the duration of her studies. When asked about the value of the life designing intervention two years ago, Grace replied: *Yes, the sessions definitely helped me. I often think about our sessions. What stands out for me, is the motivation and inspiration I got. When I get despondent, I for instance recall what we did during the making of the* collage *to inspire me. I often look at the collage and it makes me think of being something; it reminds me that I can become somebody. It helped me to realise that I want to become a nurse then and it constantly motivates me to cling to my dream. Thank you once more for giving the opportunity to learn from you but also from myself.*

DISCUSSION

Life design counselling is considered by researchers (Campbell and Ungar, 2004a, 2004b; Savickas et al., 2009; Zunker, 1998) as an effective strategy for designing an individual's life. Such a strategy can change as unique challenges, experiences and needs arise. This view is largely confirmed by the present case study, which provided a rich and dense description of how to identify and deal with the adaptability needs of an unwed pregnant teenager. The findings suggest that life design counselling is a promising strategy with long-term beneficial effects for unwed pregnant teenagers. The narrative techniques in the study seemed to augment Grace's involvement in the life design process.

The point of departure in the study was that the (career) adaptability needs of an unwed pregnant teenager can be addressed constructively through a co-constructive life design process. The study revealed the unique nature of the participant's context, the interdependent relationship between the participant and the different systems in her life, the subjective nature of her experience and the challenges faced by her as an unwed pregnant teenager.

RECOMMENDATIONS

Firstly, psychologists-in-training will benefit from the inclusion of the six phases outlined in this chapter in life design counselling curricula. Secondly, practising psychologists will likely require training in this approach as well. Thirdly, psychologists may have to refer clients to appropriate health professionals if major pathology emerges prior to embarking on career counselling per se. Fourthly, psychologists are encouraged to build on this study as it confirms the merits of a combined quantitative-qualitative approach to (career) counselling in facilitating a deeper understanding of the value of finding personal meaning, taking on personal agency, striving actively towards achieving personal growth and (co-)construction of a career and design of a life, as well as acceptance of personal responsibility in the (career) counselling process, self-construction and completing a life portrait (Maree, in press; Savickas, 2011a). Fifthly, psychologists are encouraged to conduct research in this field and to report on their findings in scholarly journals and at psychology conferences.

During this study, the researchers worked from the assumption that a co-constructive life design counselling process could address the challenges experienced by a particular unwed pregnant teenager. The approach described here equipped the researchers with the skills needed to ensure not only construction, deconstruction, reconstruction but, importantly, co-construction and self-construction, and, eventually, the spurring on of the teenager to action (Malrieu, 2003; Savickas, 2011a). The study revealed the unique nature of the teenager's context, the interdependent relationship between her and the system in which she found herself, the subjective meaning of experiences, and the challenges faced by her as an unwed pregnant teenager.

LIMITATIONS

The broader applicability, flexibility and effectiveness of a life design counselling process should be determined by repeating this study with a bigger population and more culturally diverse groups. Although steps were taken to enhance the trustworthiness and credibility of the study, the subjective interpretation of the researchers could be regarded as a limitation.

PROJECTION

Three months after the life design process, Grace seemed better equipped to confront the complexities of her life. She appeared motivated to realise specific goals that could stand her in good stead in her career development. The transcriptions of the conversations with Grace showed the effectiveness of using a life design counselling process to augment the design of a person's life. For instance, exploring Grace's past experiences, identifying her role models and discussing her success stories and strong (and weak) points most probably contributed to her increased awareness of her socialisation needs and abilities, resulting in her new positive behaviour. These conversations could also have contributed to her heightened self-insight into her experiences and perceptions.

Advice to Others Who May Wish to do this Type of Intervention

We believe that the approach described in this chapter on life designing intervention will help counsellor and client construct the client's life portrait (Savickas, 2011a) and enable him or her to design a successful life and make social contributions.

However, successful implementation of the approach will depend on the appropriate training of counsellors in the qualitative narrative tradition and perspective. Also essential is the creation of a "sacred space" (Savickas, 1989, 1998) where the therapeutic relationship between counsellor and client can develop. Counsellors will also require the skills needed to facilitate clients' reflection on their own reflections in a way that will enable counsellor and client to determine whether their understanding of the client's inner world is accurate (Rogers, 1952). Lastly, attention should be paid to the identification and interpretation of non-verbal communication and to the use of conversational modalities, for instance reformulating clients' comments and paying due attention to their questions.

CONCLUSION

The study results indicate that the approach to life design counselling described in this chapter is a useful qualitative strategy in the career counselling process. It enables counsellor and client to develop awareness of the client's Self and uncover his or her major life themes and subthemes (Maree, 2006; Savickas, 1998, 2005). The narrative approach set out here regarding life designing intervention in facilitating narrative counselling may go some way towards enabling counsellor and client to construct the client's life portrait (Savickas, 2011a) and enable him or her to design a successful life and make social contributions.

Even though the participant's circumstances and history were not changed by the life design counselling process, she did reveal a 'changed' experience in terms of some aspects of her situation. The co-constructive conversations also did not necessarily solve all her problems, but she did become more aware of the meanings she assigned to the motivation for her behaviour and her view of herself. She also showed greater insight into herself as evidenced by the following remark during the last conversation: "*I have learnt that my future is still in my hands, despite what has happened. I can still become who and what I want to become."*

In conclusion: We believe that the scope of psychology, and not only life design counselling, should be broadened to include the full spectrum of diversity in different contexts (e.g. social and financial status, gender, religion, creed and race) with the emphasis on actively engaging people in constructing personal meanings and planning for the future (Amundson, 2003). The fact that an unwed pregnant adolescent took part in the study is therefore of little importance. Furthermore, in attempting to facilitate career adaptability, psychologists should view all clients as active agents in their own personal development: counselling should therefore continue to address the needs and diversity of individual persons. Putting into practice the shift in emphasis internationally from stressing career adaptability instead of career maturity during career counselling in local contexts seems viable, timely and advisable.

REFERENCES

Ackerman, C. (2005). Promoting development during adolescence. In P. Engelbrecht and L. Green (Eds.), Promoting learner development (pp. 101-120). Pretoria, South Africa: Van Schaik.

Amundson, N. E. (2003). Active engagement: Enhancing the career counselling process. (2nd ed). Richmond, BC: Ergon Communications.

Amundson, N. (2005). The potential impact of global changes in work for career theory and practice. *International Journal for Educational and Vocational Guidance*, 5, 91-99.

Arthur, M. B., and Rousseau, D. M. (1996). The boundaryless career: A new employment principle for a new organizational era. New York, NY: Oxford University Press.

Blustein, D. L., Palladino Schulteiss, D. E., and Flum, H. (2004). Toward a relational perspective of the psychology of careers and working: A social constructionist analysis. *Journal of Vocational Behavior*, 64, 423-440.

Briggs, K. C., and Briggs Myers, I. (1994). Myers-Briggs type indicator. Palo Alto, CA: Consulting Psychologists Press.

Brosh, J., Weigel, D., and Evan, W. (2007). Pregnant and parenting adolescents' perception of sources and supports in relation to educational goals. *Child Adolescent Social Work Journal*, 24, 565-578.

Campbell, C., and Ungar, M. (2004a). Constructing a life that works: Part 1: Blending postmodern family therapy and career counseling. *The Career Development Quarterly*, 53, 16-27.

Campbell, C., and Ungar, M. (2004b). Constructing a life that works: Part 2: An approach to practice. *The Career Development Quarterly*, 53, 28-40.

Clark, M. A., Severy, L., and Sawyer, S. A. (2004). Creating connections: Using a narrative approach in career group counselling with college students from diverse cultural backgrounds. *Journal of College Counselling*, 7, 24-31.

Chope, R. C., and Consoli, A. J. (2007). A storied approach to multicultural career counselling. In K. Maree (Ed.), Shaping the story: A guide to facilitating narrative counselling (pp. 87-100). Pretoria, South Africa: Van Schaik.

Cochran, L. (1997). Career counselling: A narrative approach. California, CA: Thousand Oaks.

Cochran, L. (2007). The promise of narrative career counselling. In K. Maree (Ed.), *Shaping the story:* A guide to facilitating narrative counseling (pp. 7-19). Pretoria: Van Schaik.

Di Fabio, A., and Maree, J. G. (2012). Group-based life design counseling in an Italian context. *Journal of Vocational Behavior*, 80, 100-107.

Doan, R. E. (1997). Narrative therapy, postmodernism, social constructionism and constructivism: Discussion and distinctions. *Transactional Analysis Journal*, 27(2), 128-133.

Duarte, M. E. (2009). The psychology of life construction. *Journal of Vocational Behavior*, 75(3), 259-266.

Duarte, M. E. (2010, July). Restructuring career counseling: objectives and instruments. In R. Van Esbroeck (Convenor), Life Design Symposium. Symposium presented at the 27th International Congress of Applied Psychology, Melbourne, Australia.

Guichard, J. (2005). Life-long self-construction. *International Journal for Educational and Vocational Guidance*, 5, 111-124.

Guichard, J. (2009). Self-constructing. *Journal of Vocational Behavior*, 78(3), 251-258.

Hall, D. T. (1992). The strategic analysis of intangible resources. *Strategic Management Journal*, 13, 135-144.

Hall, D. T. (1996). The career is dead: Long lives the career. San Francisco: Jossey-Bass.

Hartung, P. J. (2007). Career construction: Principles and practice. In K. Maree (Ed.), Shaping the story: A guide to facilitating narrative counselling (pp. 103-120). Pretoria, South Africa: Van Schaik.

Hartung, P. J. (2010). Identifying life-career themes with the career-story questionnaire. In K. Maree (Ed.), Career counselling: Methods that work (pp. 161-166). Cape Town, South Africa: Juta Academic.

Hartung, P. J. (2011). Defining career services: Guidance, education, and counseling. Paper presented in P. J. Hartung (Chair). Career counseling. Definitions and new directions. American Psychological Association, 119th Annual meeting, Washington, DC.

Hartung, P. J., Porfeli, E. J., and Vondracek, F. W. (2008). Career adaptability in childhood. *The Career Development Quarterly*, 57, 63-73.

Janesick, V. J. (2000). The choreography of quality research design: Minuets, improvisations, and crystallization. In Denzin, N. K., and Y. S. Lincoln (Eds.), Handbook of qualitative research (pp. 370-396). Thousand Oaks, CA: Sage.

Malrieu, P. (2003). La question du sens dans les dires autobiographiques [The issue of meaning in autobiographical narratives]. Toulouse, France: Erès.

Maree, J. G. (2006). Manual for the CIP. Randburg, South Africa: Jopie van Rooyen and Partners.

Maree, J. G. (2008). Smarter the easy way. Pretoria, South Africa: Lapa.

Maree, J. G. (2010). *The CIP* (3rd ed.). Randburg, South Africa: Jopie van Rooyen and Partners.

Maree, J. G. (2012). A guide to reflective career counseling. [DVD]. Randburg, South Africa: Jopie van Rooyen and Partners.

Maree, J. G. (in press). *Counselling for career construction: connecting life themes to construct life portraits: Turning pain into hope*. Rotterdam, The Netherlands: Sense.

Maree, J. G., Bester, S. E., Lubbe, C., and Beck, C. (2001). Post-modern career counselling to a gifted black youth: A case study. *Gifted Education International*, 15(3), 324-338.

Niles, S. G. (2003). Career counselors confront a critical crossroad: A vision of the future. *The Career Development Quarterly*, 52, 70-77.

Oyserman, D., Bybee, D., and Terry, K. (2006). Possible selves and academic outcomes: How and when possible selves impel action. *Journal of Personality and Social Psychology*, 91, 188-204.

Powers, K., Hogansen, J., Greenen, S., Powers, L. E., and Gil-Kashiwabara, E. (2008). Gender matters in transition to adulthood: A survey study of adolescents with disabilities and their families. *Psychology in the Schools*, 45(4), 349-364.

Prins, A., and Van Niekerk, E. (2001). Theoretical perspectives in counselling. In E. van Niekerk and A. Prins (Eds.), Counselling in Southern Africa (pp. 20-57). Sandown, South Africa: Heinemann.

Rogers, C. R. (1952). Client-centered therapy. Boston, MA: Houghton Mifflin.

Savickas, M. L. (1989). Career style assessment and counseling. In T. Sweeney (Ed.), Adlerian counseling: A practical approach for a new decade (3rd ed., pp. 289-320). Muncie, IN: Accelerated Development.

Savickas, M. L. (1993). Career counselling in the postmodern era. *Journal of Cognitive Psychotherapy: An International Quarterly*, 7(3), 205-215.

Savickas, M. L. (1995). Constructivist counselling for career indecision. *Career Development Quarterly*, 43(4), 363-373.

Savickas, M. L. (1997). Career adaptability: An integrative construct for life-span, life-space theory. *Career Development Quarterly*, 45, 247-259.

Savickas, M. L. (1998). Career-style assessment and counseling. In T.Sweeney (Ed.), Adlerian counseling: A practitioner's approach (4th ed.,pp. 329–360). Philadelphia, PA: Accelerated Development.

Savickas, M. L. (2002). Career construction: A developmental theory of vocational behavior. In D. Brown (Ed.), Career choice and development (pp. 149-205). San Francisco, CA: Jossey-Bass.

Savickas, M. L. (2003). Towards a taxonomy of human strengths: Career counselling's contribution to positive psychology. In W. B. Walsh (Ed), Counseling psychology and optimal human functioning (pp. 229-249) . London, England: Routledge.

Savickas, M. L. (2005). The theory and practice of career construction. In S. D. Brown and R. W. Lent (Eds.), Career development and counseling: Putting theory and research to work (pp. 42-70). Hoboken, NJ: Wiley.

Savickas, M. L. (2009a). Career Adapt-Abilities Inventory. Unpublished working document. Pretoria. South Africa: University of Pretoria.

Savickas, M. L. (2009b, April). The essentials of life design counselling. Invited public lecture, University of Pretoria, Pretoria, South Africa.

Savickas, M. L. (2009c, April). Utilising early anecdotes in counselling in the 21st century. Keynote presentation, SA, Society for Clinical Hypnosis. Pretoria, South Africa.

Savickas, M. L. (2011a). Career counseling. Washington, DC: American Psychological Association.

Savickas, M. L. (2011b, August). A general model for career counseling. Paper presented in P. J. Hartung, (Chair), Career counseling: Definitions and new directions. American Psychological Association 119th annual meeting. Washington, DC.

Savickas, M. L. (2011c). New questions for vocational psychology: Premises, paradigms, and practices. *Journal of Career assessment*, 19(3), 251-258.

Savickas, M. L., Nota, L., and Rossier, L., Dauwalder, J. P., Duarte, M. E., Guichard, J.,...van Vianen, A. E. M. (2009). Life designing: A paradigm for career construction in the 21th century. *Journal of Vocational Behavior,* 75, 239-250.

Skovholt, T. M., Morgan, J. I., and Negron-Cunningham, H. (1989). Mental imagery in career counseling and life planning: A review of research and intervention methods. *Journal of Counseling and Development*, 67(5), 287-293.

Stead, G. B. (2004). Culture and career psychology: A social constructionist perspective. *Journal of Vocational Behavior*, 64, 389-406.

Subich, L. M. (2011, August). Tracing the evolution of career counseling theory. Paper presented in P. J. Hartung (Chair). Career counseling. Definitions and new directions. American Psychological Association, 119th Annual meeting, Washington, DC.

Super, D. E. (1957). The psychology of careers. New York, NY: Harper and Row.

Super, D. E. (1983). Assessment in career guidance: Toward truly developmental counseling. *Personnel and Guidance Journal*, 61, 555-562.

Valach, L., and Young, R. A. (2004). Some cornerstones in the development of a contextual action theory of career and counselling. *International Journal for Educational and Vocational Guidance*, 4, 61-81.

Watson, M., and Kuit, W. (2007). Postmodern career counselling and beyond. In K. Maree (Ed.), Shaping the story: A guide to facilitating narrative counselling (pp. 73-86). Pretoria, South Africa: Van Schaik.

Young, R. A., and Collin, A. (1988). Career development and hermeneutical inquiry: Part I The framework of a hermeneutical approach. *Canadian Journal of Counselling*, 22, 153-161.

Zunker, V. G. (1998). Career counseling: Applied concepts of life planning (5th ed). Pacific Grove, CA: Brooks/Cole Publishing Company.

In: Psychology of Counseling
Editor: Annamaria Di Fabio

ISBN: 978-1-62618-388-9
© 2013 Nova Science Publishers, Inc.

Chapter 10

Interdisciplinary Views on the Art Making Process in Treatment

*Nancy Slater**
Pierce College Puyallup, Puyallup, WA, US

ABSTRACT

Drawing on contemporary and historical literature, this chapter examines the role of process of art-making as the change agent for psychological and emotional healing across clinical populations and within social and cultural contexts. Through clinical practitioner observations of a client's therapeutic art-making and the client's responses to the process of art-making, understanding increases about client behavior, mental functioning and influences of stressful life experiences. This therapeutic art-making also functions to document a client's perceptions and experiences, and it functions to communicate to the observing practitioner the effects of these life experiences.

Much of the literature in psychology and counseling has focused on the final product as the primary source of information about individual functioning. The literature reviewed here demonstrates that information is revealed and data collected through observation of the art-making process, not only the art product.

Suggestions about addressing the clinical process for those who use art making in treatment and about developing research examines treatment outcomes by integrating data gathering from observations of the art-making process.

INTRODUCTION

Drawing on contemporary and historical literature this chapter examines the role of the art-making process in selected mental health disciplines. Many forms of visual art-making have been part of western mental health interventions since interest in the artwork of the mentally ill developed in Europe in the mid-1800s. Taking a view across the disciplines of

---

* Corresponding author: E-mail address: slaterna@e-arthlink.net.

psychiatry, clinical psychology, counseling, and art therapy demonstrates the differing uses of art-making. With these differing uses, the art-making process as change agent for psychological, behavioral and emotional healing cuts across clinical populations and varied social and cultural contexts.

This chapter notes that for over 100 years many in the field of psychiatry have recognized the benefits of utilizing visual art-making in treatment. From these early days, the case study research method provided opportunities for observation and analysis of patients and their spontaneous artwork, particularly in inpatient settings (MacGregor, 1989). In clinical psychology beginning in the 1940s, a different focus on art-making developed through the use of projective testing for assessment, diagnosis and treatment planning (Groth-Marnat, 2009). This became the predominant use of art-making for clinical psychology practitioners and researchers. More recently, the expressive arts/creative arts have emerged as part of the counseling discipline (Gladding, 2005). The techniques and tools in the expressive arts have been integrated into counseling practice for more than 25 years in the United States (see Degges-White & Davis, 2011; Gladding, 2005). And, art therapy, an interdisciplinary field, began as a profession in the United States and in Britain in the 1960s. This field combines the theories and practice in the visual arts with the theories and practices in mental health treatment that began with artists and art educators working under guidance by psychiatrists in the 1950s (Slater, 2010). And, earlier work in art therapy can be documented, at least back to the latter years of World War II (Hogan, 2001; Jones, 2005; Junge & Asawa, 1994).

Defining 'Process' Regarding the Use of Art-Making in Therapy

For this chapter the author is attempting to identify the role or uses of the process of art making in assessment and during treatment across four mental health disciplines. In this author's opinion and from her exploration of the use of art-making in treatment, the historical and perhaps cultural origins of each of these disciplines has a significant role in the inclusion of visual art in the practice of each of these disciplines. Therefore, the term *process* may include any or all aspects of art-making by the client/participant/patient (Betensky, 1977; Junge & Asawa, 1994; Kramer, 1976). In a broad definition of this term, the art-making process also can include verbal responses by the client during art-making, responses to the final product and/or interactions between the practitioner and client in reaction to the final product. In other words, *process* involves all aspects of the engagement of a client with art materials (media), responses by a client during art-making and responses to the final product (Hinz, 2009; Lusebrink, 1990; Slater, 2010; Wadeson, 1987). The typical type of *process* that receives the professional's attention appears to depend on the discipline/field of that practitioner or researcher. (Further discussion later in this chapter.) However the concept of *process* in relationship to making art in treatment discussed in this chapter is not part of nor connected to "Process- oriented psychology" developed by Arnold Mindell in the 1970s (see A. Mindell, 1992).

The final part of this chapter addresses the need for research about the role of the process part of art-making in clinical settings and across disciplines due to its function or potential function as a change agent for clients. Recommendations for cross-training and communication across disciplines with the goal of improving institutional efforts to facilitate effective assessment and treatment especially when art-making and/or other expressive arts are included.

ROLE OF ART-MAKING IN PSYCHIATRY

Psychiatry has a long history of attending to the 'art of the insane' (MacGregor, 1989) that began primarily as the result of remarkable individuals who obtained university degrees in art history or art and in medicine with specialization in psychiatry. Each of these specific individuals, such as Fritz Mohr, Hans Prinzhorn, and Ernst Kris in the late 1800s and early 1900s, made truly landmark contributions to the development of 'Psychiatry and Art' that continues today.

MacGregor (1989), an art historian, wrote a significant work, *The Discovery of the Art of the Insane,* that details much of the history of the relationships between psychiatry and psychology and art. To begin a look into this history, he describes that in the second half of the 19th century, "Mental disease was understood to be the result of abnormalities in the brain, and the source of emotional disorders was sought in physical lesions or irregularities in the anatomical structure of the brain". And, not until fifty years later did interest in the art of the mentally ill hold an interest in this field.

> As part of [the] process of diagnostic clarification, a final effort [during this time] was made to associate specific styles of patient art with the major syndrome groupings, and with the detailed information that was being accumulated about the symptom clusters that characterized these individual forms of mental disorder (MacGregor, 1989, p. 188).

MacGregor continues with more on this development. In Germany during the first part of the 20th century a peak in the interest about psychotic art occurred in both the fields of psychiatry and art. He states:

> Only an individual convincingly at home in both camps [artists and scientists] could have been expected to extend the new aesthetic into the realm of art produced in the context of insanity. Hans Prinzhorn (1886-1933), fully trained in art history and psychiatry, was this man.(MacGregor, 1989, p. 193)

MacGregor continues about Prinzhorn's position at the Heidelburg Psychiatric Clinic which resulted in his book on the art of the mentally ill that was intended to serve as a research tool for those in several disciplines including psychiatrists, psychologists, art theorists, art historians, and students of aesthetics. Out of this work Prinzhorn developed his own theories that were not from psychiatry, but from an integration of ideas "that formed part of the 'psychology of expression'. His ideas did not include the use of art for diagnosis, and he clearly became more aligned with the 'psychology of art'. (Prinzhorn's book (1922/1995) has remained in print since its first publication.)

MacGregor builds the connections between art and dreams that he describes: "In the early years of its development, treatment, in its examination of art, contented itself with pointing out similarities between the processes and symbols observed in dreams, in the formation of symptoms, and in works of literature and art. Our understanding of image-making process, whether 'psychotic' or 'normal', [was] immeasurably enhanced by Freud's description of the quite different modes of mental functioning characteristic of the unconscious (the primary process)" (MacGregor, 1989, pp. 249-250).

This description by MacGregor is the first to build a connection of the art-making process and psychological and emotional functioning that is reviewed in the literature for this chapter. From this, MacGregor discusses at length the valuable contributions of Ernst Kris who also attained degrees and training in art history and psychiatry. During his shortened life, Kris as a follower of Freud applied psychoanalytic theory and methods in his investigation of visual art. MacGregor writes that Kris's publications in the field of psychoanalysis and art...established a scholarly and scientific standard to describe the nature and range of problems that psychoanalysis could address on art and creativity. His discussions of psychotic art represent the first successful attempt to employ psychoanalytic insight in the understanding of a form of image and human experience even though Freud and his [other] immediate followers had little to say (MacGregor, 1989, p. 250).

As understood and practiced at that time by those involved in psychoanalysis and art including Kris, the presence of a therapist in the image-making process would change the nature of the patient's activity because the drawings done in therapy serve a different function and are usually made for the therapist and convey some type message [non-verbal communication] from the patient to the therapist.

In this author's view, this practice not to include art-making during treatment in the early years of psychiatry actually influenced practitioners to focus on analysis of the artwork and not attempt to include the process of art-making as part of the treatment. And MacGregor (1989) acknowledged that other later psychiatry practitioners such as D W Winnicott successfully included art-making with many of his clients (although he usually did not work with individuals who were psychotic). Winnicott who developed the 'Squiggle Drawing' used visual images as a means of contact between himself and the patient in the clinical session that served as a means of 'symbolic realization', not a way to convey a secret or unconscious message between his patient and himself.

Following these early years of the development of psychoanalysis and other theories in psychiatry, collections and published work on the use of art-making in psychiatric practice have been recognized for contributions to the specialization of psychiatry and art. Extraordinary examples have come from psychiatrists Dr. Marion Milner, author of *On not being able to paint* (1957/1979), Dr. Ainslie Meares, author of *The door to serenity* (1977). In Milner's book , she describes through self-observation her own efforts to overcome obstacles to paint, engaging in creative self-expression while continuing her work as a British psychiatrist. Australian psychiatrist Meares offers a valuable case history on his treatment of a young woman with schizophrenia who attempted to communicate with him through her artwork. Meares includes reflections on his own efforts to integrate this visual communication into his understanding of this patient. And Dr. Eric Cunningham Dax, from his hospital-based practice, research and teaching first in Britain and from the 1950s onward in Australia, built a collection of over 15,000 artworks by patients with schizophrenia and other psychoses. The Dax Centre collection remains utilized today throughout the world for education and research to enhance the understanding of the art of the seriously mentally ill.

Based on the origins of psychiatry utilizing interpretation of art products and case study as a method of research, and the inclusion of psychiatrists with expertise in art/art history, a foundation was built so the practitioners and educators in psychiatry may understand and gain from the uses of art and art-making in the treatment of their patients. And in recent decades through the present, a number of notable psychiatrists espouse the benefits and effectiveness of the use of art-making and artwork in many kinds of mental health treatment in different settings. This includes supporting other types of practitioners who are skilled in the use of art-making that effectively focuses on the *process* of art-making as a valuable healing component (Slater, 2010).

ON PSYCHOLOGY AND THE ROLE OF ART-MAKING

Clinical psychology with its western roots was built from philosophy and from science (experimental psychology) (Gregory, 1987; Groth-Marnat, 2009). Psychology also developed connection with medicine and psychiatry in its early days (Groth-Marnat, 1997, 2009; MacGregor, 1989). In psychology, as Groth-Marnat (2009) describes:

> The earliest form of obtaining information from clients was through clinical interviewing. At first, these interviews were modeled after questions-and-answer medical formats, but later, the influence of psychoanalytic theories resulted in a more open-ended, free-flowing style....the interviews all had these common objectives to obtain a psychological portrait of the person, to conceptualize what is causing the person's current difficulties, to make a diagnosis, and to formulate a treatment plan (Groth-Marnat, 2009, p. 66).

One of the central assumptions of this procedure is that, because many important aspects of personality are not available to conscious self-report, questionnaires and inventories are of limited value. Thus, as Groth-Marnat (1997) states:

> Using an indirect approach, 'psychoanalytic theory further assumes that symbolical expression can occur, and a person's perceptions and responses to his or her world are actually determined by inner qualities and forces…These idiosyncratic expressions of inner dynamics are most likely to occur when the person draws something [projections] on a blank sheet of paper (Groth-Marnat, 1997, p. 499).

Using Projective Tests

Psychologists with a scientific approach to interviewing, recognized problems using an unstructured style because of the recognition that reliability and validity were questionable reliability, validity and cost-effectiveness. Thus, the first standardized psychological tests were developed to overcome these limitations (Groth-Marnat, 1997).

In Germany Dr. Fritz Mohr (1874-1966) studied the art of the insane for insight into nonpathological mental processes, using psychiatric insights to answer questions about psychology. Based on recent studies at that time on the art of normal children, Mohr saw that these new approaches could be used to study 'psychotic art'. As a result, the study of children's art that was developing during the nineteenth century was moving along a course that appeared as a more advanced method of investigation. From this Mohr devised, (as cited in MacGregor, 1989), the first standardized tests to use drawings.

With this use of standardized tests came the development of projective tests. By 1926 Goodenough (as cited in Groth-Marnat,1997) developed the first formal drawing technique for assessment, the *Draw-a-Man test*. More than twenty years later in 1949, Machover was the first to formally extend drawing techniques from tests of cognitive development into personality interpretation based on projective testing theory with the *Draw-a-Person Test* (Groth-Marnat, 1997, p. 500-501).

As a result of the addition of Mohr's new approach (observation, diagnosis, and the new Kraepelinian nomenclature) that occurred in psychiatry and shortly after in psychology, it was applied to the "graphic activity of patients and the formal qualities of their drawings". From this advance, a split occurred in the study of patient art. The two approaches now developed along very different lines: One side was identified as the "diagnostic and experimentally oriented investigation of nonspontaneous drawings", and on the other, a focus on the "spontaneous drawings of psychotic patients produced freely" - outside of a clinical/treatment context, in a psychiatric hospital, at home, or in rare circumstances, as an aspect of a psychotherapeutic relationships (MacGregor, 1989, p. 193).

The Draw-A-Person test, the Kinetic Family Drawing, and the House-Tree-Person test are all 'drawing tests often used in personality assessment'. Currently, in clinical settings the DAP is the most frequently utilized projective drawing of these above drawings. The DAP is often welcomed by inhibited and nontalkative patients. It is a relatively nonverbal test (the only verbal material is contained in the thematic associations to the drawings) and therefore it is useful when language is a problem... (Handler, 1996, p. 207).

The methods of projective testing discussed here have been researched a great deal since the development of their use by psychologists in clinical treatment settings and in research. The limitations and criticisms have continued for decades within the field and by others due to lack of consistency in reliability and validity (Groth-Marnat, 1997; Handler, 1996; Kaplan, 2003; Newmark, 1996; Lilienfeld, Wood, & Garb, 2000). In addition, as Groth-Marnat (1997) describes: "Although quantitative scoring systems... have been developed and available for years, they are rarely used. ..clinicians are far more likely to use intuitive judgments based on clinical experience..." when psychologists utilize many kinds of projective tests. And, while not as much as in the recent past, this type of testing continues to be taught in graduate programs, certainly throughout the US and in other countries.

A significant difference in the use of these projective tests in comparison to the use of art-making in the other disciplines (psychiatry, counseling and art therapy) is the materials used. For these projective tests, the materials typically include blank white paper (8.5 x 11 inches/A4) and pencils (made of standard graphite with no colors). While this material limitation has been constant throughout the use of projective testing, the explanation directly relates to the necessity of excluding the number and type of variables in quantitative scoring and research protocols. As a result, projective testing is not considered as art-making by many. In addition, for some projective tests, verbal communication by the client is not included as part of scoring. Thus, much of the *process* of creating visual images is left out, and the focus is on the product. The use of projective testing with adults and children has become the dominant means of assessment, diagnosis and treatment planning with no or little attention to the use of art-making in treatment.

On the Psychology of Art

Within the field of psychology, including those discussed above whose efforts ,have been on projective testing that utilizes image-making, also have been psychologists who focus on the psychology of art including the *process* of art making with children. Those with published works in this area such as Dr. Seymour Sarason recognized the need for and argued for a greater inclusion of creative arts such as visual art in education and other community activities more than twenty years ago in the US. In his book, *The Challenge of Art to Psychology* (1990), Sarason states:

> Artistic activity is a unique, universal potential of the human organism, of all human organisms. I define artistic activity as an individual's choice and use of a particular medium to give ordered external expression to internal imagery, feelings, and ideas that are unique in some way for that individual (Sarason, 1990,p. 2).
>
> Ours [US] is not a culture that places a premium on the artistic activity of young children. Scores of child-rearing books sensitize parents to the importance of reading, writing, numbers, and 'objective' thinking as necessary for the good life. They say nothing about artistic activity as a source of personal expression, mastery, and satisfaction over a lifetime (Sarason, 1990,p. 4).

Later in this work Sarason (1990) made the connection (as other psychologists previously mentioned have made such as Groth-Marnat, 1997) between the changes after post-World War II era of growth and change. Sarason wrote:

> For a short period in the post-World War II decades, creativity as a concept, and as a basis for criticizing narrow views of intelligence, became a focus of interest. If that interest was fleeting, it was because of what I term the 'flight to measurement'. What is creativity and how do we measure it? These are not, of course, trivial questions, but focusing on them had the effect of restricting observation of this phenomenon to schoolchildren and selected groups of adults. It is really incorrect to say 'observation' if by this word we mean looking at the phenomenon in 'naturally occurring contexts'. That is quite different from looking at it in contrived situations with predetermined categories of problems and judgment. It is not that one way is right and the other wrong: each has its time and place. But the flight to measurement had several untoward effects. The first was that it drew attention away from the central questions: is creativity a normal human attribute? The second was that it did not lead to the observation of very young children or to an examination of the vast observational literature on children's play and problem solving. And the third was that it created a paradox: if creativity is indeed a human attribute observable in every young child, why does it seem to languish or disappear as the years pass and children go on to school [more advanced schooling]? (Sarason, 1990,p. 21).

And, toward the end of his book, Sarason states that he is talking about saving artistic activity as 'normal' and as a part of development – not necessarily or exclusively as a therapeutic activity, more so as an activity that is equally important as scientific activities/ learning.

And, other psychologists have addressed understanding children's art work, not focusing on measurement, however, on understanding children's engagement with art. Golomb (2004) also a psychologist, describes her understanding of children's art work, so similar to psychologist Di Leo's (1983) remarks in his work twenty years earlier. Golomb states:

> …Drawing is a language that children master in their quest to understand their world and to express their feelings. In my review of studies that focus on the diagnostic value of children's drawings, I have cautioned against using drawings as if they were an X-ray of the child's heart and mind. Although drawings may not yield to a mechanical analysis that ignores the individuality of the child artists, they can reveal to an empathic participant observer what the child's mood and what feelings he is trying to express. Indeed, a large body of literature attests to the possibility, even the desirability, of using drawings in a therapeutic context. Many experienced child therapists have used drawing in connection with other techniques (for example, play therapy and conversations) in an effort to help the emotionally distressed, and at times severely disturbed child…For some youngsters drawing is a substitute for verbal communications, for others it is an additional avenue for discovering and communicating important feelings the child harbors about herself and others (Golomb, 2004, p. 320-321).

Thus, regarding the role of psychologists who focus on ways that they can better understand and offer support and assistance, they emphasize understanding the *process* of art-making. As each has stated, this includes observing and interacting with a child client. With psychologists who work in this manner, they emphasize the uses of art-making as part of therapeutic interventions that includes use drawing and other forms of art-making as a part of assessment, too.

ON COUNSELING AND THE ROLE OF ART-MAKING

For almost ten years counseling as a mental health discipline in the US officially has integrated tools and techniques of various expressive arts into counseling practice (Gladding, 2005). With the addition of the Association of Creativity in Counseling (ACC) in the American Counseling Association, professional members address uses of creativity in counseling (Gladding, 2005). One of the strongest forces in the ongoing and committed efforts to develop ways that creativity can enhance counseling outcomes is Samuel Gladding, counseling educator, author, and past president of the American Counseling Association.

In the most recent edition of his book, *Counseling as an art: The creative arts in counseling* (2005), Gladding explains:

> When creativity is combined with the arts, this frequently results in (1) the production of a tangible product that gives a client insight, such as a piece of writing or a painting, or (2) a process that the clinician formulates, such as a new way of conducting counseling that leads to client change (Gladding, 2005, p. 3).

Gladding (2005) also developed a list of rationales for integrating the arts in counseling. A primary rationale he describes "involves energy and process. Most creative arts are participatory and require the generation of behaviors and emotions. Activity involving the creative or expressive arts gives individuals new energy and is reinforcing because it leads somewhere" (Gladding, 2005, p. 8).

While many practitioners in all mental health disciplines have utilized drawing and other expressive arts therapeutically for many years, this is a newly organized area of counselor practice. The focus appears to be on the integration of expressive arts tools and techniques within the theories of counseling practice. In addition, in the counseling literature such as Gladding's (2005) and the work of Degges-White and Davis (2011), the focus of expressive arts in counseling is primarily on therapeutic intervention with limited attention to assessment and testing. In the broad view of *process* in art-making, expressive arts counselors are attending to process. The examples presented in Degges-White and Davis (2011) demonstrate that counselors invite clients to participate actively participate and verbalize in response (if possible) to engagement with the expressive arts techniques.

Thus, in this relatively new area of practice and investigation, the question arises about education and training in the expressive arts in counseling. Gladding (2005) explains that most counselors who use visual arts in their work have received special training, for example by earning a master's degree in counseling with a concentration in art therapy or a certificate in expressive arts counseling...' Other professionals who do not want that credential compensate for the lack of overall training in using the visual arts by concentrating their practice on specific areas in which they are competent to work (Gladding, 2005, p. 89).

ON ART THERAPY AND THE ROLE OF ART-MAKING

Art therapy as a discipline has its western origins in the US and in Britain. The art therapy pioneers in Britain and the US came from related fields of art and art education actually during and after World War II through the 1960s. Some entered therapeutic work, almost by serendipity, using art in hospital or school settings. From such beginnings was created the profession of art therapy (Hogan, 2001; Junge & Asawa, 1994).

One art therapy pioneer in the US, Margaret Naumburg, developed 'dynamically oriented art therapy' that she founded as an adjunct to psychoanalytic therapy through working with psychiatrist, Dr. Nolan Lewis (Hogan, 2001; Junge & Asawa, 1994). However, others such as Edward Adamson in Britain and Edith Kramer in the US identified the art as the therapy (Hogan, 2001; Junge & Asawa, 1994).

Junge and Asawa (1994) described:

> Kramer developed a theory that established for this growing field a focus opposite that of Naumburg's. She forcefully postulated the importance of the creative process itself as a healing agent. ...Kramer's theoretical model focuses on art *as* therapy, rather than *in* as Naumburg suggests. Kramer's stress on the importance of the *art* in art therapy was something that many art therapists already believed in and practiced (Junge & Asawa, 1994, p. 31).

From these early days of art therapy, many practitioners focused on the art-making process as the most relevant part of working with clients. Training developed in art therapy at the graduate level that emphasized the uses of art-making with a client population – whether working within a psychoanalytic or psychodynamic theoretical framework or other psychological theory. Over time art therapy education made changes to meet higher education demands and improve practitioners' knowledge base in psychology including psychological assessment (Junge & Asawa, 1994). With such changes and increased rigor in art therapy education and practice, in this author's view, emphasis in approaches in the field developed that also is related to changes in mental health services. Groth-Marnat's (1997) recognition of changes in the use of projective testing in psychology are relevant here, too, "The themes and issues related to cost-effectiveness, patient-treatment matching, the use of new interview technologies…will continue to be important themes throughout the first one or two decades of the millennium."

Yet art therapists have continued to focus on the role of art-making in treatment while there has been a significant shift in attention to assessment in art therapy (e.g. Gantt, 2004; Kaplan, 2003). Art therapist Schwartz (1996) has described this continued focus so well:

> When we speak of process in art therapy we speak of the client's activity, the involvement in a creative pursuit. The therapist's perception and response to the client's activity (as well as the response to the final product of this activity) is also an aspect of this process. Process also refers to the interaction between the client and therapist as they perform their respective roles in the relationship, often referred to as the therapeutic process (Schwartz, 1996, p. 245).

Schwartz (1996) goes on to explain:

> As an observer the therapist perceives the client, the therapeutic process in progress, the client's artwork as well as the client's work of art. The process of art therapy is documented by, and reflected in, the client's art and the transformations of form and content within it, over time, due to the influence of the therapeutic relationship…(Schwartz, 1996, p. 245).

A most significant contribution to the field of art therapy that integrates the role of *process* and creates a solid theoretical framework, the Expressive Therapy Continuum, for the practice of art therapy was developed by art therapy professor emeritus, Dr. Vija Lusebrink (see Hinz, 2009; Lusebrink, 1990). Hinz (2009) describes the Expressive Therapy Continuum:

> The Expressive Therapies Continuum (ETC) represents a means to classify interactions with art media or other experiential activities in order to process information and form images. The ETC organizes media interactions into a developmental sequence of information processing and image formation from simple to complex. Image formation and information processing are categorized in a hierarchical fashion from simple kinesthetic experiences at one end to complex symbolic images at the other. The ETC is arranged in four levels of increasingly complex processing (Hinz, 2009, p. 4-5).

With further explanation Hinz (2009) states:

> The ETC is a theoretical and practical guide that describes and represents the ways in which people interact with various art media or experiential activities to process information and form images. The ETC attempts to explain the healing dimensions of various expressive experiences and the restorative power of creativity…The ETC helps clarify art therapy as not merely a modality of verbal psychotherapy, but a unique discipline in its own rights with a theoretical framework that can guide the use of art media and experiences…The Expressive Therapies Continuum represents a common

language for art therapists having diverse [psychology] theoretical backgrounds (Hinz, 2009, p. 17).

This overview of the role of process in art-making has been presented through the words of pioneer art therapists and those who followed with their research and effective clinical practices. The beginnings of the field of art therapy spread through the case study clinical and research methods as their mentors in psychiatry utilized; art therapy assessments were developed by following procedures used in the projective tests of psychology. In psychiatry those practitioners who had formal education in art or in art history encouraged and supported patients to engage spontaneously in art making that facilitates the verbal treatment process. The role of art-making has stayed consistent throughout the integration of knowledge and skills in both psychiatry and psychology.

CONCLUSION

The descriptions and observations in each of the mental health disciplines presented in this chapter provide clues about their varied development and their uses of art-making in clinical settings. The details show that history influences how and when each discipline incorporated some form of art-making into assessment and treatment. In psychology with some influences from psychiatry, the primary role of art-making began and continues to this day in projective testing. In counseling, the common inclusion of the tools of art-making and other expressive arts recently has evolved into more rigorous use of the expressive arts (including visual art-making). Especially in the past fifteen years the counseling literature has grown to include the expressive arts. In art therapy the art-making itself formed the foundation for this profession. In this field it is the practitioners who enter the field with their own developed art skills and offer art-making as healing for their clients. Thus, practitioners in each discipline have different approaches to purpose or art-making and its role(s) in treatment; this has influenced efforts for collaboration across disciplines that could have direct benefits for clients along with benefits in program development to enhance assessment and treatment, and thus treatment outcomes. Research in each discipline could answer questions such as, in what ways does this use of art-making in assessment and/or in treatment benefit various client populations? Which types of assessment using art-making are most effective? And, in terms of collaborative efforts across disciplines, what can we learn from one another that could improve our own uses of art-making as healing/effecting positive change?

REFERENCES

Betensky, M. G. (1977). The phenomenological approach to art expression and art therapy. *Art Psychotherapy, 4*, 173-179.

Degges-White, S. & Davis, N. L. (2011). *Integrating the expressive arts into counseling practice.* New York: Springer.

Di Leo, J. H. (1983). *Interpreting children's drawings.* New York: Brunner/Mazel.

Gantt, L. (2004). The case for formal art therapy assessments. *Art Therapy: Journal of the American Art Therapy Association*, *21*(1), 18-29.

Gladding, S. T. (2005). *Counseling as an art: The creative arts in counseling* (3rd ed.) Alexandra, VA: American Counseling Association.

Golomb, C. (2004). *The child's creation of a pictorial world* (2nd ed.). Mahwah, New Jersey: Lawrence Erlbaum Associates.

Gregory, R. L. (Ed.). (1987). *The Oxford companion to the mind.* New York: Oxford University.

Groth-Marnat, G. (1997/1999). *Handbook of psychological assessment* (3rd ed). New York: John Wiley & Sons.

Groth-Marnat, G. (2009). *Handbook of psychological assessment* (5th ed.). New York:John Wiley & Sons.

Handler, L. (1996). The clinical use of drawings. In C. S. Newmark (Ed.). *Major psychological assessment instruments* (2nd ed., pp. 206-293). Needham Heights, MA: Allyn & Bacon.

Hinz, L. (2009). *Expressive Therapies Continuum: A framework for using art in therapy.* New York: Routledge.

Hogan, S. (2001). *Healing arts: The history of art therapy.* London: Jessica Kingsley.

Jones, P. (2005). *The arts therapies: A revolution in healthcare.* Hove, UK and New York: Brunner-Routledge.

Junge, M. B. & Asawa, P. P. (1994). *A history of art therapy in the United States.* Mundelein, Illinois: American Art Therapy Association.

Kaplan, F. F. (2003). Art-based assessments, In C. Malchiodi (Ed.), *Handbook of art therapy* (pp. 25-35). New York: Guilford.

Kramer, E. (1976). The unity of process and product in Symposium: Integration of divergent points of view in art therapy. *American Journal of Art Therapy*, *14*(1), 13-18.

Lilienfeld, S. O., Wood, J. M., & Garb, H. N. (2000). The scientific status of projective techniques. *Psychological Science in the Public Interest*, *1*(2), 27-40.

Lusebrink, V. B. (1990). *Imagery and visual expression in therapy.* New York: Plenum.

MacGregor, J. M. (1989). *The discovery of the art of the insane.* Princeton, NJ: Princeton University Press.

Meares, A. (1977). *The door of serenity.* Melbourne, Australia: Hill of Content.

Milner, M. (1957/1979). *On not being able to paint.* New York: International University Press.

Mindell, A. (1992). *Riding the horse backward: Process work in theory and practice.* New York: Penguin.

Newmark, C. S. (Ed.). (1996). *Major psychological assessment instruments* (2nd ed.). Needham Heights, MA: Allyn & Bacon.

Prinzhorn, H. (1995). *Artistry of the mentally ill* (2nd ed.) (Trans. E. von Brockdoff). Wien-New York: Springer-Verlag. (Original work published in 1922).

Sarason, S. B. (1990). *The challenge of art to psychology.* New Haven: Yale University.

Schwartz, N. (1996). Observer, process, and product. *Art Therapy: Journal of the American Art Therapy Association*, *13*(4), 244-251.

Slater, N. A. (2010). Introduction to art therapy. In L. Bovornkitti (Ed.). *Synopsis of art therapy* (pp. 86-120). Bangkok: Bangkok Medical Journal.

Wadeson, H. (1987). *The dynamics of art psychotherapy.* New York: John Wiley.

In: Psychology of Counseling
Editor: Annamaria Di Fabio

ISBN: 978-1-62618-388-9
© 2013 Nova Science Publishers, Inc.

Chapter 11

Emotional Intelligence and Mediation: New Perspectives for Psychological Counseling Intervention

Annamaria Di Fabio[*] and Letizia Palazzeschi
Department of Psychology, University of Florence, Italy

ABSTRACT

This chapter deals with the promising role of emotional intelligence construct in mediation, offering new perspectives for psychological counseling intervention. It starts with an analysis of the literature relative to the relationships between emotions and mediation, and analyses associated with the role of emotional intelligence in mediation in particular. Then, the chapter traces the evolution of the emotional intelligence construct, also presenting the most significant and relevant theoretical models relative to emotional intelligence: the ability-based model by Salovey and Mayer (1990; Mayer & Salovey, 1997), the model by Bar-On (1997, 2002), and the model by Petrides and Furnham (2001). It goes on to describe the principal tools for measuring emotional intelligence. Furthermore, the chapter stresses the importance of promoting emotional intelligence through specific training, given that a great consent exists in the literature that emotional intelligence is a characteristic which can be increased. The chapter underlines the importance of emotional intelligence in mediation and the possible implications for training mediators and psychological counseling intervention in mediation.

1.1. EMOTIONS AND MEDIATION

An analysis of the literature shows the centrality of emotion in conflict, highlighting that the transformation of conflict necessarily involves taking emotional aspects into account (Galtung, 1996; Jones, 2005). Given the centrality of emotion and emotional communication

---

[*] Corresponding author: Annamaria Di Fabio. E-mail address: adifabio@psico.unifi.it.

in the context of conflict interaction, it can easily be understood how emotions take a major role in mediation (Jones & Bodtker, 2001). Mediators who use emotion-focused strategies may therefore be more likely to go beyond the surface aspects of the presented issues, increasing understanding of problems and facilitating the transformation of the conflict (Jameson, Bodtker, & Linker, 2010).

In the past decade, the issue of emotions has received increased attention by many scholars of various disciplines (Jameson et al., 2010; Jones, 2005; Jones & Bodtker, 2001). Despite the spread of the scientific deepening and complexity of the concept, many scholars, referring to the model by Lazarus (1991), argue that emotion consists of three basic components: a cognitive component, a physiological component, and a behavioral component (Jones, 2005).

The cognitive component of emotion refers to the process of evaluating emotional stimuli (appraisal), the physiological component of emotion regards the physiological responses related to emotion, and the expressive component of emotion concerns the behavioral expression in response to evaluated cognitive or physiological experience (Lazarus, 1991). The physiological and cognitive components of emotion are important in relation to how the emotion is experienced by the individual. The expressive element represents the way in which it is possible to communicate to others what one thinks and what one feels (Jones, 2005). Jones and Bodtker (2001) emphasize in this regard that the expression of emotions can create a conflict, and this conflict can also result from acting on the emotion in an inappropriate manner with respect to socially shared rules. The conflict can also arise from the lack of ability in decoding expressed emotions (Jones & Bodtker, 2001).

Referring to Lazarus' theory (1991), Jones and Bodtker (2001) argue that emotions result from a process of cognitive appraisal in two phases. In the first phase, individuals experience a triggering event and evaluate the event in terms of: the relevance for the achievement of one's own goals (goal relevance), the fact that this event makes it easier or more difficult to achieve their goals (goal congruence) and the impact of such a goal on the identity of the individuals (ego involvement). In the second phase, individuals focus on additional issues such as judgments of responsibility (who is the culprit), the potential to address the problem (as it is possible to effectively deal with the problem), and future expectations (if things will go in a better way or worse without action). According to Jameson et al. (2010), this model by Jones and Bodtker (2001) offers some means by which it is possible to act on the conflict. Jameson et al. (2010) argue in this regards that if a mediator is able to focus the attention of the participants on the evaluations they are doing, then the parties could have the opportunities to see the conflict from different perspectives, leading to a different emotional experience. Moreover, to identify and understand their own emotions and examine the causes in the course of a discussion could provide additional information useful to all involved parties (Jameson et al., 2010).

The same authors (2010, p. 27) also introduced "the term 'emotional experience' to capture the pragmatic essence of emotion in the conflict process and to sidestep the definitional complications inherent in any single theory of emotion", focusing in particular on how the experience of emotion influences the conflict interaction. The way people express their emotions communicate many messages to others, especially when such people are parties to a dispute (Jameson et al., 2010). In relation to the cognitive aspects of emotion, they also claim, as through facilitated discussion, the involved parties can take into account their emotional experiences and those of others, paying attention to conflict issues and their importance, helping the parties to identify possible meeting points. Strengthening the ability to communicate their emotional experiences could enhance self-efficacy and allow all involved parties to feel more able to control the process (Jameson et al., 2010).

Regarding the emotional competencies that mediators can use to recognize and deal with emotions in mediation, Jones (2005) identifies three competences: decoding the emotional experience of the parties, helping the parties to understand their own emotional experiences, and facilitating the parties to reassess emotions for removing obstacles related to the emotional experience. Jameson et al. (2010) also emphasize that the mediators are in a unique position to help the parties better understand their own emotions and those of others, and to inform the parties how their emotions can be involved in the conflict interaction. Starting from these premises, they carried out a study to identify the types of strategies that mediators use to elicit emotional communication, identifying five types of strategies to elicit emotions: granting legitimacy, encouraging emotion identification, confronting avoidance of emotion, paraphrasing emotion, and encouraging emotional perspective taking (Jameson et al., 2010). The granting legitimacy strategy occurs when a mediator verbally or nonverbally recognizes the emotions that a part is expressing. The encouraging emotion identification strategy occurs when the mediator decodes the emotions of the parties while also helping them to recognize their own emotions. The confronting avoidance of emotion strategy occurs when a mediator points out that a part is denying to experience a particular emotion and his/her behavior suggests otherwise. The paraphrasing emotion strategy consists of expressing the emotion in words, offering a different key to reading to the parties. The encouraging emotional-perspective taking strategy occurs when the mediator intentionally directs one of the parties to consider the situation from different points of view. Jameson et al. (2010) conclude their reflection by emphasizing that mediation is a method that has the potential to transform relationships; thus to understand and manage the emotions underlying the conflict is an essential element for the transformation of the conflict.

It is also interesting to underline, as an area of current research concern, the study of particular emotional aspects related to the resolution of conflict as perspective taking, such as the cognitive ability to consider the world from the perspective of another individual, and empathy, the ability to enter in emotional contact with another individual (Galinsky, Maddux, Gilin, & White, 2008). Three studies (Galinsky et al., 2008) showed that the perspective taking increased the ability of individuals to discover hidden agreements and to create resources during the discussion, and empathy could not always truly be beneficial in terms of private profit. Thus, although empathy appears essential in many areas of social life and relationships, the perspective taking can be seen to be an important element in the negotiation and thus could also be important in the context of mediation. In the literature, however, the perspective taking is also considered as a dimension of empathy (Davis, 1980, 1983); therefore, further empirical investigations are necessary in relation to mediation, and it is hoped that future studies will continue in this direction in order to better understand the possible contributions associated with the construct of empathy. An analysis of the literature suggests, therefore, the importance of emotions in conflict resolution and mediation, emphasizing the importance of emotional aspects for operators of mediation. It seems, therefore, that there is a great interest in the new construct of emotional intelligence in the field of mediation.

1.2. Emotional Intelligence and Mediation

The scientific literature on emotional intelligence has emphasized the central role of this construct in different aspects of one's life. Emotional intelligence is an element of facilitation in creating and maintaining relationships with others, enhancing the skills to understand their emotions and express them in a consistent manner; interacting appropriately with others, establishing rewarding and meaningful interpersonal relationships; acting appropriate in different experienced situations and implementing effective strategies for problem solving, managing one's own emotions in order to express them in an adaptive and context-congruent manner (Bar-On, 1997; Mayer & Salovey, 1997). People with higher emotional intelligence appear to have greater success in various areas of life (Bar-On, 1997), achieving a greater success in school (Di Fabio & Palazzeschi, 2009; Parker et al., 2004) and more easily reaching managerial or leadership roles (Lopes, Grewal, Kadis, Gall, & Salovey, 2006). Emotional intelligence is in fact also related to effective leadership (Caruso & Salovey, 2004). Managers with high emotional intelligence scores seem to collaborate better with subordinate roles, which in turn show greater organizational commitment and lower turnover intention (Wong & Law, 2002). In addition, leaders with high emotional intelligence seem more open to proposals made by their employees, tending to listen more effectively and reach agreement in disputes (Bryson, 2005).

Boland and Ross (2010) emphasize the similarity between leadership and mediation, referring to the mediation model by McGrath (1966) which suggests this parallelism. The mediation model by McGrath (1966) supports that mediation has many aspects in common with the leadership in conflict situations, highlighting how the mediator, in the same way as the leader, typically assumes control of the mediation process. The mediator also often acts as a creative agent, trying to find a solution that can satisfy all parties involved in the dispute.

Boland and Ross (2010), further underlining the link between mediation and leadership, refer to the taxonomy of mediator behavior by Jones (1989) that includes some real leadership strategies and techniques, such as: power balancing, pressuring the parties, discussing solutions, and summarizing partial agreements. These supportive-communication techniques lead to a socio-emotional leadership which is defined as a way to reduce defenses and hostility (Haynes, 1986). Already, the empirical study by Ross, Conlon and Lind (1990) showed that the mediators implement different leadership styles causing different reactions in the involved parts. The same traditional study by Landsberger (1955), which was based on observations associated with the dynamics of the negotiation groups, underlined similarities between leadership and labor contract mediation.

Boland and Ross (2010) argue that since there is a link between emotional intelligence and leadership and mediation shows similarities to leadership, it is also possible to hypothesize a link between emotional intelligence and mediation. Some scholars argue that emotion recognition and emotion regulation skills are important for the mediator (Cloke, 1993; Diamond, 2006; Retzinger & Scheff, 2006). In particular, Cloke (1993) underlines the role of mediators in reducing hostile emotions such as anger. Retzinger and Scheff (2006) suggest that selecting mediators on the base of their emotional skills or by focusing more on their training in emotional areas could be particularly important. Emotional intelligence can offer an important contribution in the management of conflict situations and could therefore be seen as an interesting variable even within the field of negotiation (Fulmer & Barry, 2004;

Ogilvie & Carsky, 2002). Individuals with higher emotional intelligence are better able to acquire information relevant to the negotiation, appear more sensitive to emotional cues provided by other people who can contain information concerning the importance of an issue or acceptability of a possible proposal (Fulmer & Barry, 2004). The same authors also underline, recognizing that emotions affect the perception of risk, individuals with higher emotional intelligence seem to be better able to more accurately assess risk on one hand, and would be more likely to take advantage of the opportunity to actively influence the emotions of counterparts on the other hand. The study by Foo, Elfenbein, Tan, and Aik (2004) analyzed the relationships between emotional intelligence of both members of couples involved in a negotiation. The results showed that individuals with higher emotional intelligence perceive a more positive experience, as is also the case in reaching a greater number of objectives with respect to their counterparts. Boland and Ross (2010) suggest that many aspects regarding the relationships between emotional intelligence and negotiation can also be applied to mediation although the negotiators have different motivations and interests with respect to mediators because the mediators, when they enter into the dispute, pursue the interests of others rather than own interests. Emotional intelligence could be a useful instrument for mediators especially in relation to the role of the leader in the mediation process (Boland & Ross, 2010). Mediators with higher emotional intelligence will most likely be able to find the emotional clues hidden by the parties, evaluate the possible consequences associated with a particular issue, and act on the emotions of the parties to facilitate an integrated problem solving and dispute resolution (Boland & Ross, 2010).

The study by Rahim et al. (2002) showed, through the use of structural equation models, that emotional self awareness and emotional self-regulation predict empathy and social skills. These factors are also related to goal-oriented work motivation and to an integrative problem-solving conflict management that attempts to integrate different points of view. The results, therefore, suggest that emotional intelligence can predict third-party conflict management strategies.

According to Boland and Ross (2010), emotional intelligence can influence mediation in different specific ways. Individuals with high emotional intelligence recognized the complexity, and sometimes the contradicting aspects, of situations.

Recognizing these emotional aspects could influence the goals that the mediator seeks for the intervention. Specifically, mediators who are more sensitive to the emotions present in long-term relationships could seek to understand and manage these issues in the conflict situation more likely than mediators who are less sensitive to these emotions (Schreier, 2002). On the contrary, mediators who have low emotional intelligence seem able to deal with only the dominant emotion displayed by the parties and not with all other found emotions (Boland & Ross, 2010).

Moreover, Boland and Ross (2010) underline that mediators with high emotional intelligence could be more sensitive to the relations between the various outcomes of the negotiation and to negative emotions within groups in mediation. The authors show that mediators with higher emotional intelligence could recognize that the parties could most likely remain unsatisfied even when the main issue is resolved in multi-issue disputes. Some studies on group performance suggest that groups whose members have higher emotional intelligence are able to better take into account the emotional aspects and, consequently, achieve a higher performance compared to groups that are composed of members with low emotional intelligence (Jordan, Ashkanasy, Hartel, & Hooper, 2002; Jordan & Troth, 2004;

Offermann, Bailey, Vasilopoulos, Seal, & Sass, 2004). Thus, since the mediators play a leading role in groups (McGrath, 1966), mediators with high emotional intelligence would be more able to find an including agreement which minimizes the dissatisfaction of the parties (Boland & Ross, 2010).

Boland and Ross (2010) underline that an agreement that takes into account the different needs of the parties could be more satisfactory for a greater number of parties. If an agreement of this kind is not obtainable, mediators with high emotional intelligence would be quite sensitive to the reactions of the parties to use techniques to try to push the parties toward a compromised solution. In addition, mediators with high emotional intelligence seem more able to use tactics to promote both the compromise and the integrative agreements (Boland & Ross, 2010). Mediators with high emotional intelligence are better able to utilize a variety of tactics based on the needs of the parties in a given moment of mediation compared to mediators with low emotional intelligence (Boland & Ross, 2010).

As underlined by Boland and Ross (2010), mediators with low emotional intelligence could instead only be considered in a negative way regarding the expression of the hostility of the parties and could believe that if the parties express negative emotions the agreement becomes unlikely. In this condition, it is possible that mediators attempt to force the parties to offer concessions by pressuring and threatening, or offer additional incentives, implementing a compensatory strategy to encourage the parties to agree (Carnevale, 1986). It is also possible that mediators with low emotional intelligence can simply have difficulty in responding to situations where the parties express negative emotions, preferring not to act in the mediation (Boland & Ross, 2010).

The empirical study by Boland and Ross (2010) analyzed how emotional intelligence can influence informal mediation through the use of a factorial design. The study had varied the emotional intelligence levels (high vs. low) and addressed whether disputant hostility was escalating or de-escalating. Among all emotions that can arise in a conflict situation, anger is probably the one that represents the biggest challenge for mediators (Slaikeu, 1996). As stressed by Boland and Ross (2010), anger can indeed influence the way a person is perceived and evaluated (Van Kleef, De Dreu, & Manstread, 2004); can generate answers charged with anger, ruin relationships, and reduce the possibility of realizing a creative problem solving (Allred, Mallozzi, Matsui, & Raia, 1997; Friedman, Anderson, & Brett, 2004; Moore, 2003); and can lead to physical aggression (Van Coillie & Van Mechelen, 2006). During mediation, the desire of individuals to interact with the parties expressing anger decreases (Van Kleef et al., 2004). Anger can lead to an escalation of hostility, leading to an increase in violent offenses and actions between the parties (Rubin, Pruitt, & Kim, 1994). For the presented above reasons related to its potential negative consequences, anger has received greater attention than any other emotion in the field of mediation (Druckman & Olekalns, 2008; Van Kleef, van Dijk, Steinel, Harinek, & van Beest, 2008). Since there was no empirical research on individual differences in emotional intelligence in the field of mediation strategies that also considered the conditions of increased or decreased hostility between the parties, Boland and Ross (2010) have empirically analyzed the condition.

The results of Boland and Ross's study (2010) indicate that mediators with high emotional intelligence are better able than mediators with low emotional intelligence to pursue the goal of reaching a comprehensive and mutually satisfactory agreement.

Mediators with high emotional intelligence also put in place, more likely than mediators with low emotional intelligence, a greater variety of tactics to help in achieving a compromise between the parties. On the contrary, the mediators with low emotional intelligence are more inclined to intervene by pressure, using compensatory tactics or not acting at all. These results suggest that individual differences in emotional intelligence can play a role in mediation processes (Fulmer & Barry, 2004; Schreier, 2002), suggesting the importance of providing training to strengthen the emotional intelligence (Di Fabio, 2010) of mediators to facilitate the mediation process (Jameson et al., 2010).

1.3. THE EVOLUTION OF THE EMOTIONAL INTELLIGENCE CONSTRUCT

Emotional intelligence can be considered as a relatively new and current research area, in constant development, which attracts attention at multiple levels (Zeidner, Matthews, & Roberts, 2004). In 1920, Thorndike defined emotional intelligence as the ability to perceive one's own and others' emotions, motives and behaviors, and to use them to act optimally. In 1966, Leuner coined the term emotional intelligence and in 1988 Bar-on formulated the term Emotional Quotient (EQ). The emotional intelligence construct since the 1990s has attracted increasing interest, generating different models and definitions.

A first proposal of articulation relative to emotional intelligence was elaborated by Mayer, Salovey, and Caruso (2000), who distinguished between mental ability models and mixed models: the first define emotional intelligence in terms of individual cognitive abilities in processing emotional information, whereas the second consider emotional intelligence as a construct which includes a mix of cognitive abilities with other characteristics such as aspects of personality.

A second proposal of articulation relative to emotional intelligence is based on different tools for detecting the construct, underlining the used type of measurement to determine the nature of the emotional intelligence model. Based on this perspective, Petrides and Furnham (2000, 2001) distinguish between trait emotional intelligence (or trait emotional self-efficacy) and ability emotional intelligence (formally defined as information-processing emotional intelligence). This distinction has no ties with the previously discussed ability and mixed models: the articulation by Petrides and Furnham is indeed based on a method of measuring the construct (self-report vs. maximum performance), and it considers the assessed construct as qualitatively different. In this perspective, trait emotional intelligence, also named trait emotional self-efficacy, concerns a constellation of emotion-related self-perceptions located primary in the personality domain. Information processing emotional intelligence refers instead to emotional abilities (for example, the ability to identify, express and label emotions). Trait emotional intelligence is therefore assessed through self-reported measures, whereas the information processing approach refers to objective maximum performance measures (Petrides & Furnham, 2000).

Finally, it is possible to consider further articulations relative to emotional intelligence which differs from the various models in literature based on the fact that they are centered on specific abilities or can globally integrate these abilities (Mayer, Roberts, & Barsade, 2008). There are three approaches in this articulation: specific-ability approaches that concern single cognitive abilities or abilities that are considered as fundamental for emotional intelligence; integrative-model approaches that consider emotional intelligence as a global ability unifying many specific abilities; and mixed-model approaches that include a wide range of non-cognitive aspects, including the emotional and social intelligent behavior and aspects relative to personality.

Among the various theoretical models relative to emotional intelligence, some are particularly significant and relevant: the ability-based model by Salovey and Mayer (1990; Mayer & Salovey, 1997), the model by Bar-On (1997, 2002), and the model by Petrides and Furnham (2001).

The first model by Salovey and Mayer (1990) includes three categories of adaptive abilities: appraisal and expression of emotion, regulation of emotion and utilization of emotions in solving problems. The first category includes the dimension of appraisal and expression of emotion in the self and appraisal of emotion in others. The component of appraisal and expression of emotion in the self is further subdivided in the verbal and non-verbal subcomponents, whereas the component appraisal of emotion in others consists of the non-verbal perception and empathy subcomponents. The second category, regulation of emotions, is associated with the subcomponents of regulations of emotions in the self and regulation of emotion in others.

The third category, utilization of emotions, includes subcomponents: flexible planning, that is the ability of modifying own program, identifying alternative solutions to deal with any problems or changes; creative thinking, that is the ability to track information in memory for problem solving; redirected attention, that is the ability to shift attention to new problems if strong emotions develop; and motivation, that is the ability of emotions to motivate in the face of tasks and changes. Subsequently, Mayer and Salovey (1997) revised their emotional intelligence model to focus more on cognitive aspects of the construct. Such revised model includes four components that develop themselves over time, ranging from basic psychological processes to higher and more integrated processes at a psychological level: 1) Perceiving Emotion; 2) Facilitating Thought; 3) Understanding Emotion; 4) Managing Emotions. According to this model, the first and the second components refer to the area named Experiential Emotional Intelligence, whereas the third and the fourth components flow into the area defined as Strategic emotional intelligence.

Another relevant emotional intelligence model is the model by Bar-On (1997, 2002). In such model emotional intelligence is conceptualized as a multi-factorial construct, in which emotional, personal and social competencies converge that determine modalities through which a person relates with itself and with others, and that support him/her in coping effectively with the environmental demands and pressures. The detection of emotional intelligence in this model is carried out through self-report tools.

Emotional intelligence develops over time; it changes in an individual's life and it can be improved through training programs. The Bar-On (1997) model is hierarchical and includes a global dimension of emotional intelligence, five principal dimensions and fifteen sub-dimensions. The principal dimensions and their fifteen sub-dimensions are as follows: 1) intrapersonal emotional intelligence, which refers to awareness of one's own emotions and ability to express one's own feelings and communicate one's own needs. It concerns: self-regard, emotional self-awareness, assertiveness, independence and self-actualization; 2) interpersonal emotional intelligence, which refers to the ability both to establish cooperative, constructive and satisfactory relationships and to understand the feelings of others. It concerns: empathy, social responsibility and interpersonal relationships; 3) stress management, which refers to the ability to control and regulate emotions. It concerns: stress tolerance and impulse control; 4) adaptability, which refers to the ability of use emotions to implement effective strategies for problem-solving. It concerns: reality testing, flexibility and problem-solving; 5) general mood, which refers to the ability to be optimistic, to feel and express positive feelings and to draw pleasure from the presence of others. It includes optimism and happiness.

Another model of emotional intelligence was developed by Petrides and Furnham (2001) who attribute importance to the measurement in the description of emotional intelligence, so they proposed the distinction between Trait emotional intelligence and Ability emotional intelligence. Trait emotional intelligence (or trait emotional self-efficacy) refers to a constellation of behavioral dispositions and self-perceptions related to emotions, stable in time and in different situations, as well as elements of social intelligence and personal intelligence, as assessed by self-report measures. The definition of Ability emotional intelligence refers to actual abilities of emotional intelligence, measured by tests of maximum performance. Petrides and Furnham (2001) use the term trait, therefore, to indicate the dispositions of the individual so as to highlight the relationship of emotional intelligence to personality and not with cognitive ability; however, with the term trait having been previously used by Mayer et al. (2000) to describe the personality traits considered in the mixed models, it was decided to specify further by defining such a construct of emotional intelligence as emotional self-efficacy. The areas of the trait emotional intelligence are: Adaptability, the flexibility and willingness to adapt to new situations and conditions; Assertiveness, the ability to express their thoughts and explain their rights by recognizing the rights of others without falling into an aggressive attitude; Emotion expression, the ability to communicate their feelings to others; Emotional management (others), ability to influence others' emotions; Emotion perception (self and other), the ability to clearly recognize and feel their own feelings and those of others; Emotion regulation, the ability to control own emotions; Impulsiveness (low), the ability to control their own impulsiveness; Relationships, the ability to establish and maintain satisfactory interpersonal relationships; Self-esteem, relative to a positive evaluation of one self; Self-motivation, the ability to guide themselves and know how to deal with adversity; Social awareness, the ability to use higher-order social skills within the social network in which one lives; Stress management, the ability to withstand the pressure and regulate stress; Trait empathy, the ability to take the perspective of others; Trait happiness, relative to the fact of finding fulfillment and happiness for one's own life; and Trait Optimism, being confident and being able to see the positive side of life.

1.4. PRINCIPAL TOOLS FOR MEASURING EMOTIONAL INTELLIGENCE

As previously mentioned, an analysis of the literature shows that there are two main types of tools for measuring emotional intelligence: an ability test and self-report measures. Among the tools that belong to the category of ability test, it is worth mentioning in particular the Mayer-Salovey-Caruso Emotional Intelligence Test (MSCEIT, Mayer, Salovey, & Caruso, 2002), whereas among the main self-report instruments it is possible to mention the Emotional Quotient Inventory (EQ-i, Bar-on, 1997), of which there is also a short version (Bar-on, 2002); the Emotional Intelligence Scale (EIS, Schutte et al., 1998); and the Trait

Emotional intelligence Questionnaire (TEIQue, Petrides & Furnham, 2004). These tools will be briefly presented below.

Mayer-Salovey-Caruso Emotional Intelligence Test (MSCEIT)

The MSCEIT (Mayer et al., 2002) is a tool for the detection of ability-based emotional intelligence which assesses the extent to which people solve tasks and problems of an emotional nature. It was built on the model of emotional intelligence developed by Salovey and Mayer in 1997 (Four-Branch Model). The MSCEIT consists of 141 items that either converge in four dimensions or branch.

The tasks related to the first branch, Perception of emotions, concern abilities to perceive and identify the emotional content from a wide range of stimuli. The first task is to assess the emotion expressed by pictures representing different features: five emotions are listed for each photo (for example, happiness, sadness, surprise, fear, excitement) and the subject must say how the face expresses the particular emotion on a 5-point Likert scale ranging from 1 = *None* to 5 = *Extreme*. The second task is similar to the above, but instead of faces, they are presented images with respect to which the subject is asked to indicate how strongly the figure expresses the various emotions shown.

The tasks related to the second branch, Facilitating Thought, concern the abilities to assimilate emotions into perceptual and cognitive processes. In the first task, subjects are presented with situations and are asked to assign a score from 1 *useless* to 5 *useful* to each of the indicated states of mind. In the second task, the subject is asked to try to imagine the different feelings described in each question and best respond, assigning a score from 1 *Quite different* to 5 *Quite similar* to each of the proposed adjectives (for example, cold, blue, sweet), even if it fails to represent the feeling well.

The tasks related to the third branch of Understanding emotions concern the abilities to reflect on and understand emotions. In the first task, the subject is asked to choose between five emotions that one feels in a given presented situation. In the second task, the subject is presented with the description of an emotion and is asked to choose the best alternative among five options of emotion for each of the submitted descriptions.

The tasks related to the fourth branch, Managing emotions, concern the ability to gain control over emotions. In the first task, some situations are presented followed by five actions; the subject is asked to express to which extent each described action is effective, from *Absolutely ineffective* to *Absolutely effective*. In the second task, some situations are still presented, followed by five possible reactions; the subject is asked to express how each of these are effective from *Absolutely ineffective* to *Absolutely effective*.

Emotional Quotient Inventory (EQ-i)

The EQ-i (Bar-On, 1997) is a self-report questionnaire for measuring perceived emotional intelligence, composed of 133 items with response options on a 5-point Likert scale format (ranging from 1 = *Not at all true of me* to 5 = *Absolutely true for me*). Based on the Bar-On model (1997), the EQ-i provides five principal scales and fifteen subscales. In particular, the five principal scales are Intrapersonal, Interpersonal, Stress Management,

Adaptability, and General Mood. The fifteen subscales are: Self-Regards, Emotional Self-Awareness, Assertiveness, Independence, Self-Actualization, Empathy, Social Responsibility, Interpersonal Relationship, Stress Tolerance, Impulse Control, Reality-Testing, Flexibility, Problem-Solving, Optimism, and Happiness.

The scale provides a total emotional intelligence score, which consists in the sum of its scores, a score for the five principal scale, a score for each of the fifteen subscale and four validity indices: Percentage of Omitted Responses, Inconsistency Index, Positive Impression scale and Negative Impression scale. Eight of the 133 items, that compose the instrument, constitute the Positive Impression scale and seven items constitute the Negative Impression scale, both aiming to determine whether the subject completing the questionnaire is responding in an overly positive or negative manner. Moreover it is possible to detect the Inconsistency Index which is calculated by summing the differences in the scores obtained for answers to ten pairs of similar items and which has the intent to detect the answers randomly given. Finally, item number 133 also evaluates the subject's tendency to respond randomly to questions: whether the subject's answer to this item is 1 or 2 the subject's results to the questionnaire are not considered valid. The answers of the participants are also not considered valid in cases when they do not respond to a certain number of items: this is detected by Percentage of Responses Omitted; in particular the results are invalidated in the case in which the percentage of missing answers is greater than 6%.

Also, a short form of the questionnaire exists, the Bar-On Emotional Quotient Inventory: the Short (Bar-On EQ-i: S, Bar-On, 2002) is composed of 51 items with response options on a 5-point Likert scale format (ranging from 1 = *Not at all true of me* to 5 = *Absolutely true for me*). The short form of the Bar-On EQ-i, choosing not to detect the complexity of the construct at the level of sub-dimensions, permits a rapid administration and handy use, while simultaneously allowing for the detection of the four main dimensions of emotional intelligence (Intrapersonal, Interpersonal, Stress Management, Adaptability).

Emotional Intelligence Scale (EIS)

The EIS (Schutte et al., 1998) is a scale for measuring emotional intelligence realized by Schutte et al. (1998), based on the theoretical model by Salovey and Mayer (1990) which is composed of 33 items with response options on a 5-point Likert scale format (ranging from 1 = *Strongly disagree* to 5 = *Strongly agree*). With regard to the construction of the scale, the authors generated an initial pool of 62 items representing the three different dimensions of the theoretical model, namely the Appraisal and expression of emotions in oneself and in others, the Regulation of emotions in oneself and in others, and the Utilization of emotions in solving problems. A factor analysis of the responses of 346 participants in the initial pool of 62 items led to the creation of a one-dimensional version of the scale composed of 33 items.

Trait Emotional Intelligence Questionnaire (TEIQue)

The TEIQue by Petrides and Furnham (2004) is a self-report questionnaire for measuring trait emotional intelligence (Petrides & Furnham, 2001). The tool is composed of 144 items with response options on a 7-point Likert scale format (ranging from 1 = *Strongly disagree* to

7 = *Strongly agree*) and is articulated in fifteen subscales organized in four factors: Well-being, Self-control, Emotionality, and Sociability. By analyzing the answers it is possible to have the fifteen subscales scores, the four factors scores, and a global score of emotional intelligence.

The first factor, Well-being, is composed of the subscale Self-esteem, Happiness, and Optimism: high scores in the Self-esteem subscale indicates a higher level of satisfaction associated with respecting themselves and their realization; high scores in the Happiness subscale indicates a feeling of well-being which results in an overall positive mood; high scores in the Optimism subscale indicates a tendency to see the positive side of life.

Also, the second factor is articulated in three subscales: the first subscale named Emotion regulation indicates the skill to manage one's own emotions; the second subscale named Stress management measures the skills to withstand the pressures and regulate the stress; finally, the third subscale named Impulsiveness (low) indicates being reflective and not acting as a prey to one's own impulses.

The third factor is composed of four subscales: Emotion perception (self and others), Emotion expression, Relationships, Empathy. The first subscale detects the clarity about one's own feelings and those of others, whereas the second subscale indicates the skill to communicate one's own feelings to others. The third subscale measures the skill to have satisfying personal relationships, while the fourth subscale indicates the skill to take alternative perspectives to one's own.

Finally, the fourth factor is articulated in three subscales: the first subscale, Social awareness, detects the skill to speak clearly, to negotiate and influence the decisions of others; the second subscale named Emotion management (others) indicates the ease of managing or influencing the emotions of others (for example, console or depress others); the third subscale named Assertiveness measures the tendency to be frank and direct, to express clearly, but not aggressively, their needs and desires.

The TEIQue has two additional subscales that that do not relate to any particular factor but are directly counted in the total score; they are the Adaptability subscale and Self-motivation subscale. The first subscale expresses the ease of adaptation of the person in situations and different and new environments, whereas the second indicates the tendency to be motivated intrinsically rather than in an extrinsic way.

1.5. PROMOTING EMOTIONAL INTELLIGENCE

An aspect that makes emotional intelligence an innovative variable in research and intervention fields derives from the fact that while personality traits are considered substantially stable (Costa & McCrae, 1992), there is a broad consensus in the literature with regard to the fact that emotional intelligence is a characteristic which can be increased (Bar-On, 1997, 2002; Cobb & Mayer, 2000; Di Fabio & Kenny, 2011; Kotsou, Nelis, Grégoire, & Mikolajczak, 2011; Mayer et al., 2002; Nelis, Quoidbach, Mikolajczak, & Hansenne, 2009; Salovey & Sluyter, 1997). There are many authors who claim that emotional intelligence can be developed through specific training (Bar-On, 1997, Cobb & Mayer, 2000; Salovey & Sluyter, 1997), but few programs provide empirical evidence of their effectiveness through rigorous evaluation (Clarke, 2006; Groves, McEnrue, & Shen, 2008; Kotsou et al., 2011;

Nelis et al., 2009). The research appears limited that is associated with evaluations of the effectiveness of training related to emotional intelligence that also includes a comparison between groups and the use of solid psychometric measuring for the detection of emotional intelligence (Groves et al., 2008).

In this regard, Nelis et al. (2009) present a study with a control group to verify the effectiveness of training to increase emotional intelligence, structured into four sessions of two and a half hours each. The results of the study by Nelis et al. (2009) showed a significant increase in the ability to identify and manage the emotions that persist at the follow-up made six months after the training.

A later study conducted by Kotsou et al. (2011) with a control group aimed to analyze not only whether it is possible to increase emotional skills through a group intervention for fifteen hours, but even whether this increase can lead to a better adjustment of mental, physical and social abilities. The results of this study showed that the level of emotional skills significantly increased in the experimental group compared with the control group, suggesting that emotional skills can be enhanced with the benefits of personal and interpersonal functioning that persist for a year after the training.

In the Italian context, according to the theoretical model by Mayer and Salovey (1997), Di Fabio (2010) developed a training in ten sessions with the aim of increasing emotional intelligence in high school students (Di Fabio & Kenny, 2011). It is possible for application in a reduced form (4 sessions) as presented in the study by Di Fabio and Kenny (2011). In such a study, in the preliminary phase of intervention, four classes of Italian high school students (91 participants) were randomly selected among those of the last year of high school in a scholastic complex. The two classes that didn't show significant difference in the mean scores of the studied variables were selected for taking part in the present study. The instruments (T1 and T2) were collectively administered in the classrooms. At T1 the measures were administered to the students of four classes as foreseen in the process for the selection of experimental and control groups. A month after the training, the initial instruments (T2) were administered both to the experimental and the control groups. The administered instruments were: the Italian version (D'Amico & Curci, 2010) of the Mayer-Salovey-Caruso Emotional Intelligence Test (MSCEIT, Mayer et al., 2002); the Italian version (Di Fabio, Giannini, & Palazzeschi, 2008) of the Emotional Intelligence Scale (EIS, Schutte et al., 1998); the Italian version (Di Fabio, Busoni, & Palazzeschi, 2011) of the Indecisiveness Scale (IS, Frost & Shows, 1993); and the Italian version (Di Fabio & Palazzeschi, 2010) of the Career Decision-making Difficulties Questionnaire (CDDQ, Gati, Krausz, & Osipow, 1996).

Each session was focused on one of the four dimensions of the MSCEIT and it was subdivided in two units. Also, there are specific preliminary sessions in the training relative to the strengthening and congruence of the emotional lexicon, and specific, final sessions relative to the reflection on emotions in general and on empathy.

The results of the study by Di Fabio & Kenny (2011) suggested that such training was effective not only in increasing both ability-based and self-reported emotional intelligence, but also in reducing indecisiveness and career indecision, (Di Fabio & Kenny, 2011).

It is important to underline, on the one hand, that more results are obtained if programs for increasing emotional intelligence are applied in a preventive manner in early developmental phases, and on the other hand, that it is possible to provide specific exercises for each age (Walsh, Galassi, Murphy, & Park-Taylor, 2002). Interventions aimed at enhancing emotional intelligence thus refer to three different areas: first, to life abilities/positive social skills; secondly, to promotion of wellness, prevention of problems, and risk reduction; and, finally, to conflict resolution and support in times of transition and crisis (Di Fabio, 2010).

1.6. Counseling and Mediation

Relying on an analysis of the literature, counseling seems to be traditionally used in decision-making and as a specific decisional domain in the resolution of in various conflict kinds in familiar, scholastics, work, economic and social domains (Messing, 1993).

Mediation is configured as a mode of conflict resolution defined as the voluntary participation in a structured, informal process in which there are two conflicting parties and a third "neutral" part who supports them to find a solution and obtain a shared agreement (Girard, Refkin, & Townley, 1985). The mediator plays a role as a facilitator in helping conflicting parties work together to find shared interests and satisfactory solutions to both parties (Girard et al., 1985; Laue, 1987). In the United States since the 1980s, mediation has been considered as a possible application area for counseling, leading to a development of mediation services within counseling centers where the counselor/mediator provided short-term intervention that allowed couples, ex-spouses, students, workers to deal effectively with interpersonal conflicts (Kessler, 1979).

The goal of mediation conducted by a counselor is to offer a place where a conflict can be addressed and resolved peacefully, so as to strengthen interpersonal relationships rather than to damage them trough the dispute and to highlight skills useful in future differences of opinion (Kessler, 1979).

In the legal domain, mediation can allow for reducing the overall burden of the complex judicial system in terms of duration and process costs (Kessler, 1979). In the United States since the 1970s, the federal courts provided mediation services in divorce cases. Subsequently, mediation has also been expanded in other kinds of legal conflicts such as domestic, neighborhood, and property disputes. During the 1990s, counseling had increasingly joined mediation when associated with legal issues related to family, particularly in separations and divorces, child custody, and domestic violence (Pearson, 1997). In Italy, mediation in the judicial system is compulsory only since late 2010 (d.lgs. 28-2010) as preliminary step to many domains in judicial cases: condo; real rights; division; inheritances; family agreements; lease; loan; rental company; compensation for damage resulting from the movement of vehicles and boats; compensation for damage resulting from medical liability; compensation for damage resulting from defamation by the press or other means of advertising; and insurance contracts, banking, financial, and business mediations.

The mediation is a short, structured process aimed particularly at making decisions that satisfy both parties, and allowing involved people to express their opinions and to facilitate the hearing of others' positions on the debated issue (Kessler, 1978). The mediator establishes a cooperative climate by identifying and recalling shared objectives, establishing rules, seeking to engage the participants, and prefiguring the way. Therefore, mediators allow for the development of a service whereby the resolution of conflict becomes not a fight to win, but a cooperative process that leads to solutions satisfactory to both parties involved (Kessler,

1979). Mediation is configured thus as a profession that involves interacting with people and helping at various levels by invoking the relational aspect. In 1983, Kelly had already emphasized that counseling skills, such as unconditional acceptance, active listening, empathy, are essential in mediation (Kelly, 1983).

In 1998, the Mediator Skills Project, a research group at the University of Georgia, in collaboration with the Voluntary Mediator Certification Project of the American Academy of Family Mediators, conducted a job analysis of the specific professional profile of mediators involved in interpersonal disputes (for example, disputes in the family, commercial, business, etc.) in order to define the knowledge and basic skills required for effective mediation (Herrman, Hollett, Gale, & Foster, 2001). The job analysis has identified 18 knowledge areas and 13 skill areas relative to the profile of the mediator regarding both legal aspects and relational aspects (Herrman et al., 2001). The 18 knowledge areas are the following: 1) The Administrative Practices/Procedures area regards knowledge of administrative structures and legal practices to be made in the mediation process. 2) The Personal Skills and Limitations area refers to the awareness of mediators in relation to their personal characteristics and how these characteristics can influence the participants, the process and outcomes of mediation. 3) The Mediation Models area relates to the knowledge of the main theories in the field of negotiation and mediation. 4) The Mediation Process area concerns the knowledge on how to facilitate and manage the mediation process (for example, knowledge about how to help participants understand how the mediation will be conducted, about forms of interaction that facilitate the implementation of a creative problem solving, about how to manage interactions with high emotional content, about how to manage time in a mediation session). 5) The Problem Solving Techniques area concerns the knowledge about how to handle creative problem solving, facilitating the identification by the parties of the conflict areas, generating ideas and opinions, considering potential solutions, selecting common solutions. 6) The Interpersonal Dynamics area refers to knowledge about how to facilitate creative problem solving, shifting the focus from competition to cooperation, identifying interests and similar goals among the participants, and managing the expression of emotions and anger. 7) The Theories of Social Change area is related to the knowledge of psychological states that accompany the conflict as hostile and competitive goals, negative attitudes and perceptions, the discrediting of the person. 8) The Conflict area concerns the knowledge related to: sources and types of conflict (for example, realistic or unrealistic conflict), cycles of conflict (for example, guilt, violence, fear), and styles of conflict (for example, from passive to aggressive), as conflict affects the groups and relationships. 9) The Communication area regards knowledge of verbal and nonverbal communication, management of emotions, and asking questions. 10) The Information Gathering area concerns the knowledge on how to obtain information from participants, particularly information relating to the fundamental problems, beliefs and emotions associated with conflict. 11) The Solution/Agreement Formation area refers to knowledge about how to create an agreement that is relevant to all participants. 12) The Cultural Issues area refers to knowledge related to cultural differences in the mediation, such as knowledge about how different cultures may react to mediation, to how people from different backgrounds communicate and solve problems, reactions to the different cultural oppression and power. 13) The Power and Control area concerns the knowledge associated with the sources of power in mediation (age, race, education, personal resources, sex, sexual orientation, physical appearance, physical abilities, professional status, etc.) and how to manage the mediation process. 14) The Inform/Disseminate/Educate/Teach area concerns the knowledge about how to explain the role of the mediator, the process and goals of mediation; the phases of problem solving and possible outcomes; and the legal fundamentals and policies relevant to the mediation and jurisdiction in the field of mediation. 15) The Alternatives to Mediation area refers to general knowledge relative to procedures of negotiation, facilitation, conciliation on the one hand, and to specific knowledge relative to how these procedures work and their possible impact in conflict resolution on the other hand. 16) The Knowledge of Resources Outside of Mediation area regards the knowledge relative to: the resources offered by the community as experts, programs and agencies; how to identify additional relevant information in relation to the needs of customers. 17) The How to Interact with Involved People other than Primary Participants area consists of knowledge about how to deal productively with other parts (such as friends or family) that could facilitate the mediation process. 18) The Ethical Issues area concerns the knowledge relative to: limits of their professional skills, ethical codes of mediation, and potential conflicts of interest.

There are 13 skill areas that emerged through a job analysis (Herrman et al., 2001): 1) The Administrative area regards the skills that refer to the steps needed to create a problem-safe, enjoyable and productive solving process in mediation (for example, encouraging all participants to engage in the mediation process, getting the information and the appropriate documentation, providing a setting appropriate to mediation, clarifying points to participants the mediation process, and explaining how the mediation interfaces with the legal processes). 2) The Mediator Error Correction area refers to the skills related to the recognition, correction and communication on behalf of the participants regarding the possible errors of the mediator. 3) The Mediation Process Management area concerns the skills to facilitate and manage the entire process of mediation, and skills concerning how to integrate a wide range of facilitation techniques and strategies, manage time, facilitate and provide answers to questions, negotiate, resolve the problem, and build possible agreements. 4) The Problem Solving area refers to the skills to encourage the parties to collaborate in the analysis of the problem and its resolution, and to create solutions that meet the needs and interests of each involved party. 5) The Relationship Management and Encouragement area is relative to the management of relations between both parties and between the mediator and the parties and includes creating an environment that fosters creative, collaborative, and productive relationships; facilitating the involved parties to recognize differences in self-respecting themselves and others; and the facilitating the self-determination of the parties. 6) The Critical Thinking area concerns the skills relative to intuitive reasoning, rational decision making, and selecting different interventions that promote creativity and collaborative problem solving. 7) The Communication area concerns the skills relative to the use of an appropriate communication style, adapting one's own communication style in relation to the different needs of participants, facilitating communication between the parties, creating a safe environment for the expression of strong emotions, and using neutral language. 8) The Information Gathering area refers to the ability to gather and organize information, facilitating the participants in identifying the information needed to reach an agreed solution, classifying information according to their relevance for the final solution, and facilitating the parties to use the information to reach and shared a stand-alone solution. 9) The Dealing with Information area regards the skills needed to facilitate the parties to recognize and understand the desired information and emotions, to identify sources of information, and to present information and options offered during the mediation process. 10) The Cultural and Diversity Competency

Skills area concerns the skills relating to the assessment of cultural differences that can affect the mediation process. 11) The Power and Control area refers to the skills to detect the various manifestations of power of the mediator and/or of participants for preventing or hindering the mediation process. 12) The Education and Dissemination of Knowledge area concerns the skills needed to provide to the parties information relative to the mediation process including the various stages of problem solving, the role of mediator, and basic legal information in the field of mediation. 13) The Ethical Issues area refers to the skills of the mediator to inform the parties about the specificity of its role and the limits of its competences.

The results of such a job analysis (Herrman et al., 2001) permit to define in detail the knowledge and skills necessary to facilitate the mediation process effectively, allowing to delineate the profile of the mediator and open new perspectives in the field associated with training this professional profile.

Also, McCorkle and Reese (2005) underline the importance that the mediator is a listener with skills related to nonverbal communication and needs to have knowledge of the role of cultural differences in mediation. Thus, one can understood how it can be essential for mediators to train on their communication skills and interpersonal relationship management (Di Fabio, in press). Mediators, as professionals who relate to people expressing needs, keep their specific intervention in focus in the foreground but can refine it through further knowledge and enrich their, communicative-relational knowledge (Di Fabio, in press).

Recently, further interesting stimuli have been proposed that link counseling and mediation. As counseling uses a narrative approach, introduced in career counseling and guidance interventions for the 21st century (Savickas, 2004, 2007; Savickas et al., 2009) changing the life and identity of a person by changing his/her story (Savickas, 2004, 2007; Di Fabio & Maree, 2012; Maree, 2007; Rehfuss, 2009), mediation has also begun using a narrative approach (Rubinson, 2004). According to Rubinson (2004), mediation:

> "is far more than an 'alternative' to litigation is a new way of telling stories about the world. These new stories are worth telling or at least exploring, and lawyers who meet the challenges of doing so enrich and expand the means through which both lawyers and clients resolve disputes" (p. 16).

A further stimulus considers mediation as part of the game theory, emphasizing the role of the mediator as a facilitator to increase cohesion between the players (Eklund, Rusinowska, & De Swart, 2007; Herrera-Viedma, Alonso, Chiclana, Herrera & 2007; Maturo, Sciarra & Ventre, 2010). The mediator is separate from each player, showing the advantages and disadvantages of a shared solution, particularly emphasizing the disadvantages of being excluded from a majority that has obtained the consent (Eklund et al., 2007; Herrera-Viedma et al., 2007; Maturo et al., 2010). The techniques used in the process of consensus, in many aspects similar to those governing the search of winning coalitions in cooperative games (Luce & Raiffa, 1957) (but the coalitions formed with the consented procedure are not only winning coalitions), are obtained with a particular dynamic procedure, based on changes induced by the maieutic and scrupulous work of the mediator. This facilitation work is near to counseling, promoting the individual's ability to make decisions independently and helping people with different interests and conflicting opinions to mediate and reach consensus.

CONCLUSION

In literature, the role of emotions in mediation has emerged (Jones & Bodtker, 2001), particularly, more recently, the role of emotional intelligence and the value of its enhancement (Boland & Ross, 2010). The aspect that makes emotional intelligence a variable worthy of interest in mediation arises from the fact that, while the personality characteristics of individuals are considered stable (Costa & McCrae, 1992), emotional intelligence is a characteristic that can be increased by specific training (Di Fabio & Kenny, 2011; Kotsou et al., 2011; Nelis et al., 2009). Some scholars suggested that it is necessary to provide more training regarding emotions as an integral part of the mediation process itself (Jameson, Bodtker, & Linker, 2010). Emotion plays a key role in conflict and, consequently, in the mediation process (Jones & Bodtker, 2011). Recognizing, understanding and comprehending emotions are considered important skills for the mediator (Cloke, 1993; Diamond, 2006; Retzinger & Scheff, 2006). In particular Retzinger and Scheff (2006) emphasize the importance of focusing more attention on training mediators in emotional areas.

In this framework, regarding the relation between emotional intelligence and mediation, studies highlight that mediators with higher emotional intelligence are better able to identify emotional cues presented by the parties, managing emotions more appropriately so that they can better facilitate a resolution of the conflict that satisfies the various parties involved in the dispute (Boland & Ross, 2010). Mediators with high emotional intelligence are better able to reach an overall agreement that minimizes the dissatisfaction of the parties, using techniques to push the parties towards a compromise solution and pursuing a goal, the overall and mutually satisfactory agreement (Boland & Ross, 2010).

It is possible, therefore, to give importance to providing specific training, starting from different components of emotional intelligence, for mediators on the basis of the training proposed by Di Fabio and Kenny (2011), for example. The latter focuses on developing the four components of emotional intelligence seemingly involved in the mediation process: a) perceiving emotions to recognize emotions of the parties and encourage a constructive expression of them; b) facilitating thought for problem solving that includes emotional aspects, promoting a resolution of the conflict, and providing a satisfactory agreement between the parties; c) understanding emotions of the conflicting parties and using them effectively in the mediation process; d) managing emotions to avoid the escalation of the conflict in mediation and promote an agreement between the parties. The deepening of emotional roles, particularly emotional intelligence, in mediation leads to thinking about the importance associated with the professionalism of the mediator and the construction of such professionalism in an intervention area regarding the relationships, both between people and the single person that expresses need.

The importance of enhancing psychological counseling soft skills for helping the mediation process is based on the awareness that it is a profession that realizes an intervention centered on relationships with people expressing needs. The mediator has obviously not requested to "be the counselor", but is rather someone who has obtained highlighted skills through advanced learning, allowing he/she to do their job better and more efficiently. Along with a mediator's communication and interpersonal skills, the areas of emotion and enhancing emotional intelligence seem to play a fundamental role in mediation domain. The latter also refers to the enrichment of mediation intervention with a psychological basis as an added value in terms of professionalism within the professional background of mediators and to the enhancement their level of professional competence to better do what their profession requires of them. In such a framework, promising perspectives open for psychological counseling in the field of mediation. Counselor psychologists can indeed deal with training mediation operators on sensitizing the psychological aspects of relationship and interpersonal dynamics, such as acquiring skills to address the psychological implications of their profession. Furthermore, counselor psychologists can have an academic training specific in the legal area as professionals bringing a transdisciplinar background of skills, able to further facilitate the success of mediation intervention, both as operators and as "nurturing" supervisors when consulting for mediators.

In conclusion, it is possible to state that the development of communication and interpersonal skills and the enhancement of emotional intelligence in the field of mediation can be placed in an intervention perspective. The latter can be characterized by an in-depth state of professionalism in which the facilitation process is a time and an opportunity of actual growth and social benefit through an increase of the adaptive autonomy of the parties in the mediation process.

REFERENCES

Allred, K. G., Mallozzi, J. S., Matsui, F. & Raia, C. P. (1997). The influence of anger and compassion on negotiation performance. *Organizational Behavior and Human Decision Processes, 70*, 175-187.

Bar-On, R. (1988). *The development of a concept of psychological well-being* (Unpublished Doctoral Dissertation). Rhodes University, South Africa.

Bar-On, R. (1997). *The Emotional Intelligence Inventory (EQ-I): Technical manual*. Toronto, ON, Canada: Multi-Health Systems.

Bar-On, R. (2002). *Bar-On Emotional Quotient Inventory: Short. Technical manual*. Toronto, ON, Canada: Multi-Health Systems.

Boland, M. J. & Ross, W. H. (2010). Emotional intelligence and dispute mediation in escalating and de-escalating situations. *Journal of Applied Social Psychology, 10*(12), 3059-3105.

Bryson, K. D. (2005). Managerial success and derailment: The relationship between emotional intelligence and leadership. *Dissertation Abstracts International: Section B. Sciences and Engineering, 66*(1-B), 614.

Carnevale, P. J. (1986). Strategic choice in mediation. *Negotiation Journal, 2*, 41-56.

Caruso, D. R. & Salovey, P. (2004). *The emotionally intelligent manager: How to develop and use the four key emotional skills of leadership*. San Francisco, Jossey-Bass.

Clarke, N. (2006). Emotional intelligence training: A case of caveat emptor. *Human Resource Development Review, 5*, 422-441.

Cloke, K. (1993). Revenge, forgiveness, and the magic of mediation. *Mediation Quarterly, 11*, 67-78.

Cobb, C. D. & Mayer, J. D. (2000). Emotional intelligence: What the research says. *Educational Leadership, 58*, 14-18.

Costa, P. T. & McCrae, R. R. (1992). *NEO PI-R professional manual*. Odessa, FL: Psychological Assessment Resources.

D'Amico, A. & Curci, A. (2010). *Mayer-Salovey-Caruso Emotional Intelligence Test (MSCEIT)*. Firenze: Giunti O.S. Organizzazioni Speciali.

Davis, M. H. (1980). A multidimensional approach to individual differences in empathy. *JSAS Catalogue of Selected Documents in Psychology*, *10*, 85.

Davis, M. H. (1983). Measuring individual differences in empathy: Evidence for a multidimensional approach. *Journal of Personality and Social Psychology*, *44*, 113-126.

Diamond, I. (2006). Therapeutic aspects of community mediation. *Dissertation Abstracts International: Section B. Sciences and Engineering*, *67*(4-B), 2220.

Di Fabio, A. (2010). *Potenziare l'intelligenza emotiva in classe. Linee guida per il training* [*Enhancing emotional intelligence at school: Guidelines for training*]. Firenze: Giunti O.S. Organizzazioni Speciali.

Di Fabio, A. & Busoni, L. (in press). *L'intelligenza emotiva nei contesti organizzativi. Training di potenziamento* [*Emotional intelligence in organizational contexts. Enhancement training*]. Firenze: Giunti O.S.

Di Fabio, A. & Kenny, M. E. (2011). Promoting emotional intelligence and career decision making among Italian high school students. *Journal of Career Assessment*, *19*, 21-34.

Di Fabio, A. & Maree, J. G. (2012). Group-based Life Design Counseling in an Italian context. *Journal of Vocational Behavior*, *80*, 100-107.

Di Fabio, A. & Palazzeschi, L. (2009). An in-depht look at scholastic success: Fluid intelligence, personality traits or emotional intelligence? *Personality and Individual Differences*, *46*, 581-585

Di Fabio, A. & Palazzeschi, L., (2010). Career Decision-Making Difficulties Questionnaire: Proprietà psicometriche nel contesto italiano [Career Decision-Making Difficulties Questionnaire: Psychometric properties in the Italian context]. *Counseling. Giornale Italiano di Ricerca e Applicazioni*, *3*, 351-364.

Di Fabio, A., Busoni, L. & Palazzeschi, L. (2011). Indecisiveness Scale (IS): Proprietà psicometriche della versione italiana [Indecisiveness Scale (IS): Psychometric properties of the Italian version]. *Counseling. Giornale Italiano di Ricerca e Applicazioni*, *4*, 13-24.

Di Fabio, A., Giannini, M. & Palazzeschi, L. (2008). Intelligenza emotiva: Proprietà psicometriche della versione italiana della Emotional Intelligence Scale (EIS) [Emotional intelligence: Psychometric properties of the Emotional Intelligence Scale]. *Counseling. Giornale Italiano di Ricerca e Applicazioni*, *1*, 61-72.

Druckman, D. & Olekalns, M. (2008). Emotions in negotiation. *Group Decision and Negotiation*, *17*, 1-11.

Eklund, P., Rusinowska, A. & De Swart, H. (2007). Consensus reaching in committees. *European Journal of Operational Research*, *178*, 185-193.

Foo, M. D., Elfenbein, H. A., Tan, H. H. & Aik, V. C. (2004). Emotional intelligence and negotiation: The tension between creating and claiming value. *The International Journal of Conflict Management*, *15*(4), 411-429.

Friedman, R., Anderson, C. & Brett, J. (2004). The positive and negative effects of anger on dispute resolution. *Journal of Applied Psychology*, *89*, 369-376.

Frost, R. O. & Shows, D. L. (1993). The nature and measurement of compulsive indecisiveness. *Behavior Research Therapy*, *31*, 683-692.

Fulmer, I. S. & Barry, B. (2004). The smart negotiator: Cognitive ability and emotional intelligence in negotiation. *International Journal of Conflict Management, 15*, 245-272.

Galinsky, A. D., Maddux, W. W., Gilin, D. & White, J. B. (2008). Why it pays to get inside the head of your opponent: The differential effects of perspective-taking and empathy in negotiations. *Psychological Science, 19*(4), 378-384.

Galtung, J. (1996). *Peace by peaceful means: Peace and conflict development and civilization.* Thousand Oaks, CA: Sage.

Gati, I., Krausz, M. & Osipow, S. H. (1996). A taxonomy of difficulties in career decision-making. *Journal of Counseling Psychology, 43*(4), 510-526.

Girard, K., Refkin, J. & Townley, A. (1985). *Peaceful persuasion: A guide to creating mediation dispute resolution programs on college campuses.* Amherts, MA: The Mediation Project at the University of Massachusetts.

Groves, K. S., McEnrue, M. P. & Shen, W. (2008). Developing and measuring the emotional intelligence of leaders. *Journal of Management Development, 27*, 225-250.

Haynes, J. M. (1986). Supervision issues in mediation. *Mediation Quarterly, 13*, 31-42.

Herrera-Viedma, E., Alonso, S., Chiclana, F. & Herrera, F. (2007). A consensus model for group decision making with incomplete fuzzy preference relations. *IEEE Transactions on Systems Fuzzy Systems, 15*(5), 863-877.

Herrman, M. S., Hollett, N., Gale, J. & Foster, M. (2001). Defining mediator knowledge and skills. *Negotiation Journal, 17*(2), 138-152.

Jameson, J. K., Bodtker, A. M. & Linker, T. (2010). Facilitating conflict transformation: Mediator strategies for eliciting emotional communication in a workplace conflict. *Negotiation Journal, 26,* 25-48,

Jones, T. S. & Bodtker, A. M. (2001). Mediating with heart in mind: Addressing emotion in mediation practice. *Negotiation Journal, 17*, 207-244.

Jones, T. S. (1989). A taxonomy of effective mediator strategies and tactics for nonlabor–management mediation. In M. A. Rahim (Ed.), *Managing conflict: An interdisciplinary approach* (pp. 221–230). New York: Praeger.

Jones, T. S. (2005). Emotion in mediation: Implications, applications, opportunities and challenges. In M. Herrman (Ed.), *Blackwell handbook of mediation: Theory and practice* (pp. 277-306). New York: Blackwell.

Jordan, P. J. & Troth, A. C. (2004). Managing emotions during team problem solving: Emotional intelligence and conflict resolution. *Human Performance, 17*, 195-218.

Jordan, P. J., Ashkanasy, N. M., Hartel, C. E. J. & Hooper, G. S. (2002). Workgroup emotional intelligence: Scale development and relationship to team process effectiveness and goal focus. *Human Resource Management Review, 12*, 195-214.

Kelly, J. B. (1983). Mediation and psychotherapy: Distinguishing the differences. In J. A. Lemmon (Ed.), Dimensions and practice of divorce mediation (pp. 33-44). *Mediation Quarterly, No. 1.* San Francisco: Jossey-Bass.

Kessler, S. (1978). *Creative conflict resolution: Participant's guide.* Atlanta. GA: Lenox Circle.

Kessler, S. (1979). Counselor as mediator. *The Personnel and Guidance Journal, November,* 194-196.

Kotsou, I., Nelis, D., Grégoire, J. & Mikolajczak, M. (2011). Emotional plasticity: Conditions and effects of improving emotional competence in adulthood. *Journal of Applied Psychology, 96*(4), 827-839.

Landsberger, H. A. (1955). Interaction process analysis of professional behavior: A study of labor mediators in twelve labor–management disputes. *American Sociological Review*, *20*, 566-575.

Laue, J. (1987). The emergence and institutionalization of third party roles in conflict. In D. J. D. Sandole & I. Sandole-Staroste (Eds.), *Conflict management and problem solving* (pp. 17-29). New York: New York University Press.

Lazarus, R. S. (1991). *Emotion and adaptation*. New York: Oxford University Press.

Leuner, B. (1966). Emotional intelligence and emancipation. *Praxis der Kinderpsychologie und Kinderpsychiatrie*, *15*(6), 196-203.

Lopes, P. N, Grewal, D., Kadis, J., Gall, M. & Salovey, P. (2006). Evidence that emotional intelligence is related to job performance and affect and attitudes at work. *Psicothema*, *18*, 132-138.

Luce, R. D. & Raiffa, H. (1957). *Games and Decisions*. New York: John Wiley.

Maree, K. (Ed.). (2007). *Shaping the story: A guide to facilitating narrative career counselling*. Pretoria: Van Schaik.

Maturo, A., Sciarra, E. & Ventre, A. G. S. (2010). Counselling: Decision making, consensus, and mediation. *Procedia Social and Behavioral Sciences*, *5*, 1770-1776.

Mayer, J. D. & Salovey, P. (1997). What is emotional intelligence? In P. Salovey & D. Sluyter (Eds.), *Emotional development and emotional intelligence: Educational implications* (pp. 3-31). New York: Basic Books.

Mayer, J. D., Roberts, R. C. & Barsade, S. G. (2008). Human abilities: Emotional intelligence. *Annual Review of Psychology*, *59*, 507-536.

Mayer, J. D., Salovey, P. & Caruso, D. R. (2000). Selecting a measure of emotional intelligence: The case of ability scales. In R. Bar-On & J. D. Parker (Eds.), *The handbook of emotional intelligence* (pp. 320-342). San Francisco: Jossey Bass.

Mayer, J. D., Salovey, P. & Caruso, D. R. (2002). *Mayer-Salovey-Caruso Emotional Intelligence Test (MSCEIT): User's manual*. Toronto, Canada: Multi-Health Systems.

McCorkle, S. & Reese, M. J. (2005). *Mediation theory and practice*. Boston: Pearson Education.

McGrath, J. E. (1966). A social psychological approach to the study of negotiation. In R. V. Bowers (Ed.), *Studies on behavior in organizations: A research symposium* (pp. 101-134). Athens, GA: University of Georgia Press.

Messing, J. K. (1993). Mediation: An intervention strategy for counsellors. *Journal of Counseling and Development*, *72*, 67-72.

Moore, C. (2003). *The mediation process: Practical strategies for resolving conflict* (3rd ed.). San Francisco: Jossey-Bass.

Nelis, D., Quoidbach, J., Mikolajczak, M. & Hansenne M. (2009). Increasing emotional intelligence: (How) is it possible? *Personality and Individual Differences*, *47*, 36-41.

Offermann, L. R., Bailey, J. R., Vasilopoulos, N. L., Seal, C. & Sass, M. (2004). The relative contribution of emotional competence and cognitive ability to individual and team performance. *Human Performance*, *17*, 219-243.

Ogilvie, J. R. & Carsky, M. L. (2002). Building emotional intelligence in negotiations. *The International Journal of Conflict Management*, *13*(4), 381-400.

Parker, J. D. A., Creque, E. R., Barnhart, D. L., Harris, J. I., Majeski, S. A., Wood, L. M.,, & Hogan, M. J. (2004). Academic achievement in high school: Does emotional intelligence matter? *Personality and Individual Differences*, *37*, 1321-1330.

Pearson, J. (1997). Mediating when domestic violence is a factor: Policies and practices in court-based divorce mediation programs. *Mediation Quarterly, 14*, 319-33.

Petrides, K. V. & Furnham, A. (2000). On the dimensional structure of emotional intelligence. *Personality and Individual Differences, 29*, 313-320.

Petrides, K. V. & Furnham, A. (2001). Trait emotional intelligence: Psychometric investigation with reference to established trait taxonomies. *European Journal of Personality, 15*, 425-428.

Petrides, K. V. & Furnham, A. (2004). *Technical manual of the Trait Emotional Intelligence Questionnaire (TEIQue)*. London: University of London, Institute of Education.

Rahim, M. A., Psenicka, C., Polychroniou, P., Zhao, J. H., Yu, C. S., Chan, K. A., . . . Wyk, R.V. (2002). A model of emotional intelligence and conflict management strategies: A study in seven countries. *International Journal of Organizational Analysis, 10*, 302-326.

Rehfuss, M. C. (2009). The Future Career Autobiography: A narrative measure of career intervention effectiveness. *The Career Development Quarterly, 58*(1), 82-90.

Retzinger, S. & Scheff, T. (2006). Emotion, alienation, and narratives in protracted conflict. In M. Fitzduff & C. Stout (Eds.). *The psychology of resolving global conflicts: From war to peace* (Vol. 1, pp. 239-255). Westport, CT: Praeger.

Ross, W. H., Conlon, D. E. & Lind, E. A. (1990). The mediator as leader: Effects of behavioral style and deadline certainty on negotiator behavior. *Group and Organization Studies, 15*, 105-124.

Rubin, J. Z., Pruitt, D. G. & Kim, S. H. (1994). *Social conflict: Escalation, stalemate, and settlement* (2nd ed.). New York: McGraw-Hill.

Rubinson, R. (2004). Client counseling, mediation, and alternative narratives of dispute resolution. *Clinical Law Review, 833*. Retrieved from www.negotiationlawblog.com.

Salovey, P. & Mayer, J. D. (1990). Emotional intelligence. *Imagination, Cognition and Personality, 9*, 185-211.

Salovey, P. & Sluyter, D. (1997). *Emotional development and emotional intelligence: Educational implications*. New York: Basic Books.

Savickas, M. (2004). Vocational psychology. In C. Spielberger (Ed.), *Encyclopedia of Applied Psychology* (pp. 655-667). Amsterdam, Netherlands: Elsevier.

Savickas, M. L. (2007). Prologue Reshaping the story of career counseling. In K. Maree (Ed.), *Shaping the story. A guide to facilitating narrative counselling* (pp. 1-3). Pretoria, South Africa: Van Schaik.

Savickas, M. L., Nota, L. & Rossier, J., Dauwalder, J.-P., Duarte, M. E., Guichard, J.,. . .Van Vianen, A. E. M. (2009). Life Designing: A paradigm for career construction in the 21th century. *Journal of Vocational Behavior, 75*, 239-250.

Schreier, L. S. (2002). Emotional intelligence and mediation training. *Conflict Resolution Quarterly, 20*, 99-119.

Schutte, N. S., Malouff, J. M., Hall, L. E., Haggerty, D. J., Cooper, J. T., Golden, C. J. & Dornheim, L. (1998). Development and validation of a measure of emotional intelligence. *Personality and Individual Differences, 25*, 167-177.

Slaikeu, K. A. (1996). *When push comes to shove: A practical guide to mediating disputes*. San Francisco: Jossey-Bass.

Thorndike, R. K. (1920). Intelligence and its uses. *Harper's Magazine, 140*, 227-235.

Van Coillie, H. & Van Mechelen, I. (2006). A taxonomy of anger-related behaviors in young adults. *Motivation and Emotion, 30*, 57-74.

Van Kleef, G. A., De Dreu, C. K. & Manstead, A. S. (2004). The interpersonal effects of anger and happiness in negotiations. *Journal of Personality and Social Psychology, 86,* 57-76.

Van Kleef, G. A., van Dijk, E., Steinel, W., Harinek, F. & van Beest, I. (2008). Anger in social conflict: Cross-situational comparisons and suggestions for the future. *Group Decision and Negotiation, 17,* 13-30.

Walsh, M. E., Galassi, J. P., Murphy, J. A. & Park-Taylor, J. (2002). A conceptual framework for counseling psychologists in schools. *The Counseling Psychologist, 30*(5), 682-704.

Wong, C. S. & Law, K. S. (2002). The effects of leader and follower emotional intelligence on performance and attitude: An exploratory study. *Leadership Quarterly, 13,* 243-275.

Zeidner, M., Matthews, G. & Roberts, R. D. (2004). Emotional intelligence in the workplace: A critical review. *Applied Psychology: An International Review, 53*(3), 371-399.

In: Psychology of Counseling
Editor: Annamaria Di Fabio

ISBN: 978-1-62618-388-9
© 2013 Nova Science Publishers, Inc.

Chapter 12

Cognitive Barriers to Rational Home Loan Decision Making: Implications for Mortgage Counseling

Jessica M. Choplin,[1,*] *Debra Pogrund Stark*[2] *and Joseph A. Mikels*[1]
[1]DePaul University, Chicago, IL, US
[2]The John Marshall Law School, Chicago, IL, US

ABSTRACT

This chapter describes the cognitive steps that consumers need to go through to make wise conventional and reverse mortgage decisions with the aim of educating mortgage counselors about these steps and to develop strategies so counselors can more effectively help lead consumers through them. These cognitive steps include: (1) learning about and understanding how mortgages operate, (2) estimating unknown quantitative values such future income and the ongoing expenses of home ownership, including insurance, real estate taxes, and repairs, (3) evaluating known attributes of the mortgage such as the interest rate and monthly payment for fixed-rate mortgages, (4) identifying how important those attributes are, (5) judging the likelihood of events such as the likelihood of unemployment in the case of younger consumers considering conventional mortgages or the likelihood that a senior will be involuntarily away from the home for more than twelve months (an event that would trigger the necessity of repaying a reverse mortgage loan) in the case of a reverse mortgage, and (6) integrating all of that information to make a decision. In reviewing these steps, this chapter describes cognitive and social psychological barriers that impede consumers' abilities to enact each step (e.g., uncertainty discounting causes consumers to minimize or ignore risks associated with uncertain events, impeding step 5). These barriers make it difficult for consumers to integrate and evaluate all of the information needed to make wise decisions (i.e., because it is uncertain, the risks of unemployment will be minimized or ignored when considering the risks of taking out a mortgage). Many of the barriers discussed in this chapter change across the lifespan so the type of counseling should vary according to the age of the

---

* Corresponding author: Jessica M. Choplin. Email address: jchoplin@depaul.edu.

consumer considering the loan product. Awareness of these cognitive steps and the barriers consumers face in taking these steps will help counselors serve their clients' needs and protect their clients from predatory loan products.

INTRODUCTION

Owing in part to the complexity of conventional and reverse mortgages, many consumers have been deceived into entering into overpriced and unaffordable conventional home loans or refinances of these loans with no net economic benefit, or have entered into high cost reverse mortgages that are not the lowest cost means to address their cash needs. One strategy to protect consumers is to require them to receive mortgage counseling. Congress has required mortgage counseling for reverse mortgages since 1998. However, only in 2008 did Congress mandate that independent counselors perform the counseling rather than parties, such as the lender, who had an interest in inducing the borrowers to enter into the loan. To further improve the effectiveness of the counseling, the Department of Housing and Urban Development enacted a counseling protocol in 2010. There is no similar federal counseling requirement for conventional home loans, but Stark and Choplin (2010) proposed mortgage counseling to better enable consumers to avoid overpriced or potentially unaffordable home loans and to aid the borrower in his or her decision making. This chapter explores cognitive and social psychological phenomena that make it difficult for consumers to judge whether mortgages—conventional or reverse—are in their best interest. Our goal is to inform mortgage counselors about the difficulties consumers face so that they can devise ways to aid consumers through these difficulties. Where appropriate, we also note possible strategies counselors might consider using to address some of these cognitive difficulties. In the conclusion section, we summarize these phenomena and strategies mortgage counselors might use to address them.

To make wise home mortgage decisions, consumers need to go through a number of difficult cognitive psychological steps. First, consumers need to learn how mortgages operate. What do they entail? While learning how mortgages operate, consumers are given a lot of information and they have to remember all of this information. This involves holding multiple pieces of information in their minds and integrating them to form coherent schemas and scripts for how mortgages work. They will have to verify what they have been told about the mortgage by the broker or lender so that they are not misled into taking out a mortgage that is not in their interests. This step might be particularly difficult for seniors considering reverse mortgages. As discussed below, not only does cognitive aging make learning this new material difficult, but also seniors may already be familiar with conventional mortgages. If so, they may make inappropriate assumptions that reverse mortgages are more similar to conventional mortgages than they actually are. The process of learning about the similarities and differences between reverse mortgages and conventional mortgages is cognitively difficult.

Once consumers understand how mortgages operate, they will need to judge whether the mortgage that they are considering will suit their needs. To make this judgment, consumers need to estimate quantitative values that are difficult to estimate. Consumers considering conventional mortgages will need to estimate their future incomes, the appreciation (or depreciation) of the property, and so forth, as well as the ongoing expenses of home ownership such as insurance, real estate taxes, and repairs. If the mortgage has an adjustable rate, they will need to estimate likely future interest rates and monthly payments. Seniors considering reverse mortgages need to estimate quantitative values such as how much money they will need, how long they might live, when they will need this money, and how much money out of the reverse mortgage proceeds they should budget for the ongoing costs of home ownership, including insurance, real estate taxes, and repairs.

In addition to estimating unknown values, consumers also have to evaluate how good or bad known attribute values are. That is, they must evaluate how good or bad the interest rate is, the monthly payment, origination fees, closing costs, servicing fees, the mortgage insurance premiums, and so forth. How good is a 5.61% interest rate? How bad is a $2,567 monthly payment? They will also need to evaluate their current income and whether the proportion of their income that would be spent on housing costs is a good or bad proportion. Seniors considering reverse mortgages will need to evaluate the benefits that they receive from remaining in their home and compare those benefits with the benefits that they might receive from living elsewhere. Seniors will need to evaluate their current fixed income, the shortfall between their limited fixed income and their needs, and the amount of money they will have after taking out the reverse mortgage. Seniors will also need to evaluate a number of attributes of the reverse mortgage such as how adequate or inadequate the amount of money they will be receiving is, and how high the costs of this reverse mortgage are; and they will need to compare these values with the amounts received and costs of alternatives.

Once consumers have evaluated how good or bad these attributes are, they will need to judge how important each attribute is to making a decision. How important is it that the origination fees are high and have been evaluated as bad? Is it important enough to conclude that the proposed loan should be rejected? How important is it to keep monthly payments low versus how important is it to incur fewer costs. If keeping monthly payments low is more important, consumers should choose a longer-term loan. If incurring fewer costs is more important, a shorter-term loan would be a better choice. For seniors choosing a reverse mortgage payment plan, how important is it to maximize the amount of money they receive now versus maximizing the amount later; and if it costs more to receive money now, how much emphasis should one put on this extra cost?

Mortgage decisions also involve probability judgments. What is the probability of getting a job transfer? What is the probability of becoming unemployed? What is the probability of defaulting on the loan? What is the probability of needing to refinance? What is the probability that the fair market value will go up or down, in case they need to refinance? If it is an adjustable rate loan, what is the probability that it will adjust upward? What is the probability that it will adjust downward? What is the likelihood that the home will require major repairs? Seniors who are considering taking out a reverse mortgage have to consider additional possibilities. What is the likelihood that they will get sick and be away from their home for more than twelve months? What is the likelihood that they will outlive the money they receive from the reverse mortgage?

Finally, once all of these cognitive steps have been completed, consumers need to hold all of this information in mind to make a decision. It is extremely difficult to hold all of this information in mind. Research has found that even with simpler decisions, consumers of all ages often avoid the complexity of decision making by shortcutting some of these cognitive steps and looking for a simple reason or justification to simply go with an option. Or they use other heuristics such as going with the option that is recognized (a shortcut called the recognition heuristic) or relying on one's mood or emotional state when considering that option (a shortcut called the affect heuristic).

These cognitive psychological steps are difficult for consumers regardless of age and so are problematic for younger consumers considering conventional mortgages. However, due to changes in cognitive and emotional processes that occur across the lifespan, older adults will, on balance, have more difficulties than their younger counterparts. While as discussed below some of these changes may operate to protect older adults, the majority of these changes operate to make older adults more vulnerable. For this reason, optimal intervention strategies designed to protect consumers from making unwise decisions will often depend on age. For this reason and also because reverse mortgage counseling is currently required and a counseling protocol is in place, whereas there is no similar national requirement for conventional mortgages, this chapter discusses in depth age-related differences in the difficulties encountered at each of these cognitive steps.

In the sections that follow, we explore each of these cognitive steps in considerable detail. These cognitive steps include: (Step 1) learning and understanding how mortgages operate; (Step 2) effectively estimating unknown quantitative values; (Step 3) effectively evaluating known attributes of the mortgage; (Step 4) recognizing which attributes are most important; (Step 5) judging the likelihood of events; and (Step 6) integrating information and making a decision.

STEP 1. LEARNING AND UNDERSTANDING HOW MORTGAGES OPERATE

Before deciding to take out a mortgage, consumers had better understand how they operate. That is, consumers need to have cognitive scripts and schemas of how mortgages operate (Stark and Choplin, 2009, 2010). Learning how they operate is a difficult cognitive task. Because optimally consumers should compare a proposed loan with all of the alternatives, the task of learning how mortgages operate is made more complex by the diversity of loan products on the market. Indeed, one could spend a career learning about alternatives, and so at some point consumers have to decide that they know enough to make a decision.

The question of how much information they should gather (see *Information Gathering* below) is then one of the primary difficulties that consumers face when they are considering mortgages. Furthermore, memory difficulties in general, and binding difficulties in particular, can cause considerable problems for consumers considering mortgages (see *Memory Difficulties* and *Binding Difficulties* below). Interference from previous knowledge can also create difficulties (see the *Interference from Previous Knowledge* below). Mortgages today are much more complex than they traditionally were and often include new and different attributes (e.g., adjustable rate versus fixed interest rates, prepayment charges, interest only loans with balloon payments versus fully amortized loans, and varying levels of down payment which can lead to costly mortgage insurance premiums). Consumers may falsely believe that they understand a loan product, because they assumed the loan product under consideration was similar to previous loan products they had seen. Likewise, seniors considering reverse mortgages may assume that reverse mortgages are more similar to conventional mortgages than they actually are. Owing in part to the fact that consumers are often motivated to trust those who are "giving" them loans (see *Motivation to Trust* below), mortgage brokers and lenders—perhaps unaware that they are doing so—are often able to use cognitive and social psychological principles that undermine consumers' attempts to understand the mortgage loans that they are considering, especially the problematic attributes. Mortgage brokers and lenders are often able to use framing (see *Framing Effects* below), confirmation biases (see *Confirmation Biases* below), argument immunization (see *Argument Immunization* below), and senseless explanations (see *Senseless Explanations* below) to undermine consumers' attempts to understand problematic attributes.

Information Gathering

The task of judging how much information to gather and when enough is known to make a decision is difficult for consumers of all ages (Gigerenzer, Todd, and ABC Research Group, 1999). Younger consumers considering conventional mortgages will, therefore, likely struggle with this issue and mortgage counselors will need to monitor their clients to make sure that they have done their homework and gathered enough information to make a wise decision even if their clients are young. The counselor can assist this process for a conventional loan by working with the borrower in the ways described in Stark (2005) to obtain the information necessary to determine if the loan is overpriced, affordable, and provides a net economic benefit to the borrower. Because of the declines in their deliberative processing abilities, older adults are particularly likely to make decisions before gathering enough information. Older adults tend to seek out less information than their younger counterparts when they are faced with a decision (Löckenhoff and Carstensen, 2007). Numerous studies have examined age differences in information search when making decisions; and a meta-analysis of twelve such studies revealed that older adults consistently examine less information overall relative to younger adults. This analysis revealed only a small loss in decision quality. However, most of the decisions explored in the studies covered by this meta-analysis were decisions for which older adults could use their existing scripts and schemas or learn relatively simple new ones.

The domains in these studies were cereals (search for nutritional information), cars, apartments, medications, health plans, physicians, diamonds (learning discriminating dimensions, e.g. color and crown proportions), stocks, and political candidates. None of the studies seemed to require participants to unlearn or significantly modify existing scripts and schemas as they would have to unlearn or modify their scripts and schemas for conventional mortgages to understand reverse mortgages. Because older adults collect less information, they may not know as much as they should before making a decision on whether or not to take out a mortgage. This is especially the case for reverse mortgages given that understanding reverse mortgages will often require individuals to unlearn or modify their existing scripts and schemas for conventional mortgages.

The tendency for older adults to gather less information as well as the fact that younger adults also struggle with this issue emphasizes the importance of the counseling session and requires the counselor to monitor how much the client understands. It also requires the counseling session to be well organized. Unimportant or less important information needs to be eliminated. Important information needs to be emphasized; and, furthermore, because consumers—especially older adults—may stop listening to mortgage counselors after receiving their limit of information, mortgage counselors should present the most important information as early in the counseling session as possible.

Memory Difficulties

Remembering particular attribute values of the mortgage one is considering (e.g., that the interest rate is 4.91%) can be difficult for consumers of all ages. It is likely to be particularly difficult for older adults and seniors, however, as they have more difficulty than their younger counterparts remembering information. An important distinction in memory research concerns the distinction between veridical memory for the details and general memory for the gist of the information.

For instance, in studies examining recall of simple verbal material, older adults show a shift toward reliance on retrieval processes that are based on gist versus the verbatim details. In one seminal study, older and younger adults read a series of short stories and then responded to questions for the verbatim details of the story or whether a certain detail was plausible (Reder, Wible, and Martin, 1986). Although older adults were equally as accurate as younger adults regarding the plausibility questions, they were significantly less accurate when responses required veridical memory for the specific details. Thus, older adults may be able to very well recall the gist of the details for a mortgage or reverse mortgage, but would have significant difficulties recalling the verbatim details.

A senior considering a reverse mortgage may get the gist from a sales pitch of a mortgage broker or lender that a reverse mortgage allows them to obtain their needed cash and that the amount borrowed will not become due until they die. But what is the gist of what a mortgage counselor tells the senior? It is likely there is no one key message from a mortgage counselor, since the counselor is not selling a product but instead tasked with explaining it. Instead, the counselor relays to the senior numerous details of how reverse mortgages work and various payment and other options under them. This is problematic in light of the problem of veridical memory of details. Seniors are likely to fail to recall the many options and considerations counselors point out on how to structure the reverse mortgage let alone whether it makes sense for the senior to enter into the transaction. For this reason Stark, Choplin, Mikels, and McDonnell (in press) recommended that the rules on reverse mortgage counseling be revised to require counselors to provide the senior with a specific written finding on whether the reverse mortgage meets the borrower's goals or not.

The idea behind this recommendation was to create a gist that seniors can recall and counter-balance the pro-reverse mortgage message they receive from the mortgage lender or broker. Short of this reform to the reverse mortgage counseling protocol, mortgage counselors should keep in mind that their clients, especially their older clients, are unlikely to remember the verbatim details and more likely to remember the gist.

Binding Difficulties

Binding difficulties are a type of memory difficulty likely to plague consumers who have been doing their homework and have been considering many alternative mortgages. Under this phenomenon, consumers will mistakenly think that an attribute of Mortgage A is an attribute of Mortgage B. For example, they might remember Mortgage B as having an interest rate of 4.91% when the number 4.91 was actually the interest rate of Mortgage A and Mortgage B has an interest rate of 5.63%. Consumers of all ages make this mistake, but it is likely to be particularly common among older adults. Jacoby (1999) reported a scam wherein binding difficulties cause older adults a great deal of harm. Scam artists find older adults with memory difficulties and then tell these vulnerable older adults something like the following: "We received your check for $1,200.00, but it should have only been $950.00. Send us another check for $950 and we will return the first check to you." In reality, there was no $1,200.00 check, but they remember sending checks out throughout their lives and they interacted with similar businesses. Some older adults then confuse these previous instances with the confident claim of the scam artist, binding a memory of sending a different check to the scam artist's fictional story. Believing the story and even having somewhat fuzzy (and it turns out false) memories of the incident, some older adults proceed to write the scam artist a check for $950. Similar binding errors are likely to occur as consumers, especially older adults, learn about alternative mortgages. They might, for example, confuse the interest rate or the origination fees of one mortgage that they considered with another. Or as happened in one legal case (*Kennedy v. World Alliance Financial Corp*), seniors considering reverse mortgages confused the loan amount that would be disbursed to them with the maximum loan amount for priority purposes relating to the lien on the mortgaged property. We thus recommend that mortgage counselors review with their clients the attributes of the proposed loan (i.e., interest rate and costs) to make sure they have not confused the attributes of the proposed loan with another loan or the attributes of the proposed loan with each other. We also recommend that mortgage counselors look at how the proposed loan compares with the general market to ensure that the proposed loan is not higher than prevailing market rates for this type of loan, and if a conventional loan, to determine based on the borrower's credit score the APR (annualized interest rate combined with certain closing costs) they should be charged, by going on www.myfico.com to obtain this (Stark, 2005).

Interference from Previous Knowledge

Mortgages today are much more complex than they were traditionally. Many relatively new features that add risks and costs to the borrower that developed with the sub-prime home loan market (e.g., the imposition of prepayment charges, interest only, non-amortizing loans with balloon payments, and adjustable interest rates) have been added. Consumers who are familiar with mortgages from the past may assume that the mortgage they are considering is similar to the ones they knew and fail to look for these new features. Similarly, a senior who is considering a reverse mortgage is likely to have taken out at least one, and possibly several, conventional mortgages in his or her lifetime.

The individual, therefore, probably knows a lot about conventional mortgages. A great deal of psychological research has documented that consumers often learn about new domains by drawing analogies from old domains. In the case of reverse mortgages, seniors may try to understand how reverse mortgages operate by drawing analogies from conventional mortgages. Some attributes of conventional mortgages such as interest rates and origination fees also apply to reverse mortgages and might serve to make the analogy particularly likely.

There are, however, a number of attributes that do not apply. Savvy seniors may catch some of the attributes of conventional mortgages that do not apply to reverse mortgages, such as the fact that at the end of the reverse mortgage process instead of owing nothing as in a conventional mortgage, they will owe a lot more than when the process started. They may also understand that their heirs will not inherit the home. They may, however, fail to understand that if they move out for a year, the reverse mortgage will become due and they will likely be unable to live in that home. They may also fail to realize that under a reverse mortgage the loan amount will increase each month to pay for mortgage insurance. Consequently, mortgage counselors should be made aware of this tendency to draw inferences from previous knowledge and to emphasize how the mortgage under consideration is different from previous mortgages the consumer may have seen, especially when the differences are disadvantageous to the consumer.

Motivation to Trust

In conventional mortgages, consumers are dependent upon mortgage brokers and lenders to "give" them the loan they need to purchase their home. In reverse mortgages, seniors who are having financial difficulties and are looking to reverse mortgages as a solution to these difficulties are dependent upon the salespeople who might be "giving" them reverse mortgage loans. Research suggests that consumers who are dependent ameliorate the fears and uncertainty associated with their situation by trusting those on whom they depend and to trust so that by reciprocity they will in turn be trusted. Future research should investigate whether or not older adults are more vulnerable to this phenomenon than their younger counterparts. There are, however, several reasons to suspect that they might be. First, older adults are often more dependent than their younger counterparts. Older adults then may suffer a disproportionate impact, even if this psychological phenomenon is the same for them as for their younger counterparts. Second, older adults tend to pay more attention to positive information (see Step 3 below) than their younger counterparts do, which could exacerbate the problem of unwarranted trust. This motivation to trust underscores the importance that the mortgage counseling be performed by individuals who have no stake in the financial transaction and can provide truly objective information and advice, as is now required for reverse mortgage counseling.

This tendency to trust those on whom they depend on will be problematic for the task of learning how the mortgage they are considering operates, if the salespeople on whom they are depending to receive the mortgage provide inaccurate or misleading information. Alternatively, as described next trusted salespeople might craft how they frame messages. They might present information so consumers look for information that confirms their claims, causing them to ignore information that would disconfirm them. They might immunize their customers from counterarguments and present senseless information. To counter this, independent mortgage counselors should be directed to correct any misleading information presented by the mortgage lender or broker and alert consumers when a lower cost alternative is available.

Framing Effects

The manner in which options are discussed or framed has a considerable effect on the decisions consumers make, and these framing effects interact with age. Contrast the positive frame (i.e., you will save money if you do) with the negative frame (i.e., you will lose money if you do not). All consumers are loss averse, but younger consumers are particularly so. The negative frame will, therefore, be salient, especially for younger adults. By contrast, older adults pay more attention to positive information and less attention to negative information relative to their younger counterparts. That is, older adults are more likely than younger adults to learn and remember information presented in a positive frame. For instance, a recent study conducted by Shamaskin, Mikels, and Reed (2010) examining the framing of health care messages found that older adults found positive messages more informative than negative, and better remembered the positive messages. Specifically, the researchers presented older and younger adults with health care pamphlets that had either positively or negatively framed health messages. As an example, for skin cancer, messages indicated that "The earlier it is detected, the better the person's chances are for full recovery" or "The later it is detected, the poorer the person's chances are for full recovery," respectively. In this study, older adults rated pamphlets with positive statements as more informative than pamphlets with negative statements. Also, older adults remembered a higher proportion of positive to negative statement relative to the young. The lesson from this finding for counselors is that the most appropriate framing will usually depend upon the age of the client. To make information salient, negative frames are more likely to be appropriate for younger than older consumers, while positive frames are more likely to be appropriate for older than younger consumers.

Confirmation Biases

Consumers have a tendency to look for information that is consistent with their prior beliefs. That is, they will look for information that confirms, rather than disconfirms, their previous beliefs. Due to confirmation biases, consumers may look over the loan documents for information that confirms their prior beliefs (e.g., that the monthly payment is what the mortgage broker or lender said it was) and fail to look for information that would disconfirm those beliefs (e.g., that the monthly payment adjusts). Or consumers who are considering a reverse mortgage may look over the loan documents for information that confirms their prior beliefs (e.g., that the loan does not become due until they die) and fail to look for information that would disconfirm those beliefs (e.g., that other events can trigger the loan to become due such as if they become ill and absent from the home for more than twelve months). Due to age-related differences in deliberative processing, older adults may be more likely to use this shortcut. In related research, for example, Mutter and Pliske (1994) presented older and younger adults with a series of case studies on psychiatric patients in which characteristics of the patient were intuitively associated with their interpretations of a Rorschach drawing. Both older and younger adults were equally as likely to report illusory correlations, such that a relationship was reported even though the patient characteristics and the Rorschach judgments were uncorrelated. Importantly, though, when presented with information that contradicted the illusory correlations, younger adults adjusted their judgments whereas older adults were less likely to adjust their judgments and were more likely to remain biased in favor of their initial judgments. Similar confirmation biases may occur when consumers are trying to learn about the mortgage products they are considering. Mortgage counselors need to be aware of confirmation biases and present information that disconfirms misinformation.

Argument Immunization

Mortgage brokers or lenders might immunize consumers from arguments against taking out a mortgage product (such as arguments made by mortgage counselors) by following a procedure first studied by McGuire and his colleagues in the early 1960s (McGuire and Papageorgias, 1961). Under this procedure, people first exposed to a weak argument for a negative decision and then a stronger counter-argument for a positive decision will be "immunized" from even stronger arguments for the negative decision. In the case of a reverse mortgage, for example, a mortgage broker might be concerned that a counselor will notice that the income from the reverse mortgage and the senior's other fixed income are not enough to cover the senior's basic needs. The broker might then immunize the senior against this concern by saying, for example, "someone might worry that this reverse mortgage will not cover all of your expenses, but it will cover your food and electricity and every little bit helps." The senior might then be less likely to listen to counselors when they enumerate all of the senior's expenses and suggest that the reverse mortgage is inadequate.

Counselors need to be aware that brokers and lenders may have used argument immunization to make consumers resistant to arguments against the mortgage product. To address this issue, counselors might ask their clients whether the broker or lender discussed with them any negative aspects of the mortgage and what they were told. If the broker or lender used argument immunization, the best way for the counselor to discuss disadvantages might be by framing the disadvantages in the form of advantages of alternatives. For example, in discussing the high cost of reverse mortgages, the counselor can refer to the lower cost of an alternative like downsizing when noting how much more costly the reverse mortgage would be.

Senseless Explanations

Inspired by a classic study by Langer, Blank, and Chanowitz (1978), Choplin, Stark, and Ahmad (2011) ran an experiment in which they asked participants to sign a consent form to participate in a study. The participants had been told earlier that the study would only take five more minutes and that they would receive one credit hour for each hour of participation. The consent form that the participants were asked to sign said something quite different. In bright red, boldface, 16-point font (while the rest of the text was in black 10-point font and not bold) one line on the consent form read, "You will receive one hour's credit for your three hours of participation." Of the eighty participants in the study, thirty-five (43.8%) simply signed the consent form and did not raise any concerns. The remaining forty-five did raise concerns about this line and were randomly assigned to three groups of fifteen participants each: a control condition, a plausible explanation condition, and a senseless explanation condition. The participants in the control condition were told that the consent form was correct and that they would be expected to participate for three hours and would only receive one credit. Only six of the fifteen participants in this condition signed. In the plausible explanation condition, participants were told that it would not apply and they were given a plausible explanation, "the consent form only reads that way because it is an old form." Thirteen of the fifteen in this condition signed. Finally, in the senseless explanation condition, participants were given the senseless explanation, "the consent form only reads that way because that is the way it was drafted." Twelve of the fifteen participants in this condition signed.

This experiment raises the concern that problematic aspects of consumer contracts might be explained away, not only by plausible explanations, but also be senseless explanations. If consumers discover problematic aspects of a mortgage, these concerns can often be allayed by explanations. In the case of reverse mortgages, for example, the provision that the reverse mortgage will become due if they fail to pay taxes or perform maintenance might be explained away by a plausible statement such as, "you can use the loan to make these payments" (not explaining that funds may be inadequate from the loan to make this payment) or even a senseless explanation such as, "you have to make those payments anyhow" (not explaining that if one lacks these funds, it is possible to sell the home and find a lower-cost place to live).

It would be impossible to reconstruct an entire conversation or conversations that the consumer has had with the mortgage broker or lender to determine all of the questions the consumers raised and all of the senseless explanations they may have received, but the counselor might ask the consumer what were the key questions he or she had raised with the lender/broker and how were these key questions answered. If the counselor learns of a senseless explanation, he or she might explain how the response was inaccurate and then emphasize how other alternatives would better address their needs.

STEP 2. ESTIMATING UNKNOWN QUANTITATIVE VALUES

It is impossible to justifiably conclude that a proposed mortgage is in the consumer's interests without estimating some values that are unknown and, likely, unknowable. For example, consumers considering mortgages will need to have as trustworthy of estimates as they can possibly get for the ongoing expenses of home ownership including insurance, real estate taxes, repairs, etc. Consumers considering conventional mortgages will need to estimate their future incomes, the appreciation (or depreciation) of the property, etc. For adjustable-rate loans, they will need to estimate future interest rates and monthly payment amounts. Seniors considering reverse mortgaged will need to estimate the amount of money they will need, how long they will live, when they will need this money, etc. The task of estimating these values is often difficult. Experience or being in a community of peers who have experience can help (see *Experience: Being in a Community of Peers* below). However, remembering budget items so that no budget items are neglected can be a challenge (see *Memory for Budget Items* below) as can estimating the cost of each of those budget items (see *Estimating Costs of Budget Items* below). Because of these difficulties, consumers often rely on heuristics—short-cuts to an answer that usually produce reasonable results, although they can also lead consumers astray—to estimate these unknown quantitative values (see *Reliance on Heuristics to Estimate Values* below).

Experience: Being in a Community of Peers

Experience putting together budgets and paying bills allows consumers who have had that experience to recall prior examples and, thereby, use those prior examples to aid in estimating similar values. This is one factor on which older adults are likely to have advantages over younger adults. Younger adults will often lack the experience of estimating the values necessary to judge whether a mortgage will suit their needs, or their experiences will not be as extensive as older adults. Older adults will have advantages, especially for realistic values that are consistent with prior knowledge. A second typical source of knowledge, if consumers lack this experience themselves, is to rely on their peers who have the relevant experience. Here again, older adults have advantages as they are often part of a community of their own same-aged peers who are likely to have experienced similar budgeting issues. Researchers have documented how seniors often create social networks that share knowledge with each other and thereby promote their own health and well-being. These social networks are also likely to promote economic well-being by providing each other with information relevant to estimating values such as those necessary to judge whether a mortgage product is advantageous. Younger adults' same-aged peers are less likely to have had the relevant experience. However, other factors are likely to create difficulties for older adults in estimating these values.

Memory for Budget Items

Older adults have greater difficulties in general recalling items from memory than do their younger counterparts. In particular, older adults are likely to have difficulties recalling budget items (e.g., that the roof will need to be replaced). Older adults show declines in memory for specific details despite preserved memory for the gist. This factor could cause older adults to neglect some budget items altogether. For reverse mortgage counseling, the 2010 reverse mortgage counseling protocol helps in this regard by having the mortgage counselor review the budget with the senior using the FIT software. However, it is possible that the senior may have expenses or sources of income not included in the FIT software for creating a budget. The counselor should endeavor to find out from the senior any such additional sources of income or expenses in the senior's life so as not to miss any budget items. Despite the fact that younger adults are less vulnerable than their older counterparts on this factor, younger adults will also often forget and thereby neglect some budget items altogether. Conventional mortgage counselors should, therefore, also be cognizant of this issue.

Estimating Costs of Budget Items

To estimate costs such as the cost of repairs, not only do consumers have to recall budget items (e.g., that the roof will need to be replaced in the next few years because it has not been replaced in twenty-five years), but they also have to estimate the costs of each of those budget items (i.e., the cost of the roof). The selective accessibility model of estimation holds that consumers estimate numerical values like these by remembering attributes of the to-be-estimated items. To estimate the cost of replacing the roof, for example, a consumer will have to remember that the roof is slate, that the slate is synthetic or Vermont-quarried, and other details. The problem is that consumers do not and cannot remember all of the attributes of the to-be-estimated items. Whether particular attributes are accessible in memory will depend upon the person's state of mind and the contextual cues that trigger memory and make those attributes accessible.

Although memory deficits could make this process more difficult for older adults, fortunately experience and expertise can assuage some of these age-related memory changes. For instance, in a study by Castel (2007), younger and older adults—some of whom were retired accountants and bookkeepers—were presented with phrases that consisted of a number, an object, and a location. When memory was later examined for the numbers and objects when presented with the location, older adults did not show a significant deficit in remembering the object information, although some of them—those who were not retired accountants or bookkeepers—did show a deficit for the numeric information. The retired accountants and bookkeepers remarkably showed incredibly well intact memory for the numeric information. Related work demonstrates older adults' strengths and vulnerabilities. In that work, older and younger adults were presented with grocery items with realistic versus unrealistic prices. Older adults demonstrated equally accurate memory for the realistic prices, but inferior memory relative to the young for the unrealistic prices (Castel, 2005). Thus, when older adults attempt to estimate values relevant to making a wise decision on a mortgage and they use their prior knowledge of budget-item attributes to do so, they are likely to do well so long as they can rely on prior knowledge and schematic supports in familiar domains, but they are likely to have difficulties when they cannot rely on these supports. Creating a realistic budget is currently required of reverse mortgage counselors under the new protocol. These experimental results suggest that mortgage counselors can rely on the older adults' experience and expertise in estimating budget items as long as the older adult can utilize prior knowledge and schematic supports in familiar domains. Younger adults lack this experience and, thereby, might have more difficulties on this factor. Conventional mortgage counselors will, therefore, need to be especially vigilant on this issue.

Reliance on Heuristics to Estimate Values

Because accurate estimates are extremely difficult and often impossible, consumers use heuristics to estimate values. As defined above, heuristics are short-cuts to an answer that usually produce reasonable results, although they can also lead consumers astray and produce systematic inaccuracies. The anchoring heuristic is probably the most well-known example of an estimation heuristic. Under this heuristic, if consumers compare the to-be-estimated value to an arbitrary number or even if they merely hear an arbitrary number presented in an unrelated context, their estimates will be biased toward the arbitrary number. Another heuristic is the availability heuristic. Under this heuristic, consumers estimate the budget items that come to mind most easily to be the largest budget items and assume that budget items that do not come to mind are likely to be small. This heuristic often produces reasonable results, because high-priced budget items are typically the ones that consumers talk about the most, the ones that are advertised more frequently, and so forth. However, relying on this heuristic can lead consumers wrong because factors other than price often affect the frequency with which these budget items are discussed. Consumers' reliance on these heuristics underscores the importance for counselors to be trained in creating realistic budgets.

STEP 3. EVALUATING ATTRIBUTES

Even if attribute values are known, it will still be unclear how good or bad those values are. How good is a 5.61% interest rate? How bad is a $2,567 monthly payment? It is often difficult to make these types of judgments and many different factors create biases for these judgments. Relative to younger adults, older adults exhibit a positivity bias that could cause them to evaluate loan product attributes through rose-colored glasses (see *Positivity Effects* below). In addition, adaptation effects, the tendency for consumers to overvalue small changes and undervalue large ones, temporal discounting, range effects, endowment effects, and binding difficulties can all cause biases in consumers' judgments of how good or bad the known attributes of the mortgage are. Each of these factors is discussed in its own section below.

Positivity Effects

Younger adults have a long life in front of them and need to pay attention to negative information so they can improve their situation for the long run. Older adults have less time and are thus more motivated to enjoy each day. This asymmetry between younger and older adults causes seniors to focus more on positive information and to evaluate attributes more positively than younger adults do. An unpublished study by the first and third authors of this chapter demonstrates this phenomenon. Twenty younger participants (mean age was 20.8 years) and twenty older participants (mean age was 72.8 years) evaluated how good or bad thirteen particular temperatures (i.e., 10°, 17°, 23°, 28°, 32°, 35°, 37°, 39°, 42°, 46°, 51°, 57°, 64°) seemed for the month of March in Ithaca, NY. The older participants evaluated these temperatures significantly better than did the younger participants. The implication of this finding for mortgage counselors is that the optimal way to describe mortgage product attributes and to compare mortgage products to their alternatives will depend upon the age of the client.

In particular, while presenting negative information about a loan product will often be effective for younger adults, it will often be less effective for older adults. Older adults will have a tendency to evaluate the attributes of the reverse mortgage they are considering more positively than they should and see the proposed reverse mortgage through rose-colored glasses. This phenomenon could potentially serve a protective function against inappropriately choosing a reverse mortgage, however, if it also causes seniors to evaluate alternatives (such as selling their homes, downsizing, or taking on a tenant or roommate) more positively. It is important for mortgage counselors to be made aware of the positivity effect on seniors and criticize reverse mortgages where appropriate, not by directly pointing out negative information about reverse mortgages, but rather by emphasizing the positive aspects of alternative ways to get the needed money such as selling their home and downsizing.

Adaptation Effects

Adaptation effects can create difficulties evaluating reverse mortgages, although they may play a protective role in evaluating conventional mortgages. Seniors considering reverse mortgages are typically on a low fixed income and have made the adjustments that they could to adapt to that income. Even if they were unable to completely adapt and need a reverse mortgage to make ends meet, research has found that consumers adapt better than they expect to adapt to situations like this and so the income that they would consider adequate, normal, or average would be lower than it would be for their middle-aged counterparts. This adaptation to lower incomes is also facilitated by social comparison effects where consumers compare themselves to similar peers such as those who are the same age and from the same socio-economic status. Once this process of adaptation to lower incomes is complete, then any small boost higher than what they consider normal or average will be considered good relative to this now lowered new average. One result of this lowered average is that so long as it boosts their income above the new lowered normal or average, seniors may be too quickly satisfied with a gain in monthly income that is either smaller than the equity in their house is worth or smaller than necessary to meet all of the senior's projected expenses. The additional money coming from reverse mortgages might be evaluated as larger than it should be and they will pay more for this additional income than they should. This might especially be the case because consumers overvalue small changes and undervalue large ones (see *Overvaluing Small Changes, Undervaluing Large Ones*).

Mortgage counselors may be able to help seniors avoid these adaptation effects by asking them to evaluate the income from the reverse mortgage relative to the income they were earning at the peak of their earnings history, especially if the increased income is inadequate compared with his or her expenses while staying in the home. Adaptation effects may sometimes play a protective function in the case of conventional mortgages where younger consumers are likely to see rising incomes. These consumers will evaluate the costs of the mortgage relative to their current incomes and the mortgage will then be less expensive relative to their future incomes.

Overvaluing Small Changes, Undervaluing Large Ones

Consumers overreact to small expenses and gains and under react to large ones. For example, a $1,000 repair expense will appear large, but an additional $1,000 added to an already very large $30,000 repair expense will not appear as large. It is as if the $30,000 bill is so bad that $31,000 could not be much worse. Even if it is a little worse, it is not proportionately worse. Their reaction to the $31,000 bill will not be equivalent to their reaction to a $30,000 bill plus what their reaction to a $1,000 bill would have been had they never received the $30,000 bill, because the extra $1,000 will appear small next to the $30,000 that they already lost. Similarly, small amounts of additional income are appreciated, but larger amounts of additional income are not appreciated proportionately as much.

Kahneman and Tversky (1984) demonstrated this phenomenon. In their study, they asked one group of participants to imagine that they were buying a calculator for $15 and a jacket for $125, but the calculator was on sale and would cost $5 less at another store that was a twenty-minute drive away, thus reducing the price from $15 to $10. They then asked participants whether they would drive the twenty minutes, and 68% were willing to do so. In another condition, they asked another group of participants to imagine that the calculator cost $125 and the jacket cost $15. They asked this group of participants whether they would drive the twenty minutes to reduce the price from $125 to $120, again saving $5. This time only 29% were willing to drive.

One effect of this phenomenon will be that bundling expenses such as third-party closing costs (which include possible appraisal fees, title search fees, title insurance, surveys, inspections, recording fees, mortgage taxes, credit checks and so forth) will cause the bundled fees to appear less large than those same expenses presented separately. In addition, the phenomena of overvaluing small changes and undervaluing large ones could cause consumers to overvalue minor savings on certain closing costs, but cause them to fail to take into proper account much higher cumulative savings that could result if they shopped around for a mortgage loan with a lower interest rate. Counselors can help reduce these effects by unbundling expenses and pointing out how much that money would be worth in other contexts.

Temporal Discounting

Consumers overvalue money received immediately and undervalue money that they could receive later. For instance, when presented with the option of receiving $10 now versus $100 in six months, consumers of all ages are more likely to choose the immediate reward of $10. This effect is problematic for consumers considering a conventional mortgage as it will often cause them to choose long-term mortgages with lower monthly payments over shorter-term loans with higher monthly payments. They will overvalue the greater short-term disposable income and undervalue the added expenses involved in a long-term mortgage. In addition, costs that are delayed appear less bad. So costs such as repairs and property taxes that are delayed will have a tendency to seem smaller than they are, as would the delayed costs of mortgage insurance. Counter intuitively, although older adults do show this effect, they do so to a lesser extent than their younger counterparts, despite the fact that their life expectancy is shorter. In one recent study, this reduced tendency of older individuals to discount the future was observed for delayed gains but not delayed losses (Löckenhoff, O'Donoghue, and Dunning, 2011). Such findings have implications for reserve mortgages. In particular, although seniors may be less vulnerable to these effects than their younger counterparts, this phenomenon might still cause seniors to opt for lines of credit payment plans under which borrowers receive mortgage proceeds in unscheduled payments or in installments at times and in amounts that they choose, potentially taking virtually all of the loan amount up front, rather than opt for a tenure payment plan under which borrowers receive equal monthly payments for as long as they live and occupy the property as their principal residence. This can be problematic in that it can lead to no more loan proceeds down the road when it is still needed and higher mortgage insurance premium costs (since it is an annual fee based on a percentage of the loan amount disbursed).

Range Effects

Extremely bad attribute values will appear less bad, if they are presented next to even worse values. Extremely high interest rates, for example, might appear reasonable, if they are presented next to even higher interest rates and a mortgage broker or lender may in fact present the interest rate of the proposed mortgage in this fashion (another reason why mortgage counselors should be aware of market interest rates and check if the proposed mortgage is at the market rate or higher than that). Likewise, for reverse mortgages this phenomenon could cause the amount of money seniors would receive monthly from a tenure payment plan to appear small next to the amount that they would receive in lump payments from a line-of-credit payment plan. This might partially explain why seniors take out reverse mortgages with tenure payment plans much less often than reverse mortgages with line-of-credit payment plans. Counselors might reduce these effects by presenting the total dollar amount the senior would receive if he or she lived to the age of 100 under each plan. Also, if a poor interest rate has been made to appear less bad next to an extremely bad interest rate, presenting an extremely good interest rate will help put the poor interest rate in perspective.

Endowment Effects

Consumers overvalue things that they already own and undervalue things that they do not. Kahneman, Knetsch, and Thaler (1990) demonstrated this phenomenon in a study in which they gave one group of participants coffee mugs and asked them whether they would be willing to sell it at dollar amounts that ranged from $.25 to $9.25. They asked another group of participants whether they would be willing to buy at these dollar amounts. They asked a third group of participants whether they would prefer the mug or the cash. Because they already owned the coffee mug, the participants in the first group valued the mug much more than did the other two groups.

The median price at which they were willing to part with the mug was $7.12. The second group, by contrast, was only willing to spend $2.87; and the third group preferred the cash until the amount of the payout was $3.12 or less. The second and third groups did not own the mug and so they valued it less.

This factor is particularly problematic for seniors considering reverse mortgages. Reverse mortgages allow seniors to keep their homes and so this option might be overvalued relative to other options such as purchasing a smaller residence that could also be valued. Consistent with this, in a recent survey by AARP the vast majority of older adults express the desire to remain living in their homes for as long as they can. Moreover, the majority of these elderly individuals who wish to "age in place" are homeowners without mortgages, hence with equity that enables them to qualify for a reverse mortgage. On the other hand, since older adults are not as heavily influenced by potential losses as are younger adults (Mikels and Reed, 2009), this may mitigate the endowment effect when it comes to their home. This in turn could make them a bit more likely to think of alternatives such as selling their homes and downsizing. Counselors might help reduce the endowment effect further by emphasizing the positive aspects of these alternatives.

Binding Difficulties

All of these systematic biases in the evaluations of mortgage attributes are compounded by binding errors, the memory error described above wherein consumers confusing attribute values from one item with the attribute values of another. If consumers mistakenly believe that the mortgage they are considering had a given interest rate or quoted fees, but those amounts were not actually attributes of the mortgage they are considering, but rather were the attributes of another mortgage they had reviewed previously, then their evaluation of the mortgage is bound to be drastically mistaken.

The consumer could end up with a mortgage that has attributes that are radically different from what he or she thought. This factor makes it particularly important that mortgage counselors review the basic economics of the proposed mortgage (interest rate, origination and other closing costs, loan amount, mortgage insurance premiums, etc.) with the consumer to make sure that what the consumer thought she or he was getting as the economic terms of the loan is consistent with the loan being proposed.

STEP 4. RECOGNIZING IMPORTANT ATTRIBUTES

Even if an attribute value is known and evaluated to be bad, the question of how important that bad attribute is will remain. Is the attribute bad enough to make it such that the mortgage is not in the consumer's best interest? Or is the mortgage, on balance, still in the consumer's interest despite the bad attribute? How important is this attribute relative to the other attributes? Normatively, consumers would know the objective importance of each attribute so that positive attributes and negative attributes could compensate for each other so that the consumer would be able to make a judgment of whether the mortgage is, on balance, in the consumer's interest or not. Unfortunately, such compensatory algorithms are cognitively complex and extremely difficult. This is true for all consumers, but especially for older adults (see *Compensatory Weighting Is Computationally Complex* below). Therefore, consumers will generally use noncompensatory strategies instead (see *Use of Noncompensatory Choice Strategies* below). Consumers are also vulnerable to placing inappropriate weight on attributes owing to factors that should be irrelevant such as evaluability, dominance, and conversational norms.

Compensatory Weighting Is Computationally Complex

Weighted additive models of decision making hypothesize that decision makers score the importance of each attribute dimension and multiply this importance score by the score of how good each attribute value is.

The product of these two scores will then be summed to give a score of how good the choice is as a whole. This type of model involves compensatory weighting because strengths on some attributes can compensate for weaknesses on others, but it is extremely computationally complex because consumers use every piece of information. Few consumers of any age are able to carry it out completely.

The difficulty of carrying it out is even more difficult for older adults. In fact, research indicates that older adults prefer strategies that are generally less computationally demanding. For instance, a study by Mata, Schooler, and Rieskamp (2007) examined the decision strategies used by older versus younger adults. In this study, older and younger adults had to decide which of two diamonds was more expensive by considering how each diamond fared on eight different dimensions. The attributes for each diamond were hidden and the participants were free to view as many attributes for each diamond in any order they liked before making their decisions. The researchers were thus able to examine different strategy use and found that few consumers used a compensatory strategy, but older adults were even less likely to use compensatory weighing strategies relative to younger adults. Stark et al. (in press) argued that the difficulties consumers face in using compensatory strategies could be overcome for reverse mortgage counseling by reforming the counseling protocol to require the mortgage counselor to provide a suitability determination to the borrower regarding the reverse mortgage based upon specific criteria set forth in a new mortgage counseling protocol. The following were the four criteria proposed in Stark et al. (in press): To make a finding of "suitability," the mortgage counselor would need to conclude based on information received from the senior that: (i) the reverse mortgage proposed is likely the lowest cost means for the senior to obtain the necessary funds to meet all of their expenses and live in the home, (ii) the senior's reported physical condition and appraiser's reported condition of the senior's home make it likely that the senior can remain in the home for the period of time the senior hopes to be able to, (iii) the funds to be received under the reverse mortgage will be adequate for the senior to pay for all of her reasonably anticipated expenses to be able to live in the home for the period she desires, and (iv) the senior is aware that by entering into this loan there is less chance the senior's heirs will inherit any equity in the home. The bulk of the information needed to make the suitability determination can be obtained under the existing mortgage counseling protocol set up in 2010 by HUD, including the use of the Financial Interview Tool and Benefits Check-up. One could even create an algorithm score based on the suitability criteria that would be compensatory so that consumers' judgments would be compensatory as long as they used that score and suitability determination. Short of such a legal reform, mortgage counselors should be aware that their clients are likely to have difficulties using compensatory strategies.

Use of Noncompensatory Choice Strategies

To avoid the computational complexity of compensatory weighting, consumers often use alternative strategies such as the *elimination-by-aspects* strategy. Under this strategy, consumers focus on one dimension (i.e., the one they judge to be the most important) first and eliminate options that are low on that dimension. Once those options are eliminated, the choice set is smaller. If there is more than one option remaining, they will choose another dimension (i.e., the second most important) and repeat this process until the choice set is narrowed down to one option. This strategy will inevitably neglect some dimensions that might be important. Consumers who use this strategy will likely never even look at dimensions below the few they assume are the most important.

An even simpler strategy is the "Take The Best" strategy, which involves choosing an option based on one discriminating attribute. In making a decision, a consumer who uses this strategy would examine attributes in the order of perceived importance. If there is a best option on that dimension, stop and pick that option (e.g., look at interest rates, take the best option on that attribute and don't worry about the other attributes). Only if two options are identically best on that dimension would the consumer look at the second most important attribute, and so on. At that point, the information search ends and the better option is chosen. So, if the consumer judges interest rates to be the most important attribute and the quoted interest rate is the best of the interest rates the consumer reviewed, then the consumer would fail to look at other attributes. All consumers have a tendency to use these types of non-compensatory strategies, but Mata et al. (2007) found that older adults used simpler strategies, such as Take The Best, more often than the younger adults. Thus, relative to younger adults, older adults are more likely to use simpler non-compensatory strategies and less likely to use effortful compensatory strategies that could result in inferior choices. Mortgage counselors can play an important role in enabling consumers to take a broader perspective as they are financially sophisticated and more capable of taking a wider variety of variables into account in evaluating prospective loans.

Evaluability

Research suggests that consumers often judge how important an attribute is by how easy it is to evaluate that attribute. Hsee (1996) demonstrated this principle in an experiment in which he asked participants how much money they would spend on dictionaries. In one condition, participants identified how much money they would be willing to spend on each of two dictionaries. Dictionary A defined 10,000 words and its condition was as good as new, while Dictionary B defined 20,000 words and had a torn cover. In the other conditions, participants only identified how much money then would spend on one of these dictionaries and never saw the other one. Participants were unable to judge how good 10,000 words was when dictionary A was presented alone, so the participants who judged Dictionary A alone said that they would be willing to spend an average of $24 on Dictionary A, while the participants who judged Dictionary B alone were willing to spend an average of $20 on Dictionary B. By contrast, the participants who saw both dictionaries and judged how much they would be willing to spend on each of them were only willing to spend $19 on Dictionary A and were willing to spend $27 on Dictionary B. Hsee proposed that the reason for this reversal (called the evaluability hypothesis) is that attributes that are easily judged as good or bad are often incorrectly given greater importance, whereas those that cannot be easily judged are ignored. Consumers may be particularly likely to give greater importance to evaluable attributes like interest rates which can be compared with other interest rates being offered as contrasted with less tangible attributes such as prepayment charges which only apply if the loan is paid off early (an event that is harder to evaluate than interest rates which apply right away and for certain). Indeed, the borrower may not even be aware of the existence of a prepayment charge as the consumer is of an interest charge. Mortgage counselors can help consumers evaluate these attributes by making them aware of their existence and presenting comparison values so that they can be evaluated.

Dominance

Consumers overvalue attributes in which one attribute is clearly better than another, even if that attribute is not very important. It is as if the ease of recognizing how good it is causes consumers to place greater importance on the attributes on which it is so good and to ignore other attributes. Ariely and Wallsten (1995) found evidence for this phenomenon, and subsequent research suggests that older adults may be even more likely to rely on dominance to reduce computational complexity than their younger counterparts. Mortgage counselors should be aware of the power of dominance effects and compensate for them by spending most of their time during the counseling session on the most important attributes. Counselors will thereby be using conversational norms to compensate for these dominance effects.

Conversational Norms

Conversational norms dictate that a speaker should talk about topics that are important and ignore topics that are not. The amount of time a salesperson spends talking about an attribute of a mortgage should then be a cue to its importance. Unscrupulous salespeople can subvert this strategy by focusing primarily on relatively unimportant attributes. When selling reverse mortgages, for example, a salesperson might spend a great deal of time talking about the many uses the senior can make with the loan proceeds rather than focus on more important attributes such as whether the amount of the loan is adequate to meet the seniors projected future needs and whether this is the lowest cost basis to likely obtain the necessary funds. Mortgage counselors need to be aware of conversational norms and make sure that they spend more time on the most important aspects of the mortgage under consideration and that they spend a great deal of time determining the suitability of the loan for the consumer.

STEP 5. JUDGING PROBABILITY

Whether or not a loan product is in a consumer's interest will often depend upon the probability of various events. If it is likely that the consumer might become unemployed, then a conventional mortgage is unlikely to be a good idea. The likelihood of a job transfer would also affect whether a mortgage is a good idea. Consumers may need to refinance, and this likelihood may affect which loan product is most suitable. Furthermore, the likelihood of a refinance will depend on the likelihood that interest rates or other loan attributes become more or less expensive over time. Whether or not a refinance will be possible will depend on the likelihood that the fair market value will go up or down over time. Whether or not an adjustable rate loan is acceptable will depend on the likelihood that the rate will adjust upward. In addition, the costs of homeownership are often uncertain. Many repair costs are unknowable in advance. The furnace many need to be replaced, or it may not need to be. The roof will need to be replaced eventually, but the likelihood that it will need to be replaced next year is uncertain. Whether a reverse mortgage is in the senior's interest will depend on the likelihood that he or she will get sick and be away from their home for more than twelve months. These examples demonstrate that probability judgments are inescapable in determining whether loan products are in the consumer's interest. Unfortunately, there are many barriers that make it difficult for consumers to objectively evaluate these risks. Many consumers are overly optimistic (see *Optimistic Bias* below) or they make these judgments based upon how they are feeling in the moment, rather than making an objective judgment based on the facts (see *Risk-as-Feelings and Affect Heuristics* below). Alternatively, consumers might take a more cognitive approach to these probability judgments by relying upon memory of similar prior events (see *Memory-based models* section below). Unfortunately, this strategy is susceptible to various types of memory biases (e.g., see *Unpacking Principle* below). In addition, probability judgments are vulnerable to biases such as uncertainty discounting and risk aversion, which might place the consumer at risk or in some circumstances serve a protective function.

Optimistic Bias

Research has found that consumers have a tendency to be overly optimistic—overestimating the likelihood that good things will happen to them and underestimating the likelihood that bad things will happen to them. This phenomenon was originally demonstrated in a study by Weinstein (1980), who asked undergraduate students to judge the likelihood that events such as divorce, developing a drinking problem, owning their own home, and living past 80 years old would happen to themselves and also the likelihood that these events would happen to their average classmate. Weinstein's participants judged good events (i.e., owning their own home and living past 80 years old) more likely to happen to themselves than to their average classmate, and they judged bad events (i.e., divorce and developing a drinking problem) more likely to happen to their average classmates than to themselves.

This bias may be particularly problematic for older adults. Not only do older adults emphasize and better remember positive information with advanced age, there is some evidence that their optimism also increases with age. Thus, older adults might be particularly vulnerable to this optimistic bias. Older adults may, for example, be even more optimistic than their younger counterparts in judging the likelihood of necessary home repairs. Mortgage counselors need to be made aware of the optimistic bias especially when counseling older clients. They might also keep objective statistics on the likelihood of a variety of aversive events available to present to overly optimistic clients.

Risk-as-Feelings and Affect Heuristics

Loewenstein and colleagues' risk-as-feelings model of risk assessment holds that consumers' emotional reactions and momentary feelings can affect not only their cognitive probability judgments of risk but also the degree to which they behave in risky ways (Loewenstein, Weber, Hsee, and Welch, 2001). In a similar vein, other researchers have proposed that consumers judge risk and make risk-related decisions using an "affect heuristic," under which they use their emotional reactions and momentary feelings as guides for their judgments and decisions. Alhakami and Slovic (1994) or example, observed that even though subjective feelings about an activity cannot alter the objective risks associated with that activity, the degree to which participants liked an activity and had positive feelings about it was nevertheless associated with perceptions of how risky the activity was. Alhakami and Slovic interpreted this phenomenon as an effect of the liking and positive feelings acting on perceptions and judgments of risk. These models would suggest that instead of carefully considered judgments that take into consideration actual circumstances, consumers' judgments of the risks associated with mortgages might rather be affected by their emotional reactions and momentary feelings. In the case of a reverse mortgage, for example, the senior's assessment of the likelihood that he or she may become ill for more than twelve months or the likelihood that needed repairs to his or her home will exceed his or her means might be the result of momentary feelings, rather than being assessments based on facts.

Owing to cognitive decline associated with aging, older adults prefer strategies that are less cognitively demanding and they take less information into account when making decisions. As such, older adults might be more likely to use this strategy than their younger counterparts because it requires minimal cognitive resources to use. Using emotional reactions and momentary feelings to judge likelihood can be problematic because irrelevant momentary factors can affect the emotions a consumer is experiencing and thereby make a risky decision appear less risky and more attractive. On the other hand, using the affect heuristic could also be a strength for older adults, who have been shown to do better than younger decision makers when making decisions from the "heart" rather than the "head." Their better performance is because older adults have had many experiences that will cause the positive or negative emotional reaction. Mortgage counselors might capitalize on older adults' better-tuned emotional reactions. One way to do this is by describing risks using frequencies (e.g., 10 out of 100 people encounter difficulties) rather than probabilities (e.g., 10% encounter difficulties) because raising frequencies creates a greater emotional reaction. Similarly, using yellow flags as is currently done on the FIT can also create a greater emotional reaction that will assist a senior in using his or her emotional reaction in a constructive fashion.

Memory-Based Models

Many theories of how consumers judge the likelihood of events, or the support for hypotheses about the likelihood of events, hold that consumers make these judgments by retrieving cognitively available or representative exemplars (Dougherty, Gettys, and Ogden, 1999; Tversky and Kahneman, 1974; Tversky and Koehler, 1994). These accounts suggest that consumers might judge the likelihood of an event, such as the likelihood that their home will require repairs, based on their ability to retrieve cognitively available and representative exemplars of times that their home or homes of people they know have required repairs. Typically, this is the only strategy available to consumers to make likelihood judgments of this type, but it leaves them vulnerable to systematic biases in these judgments; that is, their judgment will be biased by their prior personal experiences or those of others they know.

Older adults may be particularly vulnerable to the biases created by this strategy for judging likelihood for two reasons. First, it is computationally complex. Consequently, older adults might retrieve fewer exemplars than would their younger counterparts.

For instance, age differences are often observed on the category exemplar generation (CEG) task, in which participants study a list of exemplars for given categories and then are later asked to recall as many exemplars for each category. On this task, older adults have been shown to retrieve significantly fewer exemplars from memory relative to their younger counterparts. Moreover, the CEG task appears to be related to fluency, that is, the ability of individuals to spontaneously generate as many exemplars for a given category in 60 seconds. On fluency tasks, older adults typically generate fewer exemplars than younger adults. Second, the positivity effect (see *Positivity Effects* in Step 3 above) may systematically bias the exemplars that older adults do retrieve such that they recall more positive outcome exemplars. If so, older adults' likelihood judgments might be systematically biases to be rosier than warranted. For instance, Kennedy, Mather, and Carstensen (2004) examined how a group of nuns recalled personal information recorded fourteen years earlier. In 1987, the researchers administered a questionnaire on healthy activities, mental health, emotions, and loneliness to a group of nuns of various ages. Fourteen years later, they administered the survey to the same nuns, asking them to respond retrospectively as they would have in 1987. They found that the older nuns remembered their past responses to be more positive than they had previously reported. This reinforces the earlier point of the difficulty older adults have with estimating probabilities and biases towards more positive judgment than might be realistic. Mortgage counselors need to be aware of these memory biases and how they affect likelihood judgments and keep objective base rate information on the likelihood of bad and good events happening to consumers.

Unpacking Principle

There are numerous scenarios under which aversive events may occur (e.g., a home might require repairs). Imagining or recalling all of the scenarios under which these outcomes could occur is difficult, if not impossible. The impracticality of imagining or recalling these scenarios makes it such that consumers will judge outcomes such as these as more likely if the scenarios under which they might come about are unpacked. For example, if a consumer has been living in their home and few home repairs have been required, the possibility of necessary home repairs might seem remote until all of the scenarios under which home repairs might become necessary are unpacked: The roof may need to be replaced because it has not been replaced for twenty years, the tree could fall down and smash in the front window, a water leak could cause extensive water damage, and so forth. Once these scenarios are unpacked, outcomes will seem much more likely. Therefore, it is important for counselors to unpack these scenarios. The advantages of doing so should be weighed against the risks of information overload. Although consumers of all ages are vulnerable to the inability to imagine or recall scenarios, older adults might be particularly vulnerable. In addition to robust age-related general declines in episodic memory, the conscious retrieval of specific past events, older adults have been shown to generate fewer episodic details relative to younger adults for past events. Evidence also indicates that the generation of fewer episodic details is observed when older adults imagine future scenarios. One factor that might offer some protection for older adults was discussed in the section on estimating quantitative values above. Older adults typically have more experience and, therefore, may have had personal experiences with many of the scenarios under which outcomes may have occurred. In addition, older adults typically belong to a community of peers who may have experienced such scenarios. Older adults may at times be able to rely on these personal experiences or experiences of their peers to bring scenarios to mind.

Uncertainty Discounting

Consumers typically minimize or even ignore the risks associated with uncertain events. For example, whether a home will require repairs is an uncertain possibility. As such, it is unlikely to be taken as seriously as it should. Consequently, to the extent feasible, mortgage counselors should use data on the typical relevant uncertain events to counter this phenomenon. Older adults may be particularly vulnerable to uncertainty discounting because of ambiguity. In particular, older adults have been shown to perform more poorly on ambiguous decision-making tasks, such as the Iowa Gambling Task (IGT; Zamarian, Sinz, Bonatti, Gamboz, and Delazer, 2008). In the IGT, participants select a series of cards one at a time from their choice of four available decks. Each selection results in either a gain or loss of money, and two of the decks have large gains but even larger losses whereas the other two decks have small gains and even smaller losses. Thus, drawing from the former decks would result in overall cumulative loss, but drawing from the latter decks overall cumulative gain. Participants, however, are unaware of these distinctions but can learn them over the course of drawing the cards. Although past results have been mixed, the overall pattern of results suggests that older adults do not perform as advantageously as younger adults on the IGT, suggesting that older adults have more difficulty making good decisions under ambiguous circumstances.

Risk Aversion

Consumers fear losses such as losing their homes more than they appreciate gains such as the money that they could receive from taking out a second mortgage or a reverse mortgage (Kahneman and Tversky, 1979). This greater fear of losses than appreciation of gains causes consumers to avoid risk. This risk aversion could potentially be a protective factor, if it were to cause consumers to avoid mortgages on the grounds that they are too risky. Although early research suggested that older adults may show increased risk aversion, the amassing literature over the years indicates that there are virtually no age differences in risky decision making (Mather, 2006). However, a few recent findings suggest that the frame of the risky decision may make a difference, with one study finding that losses do not loom as large for older adults (Mikels and Reed, 2009), and another study finding that positive frames result in decreased risk taking for older adults (Weller, Levin, and Denburg, 2011). Given the ambiguities in the literature, it is clear that more research is needed to understand how older adults approach risky decisions.

STEP 6. INTEGRATING INFORMATION AND DECIDING

Once a consumer has studied the proposed mortgage and understands how it operates; has estimated unknown quantitative values such as future income and the ongoing expenses of home ownership; has evaluated particular known attributes of the mortgage such as the interest rate; and recognized which of those attributes is important; and has judged the likelihood of events such as repairs, he or she must then integrate all this information into a decision. The task of integrating the information and coming to a decision is difficult for younger consumers considering conventional mortgages, but is particularly difficult for seniors considering reverse mortgages (see *Integrating Information Is Computationally Complex* below). Research has found that one result of this difficulty is the tendency to avoid making decisions (see *Decisional avoidance* section below), which in some cases could play a protective function, but could also cause harm. Often when consumers do make decisions, the decisions are not really based upon a complete integration of all of the information that should be taken into account. Instead, consumers will rely on shortcuts such as fast and frugal heuristics, affect heuristics, and reason-based decision making under which consumers merely look for a single reason or justification for the decision rather than thinking through all of the necessary information.

Integrating Information Is Computationally Complex

To come to a decision after gathering all of the necessary information, consumers need to integrate it. Ideally, consumers would use compensatory weighting as described in the Recognizing Important Attributes section above to come to an understanding of how good this reverse mortgage is as a whole compared with alternatives. As noted above, doing so is computationally complex. Furthermore, some of the loan attributes are themselves complex and require one to integrate information from multiple sources before the attribute value can be calculated and then evaluated. The value of a reverse mortgage is an example of such a complex attribute. To calculate the value of a reverse mortgage, seniors have to take the amount of money from the reverse mortgage and add that quantity to the value of staying in their homes. To calculate the value of staying in their homes the senior would need to calculate the expected value which would be what rent on that home would be plus the emotional value attached to the place where they have been living times the length of time they will stay there minus the expenses of staying there. Calculating the length of time that they will stay there requires an understanding of probability and survival rates. These calculations exceed the capacities of all but the most savvy consumers.

Decisional Avoidance

The complexities involved in integrating information can cause consumers of all ages to avoid making decisions, but research has documented that older adults have a greater tendency than their younger counterparts to do so. In much of this work, the older the individual, the more likely they are to choose not to make various decisions and defer to an authority figure. For instance, Curley, Eraker, and Yates (1984) presented participants with a hypothetical scenario in which the person was having trouble walking several blocks that led to leg pain.

The participants then had to decide whether or not to have a risky treatment, or to not make the decision and let their physician decide. Not only was increased age associated with increased decision avoidance, but a remarkable 52.9% of the older group (70 to 86 years of age) chose to avoid the decision. There are several potential reasons for this. Older adults may prefer to avoid the negative emotions that can occur when considering two conflicting options.

For instance, decision avoidance has been shown to produce less negative affect than choosing an option for high-conflict decisions. In contrast to this emotion regulatory explanation, it is also possible that older adults may prefer to avoid choosing an option because they may doubt their judgment, given the cognitive decline associated with older age.

This factor could protect consumers, if it were to prevent them from taking out mortgages that are not in their interests. Unfortunately, it could also prevent them from taking out mortgages that are in their interests or their financial situation could deteriorate while they avoid the decision. The phenomenon of deferring to an authority figure can be problematic, if the authority figure's advice is tainted by self-interest (as a mortgage broker or lender's could be). This underscores the need for consumers to also meet with independent mortgage counselors whose presentation of information and findings should not be tainted.

Fast and Frugal Heuristics

Research has found that consumers reduce the computational complexity of making decisions by relying on fast and frugal heuristics (Gigerenzer et al., 1999). One such heuristic is the recognition heuristic. Under the recognition heuristic, consumers choose the option that they recognize. Maybe they heard about this lender because a friend took out a loan from this lender. Maybe they heard about this lender from an advertisement. Maybe a known celebrity endorsed the loan. Consumers might use the simple fact that they recognized the lender as a cue that the loan is safe and should be chosen. This strategy will often work. Usually, if a product is recognized it is because other people have used it. If so, someone along the way must have looked into the details. Also, so many people would have been unlikely to use it if they had heard of others having problems. The fact that the product is recognized is then often a good cue that the product is unproblematic and reliable. It can also lead consumers astray, however, and it could cause them to choose loan products that are not in their best interests. In addition, the fact that the government "insures" the loan might inappropriately be used as a cue that the loan is unproblematic.

Research has documented that older adults are able to use the recognition heuristic to make good decisions in a manner similar to younger adults (Pachur, Mata, and Schooler, 2009). However, also revealed in this work are instances when recognition knowledge leads to a bad decision and older adults show a diminished ability to go against the use of recognition more often than the young. That is, older adults show a reduced ability to suspend the use of the recognition heuristic.

Affect Heuristic

Research has found that consumers often make decisions based upon their affective state (i.e. their emotional state). Slovic, Peters, Finucane, and MacGregor (2005) introduced the concept of the "affect heuristic" and suggested that relying on affective impressions when making decisions may be much easier and much more efficient relative to relying on analytic memory-based processes. Moreover, they speculate that reliance on emotional reactions may be especially beneficial for complex decisions as well as when resources are limited. That is, using affect is more efficient in certain circumstances—such as with advanced age—relative to deliberative processes. In fact, older adults often make better decisions when relying on the affect heuristic relative to deliberative strategies. Although the affect heuristic is helpful for older adults and allows them to make better decisions than they otherwise would, it might also mean that seniors have not thought out all of the ramifications of taking out a reverse mortgage before doing so. Mortgage counselors then should not discourage their older clients from using the affect heuristic as it could be useful, but they should also keep an eye on problematic issues that the older adult may not have considered due to reliance on the affect heuristic.

Reason-Based Decision Making

To avoid the complexity of integrating information and determining the best choice, consumers will often look for reasons to justify their choice. They will often do this by appealing to one salient attribute at the expense of all other attributes. In conventional mortgages, for example, consumers often appeal to the monthly payment in making a choice to take out the mortgage. Similarly, seniors may decide to take out a reverse mortgage based on a reason or justification (e.g., they need the money) without considering all of the pros and cons. Older adults may be particularly likely to use this strategy to make decisions, because their deliberative processing capacities have diminished. As noted, older adults seek less information than their younger counterparts and use simpler decision strategies for information search. This suggests that older adults base their decisions on fewer attributes and would thus likely appeal to one or two attributes when later justifying their choice. However, research is needed to determine if older adults would justify their decisions in such a manner. This phenomena of focusing on only one or two attributes when coming to a decision underscores the need for the mortgage counselor to review with their clients all of the key attributes and factors that should be considered when deciding to enter into a specific mortgage and to make a suitability determination, if the law is revised to permit or require this, that the senior can focus on.

CONCLUSION

In this Conclusion section, we will summarize the possible strategies that mortgage counselors might consider using to address some of the cognitive difficulties consumers face in accomplishing the 6 steps outlined in this chapter. These possible strategies are gleaned directly from scientific research on the psychology of judgment and decision-making. The scientific research to date supports the view that these strategies are likely to be successful. However, these strategies have generally not been tested directly on populations seeking mortgage counseling. We are, therefore, presenting these strategies not as surefire techniques that are guaranteed to work, but rather as tips for mortgage counselors to consider and try out as they attempt to improve their craft of counseling these consumers.

To address the difficulties consumers face completing Step 1 under which consumers need to learn and understand how mortgages operate, mortgage counselors will need to educate their clients. To address the fact that consumers typically do not gather as much information as they ought to before making a decision, mortgage counselors should make the counseling session as organized as possible (Löckenhoff and Carstensen, 2007). Less important information should be eliminated; and the most important information should be emphasized.

The most important information should be presented at the beginning or at the very end of the session as information presented in the middle will not be remembered as well. Since consumers—especially older consumers—have difficulties remembering many specific numbers and facts, the counseling session should have a gist that consumers can glean and take away from the session, such as a suitability determination (Reder et al., 1986). Although the mortgage counselor should also review the details of the loan as due to binding difficulties there will be the possibility that consumers might have confused the loan being considered with attributes of a loan they had previously considered (Jacoby, 1999). If the client has had previous experience with loans, the counselor should emphasize the ways that the current loan differs from the previous ones the consumer has experienced. When and if it is permitted by the counseling protocols, counselors should alert consumers to lower cost alternatives, including for a conventional home loan, determining the borrower's credit score and based on that the APR they should be charged for the loan (Stark, 2005).

The counselor should also review with the borrower under a conventional home loan the borrower's existing and anticipated income and expenses and the costs of the proposed loan to determine if the loan is affordable (Stark, 2005). If the loan transaction is a refinance of an existing conventional home loan, the counselor should also review with the borrower whether in light of the costs of obtaining the new loan and the anticipated period the borrower will keep the new loan in place (and certain other factors) the new loan will provide a net economic benefit to the borrower (Stark, 2005).

The optimal way of discussing the loan is likely to differ depending upon the age of the client (Shamaskin et al., 2010). Younger clients pay more attention to negative information and so less-than-optimal attributes of the loan might best be presented as negatives of the loan being considered. Older clients pay more attention to positive information and so less-than-optimal attributes of the loan might best be presented as the positives of alternative options. Presenting the less-than-optimal attributes of the loan as the positives of alternatives might also be effective in some situations at countering argument immunization and senseless explanations (Choplin et al., 2011; Langer et al., 1978; McGuire and Papageorgias, 1961). Counselors should be aware of confirmation biases and present information that disconfirms misinformation (Mutter and Pliske, 1994).

To address the difficulties consumers face completing Step 2 wherein consumers need to estimate unknown quantitative values, counselors should have statistical norms available on which consumers can anchor their estimates (Tversky and Kahneman, 1974). Counselors should also be ready to help consumers create realistic budgets. In situations where consumers have experience with budget items or they have peers who have this experience, counselors should call upon that experience and ask probing questions for items that might be unique to a particular client (Castel, 2007).

To address the difficulties consumers face completing Step 3 where consumers need to evaluate the known attributes of the loan as good or bad, counselors will need to be careful about how information is presented. Because additional amounts added to bundled expenses are often evaluated less large than they would have been had they not been bundled (Kahneman and Tversky, 1984), counselors might unbundle expenses such as third-party closing costs, servicing fees, and financing expenses. Presenting present value figures might help consumers avoid temporal discounting effects (Löckenhoff et al., 2011) and presenting better attribute values than the attributes of the loan being considered might help consumers avoid range effects (Hsee, 1996). Because evaluations differ across the lifespan, counselors might tailor their presentation to the age of the client, stressing negative information for younger clients and stressing positive information of alternatives for older clients (Kennedy et al., 2004; Shamaskin et al., 2010). Counselors will also need to be aware of their clients' financial situations and the incomes and expenses to which they have adapted as adaptation effects can make relatively low payouts appear higher than they should or make high expenses appear lower than they should.

In Step 4, clients need to recognize which attributes are most important. This step is made complicated by consumers' difficulties accomplishing compensatory weighting in which a bad value on one attribute can be compensated by a good weighting on another attribute so that the mortgage can be evaluated as a whole (Mata et al., 2007). Elsewhere in an article on proposed legal reforms to the reverse mortgage counseling protocol, we argued that mortgage counselors should be required to make a suitability determination and communicate this to the borrowers they are counseling which would be based upon compensatory weighting and provide an easy heuristic for the seniors in deciding whether to take out the reverse loan or not (Stark et al., in press). Short of such a reform, there are several strategies that mortgage counselors may try. Presenting comparison values and ranges of values of alternative loans that are currently on the market would help consumers evaluate the attribute and thereby raise its importance (Hsee, 1996). Avoiding presenting single bad exemplars (e.g., a single very high interest rate that would make the moderately high interest rate in the proposed loan look reasonable) which could create a dominance effect and raise the importance of that attribute out of proportion to other attributes (e.g., prepayment charges, length of the term of the loan; Ariely and Wallsten, 1995). Finally, counselors can use conversational norms to cue the importance of each attribute by spending the most time discussing the most important attributes of the loan such that the proportion of time spent on each attribute reflects the importance of each attribute.

In Step 5, clients need to judge the likelihood of events such as the likelihood of unemployment or the home needing repairs. Counselors might keep objective base rate information available to show clients as it may in some cases provide an anchor value (Tversky and Kahneman, 1974) that could help avoid optimistic biases (Weinstein, 1980), reliance on faulty memory (Dougherty et al., 1999; Tversky and Kahneman, 1974; Tversky and Koehler, 1994), or uncertainty discounting (Zamarian et al., 2008). Consistent with the risk-as-feelings model (Loewenstein et al., 2001) and the affect heuristic (Alhakami and Slovic, 1994), presenting risk using frequencies, rather than probabilities, or using symbols such as stars or flags can in some cases help consumers appropriately tap into their emotional reactions to viscerally understand risk. In some situations, unpacking scenarios by which an event can occur can help clients understand risk. For example, clients may better understand the likelihood that the home may need repair, if rather than being queried about the generic likelihood of repairs they are queried about specific items that may need to be repaired or replaced such as the likelihood that the roof will need to be repaired and the likelihood that the furnace will need to be replaced and the likelihood that a flood control system may need to be installed and so forth. They may further better understand this likelihood, if specific scenarios under which these items may need to be repaired are outlined (e.g., the likelihood of a severe thunderstorm damaging the roof which would then need to be repaired).

Helping clients achieve Step 6 in which they need to integrate information to make a decision is particularly difficult as this task exceeds the capacities of all but the most savvy consumers and even those savvy consumers are not performing this task on the fly, but rather relying upon prior experience (Gigerenzer et al., 1999). The difficulty of performing this task underscores the need for an experienced mortgage counselor to guide the client through the process, methodically presenting all of the important information in a manner that clients can comprehend and integrate to make a decision in their own best interest. If information is presented in an unbiased manner, the clients' emotional reactions will often be an efficient way of integrating large amounts of information (Loewenstein et al., 2001). Mortgage counselors who are aware of the six necessary steps that consumers need to accomplish to make rational home loan decisions and the cognitive barriers that consumers face in attempting to accomplish them will be in a much better position to help their clients through this process.

REFERENCES

Alhakami, A. S., and Slovic, P. (1994). A psychological study of the inverse relationship between perceived risk and perceived benefit. *Risk Analysis*, 14, 1085-1096.

Ariely, D., and Wallsten, T. S. (1995). Seeking subjective dominance in multidimensional space: An explanation of the asymmetric dominance effect. *Organizational Behavior and Human Decision Processes*, 63, 223-232.

Castel, A. D. (2005). Memory for grocery prices in younger and older adults: The role of schematic support. *Psychology and Aging*, 20, 718-721.

Castel, A. D. (2007). Aging and memory for numerical information: The role of specificity and expertise in associative memory. *Journal of Gerontology: Psychological Sciences*, 62, 194-196.

Choplin, J. M., Stark, D. P., and Ahmad, J. (2011). A psychological investigation of consumer vulnerability to fraud: Legal and policy implications. *Law and Psychology Review*, 35, 61-108.

Curley, S. P., Eraker, S. A., and Yates, J. F. (1984). An investigation of patients' reactions to therapeutic uncertainty. *Medical Decision Making*, 4, 501-511.

Dougherty, M. R. P., Gettys, C. F., and Ogden, E. (1999). MINERVA-DM: A memory process model for judgments of likelihood. *Psychological Review*, 106, 180-209.

Gigerenzer, G., Todd, P. M., AND ABC Research Group. (1999). Simple heuristics that make us smart. New York, NY: Oxford University Press.

Hsee, C. K. (1996). The evaluability hypothesis: An explanation for preference reversals between joint and separate evaluations of alternatives. *Organizational Behavior and Human Decision Processes*, 67, 247-257.

Jacoby, L. L. (1999, May–July). Deceiving the elderly: Effects of accessibility bias in cued-recall performance. *Cognitive Neuropsychology*, 16, 417-436.

Kahneman, D., Knetsch, J. L., and Thaler, R. (1990). Experimental tests of the endowment effect and the Coase theorem. *Journal of Political Economy*, 98, 1325-1348.

Kahneman, D., and Tversky, A. (1979, March). Prospect theory: An analysis of decision under risk. *Econometrica*, 47, 263-291.

Kahneman, D., and Tversky, A. (1984). Choices, values, and frames. *American Psychologist*, 39, 341-350.

Kennedy, Q., Mather, M., and Carstensen, L. L. (2004). The role of motivation in the age-related positivity effect in autobiographical memory. *Psychological Science*, 15, 208-214.

Langer, E. J., Blank, A., and Chanowitz, B. (1978). The mindlessness of ostensibly thoughtful action: The role of "placebic" information in interpersonal interaction. *Journal of Personality and Social Psychology*, 36, 635-642.

Löckenhoff, C. E., and Carstensen, L. L. (2007). Aging, emotion, and health-related decision strategies: Motivational manipulations can reduce age differences. *Psychology and Aging*, 22, 134-146.

Löckenhoff, C. E., O'Donoghue, T., and Dunning, D. (2011). Age differences in temporal discounting: The role of dispositional affect and anticipated emotions. *Psychology and Aging*, 26, 274-284.

Loewenstein, G. F., Weber, E. U., Hsee, C. K., and Welch, N. (2001). Risk as feelings. *Psychological Bulletin*, 127, 267-286.

Mata, R., Schooler, L., and Rieskamp, J. (2007). The aging decision maker: Cognitive aging and the adaptive selection of decision strategies. *Psychology and Aging*, 22, 796-810.

Mather, M. (2006). A review of decision-making processes: Weighing the risks and benefits of aging. In L. Carstensen and C. Hartels (Eds.), *When I'm 64* (pp. 145-173) Washington, DC: National Academies Press.

McGuire, W. J., and Papageorgias, D. (1961). The relative efficacy of various types of prior belief-defense in producing immunity against persuasion. *Journal of Abnormal and Social Psychology*, 62, 327-337.

Mikels, J. A., and Reed, A. E. (2009). Monetary losses do not loom large in later life: Age differences in the framing effect. *Journals of Gerontology Series B: Psychological Sciences and Social Sciences*, 64, 457-460.

Mutter, S. A., and Pliske, R. M. (1994). Aging and illusory correlation in judgments of co-occurrence. *Psychology and Aging*, 9, 53-63.

Pachur, T., Mata, R., and Schooler, L. J. (2009). Cognitive aging and the adaptive use of recognition in decision making. *Psychology and Aging*, 24, 901-915.

Reder, L. M., Wible, C., and Martin, J. (1986). Differential memory changes with age: Exact retrieval versus plausible inference. *Journal of Experimental Psychology: Learning, Memory and Cognition*, 12, 72-81.

Shamaskin, A. M., Mikels, J. A., and Reed, A. E. (2010). Getting the message across: Age differences in the positive and negative framing of healthcare messages. *Psychology and Aging*, 25, 746-751.

Slovic, P., Peters, E., Finucane, M. L., and MacGregor, D. G. (2005). Affect, risk, and decision making. *Health Psychology*, 24(4, Suppl.), S35-S40.

Stark, D. P. (2005). Unmasking the predatory loan in sheep's clothing: A legislative proposal. *Harvard BlackLetter Law Journal*, 21, 129-162.

Stark, D. P., and Choplin, J. M. (2009). A license to deceive: Enforcing contractual myths despite consumer psychological realities. *NYU Journal of Law and Business*, 5, 617-744.

Stark, D. P., and Choplin, J. M. (2010). A cognitive and social psychological analysis of disclosure laws and call for mortgage counseling to prevent predatory lending. *Psychology, Public Policy, and Law*, 16, 85-131.

Stark, D. P., Choplin, J. M., Mikels, J. A., and McDonnell, A. S. (in press). Complex decision-making and cognitive aging call for enhanced protection of seniors contemplating reverse mortgages. *Arizona State Law Journal*.

Tversky, A., and Kahneman, D. (1974). Judgment under uncertainty: Heuristics and biases. *Science*, 185, 1124-1131.

Tversky, A., and Koehler, D. J. (1994). Support theory: A nonextensional representation of subjective probability. *Psychological Review*, 101, 547-567.

Weinstein, N. (1980). Unrealistic optimism about future life events. *Journal of Personality and Social Psychology*, 39, 806-820.

Weller, A., Levin, I. P., and Denburg, N. L. (2011, October). Trajectory of advantageous decision making for risky gains and losses from ages 5 to 85. *Journal of Behavioral Decision Making*, 24, 331-344.

Zamarian, L., Sinz, H., Bonatti, E., Gamboz, N., and Delazer, M. (2008). Normal aging affects decisions under ambiguity, but not decisions under risk. *Neuropsychology*, 24, 645-657.

Index

D

E

F

I

Q

R

S

T